THE YALE-HOOVER SERIES ON AUTHORITARIAN REGIMES

THE ART OF THE BRIBE

CORRUPTION UNDER STALIN,

1943–1953

JAMES HEINZEN

Hoover Institution
Stanford University
Stanford, California

Yale UNIVERSITY PRESS
New Haven and London

Published with assistance from the Mary Cady Tew Memorial Fund.

Yale University Press books may be purchased in quantity for educational, business, or promotional use. For information, please e-mail sales.press@yale.edu (U.S. office) or sales@yaleup.co.uk (U.K. office).

Set in Sabon type by Integrated Publishing Solutions, Grand Rapids, Michigan.
Printed in the United States of America.

Library of Congress Control Number: 2015959466
ISBN 978-0-300-17525-7 (hardcover : alk. paper)

A catalogue record for this book is available from the British Library.

This paper meets the requirements of ANSI/NISO Z39.48-1992 (Permanence of Paper).

10 9 8 7 6 5 4 3 2 1

Contents

Part III

Acknowledgments

I am grateful to the many organizations and agencies that helped to fund research for this project: the National Endowment for the Humanities (NEH), the Library and Archives of the Hoover Institution on War, Revolution, and Peace of Stanford University, including its Archives Summer Workshops, the National Council for Eurasian and Eastern European Research (NCEEER), the Kennan Institute of the Woodrow Wilson Center, and the Open Society Archives (OSA) at Central European University (Budapest). At Rowan University my deans, Jay Harper, Parviz Ansari, and Cindy Vitto provided me with research and travel support.

I would like to thank the following people, who generously read parts of my manuscript, conference papers, or articles in draft form, and offered valuable advice and suggestions: Yoram Gorlizki, Stephen Kotkin, David Brandenberger, Paul Gregory, Eugene Huskey, Benjamin Nathans, Peter Holquist, Jeffrey Jones, Wendy Goldman, Don K. Rowney, Alfred Rieber, Andrei Markevich, Mark Harrison, Vanessa Voisin, Leonid Borodkin, Golfo Alexopolous, Kathryn Hendley, Juliane Fürst, Robert Weinberg, Becky Griffin-Heinzen, and Bill Heinzen.

Paul Gregory invited me to wonderful workshops on Stalinism that he organized at the Hoover Archive at Stanford. The seminars were stimulating and collegial, and provided me with access to the Hoover's amazing collections and staff, including its directors Eric Wakin and Elena Danielson, archivist Lora Soroka, and the director of the reading room, Carol Leadenham. I am grateful for the assistance of several professional Russian archivists and staff, including Galina Gorskaia, Nina I. Abdullaeva, Elena A. Tiurina, Tatiana V. Tsarevskaia, and the staff and archivists of the Russian State Archive of Socio-Political History (RGASPI) and the State Archive of the Russian Federation (GARF). My excellent research assistants at Rowan University were Melissa Ambricco Schwartz, Gregory Hopely, Edward Purcell, and Caressa Lynch.

Special thanks to Peter Solomon, who over the course of more than ten years has offered unstinting encouragement as I wrote this book. He read the entire manuscript and numerous conference papers, patiently offering advice. I am grateful, too, to David Shearer. Our marathon lunches have helped to shape the way I think about Soviet history. Dave read large chunks of the manuscript, often in very rough form, and offered valuable suggestions about every dimension of the book. To a person, my remarkable colleagues in the history department at Rowan University are wonderful people, as well as excellent scholars and teachers. Special thanks to department chairs, Bill Carrigan, Edward Wang, and Joy Wiltenburg, and to Denise Williams, the department secretary. As I was nearing completion of this project, William C. Jordan, Philip Nord, and David Abraham unexpectedly took the time to share their expertise on everyday corruption. I also want to thank Beverly Michaels, the copy editor for Yale University Press, whose careful reading of the manuscript has made the book much better.

Becky Griffin-Heinzen gave advice and read every chapter multiple times, immeasurably improving the book in every respect. To her I owe the greatest debt, in this and in all things great and small. My children, Conor Heinzen and Jay Heinzen, have provided me with enormous inspiration over the years as they have demonstrated curiosity, courage, and great humor. To them this book is dedicated.

Some parts of this book have been published previously. An expanded version of chapter 3 was published as "The Art of the Bribe: Corruption and Everyday Practice in the Late Stalinist USSR," in *Slavic Review* 66, no. 3 (2007). The basis of chapter 4 appeared as "Thirty Kilos of Pork: Cultural Brokers, Corruption, and the 'Bribe Trail' in the Late Stalinist Soviet Union," *Journal of Social History* 46, no. 4 (2013). Chapter 6 appeared in a longer form as "Informers and the State under Late Stalinism: Informant Networks and Crimes against 'Socialist Property,' 1940–1953," *Kritika: Explorations in Russian History* 8, no. 4

(2007). Sections of the fifth chapter first appeared as "A Campaign Spasm: Graft and the Limits of the 'Campaign' against Bribery after the Great Patriotic War," which appeared in *Late Stalinist Russia: Society between Reconstruction and Development,* edited by Juliane Fürst (2006).

Each of the people named here deserves credit for helping to write this book. All the blame for its shortcomings, needless to say, lies with me alone.

Introduction

SINCE THE COLLAPSE of the Soviet Union in 1991, traditions and practices of bribery inherited from the Soviet era have continued to permeate nearly every sphere of life in contemporary Russia. Despite a great deal of interest in the corruption and black markets that marked the final decades of the Soviet Union, little attention has been devoted to the phenomenon during the important years between World War II and Stalin's death in 1953. Following the chaos of the war itself, these postwar years, known as "late Stalinism," were pivotal in the evolution of corruption in Soviet times. By the midpoint of the war in 1943, illegal underground economic activity, the theft of state property, and bribery were significant sources of concern for Communist Party leaders, as they seemed to have become more deeply entrenched in Soviet life.

The Soviet Union under Stalin was an extremely repressive regime that nevertheless experienced great difficulties maintaining discipline among its own officials. This paradox—that bribery practices were widespread during the very apogee of the Stalinist dictatorship—lies at the heart of this study. Bureaucrats bartered with common citizens (and with each other) in exchange for their services. Such negotiations were part of the dodging and cajoling that shaped individuals' relationship with Soviet state actors. By 1943, the Stalinist party-state struggled to understand the roots of an upsurge in this informal behavior among its

1

officials and took steps to try to bring it under control. At the same time, however, the regime unintentionally created conditions in which illegal deals between Soviet officials and citizens could flourish.

Few scholars have written about corruption and economic crime in this period, even when they have studied other types of crime.[1] The overriding assumption was that the late Stalin period saw little real corruption among officials. Most Kremlinologists and contemporaries assumed that officials were too intimidated to risk engaging in bribery.[2] After a burst of highly publicized trials of bribe takers in the early 1920s, bribery, it was thought, was largely dormant during the Stalin years. In this sense, it was implied that there was a sharp break between two periods: the "stagnation" era of Brezhnev and his immediate successors (1964–1985) was brazenly venal, with its graft, abetted by political sclerosis and bureaucratization at all levels, while corruption in the Stalin years was relatively unusual, and even something of an aberration. This study directly challenges that view.[3] The postwar Stalin period, in fact, prepared the ground for the blossoming of the corruption of "mature socialism" in the 1960s–1980s.

Those who seek to understand the roots of the corruption that infected the Soviet Union during the Brezhnev years should look earlier, to the postwar Stalin period. Neither bribery nor other types of corruption appeared for the first time during late Stalinism, of course. The prewar years witnessed many of the same opportunities for embezzlement of state property, illicit networking, and black market activity that were prevalent in the late Stalinist years.[4] During the postwar period, these activities and the dictatorship's reaction to them, however, were characterized by features that both linked them to, and distinguished them from, what came before. World War II and the postwar crises shaped the nature of corrupt activities in the late Stalin years (and beyond).

What constituted corruption in the Soviet context? I have chosen a classic and relatively specific definition of corruption: the abuse of one's official position for the purpose of self-enrichment or other material advantage. Naturally, all definitions of criminal behavior, even this ostensibly straightforward one, contain ambiguity. Nevertheless, this definition of corruption would include bribery, the theft of state property for personal use by officials, the embezzlement and misappropriation of government funds, and certain types of abuse of office for personal gain.

Within this larger framework of official corruption, though, I have chosen to put the *offering and solicitation of bribes* at the center of this book. Bribery (the word is *vziatochnichestvo* in Russian) is typically defined in law as gifts of any kind of valuables, whether in money or in kind (such as food, goods, or services), that improperly influence the judgment of public officials to the benefit of the giver. Bribery and corruption are not synonymous terms, yet bribery represents the paradigmatic variety of corruption. In the Soviet Union, it was the much-reviled bribe-taking official who symbolized corruption in the popular mind and in popular culture. To be sure, other kinds of abuse of office were abundant. Yet when the Soviet state periodically attacked the "scourge of corruption," it was the bribe-taking official who bore the brunt of authorities' rhetorical venom.

The Art of the Bribe examines several critical dimensions of the post-war Soviet world during the last years of Stalin's life. Like all periods of transition, late Stalinism shares many elements with earlier years. It is evident, however, that the war's devastation deeply scarred Soviet society and state structures. Informal mechanisms for getting things done embedded themselves into party and state institutions that had been weakened, providing fertile soil for illicit relationships based on bribery. At the same time, the war etched new patterns into daily struggles.

An investigation of bribery, which involved people from across the social spectrum, provides an opportunity to explore the dynamic interplay of state, society, and criminality. The phenomenon of the bribe sheds light on the social and political consequences of Stalinism and the textures of everyday life. More broadly, an exploration of corruption probes the dysfunctions of dictatorships and the limits of authoritarian states. This research describes and explains the opaque and hard-to-study unofficial relationships found in closed societies that lack open political competition, a free press, and an independent judiciary.

In the Stalinist USSR, bribery was simultaneously enabling and disabling. Bribery and other forms of official corruption could serve as a source of stability in the near term, cementing networks of unofficial partnerships and "greasing the wheels" to enable the distribution of scarce goods and services to the population via a vast "shadow economy." Well-placed bribes allowed some people to soften the hard edges of their lives in exceedingly difficult circumstances, even if they were paid at substantial risk and a high price. Bribery, this book argues, was an integral part of an unofficial but essential series of relationships upon which much of Soviet society and state administration relied in order to function.

Yet, in the long term, bribery (and the perception that the state was doing little to punish corrupt bureaucrats) was also a destabilizing factor with significant costs, exacerbating shortages, contributing to popular cynicism about state institutions and indeed all state authority, and tarnishing the revolutionary state's image abroad. The belief that scarce goods were distributed on the basis of illegally purchased access, rather than need or demand, undermined the party's promise to provide for all equally. Bribery in judicial and law enforcement institutions could sow doubt about the impartiality of justice and even the legitimacy of the state. Party leaders, acknowledging that a corrupt bureaucracy and economic administration can weaken the state's ability to implement policies, tried, albeit inconsistently, to rein in misbehaving officials.

When seeking to explain the reasons for persistent corruption in the Soviet Union, one must discard the usual stereotypes: somehow "defective" national, ethnic, or racial "character," or primitive notions of historical continuity.[5] Explanations that focus on the immorality of certain "bad-apple" individuals, or on the essentially corrupt (and corrupting) nature of either capitalism or communism, are also unsatisfying. Instead, as James Scott has argued, the most fruitful avenues are two: first, the structural factors that provided opportunities and incentives for individuals to offer unlawful gifts and for officials to accept them; and second, the values, shaped by culture, that helped to define acceptable (and unacceptable) relations between officials and the people they were charged with serving.[6]

Bribery has figured prominently in a modern world characterized by large, sprawling states and bureaucracies, and it is by no means confined to Soviet-style systems.[7] This study's findings have implications beyond the bounds of Soviet history or authoritarian regimes. "Corrupt" relationships between official and citizen have endured in all socioeconomic and political systems, whether socialist or capitalist, dictatorial or democratic.[8] (There is, of course, no perfectly rational state bureaucracy; there are only varying degrees of irrationality.) Structural factors common to many societies also encouraged corrupt practices in the Soviet Union: a power structure that shielded elites from prosecution to some degree; a poorly paid and trained officialdom; widespread shortages and poverty; and the absence of any opposition parties or independent media, denying people these means to influence policy making and expose wrongdoing.

Nevertheless, thanks to the nature of the Stalinist state and economy, bureaucrats found themselves with bountiful opportunities to profit at the expense of the state—and the population they were serving. Opportunities for theft and self-enrichment were rife in the bedlam of the five-year plans. The command economy bred bribery, embezzlement of state property, and other crimes by officials. In a rigorously hierarchical and inflexible system, administrators had tremendous incentive to fulfill plan quotas by any means, especially in light of harsh punishments for failure to do so. Black markets in scarce goods and services thrived.[9] Economic factors that contributed to the situation included nationalized property and infrastructure, the regime's efforts to eliminate nearly all capitalist relations, and the strictly centralized planning system with its bottlenecks and chronic underproduction. A pervasive, intrusive, and arbitrary state apparatus that controlled the allocation of immense resources allowed state officials myriad possibilities to trade on their positions.[10]

During wartime, the regime faced extraordinary new challenges. The political education of party cadres was suspended amid the fighting. Nine million Communist Party members were killed in the war. Millions more were brought into the party, most of whom had no political training whatsoever beyond their time at the front.[11] Party leaders struggled to re-impose ideological purity on cadres, many of whom, in their eyes, had become complacent. Authorities targeted an uptick in bribery and other forms of malfeasance practiced by new (and experienced) officials.

The state machinery itself saw radical transformations during the war. By necessity, the party leadership had chosen to decentralize control over parts of government and economic administration. Decentralization granted local officials greater power and scope to make decisions at the grassroots. Local leaders were left to improvise amid countless emergencies. In some places, formal state structures became more indistinct and, at times, barely functioned. Once the war concluded, the party had to rebuild its authority locally. Controls over the population had also been relaxed during the conflict, and party officials struggled to re-impose and rejuvenate mechanisms of strict control.[12] This wartime weakening of state institutions led to an increase in personalized relations, which were themselves vehicles for myriad varieties of under-the-table, frequently illegal dealings.

At the same time, the late Stalinist period of stabilization strengthened the power of new economic elites who demanded, and often received, more leeway to take advantage of their positions. Much of officialdom benefited from the postwar stabilization in ways they had not in the 1930s, solidifying their status and enjoying the fruits of the victory. Bribery existed alongside well-established phenomena such as patronage and special access to scarce goods and services. Some elites coerced payments from their subordinates, and from the general population, often with little interference from the party supervision and law enforcement agencies that were at least partially aware of these dubious activities. As Vera Dunham has argued, the postwar reconstruction period saw the emergence of a relatively stable and loyal "middle class" who, in exchange for their tacit obedience to central authority, had expectations of greater access to material goods.[13] Yet quite often these desirable consumer goods could only be obtained (and supplied) through shadow "markets," which were often but not always illegal.

BRIBERY IN THE POSTWAR LANDSCAPE

This book is divided into three parts. The first part examines the landscape of the bribe in late Stalinism. One of this study's aims is to expand our field of vision to include not simply economic and political elites, but also the attempts of ordinary Soviet people informally to navigate systems of power. Many of the stories in this book involve people who tried to use bribes to extract themselves from abysmal situations: the woman who offered a judge a bribe after her husband was sentenced to seven years in prison for petty theft; the factory manager who paid off an auditor when he could not fulfill impossible plan targets; the family, evacuated from Moscow after the Nazi invasion of June 1941, that could not return to the city without paying an extra "fee" to a railroad conductor; the demobilized soldier whose apartment was seized by a government agency during the war, and whose family would be left homeless unless he made an under-the-table payment to get it back; and the court consultant who had to buy penicillin for her sick husband on the black market, paying with the cash she acquired by quietly accepting the occasional "gift."

Any study of corruption should focus on the agencies of law enforcement, including the courts, the offices of the state prosecutor (known in the USSR as the procuracy), and the police. Judges, prosecutors, and police play a dual role in an exploration of corruption: they can both expose *and* accept bribes; prosecute *and* deliver illegal payments; attack *and* abet corruption.[14] Ultimately, Soviet law enforcement and criminal justice agencies, while they were the leading investigators of corrupt acts, also ranked among the foremost venues for such deals. The challenges of Soviet life related to housing, documentation, employment, and other essentials—together with the illicit transactions and wheedling that Soviet people sometimes undertook to acquire them—all converged in the legal system. To take one example explored in these pages, the mass arrests for petty property and economic crimes characteristic of postwar Stalinism provided mass opportunities for citizens and legal officials to make under-the-table deals for leniency, with payments often disguised as "gifts of gratitude."

The book's second part moves beyond questions of economy and governance (or misgovernance) to examine notions of what Catriona Kelly has called "self-interested giving" as a cultural issue with deep roots.[15] Research informed by anthropological and sociological concerns has begun to analyze popular perceptions of gift giving to officials, and the way these perceptions interact with—and sometimes conflict with—law codes.[16] Persistent tensions among official ideology, popular attitudes, written law, and customary practices are common to many societies. In this book, bribery is explored in part as a vehicle for investigating why and how individuals developed relationships with officials.[17] In undertaking a social-historical approach to the bribe in the postwar years, including popular perceptions of bribery, the study aims to expand our understanding of crime and daily life in the postwar USSR.

The sociologist Alena V. Ledeneva has examined certain informal social and economic practices in the 1980s–1990s USSR and Russia. Of particular relevance for this study, she has insightfully explored the practice of *blat,* a colloquial term meaning the mutual exchange of favors based on "pull," friendship, acquaintance, or other personal or professional ties. People tried to use their connections to help them get things in short supply, including food, clothing, residency documents, and desirable work.[18] Some Soviet people also had patrons who could help them advance in their careers or protect them from punishment. Yet blat and patronage could not help most people gain access to everything they needed or wanted. Nor were they the same as bribes. As Ledeneva notes, bribery and blat were related but distinct phenomena. People who lacked useful contacts or the right "friends in high places" often chose to resort to a payment under the table—a bribe. For many people who were in a difficult position, or who did not have good connections, blat was simply not an option. Even those who had excellent contacts in some areas might have needed to pay bribes in others—to maneuver through the criminal justice system, for example, or to secure a good job or an apartment. Moreover, many officials wanted cash rather than favors to compensate them for taking risks. The ubiquity of bribery in the postwar USSR is testament to the fact that blat could hardly solve all problems for all people.

How, then, did people enter bribery deals? And how did popular understandings of bribery transactions shape people's choices? These practices—what I call "the art of the bribe"—are explored on these pages as a type of negotiation between ordinary people and state officials, one that sometimes involved elements of coercion. My work sets out to identify the unspoken "rules of the game," including the rituals, outlooks, and ethics that guided the practices of bribery.[19] Archival and published sources reflect the diverse and, at times, contradictory ways that individuals came to understand bribery and the state's efforts to fight it. Popular reactions to bribery were as diverse as Soviet society itself, ranging from patriotic outrage that individual bureaucrats had betrayed the ideals of the motherland, to concern about the fraying connections between the laboring masses and the socialist state, to a growing cynicism about the emergence of a class of privileged officials who considered themselves as above the law. Nevertheless, many people could justify giving or accepting bribes in certain situations. In other cases, officials said that they simply could not refuse a gift from a petitioner, an attitude that is discussed in chapter 4. A blurred line separated "acceptable" from "unacceptable" behavior. What distinguished "gifts" or "favors" from bribes in the popular imagination?

Historians of the Soviet Union lack the kinds of etiquette books and how-to manuals produced in many societies to offer help to those who wished to present gifts to influential people, whether legally or not.[20] This study offers something of a "reverse-engineered" guidebook, one that describes the social practices for offering bribes in the postwar Stalinist landscape. It gleans insights from the informative (though imperfect) documents produced by the legal agencies that were charged with exposing, prosecuting, and trying people involved in bribery. Some of our most fruitful sources, including court records, allow the accused to speak for themselves, albeit under less than ideal circumstances.[21]

Using these lively materials, this part of the book takes a unique approach. It examines bribery from the vantage point of the *participants*, and not exclusively from the point of view of prosecutors, the highly restricted press, or even those accepting the bribes.[22] In studies of graft, most scholars are interested in "political corruption," by which they typically mean crimes by high-level officials with access to substantial power. Social scientists have usually focused on the nature of "top-down" patron-client relationships in government and economic structures. When they discuss bribery, their point of reference is nearly always the state officials who abuse their offices. The *givers* of bribes, on the other hand, have been nearly invisible in scholarly studies.[23]

A starting point for such an approach is to acknowledge that actions deemed illegal by law codes may not be seen that way by citizens themselves. That which is labeled "corruption" is peculiar to a given time, place, culture, and political environment. Recognizing that state authorities and social actors often disagree about what constitutes corruption, Arnold Heidenheimer developed a useful color-coded scheme that differentiates between "white," "grey," and "black" offenses, depending on the degree to which state authorities and the population condemned a particular action.[24] "Black" corruption, the most serious form, is condemned by ruling elites and public alike; "white" offenses are petty, and neither a majority of the public nor elites would choose to punish them; and "grey" corruption falls in between these two more obvious extremes. Grey corruption involves behavior that elites normally regard as outside the boundaries of the acceptable, while ordinary people often consider it acceptable, or are undecided. In much of the Soviet period, including the postwar years, the offering of gifts to officials often falls into this "grey" category.[25]

The regime's attempts to understand the causes and extent of bribery—

and its largely ineffective efforts to control it—are at the center of the book's third part. One of the Bolshevik Revolution's great ambitions was the ideal, long held by the Russian intelligentsia, of wiping the country clean of corrupt state *chinovniki* (bureaucrats). This lofty goal was pursued zealously in the first years of the new regime. But the party faced serious challenges. Traditional practices of gift giving to officials were intertwined with longstanding patterns whereby bureaucrats squeezed extra income from the population they were supposed to serve. These mutually reinforcing practices presented formidable obstacles to eliminating such abuses from the machinery of administration. It became clear almost immediately that bribery practices and culture had transitioned across the revolutionary divide essentially unscathed. Authorities soon understood—much to their chagrin—that "socialist" varieties of administration and economic structures were just as likely to provide fertile soil for the seeds of corruption as "capitalist" variants, despite the state's attempts to stigmatize this behavior. Uneven prosecution did little to help the situation.

Like many states, the Soviet regime tried to pinpoint the causes of bribe-taking, classify the acceptance of gifts by officials as unethical and illegal, and transform administrative culture. Despite the threat of severe punishment, however, some civil servants continued to enrich themselves at public expense. The regime reacted with alarm to evidence that bribery—like many social ills, including alcoholism, domestic violence, and prostitution—proliferated after World War II.

Centrally directed, national campaigns mobilized various agencies to combat persistent crime among officials. Soviet ideology lent a particular coloration to these efforts. The party held that bribery—like all forms of corruption by officials—was wholly alien to a socialist society, a dying relic of "capitalist mentalities." For this reason, the most unsettling question from the regime's perspective was: why does this reprehensible criminal behavior persist under newly built socialism? In official rhetoric produced after the war, bribery was characterized as rare and on the verge of eradication, limited to a few self-serving and "backward" individuals. Bribery and other forms of corruption (like all crime) were said to be in the process of dying out as living standards improved and the socialist "consciousness" and cultural level of the population grew. How, then, could Soviet officials, the models of the "New Soviet People" who had served heroically in a noble war to save the Soviet Union—and the world—from fascism, continue to commit these crimes more than a full generation after the triumph of the October Revolution?

SOURCES

In undertaking any study of corruption, the historian faces special challenges with regard to source material. Individuals rarely admit to participating in illegal deals, especially accepting bribes. Moreover, most states regard corruption as an embarrassment, and do little to publicize it. Bribe-taking has long been considered shameful in most societies, and the Soviet Union was no exception. Before 1991, the sources for studies of corruption in the late Stalinist USSR were largely limited to the sometimes interesting but quite brief newspaper accounts, the law codes themselves, circumscribed if often insightful articles in the specialized legal press, and a small number of émigré memoirs. This study uses all of this existing published source material from the period.

The shortage of sources was a particular problem for students of the postwar Stalin years, the most impenetrable, least known, and most difficult-to-examine period in all of Soviet history. The quality of official material about crime and the legal system became worse than ever after the war. Inside the Soviet Union, the very topic of crime in Stalinist society was largely taboo, precluding serious public discussion of its causes or extent.[26] Crime statistics remained a state secret. And reliable sources documenting daily life after the war were almost impossible to find.

Before the fall of the Soviet Union in 1991, historians lacked access to the kinds of archival sources that would enable the detailed investigation of bribery and other forms of unlawful "entrepreneurial" activity "from the inside out." With the collapse of communism and the partial opening of many classified archive collections, new material can help us lift the veil of secrecy. We have a rare opportunity to study bribery using documentation gleaned from the archives of a regime that unraveled, to some extent, as a consequence of pervasive corruption.

This book examines its subject in large part through the lens of criminal justice, police, and "party control" agencies that played an important role after the war. Critical materials are located in the archives of the USSR Procuracy General's office, which are housed in the State

Archive of the Russian Federation (GARF). The procuracy played the leading role in investigating and prosecuting all varieties of abuse of office. While wrestling with malfeasance in its own ranks, the procuracy provided regular overviews of the national "battle against bribery." The archives of the USSR Ministry of Justice and USSR Supreme Court (also located in GARF) contain material including transcripts of criminal proceedings, witness statements, and copies of appeals. Correspondence among government agencies, including the Ministry of Internal Affairs and the domestic police force, can be quite valuable. Discussions touch on sensitive issues that could never be referenced in the press, such as the investigations of high-ranking judges and other personnel accused of taking bribes. An exceptional feature of this material is that some people implicated in bribery schemes talk about their actions from their own perspective. This type of documentation is something of a rarity. Such documents (though imperfect and sometimes one-sided) allow for an exploration of some key questions, including the social context of these activities, the rationalizations and motivations of those implicated, and the construction of narratives about "fallen" officials.

The former Central Party Archive—the Russian State Archive for Social and Political History (RGASPI)—contains a variety of rich materials, including the collections of the Party Secretariat, the Politburo, and other key departments such as the Department of Administrative Organs (which supervised the legal and security agencies), the Organizational Bureau (Orgbiuro), and the Cadres Department. Documentation includes investigations, meeting minutes, and correspondence between party officials and the leadership of the legal agencies. Another partially accessible collection of sources comes from the archive of the Central Committee's Party Control Commission (KPK), a body that was responsible for investigating the actions of party members who were accused of moral, ideological, or criminal infractions. Reports and other documents from the Ministry of Internal Affairs department responsible for coordinating the expansive secret informant network charged with rooting out economic crimes (OBKhSS) are also valuable sources.

The years of postwar Stalinism lack the kinds of grand spectacles that rocked the 1930s, a decade of show trials, violent party purges, frenetic construction of industry, bloody forced collectivization of agriculture, and famine.[27] By the end of the war, the purges and the witch-hunts of Trotskyites and other "enemies of the people" had mostly subsided (although versions of such repressions were repeated in the newly conquered and re-occupied areas of the western borderlands).[28] In the absence of such drama, nearly all studies of late Stalinism until relatively recently dealt with high politics and Cold War foreign relations: political intrigues in the Kremlin, Soviet policy toward China and the "Third World," the Korean War, and Stalin's military and ideological stance toward Europe.[29]

And although historians have long been interested in the military aspects of World War II, their work had typically isolated the war itself from its social consequences inside the USSR. Several important new studies of late Stalinism have challenged this standard, firmly situating the period in the wake of the wartime catastrophe. In turn, the social history of the period has developed rapidly with a number of compelling studies.[30] Numerous excellent works on aspects of postwar society, economy, and reconstruction have appeared in recent years.[31] Some of the most fruitful work on the late Stalin period merges a discussion of the peculiarities of postwar politics with an understanding of the larger situation inside the country.[32] It is also the case that, with the exception of the meticulous studies of Peter Solomon and Yoram Gorlizki, and the pioneering interpretations of Soviet law by John Hazard and Harold Berman, historians have not given the postwar Stalinist legal system the attention it deserves.[33] This is the case, paradoxically, despite immense interest in chronicling the Gulag and the instruments of police repression in the 1930s.[34] In its reconstruction of informal arrangements in the Stalinist economic system, Joseph Berliner's groundbreaking 1957 treatment of Soviet industrial management remains a very influential study. Mining interviews with émigrés, Berliner observed that secret relationships were rife among managers desperate to meet unrealistic plan targets. Enterprise managers in the Stalin-era USSR took advantage of personal connections, sold and bartered excess equipment and materials, padded statistics and undertook other shady (if usually not strictly illegal) practices in chaotic conditions.[35] One of Berliner's major contributions was to show that these activities were often "entrepreneurial" efforts taken by managers amid the perpetual state of confusion that typified the planned economy. Unlike the present study,

Berliner's research did not concentrate on self-profiting crimes by officials, such as outright theft, bribery, and embezzlement, but rather focused on the actions undertaken "in the interest of production" (*v pol'zu proizvodstva*) (which, no doubt, his interview subjects were more comfortable discussing).

In his classic work on the Soviet illegal economy (which he called the "second economy") and its relationship to the Brezhnev-era "kleptocracy," Gregory Grossman in the late 1970s noted the strong likelihood of "a close organic connection between political-administrative authority, on the one hand, and a highly developed world of illegal economic activity, on the other."[36] After the war, similarly, officials were sometimes deeply involved in shadow markets, both protecting and profiting from these connections even as they denounced them. The bribe, as this study shows, was an essential element of that second economy in the period of late Stalinism (as it would remain in later decades).

This book moves beyond this interest in unofficial relationships in the economy by detailing how shadow markets also operated inside the offices of public administration.[37] Illicit market mechanisms penetrated state bureaucracies outside the economy, including the legal system, to enable transactions between Soviet people and officials. Ordinary people could obtain official favors with bribes on shadow "markets" trading in state services, just as they could surreptitiously purchase needed goods and services outside the sanctioned channels.[38]

THE CHAPTERS

Part I comprises the book's first two chapters. The first chapter argues that a critical turning point in the development of the patterns of bribery that typified the later Soviet era was World War II and its aftermath. The extraordinary disruption of the war and the immediate postwar years made surreptitious contacts between Soviet people and local officials more likely. The dislocation of populations; poverty; epic shortages of housing, food, and transportation; new pressures on the legal system; and breakdowns in distribution all created conditions that were conducive to officials' profiting from their offices. Bribery lubricated the official and unofficial economies alike in ways that helped the system function. This does not mean, of course, that all people participated in it, nor that the entire system was wholly corrupt. Who participated, why, and to what ends? (Due to the secret nature of bribery transactions, determining the absolute numbers of bribes offered or accepted is not possible in any system, of course, just as it is impossible to determine the overall size of the black market or other illegal economic activity in any country.)

Chapter 2 shifts the focus to bribery among law enforcement and criminal justice officials. The enormous number of arrests for nonpolitical crimes, and the influx of those cases into the courts, provides context for an upsurge of deal-making in the overwhelmed legal agencies. Arrests gave rise to appeals, protests, and complaints. The sheer volume of cases created opportunity for judges and prosecutors to accept illicit gifts in exchange for reducing sentences or reviewing decisions, if they were willing to take the risk. In this sense, Stalin's crackdown on the theft of "socialist property," profiteering, and other economic and property crimes unexpectedly increased the prospects for offering and accepting bribes. Many petitioners, having lost confidence in the official channels, turned to potentially dangerous deals with officials.[39]

In part II, the third and fourth chapters turn to an examination of popular perceptions of the bribe, situating the practice within traditions of gift giving to officials. Chapter 3 argues that it is productive to evaluate bribery as a type of negotiation shaped by personal and collective values, rather than simply as a contemptible act to be condemned morally. As such, the scope of actions labeled as "bribery" in this study is not framed exclusively by the Soviet criminal code, but also by the outlooks, customs, social obligations, and practices of petitioners and officials.[40] The chapter explores the micro-level of everyday interactions. How did people decide who to give gifts to? What kinds of assumptions did they bring to the negotiations? And how did petitioners and officials justify their actions, both as givers and as acceptors of gifts? In this context, the fourth chapter closely examines the case of a Georgian judge on the USSR Supreme Court, Levan K. Chichua, who was arrested for accepting bribes in 1949. Chichua's story sheds light on contested notions of gift giving, bribery, and social reciprocity. The idea of the "cultural broker" as a key figure in the Soviet courts is also introduced here. Cultural brokers were individuals who had familiarity with both the Soviet legal system and local traditions and practices, and who prospered by moving back and forth between them, negotiating deals while bridging cultural gaps.

The four chapters of part III treat several dimensions of the Stalinist state's inconsistent efforts to attack bribery in Soviet society. As chapter 5 shows, beginning in mid-1943 and accelerating in the following years, concern was building among law enforcement and party authorities that bribery was becoming more prevalent. A postwar "campaign" expressed the goal of eradicating this scourge from the Soviet landscape. Why was the bribe such a source of disquiet? Authorities expressed anxiety that its existence could erode the legitimacy of institutions and, ultimately, of the regime itself, in the eyes of the population. An antibribery drive was launched in 1946, and periodically (if briefly) re-energized over the next six years; the main, but not exclusive, target was corruption in the courts and in the branches of the state prosecutors' office. This "campaign," however, was seriously flawed in practice, not least of all because it was waged in complete secrecy. Why were authorities so slow to pursue bribery, and to allow public discussion of the problem? An analysis of the contentious internal conversations surrounding the postwar "struggle against bribery" provides insight into official attitudes toward the crime, and hesitation by central party officials and the legal agencies to press forward enthusiastically with measures to control it. As chapter 6 shows, in the years between the start of World War II and the death of Stalin, the Soviet regime relied on a vast network of secret informants in its efforts to halt what it considered to be a veritable epidemic of crimes against state property and the socialist economy. Alongside regular police work, the informant network was the primary tool for uncovering the corrupt activities of Soviet officials. What were its strengths and weaknesses?

An explosive bribery scandal in the Soviet high courts, one of the major corruption cases of the Stalin period, is the subject of chapters 7 and 8. This virtually unknown series of cases resulted in the conviction of more than a dozen of the country's leading judges and hundreds of other people for bribery. These final chapters trace these investigations, which I call the "Affair of the High Courts," from their origins in 1947 to the final trial in 1952. Prosecutors charged top judges in the supreme courts of the USSR, the Russian, Ukrainian, and Georgian republics, and the Moscow City Court, as well as judges serving in several other important regional courts. The investigations were conducted completely in secret; neither the charges nor the associated trials were ever mentioned in the press.[41] An exploration of these cases links an investigation of Stalinist high politics with an inquiry into the construction of narratives of corruption and deviance, and the repression of the judiciary after the war. These cases have never before been the subject of in-depth study. What can the prosecution of prominent jurists tell us about the politics of fighting corruption and the methods of the regime in the late Stalin period?

I

1 The Landscape of Bribery and Corruption in the Shadows of Stalinism

AT THE CONCLUSION of World War II, the Soviet Union hardly looked like the victor. Devastated by nearly four years of incredible destruction, the country was depleted, the people impoverished and frequently starving. Up to twenty-seven million people, mostly noncombatants, were killed, leaving millions of orphans. Millions more were homeless. The war left two million invalids in its wake. Even before the Nazi invasion, food supplies, consumer goods, and housing had been scarce, of poor quality, and unevenly distributed. Despite the rapid modernization of heavy industry, living standards had declined sharply during the 1930s. In 1946, the harvest failed, leading to a famine in important agricultural regions that lasted until 1948, taking the lives of one to two million Soviet people, according to the best estimates.[1] Malnutrition and disease afflicted much of the rest of the population.

On this postwar stage, many types of corruption were found at all levels of society and economic life. In a wide variety of ways, government officials in civilian society acted as unofficial entrepreneurs, using their positions to make deals and enrich themselves at public expense. Working within the structures (and around the rules) of a planned economy, they misappropriated and resold government property, embezzled funds, traded access to privileges, offices, and scarce or valuable goods, and negotiated deals that involved bribes. Some relied on informal acquaintanceship or patronage networks to cover up suspect activity, or to obtain materials needed to perform their jobs and fulfill unrealistic plan targets. In so doing, officials exposed themselves to charges of bribery (*vziatochnichestvo*), embezzlement (*rastrata*), profiteering in scarce goods (*spekuliatsiia*), abuse of office (*zloupotreblenie sluzhebnym polozheniem*), and other violations of the criminal code. Many types of activities that central authorities labeled as corruption were inextricably woven into the fabric of Soviet life at all levels throughout the Stalin period (and beyond).

Even before the end of the Great Patriotic War (as World War II was known in the Soviet Union), Communist Party and Soviet governmental bodies declared forms of corruption to be a major problem and issued new measures to combat an uptick in bribery and other white-collar crimes. They also stepped up efforts against theft of state property and economic crimes such as profiteering in scarce products, the acquisition and resale of items known as "speculation." This chapter opens with a brief survey of informal reciprocal practices involving illicit exchanges between officials and citizens in late Imperial Russia and the first decades of Soviet power. It then moves on to an overview of the major varieties of official corruption in the postwar Stalin years, before shifting into a deeper exploration of the central focus of this book, the bribe. The bulk of the chapter uses recently declassified archival records to explore those hybrids of bribery that were almost never publicly discussed, but that were the most common, and the most significant, in the period of postwar Stalinism.

"WHAT DO WE HAVE HANDS FOR?" LATE IMPERIAL AND EARLY SOVIET BRIBERY PRACTICES

The Soviet regime neither invented corruption nor introduced it to the Russian imperial space, of course.[2] It certainly will surprise no one that practices that would be labeled as bribery in the Soviet Union had antecedents in tsarist times. One of the most important of these was *otkormlenie*, or "feeding from one's office" (also known as *kormlenie ot del*), a widely accepted practice whereby the veritable army of officials would supplement their small salaries by accepting gifts from the population in exchange for services.[3] Officials would expect a bottle of alcohol, a meal, a jar of honey, or another gift from petitioners who asked for assistance. In his study of serfdom in Tambov province in the early nineteenth century, Stephen Hoch describes a system of cash gifts accepted by tax collectors that can be regarded as widespread solicitation of bribes from the peasant population. Before one could pay taxes, one had to offer a gift or money to a whole slew of bureaucrats. Police officers also took bribes to supplement their meager salaries.[4] Peasants gave gifts such as eggs, paper, or candles to bureaucrats to ease their contacts with state agents who often made unreasonable and onerous demands. In the words of Nancy Shields Kollmann, referring to an earlier period, "Gift-giving had a reciprocal effect, understood by all."[5]

These traditions of gift exchange muddied the always blurred border between corrupt and non-corrupt acts, in the eyes of the law, of officialdom, and of the population itself. Otkormlenie, for example, was seen by some as a type of coercion, while others saw it as a legitimate way for officials to receive fees for services rendered.[6] Some people regarded their gifts to officials as involuntarily given, a kind of extortion. Others had reason to make gifts freely, seeing their offerings as perfectly acceptable "tokens of appreciation" that enabled smooth relations in the future. Such determinations as to whether these acts were "corrupt" were based on local customs, precedents, and concrete circumstances.

The practice of "feeding" served several functions in Russian society. For one thing, it provided supplementary income to lower officialdom. Gifts to local authorities also allowed individuals to cut through the Imperial administration's unending labyrinth of laws, regulations, and rules by establishing a personalized relationship between official and subject based on reciprocity. Aware of local officialdom's pathetically low pay, some people took pity on the impoverished bureaucrats trying to supplement their miserly incomes, and thus were tolerant of these unofficial gifts. In other cases, higher authorities simply understood that, were it not for such grazing from the local population, officials might turn to less acceptable ways to earn money. The Governor of Kiev province, I. I. Fundukel', for example, knew that big landowners paid off local police forces. Yet, the Governor did not put a stop to the practice because he reasoned that if the police did not take payments from the landowners, they instead would accept bribes from the local thieves.[7]

A second practice common to the tsarist bureaucracy can be seen as a precedent for certain varieties of bribery common in Soviet institutions. Podnoshenie (from the verb podnosit', to bring) was the giving of desirable gifts to one's superiors in an organization as a way of ensuring one's rise through the ranks or guaranteeing one's position. Strict hierarchies—the vertically ascending, ossified layers of administration—encouraged payments up the pyramid of power by those occupying the lower rungs.

These practices of "*feeding*" and "*bringing gifts*" meshed neatly together, reinforcing one another. Thus, lower-level officials took from the population (otkormlenie) in part in so they could embellish the offerings they brought to their bosses (podnoshenie). These relationships constituted a veritable "food chain," as superiors fed off their minions in the bureaucracy, who in turn fed off the population. It was this food chain—this dependence of ordinary people on (sometimes voluntary) payments to grasping state officials for their everyday needs, and those officials' subsequent payments to ever higher (and, perhaps, more venal) rungs of the hierarchy—that Soviet revolutionaries later sought to break up.

Why was the acceptance of bribes a widespread practice in Imperial Russia? Salaries of lower officialdom remained quite low, sometimes below subsistence level. Low incomes provided incentive to bureaucrats to "feed from" the population. Yet low salaries alone cannot account for pervasive bribery, which could occur even among relatively well-paid government elites.[8] Poor levels of education and inadequate professional training played their parts, to be sure. Young and inexperienced people were appointed to positions in the provinces, where, either unaware of professional ethics or unwilling to be guided by a sense of professional responsibility, they regarded their offices as an opportunity for self-enrichment. Absent a knowledge of—or respect for—the law, many officials did not consider it wrong to accept payments as a reward for doing their jobs. Complex and contradictory rules, the personalization of relationships, the poor training of police, judges, and other officials, and huge amounts of red tape in the administration and the legal system also provided fertile ground for the spread of dubious practices.[9] These factors were all very much in play in Soviet bureaucracies as well.

Richard Wortman has detailed the development of a Russian "legal consciousness" in the nineteenth century, which emerged with the growth of legal education and training for lawyers and jurists. This consciousness could be observed primarily in the higher levels of the legal administrations, and resulted in some increase in ethical responsibility among judicial and procuracy professionals.[10] Nevertheless, the reforms of mid-century and changes in the mentalities of some officials could not break the hold of the traditional practice of gift exchanges between civilians and officials. Nor, as Wortman points out, did they result in an increased respect for the law among many officials. As Catriona Kelly notes, by the late nineteenth century, there was widespread social and legal toler-ance for gifts to officials.[11] Bribery so deeply permeated some offices that audits often revealed that entire bureaus were infected; whole offices were fired, and entire departments were shut down.[12] (Imperial laws on bribery will be discussed in chapter 3.)

Most of the Russian literary and political intelligentsia were enraged by what they regarded as rampant government corruption, incubated and sheltered by a rotten autocracy that used legal institutions as a tool of domination; they spared no wrath in lambasting it. In his magazine, *The Bell (Kolokol)*, the journalist and literary critic Aleksandr Herzen wrote scathing indictments of individual bureaucrats whose bribery, embezzlement, and other dirty dealings had been leaked to him, often anonymously. He exposed what he called bureaucrats' frauds, moral turpitude, and servility, and other miscarriages of justice (often by pub-lishing documents). Bureaucrats, he said, had been bought off by the autocracy: "People who take bribes will never rebel."[13]

Nineteenth-century Russian literature is a rich source of prototypes of the bribe-taking imperial official, with contemptuous if hilarious vi-gnettes depicting Russian subjects' frustrating, and often absurd, inter-actions with venal *chinovniki* (a derogatory word for state bureaucrats), typically implying their greed and sloth. Sketches of the unabashedly corrupt provincial office holders by Nikolai Gogol', Anton Chekhov, and Mikhail Saltykov-Shchedrin are timeless. A banned comedy by Vasilii Kapnist by the name of *Iabeda* contains the immortal lines, sung by the bureaucrat-protagonist: "There is nothing to it/Take whatever you can/What do we have hands for/If not that we can take?"[14]

Stereotypes of the especially corrupt Russian functionary emerged largely from the struggle between a frustrated intelligentsia and an ar-bitrarily repressive bureaucracy.[15] The judges, court clerks, and police officers who harassed and persecuted writers and activists were targets for especially bitter invective, most memorably in the stories of Gogol'. Liberal critics of the autocracy also decried the venal petty official as a symbol of Russian backwardness. There is scarce evidence to indicate that Russian bureaucrats as a group were significantly more corrupt than bureaucrats in similar positions in other European countries. The ideal Weberian bureaucracy with its perfectly honest, disinterested, and professional officialdom was just that—an ideal. Corruption among Russian bureaucrats certainly existed, and was tolerated by some despite reformers' efforts to fight it. But it is not possible to demonstrate that Russian officialdom was *especially* corrupt. It is certainly true, however, that the practice of demanding gifts in exchange for services (and wealthy elites' and businessmen's attempts to buy off officials) was a target of special venom from the revolutionaries who were intent on destroying the tsarist state.

"ON THE BRIBERY FRONT" AFTER THE BOLSHEVIK REVOLUTION

Upon taking power in 1917, the new Soviet regime wasted little time issuing legislation condemning relationships between citizens and officials (and among officials themselves) based on illicit gifts or cash. The first Soviet anticorruption law, "On Bribery," was published on May 8, 1918. The legislation essentially defined the act of the bribe just as tsarist legislation had—as a gift of any kind to an official intended to distort their judgment as they acted in their official capacity. Yet unlike tsarist law, which did not punish the givers of bribes in most circumstances, all parties in a bribe transaction—givers, acceptors, and intermediaries—were subject to the same stiff penalty: typically five years of imprisonment with hard labor. Like all Bolshevik laws in this period, early legislation targeting crime by officials had a rigid class character. Offenders from the "exploiting classes" were usually punished with especially harsh forced-labor assignments.[16] There was little the regime could do to quash such practices, however, which by all accounts continued to infuse the lower levels of administration.

A new Criminal Code of the RSFSR took effect on July 1, 1922. People convicted of acting as intermediaries were to receive a two-year minimum sentence, sometimes with the confiscation of property. Bribe givers got up to three years. Those who accepted bribes in the absence of aggravating circumstances could receive up to five years in prison, sometimes with the confiscation of their property; aggravating circumstances resulted in a minimum of three years in isolation. The Code allowed for the possibility of the death penalty in the most serious cases. (The provision allowing for capital punishment was annulled in 1927, in honor of the tenth anniversary of the October Revolution.)[17] In a shift from tsarist legal practice, Soviet courts usually assigned the most severe sentences to those who offered the bribes, rather than to those who accepted them, because the authorities claimed that the businesspeople (known in this period as Nepmen) who gave bribes were the real danger to Soviet power. Soviet officials, on the other hand, were regarded as basically honest people who had succumbed to temptation but were redeemable (as long as they were not themselves descended from the exploiting classes). The legal statutes codified this difference, assigning more severe punishments to the givers rather than the takers of bribes.

Several areas of life became common arenas for deals involving bribes. For example, bribery appears to have been widespread in the housing department of the Moscow city soviet, which was responsible for assigning apartments to city residents. For those who needed an apartment, a payment under the table at a Moscow housing bureau could trim waiting time from four months to twenty-four hours.[18] Bribery was also common in rail transportation, where, by some accounts, simply obtaining a ticket on a passenger train required an extra payment. The Cheka (the political police) issued an order on January 12, 1922, noting "bribery on the railways of the RSFSR has recently become extremely widespread and is doing colossal harm to the Republic."[19] Bribery was common in other areas as well. Enterprise managers paid railway employees to ensure delivery, to guarantee the fastest routes, to hitch and unhitch freight cars, and to ensure that food for their staff would be delivered. A very poorly paid rural police force entered deals involving extra payments or "gifts" of moonshine. Reports of judges swapping favors in exchange for alcohol and food pervaded local and central investigations of the judiciary. And in rural areas, long-established forms of reciprocity among peasants and officials were labeled "bribery" by a regime intent on eradicating the "uncivilized vestiges" of the tsarist past.[20]

Why did the Bolsheviks condemn bribe-taking officials with such vigor? In part, for the same reasons that other states have done so— bribery weakened central state control over the administration and the economy. Pervasive bribery within Soviet institutions would undermine the state's power and reach, both because it could sap the legitimacy of the new government in the eyes of the population, and because a corrupt bureaucracy could not be counted on to carry out its policies.

Yet the regime also had other reasons for targeting bribery. In Bolshevik eyes, bribery had been among the worst crimes of the Imperial era. It represented the flagrant use of cash by the wealthy to purchase official favors, subvert justice for common people, and buttress the power of their class to exploit the laboring masses. The bribe was a highly accessible metaphor for the control of the entire state by the rich, at the expense of the poor. Bribery perfectly symbolized the chasm between "the state" and "the people" under capitalism; socialism would wipe away this division. In the Bolshevik worldview, it persisted under the tsars not only because it had been tolerated by the state, but because it had been, indeed, a key part of the state's central nervous system. Under capitalism, bribery was absolutely *essential* for the survival of the entire system.

To the new regime, the bribe thus held great symbolic importance: it epitomized capitalism in general, as the bourgeoisie "bought" officials. This language of "buying" (*podkup*) the state is precisely the wording that was used. Under capitalism, people's consciences and loyalties (like everything else) were for sale. Bribery under the Old Regime was described, and denounced, in the language of markets: the buying and selling of favors and access, the intermediaries acting as brokers, the profits and commissions, all founded on the idea that both offices and office holders were perennially for sale to the highest bidder. Socialism promised an end to what one commentator called "the spirit of venality" through the eradication of capitalism.[21] The overthrow of capitalism meant liberation from the power of the underhanded, secret, backroom deals that preserved the position of the exploiting classes. These early anticorruption efforts were framed by notions of pervasive class antagonism, like nearly everything that the Bolsheviks did.

For the Bolsheviks, bribery also typified the *moral* decay of capitalism. Corrupt relationships formed the rotten core at the center of the old world. From this perspective, the assault on bribery was an important part of the attempt to create a new model official—rarely met in Imperial Russia—the upright and impartial bureaucrat who would understand his duty to serve the laboring people rather than the grasping bourgeoisie.[22]

By the end of the 1920s and the beginning of the 1930s, there was an upsurge in concern about bribery among party and legal authorities, which coincided with Stalin's violent attempt to rid the countryside of capitalist "elements" through the collectivization of agriculture. A spike in bribery was again blamed on the enemies of socialism, in this case the so-called "kulaks," the supposedly "rich" peasants who resisted the state's seizure of their land, tools, machinery, and animals. According to official explanations, kulaks attempted to keep their land by buying off procurement agents and local authorities with gifts of food and (especially) alcohol.[23] Bribery, then, was again described by party authorities as a tool of class war, as capitalist elements such as kulaks used every available weapon to stop the consolidation of power by "the people."

During the mid- and late-1930s, however, law enforcement appears to have shifted its attention away from the problem of bribery. Prosecutors likely began to neglect the crime for several reasons. One important factor was the official claim that bribery, like many crimes, had been all but eliminated from Soviet society in the socialist era, with only a few unusual exceptions. This explanation gained currency especially with the end of collectivization and the declaration that socialism had been "built" in 1936. Since bribery was regarded as a remnant of the all-but-dead capitalist system, it *should* have been nearly extinct. Only scattered "saboteurs," "kulaks," "wreckers," certain parts of the pre-revolutionary intelligentsia, and other "enemies of the working people" would even consider engaging in this vile act.

Furthermore, the political priorities of the regime had entered a new phase. In the firestorm of terror and witch-hunts, police obsessively focused on arresting "political" criminals and rounding up dangerous "social marginals." Party leaders now aimed to prosecute Trotskyites and other "traitors" charged with "counterrevolutionary" crimes under Article 58 of the 1926 RSFSR Criminal Code, which covered various crimes against the state. In this period of hyper-vigilance against "enemies of the people," the crime of bribery was barely on the radar screen of the party and police. When it *was* exposed, bribery, like all white-collar crimes in the 1930s, was treated by the authorities as a consciously anti-Soviet act, undertaken to undermine socialism. Just as in the 1920s, bribery was considered an attack on the entire social and economic system, not merely a dying cultural artifact or a product of petty greed or individual desperation.

On the eve of World War II, then, bribery officially continued to survive only among a small, "backward" segment of Soviet society, a tiny slice of the population still infected with the poisonous but dying remnants of "bourgeois" ideology and the avaricious habits associated with private property. Despite official proclamations, of course, bribery continued to occur in the 1930s. The varieties and venues were largely the same in the 1930s as they had been in the previous decade. The courts, the police, housing, food collection agencies, inspectorates, industry, the military, and the collective farms were all places where ordinary people and officials made deals to slice through procedures and rules, obtain release from obligations, or otherwise grease the wheels to circumvent official regulations.[24]

Fundamentally, the Bolsheviks believed that if they could destroy capitalist infrastructure and corporations, and break the nexus between the government and private capital, then corruption would have no soil in which to establish its roots. They correctly identified bribery as a *deal* between at least two (usually willing) parties. But the argument that bribes were passed only among wealthy, greedy scoundrels, in whom the legacy of capitalism had not died, misinterpreted the nature of social life. The poor and desperate—both impoverished bureaucrats and downtrodden common people—also made deals, as did members of the emerging middle classes and professions. The Bolsheviks' analysis, heavily laden with moral and ideological condemnation, blinded them to the multiple functions and causes of bribery in tsarist and early Soviet society. This core belief, that good, honest, devoted Soviet citizens would never enter illegal deals with officials, was a major misunderstanding. Similarly, the fantasy that bribery cannot exist in a socialist country missed the fact that such relationships had existed as long as there had been states, and showed no signs of disappearing.

A POSTWAR BAZAAR OF CORRUPTION

In the period of postwar Stalinism, most of the crimes treated in this study as "corruption," including bribery and abuse of office, fell under the category of what the 1926 RSFSR Criminal Code called "crimes by officials acting in their official capacity" (*dolzhnostnye prestupleniia*). The crime of "abuse of office," for example, tended to serve as a catch-all for charging officials with crimes resulting in material harm to the state that did not fit neatly into other articles of the criminal code. Abuse of office (Article 109 of the RSFSR Criminal Code) was defined as any action by an official that interfered with the proper operating of an institution or enterprise and that caused it material loss or damaged public order. Authorities complained that many people who should have been convicted of crimes that were more serious were instead charged with abuse of office. A procuracy report noted, for example, that courts too often convicted store managers who had embezzled funds of abuse of office rather than theft of state property, with its much harsher penalties.[25] The numbers of convictions for abuse of office grew from 47,000 in 1940, to 48,500 in 1944, to 72,000 in 1946, peaking at 82,000 in 1947.[26]

The most significant postwar law that touched upon infractions by officialdom targeted the theft of "socialist and societal" property. The expression "socialist and societal (*obshchestvennoi*) property" covered state property, and property controlled by collective farms, trade unions, clubs, and other so-called "cooperative organizations." The term "socialist property" was essentially synonymous with "state property."

An extremely harsh *ukaz* (decree), issued on June 4, 1947 (known as the June 4 law), mandated a seven-year minimum sentence for the theft of state property, a crime for which the minimum penalty had previously been three months' imprisonment.[27] The infamous decree of June 4 called for sentences of ten to twenty-five years for repeat offenses, "group" offenses, and thefts in especially large quantities.[28] (The death penalty had been abolished a few weeks earlier, in May 1947.) Before 1947, these crimes were addressed in the criminal code by Article 116, which covered embezzlement and misappropriation; by Article 162, which covered theft and pilfering of state property; and by the law of August 7, 1932. According to a report sent to Stalin and Georgii M. Malenkov by USSR Minister of Justice Gorshenin, material losses due to theft of state property were estimated at nearly 1.5 billion rubles in 1948 and over 1.2 billion rubles in 1949. As Gorshenin noted, however, due to inefficiencies in detecting and recording theft, the actual figures were surely much higher.[29]

Annual convictions union-wide by the regular courts for theft of state property in this period ranged from more than 454,000 at the height of the campaign against theft of state property in 1947, to about 180,000 in 1952.[30] Inside party ranks, abuse of office and theft of socialist property were also commonly punished infractions; between 1946 and 1951, approximately 180,000 people were excluded from the Communist Party for such violations.[31] Among expelled party members, theft of state property represented the largest proportion of the fifteen categories of infractions that could result in expulsion. In these years, between 27 percent and 31 percent of those expelled had been removed for abuse of office or theft of state property.

In fact, the 1947 decree on the theft of state property engendered a classic Soviet campaign: a short period of mass arrests in the months following its publication, followed by a gradual drop-off in prosecutions as the campaign lost steam. The campaign swept up three categories of Soviet subjects. First, between 1947 and 1953 the decree led to the arrests of hundreds of thousands of collective farmers (*kolkhozniki*) accused of stealing food, animals, or grain from collective farms in the wake of the 1946 famine. The decree seems to have had its genesis in this massive pilfering of produce from collective farms by hungry collective farmers during crop failures. In addition to collective farmers, hundreds of thousands of industrial workers accused of stealing factory or enterprise property were also charged under the June 4 decree.[32]

Yet people from a third social category—officials and white-collar employees—were also arrested *en masse* under the June 4, 1947 ukaz. This third type of property crime has received less attention from scholars who have discussed the June 4 law. As the data show, only one-half of those arrested for theft of state property between 1947 and 1952 were workers or collective farmers; among the remainder, a great many were officials. Tens of thousands of officials were arrested, convicted, and given long mandatory sentences for various types of theft of state property in the course of their duties.

We should think of the June 4 decree on the theft of state property not exclusively as a measure directed against theft by peasants and workers, but rather as a three-pronged attack that included white collar employees, such as auditors, bookkeepers, and the directors of enterprises, stores, warehouses, and collective farms. Why did this law target officialdom? The theft of state property was growing during the war and in its aftermath, and this was purported to be highly detrimental to state interests.[33] Soviet authorities claimed that the socialist ownership of the means of production, a critical foundation of Soviet society, was responsible for its scientific and engineering achievements, which contributed to victory in World War II.

Moreover, procurators discovered that officials were at the center of many theft schemes. Quite often the largest-scale and best-organized crimes involved officials in key roles. They were able to facilitate crimes through bookkeeping maneuvers, by covering up thefts from warehouses, by passing on goods to speculators, or by exploiting their connections or positions to mask crimes and benefit themselves. As early as late 1946, when food procurement authorities were complaining about the volume of thefts from collective farms, many of them blamed not only peasants, but also officials. In September 1946, for example, the deputy Minister of Procurements for the USSR, V. Dvinskii, complained to the Council of Ministers that "in the majority of cases" officials responsible for protecting produce that had been stolen, such as the managers of warehouses and supply points, were involved in the thefts.[34] In a letter to Beria dated December 30, 1946, Justice Minister Rychkov detailed several major cases of grain theft. In nearly every case, prosecutors alleged that an official, such as a collective farm chairperson or a state farm director, was the driving force in the scheme.[35]

The regime's focus on defending state property, combined with the general postwar chaos, created an environment in which efforts to crack down on theft of state property resulted in the large-scale arrests of officials. One can argue that the June 4 decree was part of an anti-corruption effort aimed especially at the middle and lower levels of the bureaucracy, buttressed by a sense among some law enforcement and party authorities that theft by officials was spiraling out of control. This is not to say that the June 1947 law, which was drafted and revised by Stalin himself,[36] was designed *primarily* to target officials suspected of stealing state property. More likely, authorities conceived the decree during the 1946–1947 famine to update the August 1932 law on theft of state property, which was used to prosecute desperate peasants stealing food during the famine that followed collectivization. The August 1932 law on theft had imposed minimum sentences of ten years in prison for theft of state property (at that time mainly the theft of grain and animals from collective farms), and allowed for capital punishment in particularly heinous cases. Convictions peaked in 1933, and then quickly trailed off.[37] The June 4 law went far beyond the August 1932 law, and subsumed several white-collar (*dolzhnostnye*) crimes, including embezzlement and misappropriation of funds or state property (under Article 116), which earlier had not been categorized as property crimes in the criminal code. Therefore these crimes were now punished much more severely, normally with sentences of at least seven years.[38] The June 4 decree's utility in punishing official malfeasance likely became more apparent as it was applied in practice.[39]

THE CRIME OF BRIBERY—HISTORICAL BACKGROUND

Within the larger context of the crackdown on crimes by officials, bribery had its own interesting peculiarities. Remarkably, the punishments set out in the 1926 RSFSR Criminal Code were unchanged until 1953 (and beyond; the first revision came with the new criminal code of 1960), despite enormous political and economic changes. Two articles of the 1926 RSFSR Criminal Code covered bribery (vziatochnichestvo), which the law defined as an inducement that improperly influenced the performance of an official's public function to the interest of the giver.[40] People who had *accepted* bribes were charged with Article 117, while the *offering* of bribes and the act of serving as an intermediary in a bribery transaction were covered under Article 118. The criminal code categorized bribery as a *dolzhnostnoe prestuplenie*—a crime by officials carried out while serving in their official capacity. The code did not categorize bribery as an economic crime (such as speculation) or a crime against socialist property (such as theft).

The distribution of bribes was often, to be sure, at the heart of schemes facilitating speculation, embezzlement, and the diversion of state property. The law recognized that a bribe could be offered as cash, or it could be in the form of other products (or services) of value, including "cattle, grain, clothing, manufactures, and food."[41] The law stipulated that even if officials simply accepted gifts to do what the law required them to do, they had committed the crime of bribery. Officials could not be "rewarded" for doing something that was part of their normal responsibilities. Officials charged with bribery often made this defense— that they had not committed a crime; rather, they merely accepted a gift of thanks after doing their jobs properly. In contrast to Imperial law, Soviet law considered even such an after-the-fact reward to be a serious crime, punishable under the articles on bribery.

Before 1946, it was possible for a bribe-taking official to receive five to ten years in prison under aggravating circumstances, though a sentence this severe was quite rare. The majority of those convicted for accepting or offering bribes before 1946 were sentenced to between six months and two years of imprisonment, probation, or workplace labor. After the onset of a crackdown in the summer of 1946, punishments were toughened somewhat (though the laws did not change), and most of those convicted for offering or giving bribes were sentenced to between two and five years, or up to ten years under aggravating circumstances.

It is not possible to determine with precision the absolute level of bribery in a society as secretive as the Stalinist USSR. (Even in democratic societies, with a free press and relatively accessible crime data, calculating the amount of illegal economic activity poses enormous challenges.) Nevertheless, both anecdotal and archival evidence indicate that the phenomenon was widespread after the war. Although crime statistics cannot possibly tell the whole story, between 1945 and 1953, the largest number of people convicted for bribery union-wide in a single year was only about 5,600 (in 1947), a figure that clearly understates the extent greatly, as is always the case in deals of this type.[42] As is common everywhere, only a small proportion of instances of bribery were ever discovered or prosecuted by law enforcement. In the USSR, the venues for bribery were enormously diverse, and the various schemes were usually quite difficult to uncover.[43] The discrepancy between the actual volume of deals and the number of convictions was due in part to the challenges that law enforcement faced in discovering—and then in prosecuting—the crime. A bribe is a secret arrangement without witnesses, typically involving only two people (or sometimes three, if an intermediary acts as facilitator). Moreover, as Susan Rose-Ackerman has noted, "Both sides to the deal have an interest in blurring the meaning of the payment in the eyes of the outside world while keeping it quite explicit between themselves."[44] It was to both parties' benefit to have a successful transaction remain forever undiscovered.

REELING FROM THE WAR

In September 1946, less than eighteen months after the triumphant conclusion of the war, the lead editorial in *Sotsialisticheskaia zakonnost'* (*Socialist Legality*), the monthly journal of the USSR Procuracy, the Ministry of Justice, and the Soviet Supreme Court and the major journal for legal professionals, unleashed a thunderous denunciation of those Soviet officials who had failed to learn the lessons of the heroic war experience. Bribe-taking officials were taken to task and condemned as a significant threat to the postwar order. The editorial blamed an alarming upsurge in bribery on the actions of a small minority of morally corrupted officials who lacked sufficient patriotic feeling and sense of duty. In a period of postwar hardship, these few flawed bureaucrats exploited the situation. "During the Great Fatherland War, the well-organized, precise activities of all rungs of the state mechanism enabled the successful resolution of the military tasks that stood before our country," the article declared.[45] The editorial quoted Stalin's speech of November 6, 1942, which praised the work of the Soviet people on the home front: "All of our complicated organizational and construction work resulted not only in the transformation of the country, but of the people themselves. People became smarter, stronger, more disciplined; they learned how to work in a military way, [and] they came to fully understand their duties to their Fatherland." Echoing Stalin's words, the editorial affirmed that the state apparatus had played a major role in this crucial work. Ominously, however, the author warned that certain parts of the state administration are still "not completely free of people who lack feelings of civic duty, [nor is the administration free of] all kinds of random elements, slackers and crooks who steal socialist property, undermine the rules of the socialist community, and violate government discipline."

The authors went further, singling out bribe-taking officials. These criminals are morally weak and have no place in Soviet society. Officials who accept bribes corrode the ability of the party to protect state property and to distribute goods to the people according to the plan: "Criminal and morally unstable elements, who have surfaced in the state and economic apparatuses, frequently choose to abuse their offices, accepting and extorting bribes for the purpose of stealing socialist property. In this period of reconstruction, bribe takers destroy the normal work of the state and economic apparatuses, undermining state discipline and its strictly planned foundation, the immutable law of the Soviet economic system." The editorial denounced these bribe-taking "elements" as "parasites and the enemies of socialism."

The reality, however, was much more complex, and, in fact, much more serious than this righteously indignant piece would imply. The war and its aftermath represent a largely unrecognized turning point in fueling the kind of corruption that proved to be a hallmark of later periods of Soviet history. Certainly, such criminality existed before 1941. In the early 1930s, the introduction of the five-year plans and the collectivization of agriculture stimulated the growth of black markets and other informal institutions inside the socialized economy. The period of war and postwar restabilization, however, witnessed conditions that helped to accelerate and reinforce existing patterns of underground economic activity and corruption. These years created new opportunities for entrepreneurial officials who controlled the distribution of scarce goods and services to join in illegal deals with desperate Soviet subjects, and with each other.[46]

Indeed, the Great Patriotic War and the immediate postwar years provided fertile ground for bribery. Beginning especially in 1943, according to archive sources, the various permutations of crimes by officials began to flourish. The conditions that established the framework for this increased corruption had roots—or took on a more pronounced form—during the war.[47] The dislocation of populations, poverty, extraordinary shortages of housing and food, the disruption of the courts and the legal system, breakdowns in goods distribution, and famine put many Soviet people at risk, while tempting officials to benefit from their offices. In the words of one Ministry of Justice report, the "general moral uplift in the country" at the beginning of the war was one major reason for a decline in crime between 1941 and 1943.[48] By 1944, however, arrests for many types of crime, including theft of state property, abuse of office, and bribery, had grown significantly. As of 1947, the number of convictions for crimes by officials had risen 40 percent beyond the prewar level.[49] This increase remained a major concern for authorities during late Stalinism and indicates, at the very least, that law enforcement was paying more attention to these activities.

Rather than attempt to challenge or even overthrow their rulers during the desperate postwar period, Soviet subjects sought ways to cope with exhaustion and poverty. In this environment, illicit deals with officials were a vital tool for survival. As people yearned for (and increasingly expected) peace, stability, shelter, and work as rewards for their wartime sacrifices, they made quiet if illegal agreements with local officials who were in a position to help them. Well-placed bribes lubricated the shadow economy and the official economy alike.

Law enforcement authorities identified the period between 1943 and 1946 as a time when bribery reappeared as a serious problem in many areas of Soviet life. The characteristic view of most of the 1930s—the notion that bribery had all but vanished from Soviet society—was essentially absent from internal party and law enforcement discussions of crime after the war. An instruction of the USSR Procurator General in mid-1946 alluded to the rosy prewar view: "During the years of Soviet power, until the beginning of the war for the Fatherland, bribery in our country had been almost completely liquidated; the organs of the procuracy deserve much of the credit for this."[50] One sees here echoes of the official line—that the state had all but wiped out bribery before the war. The procuracy itself claimed credit for the successes in repressing bribery before 1941, while glorying in its absence.

Yet, as the same 1946 instruction phrased it, "Recently the situation has changed for the worse. One must recognize that this, one of the most disgusting of crimes, has again become quite widespread." Bribery "has appeared even in certain departments of the procuracy itself, that is, in precisely those agencies which are called upon to wage a merciless battle against this crime, which is so dangerous to the state." For the procuracy to acknowledge a spike in the crime's prevalence during the war, therefore tarnishing its own self-proclaimed record of success, would indicate that the situation may have become very severe indeed.

Those areas where bribery was pervasive highlight the fault lines in postwar Soviet society. Severe fractures in systems of production, distribution, documentation, supply, transportation, and (as will be discussed in later chapters) law enforcement gave birth to informal (and often illegal) relationships between Soviet subjects and officialdom. Such relationships played a role in many central areas of Soviet life: housing, the railroads, branches of local administration, and the workplace. One could argue that, in fact, the bribe served many critical social and economic functions, acting as a way to help people try to cope with crises and improve living standards.

GETTING THINGS DONE: THE VARIETIES AND FUNCTIONS OF THE BRIBE

Who took the opportunity to engage in gift exchanges with officials after the war, and what were their motives? In which arenas of Soviet life was it most prevalent? What were its functions in postwar Soviet society? Most cases of bribery that were prosecuted featured middle- and lower-level officials trading in relatively small amounts of money or valuables with people at all social levels, from struggling collective farmers and industrial workers to comparatively well-off directors of stores and factories.

A study of the landscape of bribes can be structured according to the purposes they served and the motives people had for offering them. Deals based on the exchange of bribes enabled people to maneuver in a society governed by multiple levels of a highly arbitrary and disorganized state bureaucracy. Perhaps the best term to describe state administration in the late Stalinist period is the Russian word *proizvol*, which conjures up a bureaucracy that is at once powerful, repressive, excessive, and unpredictable.

In the interest of grouping the many possible types of bribes, we have created four general (sometimes overlapping and by no means mutually exclusive) categories. Two of these were more common in daily life, and the other two were mainly related to the workplace. The first variety of bribery common in everyday life involved illegal deals that people arranged to obtain what they believed the state *lawfully owed them,* whether it was housing, social benefits, employment, or transport. Soviet people paid a second kind of bribe to acquire services *outside the law*—to avoid taxes or other state obligations, or to acquire needed documents or registrations. At the workplace, people in positions of authority undertook a third type of bribery in order to supplement their income, leveraging their positions and power to extract "tribute" from subordinate employees. Such tribute often took the form of payments *from* one's subordinates, part of which would then be paid *to* those further up in the hierarchy, a variation on the phenomenon of podnoshenie, or "the bringing of gifts." Finally, managers resorted to various forms of under-the-table payments to help them meet production quotas in a chaotic and extremely inefficient economy.

Chapter 2 will investigate bribery in the opaque and often outrageously punitive law enforcement and criminal justice systems.

DOCUMENTS AND APARTMENTS

Striking deals with officials could help Soviet people overcome the challenges presented by intransigent government bureaucracies. The first category of bribe was aimed at obtaining something that one had a right to under the law, but could not obtain due to unyielding, incompetent, or overburdened officials. Such payments helped people extract basic necessities, including important documents, housing, and transportation, from confounding bureaucracies.

Individuals were entirely dependent on government agencies for crucial documentation pertaining to their work history, identity, and residency, including internal passports. The wholesale destruction of personal paperwork and government records during the war only deepened the population's need for layer after layer of documentation. Disputes over these documents—or over their loss and replacement—could pass through multiple departments of local or municipal administrations, whose staff were perfectly positioned to demand an illegal "fee" to resolve problems. Individuals were at a huge disadvantage in dealing with the state bureaucracy, which often failed to review problems fairly or in a timely manner. Pensioners, families with children, invalids, and people who were ill, were all eligible for state subsidies, for example. Some officials created obstacles to block these people from receiving the benefits they were due, facilitating the process only if they received a valuable gift. Applicants had to pay to speed up stalled paperwork. In a 1949 case in the Izmailovskaia *oblast'* of the Ukrainian SSR, a bookkeeper in a regional finance office received a two-year sentence for refusing to disburse subsidies to women with children unless they made an extra payment on the side.[51]

One of the major motivations behind this type of payment came from the Soviet Union's extraordinary postwar housing crisis. There were great challenges involving access to apartments. According to procuracy statistics, illegal payments related to housing problems were the second-most-common type of bribe in the postwar years, surpassed only by bribes paid to law enforcement personnel. A February 1947 study by the RSFSR Procuracy found that fully one third of the 404 individuals in its sample of people arrested for taking bribes were employees of housing administrations.[52]

Apartments were one of the USSR's scarcest and most coveted commodities. Availability of housing was already at a critical level in the 1930s, when millions of people poured into the new industrial sites and the older, established cities.[53] The war exacerbated the shortage as enormous quantities of housing stock were ruined. Just after the end of the war, for example, a justice official in the Belorussian SSR reported that "according to data collected by the extraordinary state commission to determine and investigate atrocities committed by the German-Fascist invaders and their collaborators, in the city of Minsk 80 percent of buildings were destroyed, 90 percent of all buildings were destroyed in Vitebsk, 95 percent in Polotsk, 85 percent in Gomel, and 70 percent in Mogilev." The historian Karl Qualls notes that in Sevastopol', only 16 percent of residential buildings were usable. In all, housing for perhaps twenty-five million people was destroyed.[54] Adding to the confusion, military and civilian authorities had evacuated more than sixteen million people eastward to the interior of the country after the German invasion of June 22, 1941. When they returned home, some evacuees found that they needed to pay bribes just to get permission to reside in the towns from which they had fled.

Once they returned to their home cities, people scrambled to reclaim their apartments. Yet much of the surviving housing stock had been taken over by state or military authorities, who frequently tried to block people from regaining possession, despite their complaints to city government. People sometimes had to bribe housing bureau employees to regain access to their own apartments (or to keep from being removed from them). Justice agencies noted that this situation created "unhealthy moods and dissatisfaction," including fury over the secret payments and "gifts" solicited by housing officials. In November 1943, the head of the housing administration of the Voroshilov region in the city of Baku was convicted and sentenced to seven years in prison for accepting a 3,800-ruble bribe to exchange a citizen's "small" living space (eighteen square meters) for a "large" space (thirty-six square meters).[55]

By war's end, the tremendous scarcity of apartments made housing officials highly sought-after partners for bribes. Between 1945 and 1948, 8.5 million demobilized soldiers swamped the country's available housing, greatly exacerbating an already critical situation. The military demobilized 4,800,000 soldiers between May and December 1945 alone. The demobilization put enormous pressure on both urban and rural housing stock. It is not surprising that many veterans had great difficulty finding apartments.[56] In 1946, investigators accused an inspector in the Tbilisi (Georgia) housing bureau of extorting money from soldiers returning from the front who needed places to live. The case was suspended when the inspector went into hiding to evade the police.[57]

An Odessa newspaper described the shame of wounded veterans forced to make valuable "gifts" to receive a place to live.[58]

In Moscow, the housing situation was extremely dire. In 1943–1944, hundreds of thousands of evacuees returned to the city. German bombardments had damaged over 20,000 residential buildings in the capital city.[59] Many Muscovites returned from evacuation to find that branches of national agencies or, more often, the housing department of the Moscow City Soviet, had assigned their apartments to other people or institutions. The new occupants frequently refused to vacate the space when the original tenants returned. These circumstances provided the employees of the Moscow housing administration with tremendous opportunities. When people could not resolve their disputes through the city housing departments, they could take up matters in the courts, which soon became embroiled in thousands of housing cases. Indeed, in late 1944 police arrested several judges in Moscow for accepting bribes from returning evacuees who rightly had demanded the return of their living space.[60]

The chair of the USSR Supreme Court, Ivan T. Goliakov, recalled that the mass return from evacuation created great confusion.[61] Often, he wrote, different housing officials and judges had given both sides in these disputes the right to occupy the same space. These decisions gave rise to "endless disagreements that frequently involve the meddling of ranking employees of ministries and administrations." In many cases, Goliakov went on, even after reviewing the "confusing and contradictory documents" the courts simply could not establish who genuinely had the right to occupy an apartment.[62]

In a letter to Stalin of September 18, 1947, S. N. Kruglov, the head of the Ministry of Internal Affairs (MVD), described multiple instances of bribery that the police had discovered in the Moscow housing administration.[63] He wrote that the director of the housing administration for the Tagansk region of Moscow "illegally offered living space to a certain citizen Merzliakov, for which she received a bribe of 7,000 rubles from him."[64] In another case, Kruglov reports, the director of a regional housing department in Moscow and his bookkeeper illegally granted apartments—and illegally registered residency documents (*propiski*)—for various people from whom they received bribes.

In a tragic case documented in the records of the USSR Procuracy, a certain Nikolai K. Akulov took drastic action when he was unable to recover his apartment after he returned from the army in 1944.[65] Akulov had been the commander of the guard at the Kremlin since 1933. Denied access to his former living quarters on Moscow's Meshchanskaia Street, apparently because someone else had paid a bribe to a powerful person, he lived with his wife and two small children as squatters in an abandoned apartment while they waited for permission to live in their previous quarters or to obtain a new flat. On November 22, 1949, the police, following an order by the procuracy, "violently" evicted the family of squatters, according to a letter sent to Beria by Akulov's wife. For two months, they lived in a hallway. Their son could not attend school. "Unable physically to handle it," Akulov and his family very reluctantly moved in with his mother-in-law in one ramshackle, "half-destroyed" ten-square-meter room. With the room too tiny for a bed, they all slept on the floor. In the winter, snow came in through the walls. Finally, on January 11, 1951, Akulov killed himself. He left a despondent note that revealed his frustrated expectations after the war, including his belief that unchecked bribery was one of many negative phenomena that were disfiguring Soviet society: "I gave all my work, all my strength, my health, and the well-being of my family, and for all that I have nothing. There is no reason to go on—it is already too much. I do not want to blame anyone, but the laws do not convict anyone. Selfishness and sycophancy, bribery and bureaucratism are everywhere in abundance. We'll never reach communism with this kind of a showing." The Procurator General Grigorii N. Safonov himself became involved in the investigation, though he evinced no sympathy for the pleadings of Akulov's wife. "Judging by Akulov's behavior before his death," Safonov wrote, "his suicide was obviously the result of his disturbed psyche." (The files provide no evidence of what became of Akulov's wife and children.)

Records from a procuracy investigation reveal a fascinating twist on the prevalence of bribery in the distribution of scarce living space. A case first uncovered in 1950 shows that by the late 1940s, a secondary, shadow housing "market" had formed for Moscow elites (and the emerging middle class) to upgrade their apartments to larger and better spaces. To jump wait lists and secure improved apartments, privileged elites passed illicit payments to housing administrators, sometimes through professional underground "brokers." A glimpse into this illegal market for elite housing is provided in documents describing one particularly extensive scheme. In January 1951 USSR Procurator General Safonov outlined a major scandal in a letter to Stalin, Malenkov, Nikita S. Khrushchev, and Lavrentii Beria.[66] Tipped off by an anonymous letter received by the newspaper *Vecherniaia Moskva,* the procuracy had uncovered an operation involving large illegal payments, passed via intermediaries to employees of the housing department of the Moscow Soviet, by hundreds of prominent individuals. Included among them were well-known artists, musicians, and actors, as well as high-ranking officers in the military. (An intermediary who worked in the housing department of the Ministry of the Navy was also implicated.) The list of those involved reads almost like a "Who's Who" of Soviet artistic elites: the writer Konstantin Simonov, perhaps the Soviet Union's most famous active literary figure, and the head of the Union of Writers until early 1950, paid 25,000 rubles; the violinist Marina Kozolupova paid 5,000 rubles through an intermediary; the beloved singers Shul'zhenko and her husband Koralli paid 8,000 rubles to arrange for an apartment upgrade; the pianist Iakov Flier paid 2,800 rubles for help obtaining an apartment; a certain Garkavi, apparently the actor who played Goering in the famous film *Stalingradskaia bitva,* set at the battle of Stalingrad, paid 4,850 rubles for similar assistance.

In addition to artistic elites, renowned figures from the armed forces were implicated. Mavriky Slepnev, who was among the first group of people given the title "Hero of the Soviet Union," paid 3,000 rubles to an intermediary to arrange an apartment exchange. A certain General-Major Ivanov gave between ten and twenty thousand rubles. Perhaps the most unusual name on the list? The son of Metropolitan Nikolai (one of the leaders of the Russian Orthodox Church), who forked over 28,000 rubles—the largest sum of all—to a middleman, in hopes of getting superior living space.

There is no evidence that any of these people were punished; indeed, Konstantin Simonov became a member of the Central Committee in 1952.[67]

Apart from the fact that it was the privileged rather than ordinary people who were caught up in this investigation, another peculiar twist is worthy of attention. One person who was deeply involved was Vera Vasilievna Chapaeva, the adopted daughter of Vasilii I. Chapaev, the revered Civil War hero-soldier who had died on the battlefield in 1919 at the age of 32.[68] At the age of 36, Vera Chapaeva was a highly placed intermediary in these deals, albeit one with a storied past. The fact that Chapaeva, Simonov, and other honorary heroes of Soviet culture were involved in this scheme testifies to the ubiquity of bribery and its "markets." Procurator General Safonov reported the details of the schemes directly to Stalin. (Stalin's response is unknown.) How could esteemed generals and great writers who had honored the heroic Soviet people's struggles against fascism still be infected with a "bourgeois worldview"? How could the great Chapaev's daughter, of all people, still have harbored "the remnants of a capitalist mentality"? The war (and the revolution) produced heroic myths galore, among them the myth of Chapaev, the selfless everyman fighter who sacrificed his life to battle the dark enemies of the Revolution. The irony is particularly pronounced, then, to see so many of the artists who helped to disseminate those heroic myths—together with those who were themselves lionized—involved in a base, criminal case like this.

Several of the intermediaries involved in the case accumulated tremendous financial gains as they successfully cultivated their niche. Catering to the elite, they trumpeted their connections and shopped their expertise. In the apartment of one broker, a certain Shul'gina, investigators found a typed list of more than 450 clients. Shul'gina was said to have earned over 800,000 rubles in three years, which amounted to approximately a thousand times the average worker's monthly salary at the time. Another wildly successful broker, S. M. Iurkova, kept a card index of clients that included more than 1,200 names.

Intermediaries with connections in the Moscow housing offices had yet another layer of people working for them: "recruiters" (*verbovshchikov*) who searched for potential clients. These recruiters acted as a kind of intelligence network for the intermediaries. Shul'gina hired seven people, including Chapaeva, to find clients for her. Ultimately, the intermediaries received between two and ten years in prison.

Two of the employees of the Housing Department of the Moscow Soviet who were implicated in this case, Mishin and Suiazov, had been under suspicion by the Moscow city procuracy for years, according to the testimony of Sergei Zheleznikov, who was himself arrested for bribery in 1948. Zheleznikov told investigators that housing department employees simply silenced the investigators who questioned them by upgrading their apartments. One investigator, for example, wanted to move out of his dingy basement apartment, so Suiazov provided the investigator with a much nicer apartment in exchange for dropping the case against him. In another instance, Suiazov bought off an employee of the economic police of the MVD (OBKhSS). Zheleznikov testified that individuals to whom Suiazov gave "splendid" apartments were "people who occupied high leadership positions, directors of stores, and so on."[69]

All of these cases underscore the reality that privileged and poor alike deployed the strategy of "buying" officials' help. Illegal payments by artistic and military elites belied the official explanation that only the most backward, least politically aware stratum of Soviet society would stoop to bribery. The truth was uglier: the political, social, and cultural elites seemed just as willing to participate in illegal schemes to improve their lives as the "backward" masses.

A DESPERATE SCRAMBLE ON THE RAILROADS

During and after the war, mass evacuation and damaged transportation systems intersected to help produce lucrative income opportunities for railroad officials. Sixty-five thousand kilometers of tracks were destroyed during the war.[70] The historian Rebecca Manley has detailed examples of how people evacuated from the path of the German invasion often had to pay bribes to obtain registrations giving them the right to live in the city of Tashkent, one of the main destinations for war refugees. While the family members of famous writers, including Nadezhda Mandelstam and Lydia Chukovskaia, were able to use their connections to obtain permissions, ordinary people had to resort to paying bribes. What is more, after the war the mass return of refugees produced a huge strain on the disrupted railroad network, fueling enormous demand for tickets. Transport workers had virtually unlimited opportunities to make deals for extra payments. Families returning from Siberia or Central Asia required numerous documents, which generated another rich source of illegal income; those without effective personal connections were at the mercy of officials.[71] Railroad employees demanded an extra "fee" to sell tickets; often they extracted another payment to transport or retrieve baggage. Soldiers returning from abroad by the millions nearly all traveled by train. Grigori Chukhrai's wonderful film *Ballad of a Soldier* vilifies a railway agent who demands a can of meat from a serviceman in exchange for passage. In the spring of 1946, several employees at the Chita station of the Zabaikal railroad were arrested for taking bribes to allow passengers to ride without a ticket.[72] The escort of a special train with citizens re-evacuated from Krasnodar to Leningrad allegedly extorted bribes from certain passengers, threatening to kick them off the train. In addition, he collected bribes for carrying passengers illegally. A judge sentenced him to five years in prison. *Pravda* reported on August 1, 1946, that a cashier on the Kherson railroad line received eight years in prison for illegally selling seventy-one tickets at highly inflated prices.[73] Nevertheless, as the Minister of Justice himself noted in 1946, only a small proportion of bribe takers who operated in the railroad system were ever charged with a crime, a statement consistent with observations made by law enforcement about other sectors of the economy as well.[74]

Although the problem was not resolved, conditions doubtless improved as the volume of traffic decreased and railroad lines were rebuilt, reducing (but by no means eliminating) opportunities for employees to demand special "fees." Statistics from the Ministry of Justice put the number of people convicted for bribery on the railways at 729 in 1948, 560 in 1949, and 370 in 1950. These numbers greatly understate the extent of the problem. A major 1948 Supreme Court review of criminality in the USSR affirmed that "bribery is widespread in transportation," despite declining numbers of convictions.[75]

DEALING IN SHADOW MARKETS: DOCUMENTS, DIPLOMAS, AND FOOD QUOTAS

Although many ordinary people paid bribes simply to get what they believed the state owed them (such as legitimate official documents, apartments, and service on the railways), a second variety of bribes was offered by citizens to compensate functionaries for providing services *outside* the law. Payments to obtain something unlawfully, to resolve a problem illicitly, or to evade potential trouble, make up this second category of bribes, which includes the acquisition of false documents, improper access to higher education, and the avoidance of food collection quotas.

While Soviet citizens sometimes had to pay under the table to get documents they were rightly owed, phony documents could also at times be secured through bribes to government employees. The mass movement

of people after the war produced a large demand for false internal passports and residency permits among people who desired to live in the
cities.[76] In 1945 and 1946, several employees of an office for internal
passports in the town of Babushkin, Moscow oblast', were convicted
of providing fake passports to thirty-one people in exchange for bribes.
The employees had also issued fifty counterfeit residence permits, including some provided for "recidivist thieves" who likely had been released during the July 1945 amnesty from the Gulag but who had lost
their right to live near large population centers.[77] The historian Don
Filtzer notes cases of officials in personnel departments who accepted
payments to issue fake passports, or to provide illegal papers to workers
who had been fired or had quit without permission, falsely documenting that they had legitimately left their jobs. Another employer would
be unlikely to risk hiring a worker without these official papers.[78]

Instances of citizens greasing the palms of bureaucrats to obtain falsified documents are legion. In the Ukrainian SSR, investigators documented numerous illicit payments to employees of the offices of ZAGS,
the government bureau that registered births, marriages, and deaths.
In 1948, for example, a certain V. P. Daniliuk paid a bribe to be issued
a document declaring that he was born in 1926 rather than 1928, enabling him to avoid mandatory military service. Daniliuk also allegedly
offered a bribe in an attempt to obtain falsified military identification
papers stating that he was registered with the army reserves.[79] According to a 1951 review by the Party Control Commission (KPK), the chief
of the personnel department in an MGB office took a bribe to issue a
document falsifying an employment record, obscuring an unpleasant
disciplinary action in one man's work history.[80] Police officials could
produce papers that falsified residence or work histories, or that hid a
criminal record.

In a system that frequently demanded documentation to confirm
health history, medical personnel enjoyed a great deal of power. Doctors could issue papers declaring a person seriously ill or an invalid to
gain them an exemption from military service, to obtain permission to
switch jobs, to excuse tardiness or absence from work, or to get access
to medical, disability, or pension benefits.[81] Bribes to doctors enabled
people to escape undesirable work or military assignments. For example, an investigation found that between 1942 and 1946 three senior
inspectors at a medical clinic in Leningrad had issued fictitious docu-

ments pronouncing several individuals to be permanently injured so they could avoid work assignments and receive unjustified benefits. Twenty bribe givers were charged in the case.[82] In 1946, a dentist in a factory polyclinic in Stalingrad allegedly accepted sixteen kilos of apples and fifty rubles to draw up paperwork attesting that an employee was ill in order to cover up his unexcused absences. According to a procuracy report, personnel departments were warned to scrutinize medical documents closely, as it was commonplace for doctors' reports, which employees offered as excuses for missing work, to be obtained through bribery. A 1951 investigation found such a situation in Rovno. The secretary of that city's central polyclinic was alleged to have taken bribes of 500 to 1,500 rubles to issue papers falsely stating that people who had quit their jobs without proper permission were actually invalids.[83]

Veterinarians were also in a position to profit. In 1946, a veterinary inspector took rewards of 3,000–5,000 rubles from traders to give improper permission for the sale of the meat of breeding livestock and other animals that had been slaughtered too young. Similarly, veterinarians could accept money to approve rancid meat for sale at market. In October 1949, a veterinarian from Izmailovskii oblast', Ukrainian SSR, was convicted of systematically extorting *magarych,* that is, gifts of drinks and food, from citizens who asked him for veterinary help for their cattle. *Magarych* is an Arabic word that means gifts of meals given when buying something, often horses. The term was used colloquially to denote a gift of food or drink improperly given to an official in exchange for some service to the petitioner.[84]

Higher education was another fruitful venue. For example, in exchange for illegal payments, the director of the faculty at the Khar'kov Dental Institute, the head of its patient reception area, and the chief of its laboratory all issued certificates incorrectly stating that eleven students had passed their examinations. The institute reserved some spots for the children of soldiers who had died at the front. Prosecutors alleged that the deputy Minister of Health, Belousov, paid a bribe to have one of these reserved spots given to the daughter of a close friend, even though she had failed two exams. An anonymous letter came in to the Party Control Commission alleging that the improper actions of deputy Belousov had cost the letter writer a place as an incoming student in the institute.[85]

The crisis in agriculture helped shape the conditions for another kind of shadow deal between citizens and officials. According to an investigation, collective farmers and *kolkhoz* officials offered bribes to employees of the Ministry of Food Collection to avoid obligatory deliveries of food to the state. Especially during the 1946–1947 famine, farmers paid collection agents to reduce or overlook quotas for deliveries of meat, grain, or other produce. The collection agents would issue receipts for food that peasants had never delivered, declaring that the farmers had met their obligations.[86] In Riazan' oblast', investigators found that collection agents "regularly took bribes from collective farmers to write fictitious receipts for potatoes that had supposedly been gathered."[87] Farmers paid collection agents to release them from meat requisitions in Krasnodar *krai*. Many collective farm leaders became adept at buying off local authorities.

SHADOW ECONOMIES ON THE JOB

Bribery in the workplace took many forms and served numerous functions, allowing people to secure and retain jobs and to advance in their careers. Payments allowed employees—both managers and the rank and file—to earn extra income from their positions. Bribes could also protect them from the unwanted attention of the inspectors, controllers, and other authorities who were constantly looking over their shoulders. In a system where auditors had an almost omnipresent role, monitoring the activities of an enormous bureaucracy, many of these "checkers" were well positioned to arrange mutually beneficial deals.[88] In numerous cases reported in legal and party archives, managers, bookkeepers, and other employees made payoffs to cover up evidence of misappropriated funds or goods that had gone missing, often for resale on the black market. A 1949 case involved a compliance inspector in the Ministry of Finance in Odessa who allegedly extorted bribes when his audits found evidence of missing money. As the chief of the MVD put it to Stalin in 1947: "Bribery is undertaken by employees in agencies of internal control, who take bribes to hide crimes that they expose—theft, embezzlement, shortfalls of funds—and by the procurement officers who acquire food and who are employed in various establishments and enterprises."[89]

At other times, employees made payoffs to disguise secret enterprises that they operated to produce goods for the black market, or to hide illicit income earned on the side through the improper use of their enter-prise's machines and tools. Collective farmers paid inspectors to cover up their personal use of the farm's agricultural equipment, for example. In 1946, a Lithuanian collective farmer was said to have paid 2,000 rubles to the chair of the local soviet executive committee to hide the fact that he was using a milling machine and a threshing machine for his own profit.[90] In this period, these enterprises typically appear to have been small-scale operations, involving a few people.

The influx of trophy goods from eastern Germany provided a huge boon to the underground economy. Occupying soldiers stripped homes and apartments of their belongings and sent them back to the Soviet Union. Much of this loot—furniture, artwork, carpets, jewelry, pianos, bicycles, and automobiles—ended up on the black market. Traders ille-gally sold and re-sold and distributed it, pumping enormous amounts of scarce and luxury goods into the illegal or semi-legal shadow econ-omy. The acquisition and distribution of trophy goods were often tech-nically illegal acts, enabled and covered up by bribes. Much of this black market trophy loot ended up in the homes of soldiers, and espe-cially officers. Other goods found their way inside newly constructed dachas for party, military, and artistic elites. Not surprisingly, their ac-quisition was often smoothed—or covered up—with bribes.

Another branch of the economy that was especially rife with under-the-table payments was the production and supply of consumer goods. So-called "handicraft cooperatives" provided fertile soil for schemes in-volving elaborate webs of bribes. The Stalin-era economy, concentrated as it was on heavy industrial and military production, badly neglected consumer goods. Although they were in great demand, the country's under-developed light industrial enterprises produced woefully inade-quate quantities. One way to provide goods in short supply was the establishment of artisanal cooperatives (*promyslovaia kooperatsiia*), operated and regulated by the state, which united small handicraft work-shops (*tsekhy*) to produce consumer goods. Artisans in these official workshops produced scarce items such as clothing, household goods, and building materials.

Behind the scenes, however, these cooperatives faced major problems with their formal operation. In 1949–1950 a major investigation of cor-ruption in several handicrafts cooperatives in Moscow oblast' revealed a tangled matrix of bribery that stretched from the suppliers of raw

materials, to the bosses of the shops, to the head of the union of cooperatives, to the engineers and bookkeepers.[91] The cooperatives under
investigation were supposed to turn out consumer products that either
were daily essentials or improved the quality of life for Soviet people—
furniture, rubber boots, toy balls, and plastic tablecloths, for example.
The desirability of good toys for children, decent furniture, house
wares, and shoes for a working- or middle-class family cannot be overstated. Artisan workshops required hard-to-get raw materials, including wood, plastic, rubber, and zinc. In the case of the cooperative enterprise in Moscow oblast', the "socialist" workshop under investigation
had actually long disguised an illegal "capitalist" business within it.
The illegal workshop managed to acquire needed supplies, produce
goods that were in tremendous demand, locate its market niche, and
find plenty of buyers.

The workshop's successes were due in no small part to the fact that,
in addition to buying off suppliers of raw materials, their organizers
paid hundreds of thousands of rubles in bribes to officials at every rung
of the cooperative system. The procuracy alleged that the complex
scheme resulted in the illegal appropriation of state resources worth
over five million rubles. The procuracy, which put its best investigators on the case, sent reports on this operation directly to Stalin. It is
safe to say that such workshops involving the subterranean production
of consumer goods were by no means a rarity around the country; the
liberal payment of bribes to key officials enabled these enterprises to
prosper.[92]

"BRINGING GIFTS" IN THE WORKPLACE

Many archival sources describe and decry the phenomenon of podnoshenie, the traditional practice of "bringing gifts" to one's superiors
at work. This Sovietized institution had antecedents deep in the tsarist
period (as was discussed at the beginning of this chapter).[93]

Practices of podnoshenie not only crossed the 1917 revolutionary
divide in their own, vibrant Soviet forms; they also survived the war
unscathed, if not strengthened. In Soviet times, podnoshenie translated
into a pyramiding structure of bribery. State employees at lower levels
of a bureaucracy fleeced individuals, substantially increasing their own

incomes, then made regular payoffs to their superiors up the hierarchy. They participated in this process in order to acquire and keep their jobs, to establish trust and cement networks, and to move up the career ladder. This phenomenon resulted in large part from the absence of meritocratic mechanisms for career advancement, and the resulting dependence of most employees on the unpredictable actions of their workplace superiors. Economic and party elites at the apex of the hierarchy stood to benefit from the "donations" of many tiers of employees below them, who were dependent on them for job security. A procuracy investigation referred to this practice as "the giving of gifts to bosses or other 'necessary people.'"[94] Generous gifts to one's superiors could include services such as organizing banquets or otherwise "entertaining necessary people." It is not entirely clear whether employees thought that these payments to superiors were voluntary or coerced. Surely, some employees believed that they simply had no choice but to line the pockets of their bosses if they wished to preserve their jobs or move up the ranks; others hoped to establish positive, reciprocal personal relations by flattering or otherwise pleasing supervisors with freely offered presents.

In the retail economy, where the state completely managed the production and distribution of goods, unofficial relationships flourished. As Stephen Kotkin has put it, "Socialist trade was a veritable school for insider theft."[95] In one variety of podnoshenie, people would *pay a bribe* to obtain a job where they could *accept bribes*—a kind of speculative investment in future income. Ambitious people could make deals to secure a valuable position, such as manager of a retail store or chief of a warehouse, jobs that could be prime sources of self-enrichment.[96] In December 1949, the director of an agency supervising one branch of the retail trade network for the city of Moscow was alleged to have accepted a bribe of 11,000 rubles, ten chairs, two mirrors, a bed, a table, a lamp, and a radio receiver in exchange for appointing someone to the post of director of Store No. 41. Similarly, a June 1952 report sent to Procurator General Safonov noted that five people in Krasnovodsk had paid bribes to obtain profitable jobs as the directors of retail shops.[97] Prosecutors alleged that these store directors benefited in several ways from their positions. They received kickbacks from employees who overcharged customers for goods that were in short supply, embezzled a slice of the store's income and sales, and profiteered on the black market by trading in any scarce products sold by their store. The five store managers were sentenced to ten years in prison.

The food industries, which controlled scarce products in great demand, were particularly hospitable territory for corruption.[98] To be sure, the disastrously low level of food production in the years after the war undoubtedly gave rise to close scrutiny of food industries, which was likely to uncover wrongdoing and pinpoint scapegoats. And although in some cases there may have been political reasons to target certain officials who got on the wrong side of local elites, internal correspondence demonstrates that the kinds of arrangements uncovered by these targeted investigations were thought to be quite widespread.

An unsigned letter of October 2, 1946, denouncing the managers of certain retail bread stores—and indeed the leadership of the country's bread production and distribution network (known as "the Bread Trust")—provides details of what seems to have been a typical practice in retail trade.[99] First an aspiring candidate had to pay a bribe to a high-ranking official in the Bread Trust to obtain a job as a store director. Describing a truly competitive "market" (both for jobs and for the income they brought), the letter explains that the more one paid, the more lucrative the director's position one could buy. A position running a busy store was the most expensive to obtain, but it would make for the most valuable long-term investment. Further illicit payments would guarantee a steady supply of quality goods. The letter neatly summarizes the system, claiming that the head of a bread baking trust received between 1,000 and 2,000 rubles from each employee in Store No. 110. To fund these kickbacks to their boss, salespeople overcharged customers, to complete the food chain. "Everywhere there is deception of the consumer. . . . [The store director] Doktor is afraid of nothing. He takes bribes from the salespeople, and the salespeople deceive the consumers."

A similar denunciation came in early 1951 from two people who alleged that the director of the Moscow Central Department Store (TsUM) took bribes from employees and salespeople. This allegation has the ring of truth,[100] and certainly abundant anecdotal evidence testifies to the existence of profitable relationships in retail trade established on the basis of bribery.[101] Salespeople paid their bosses for the right to steal with impunity from customers and from the store itself. A blistering anonymous denunciation alleged similar wrongdoing in Store

No. 50, claiming that the director demanded bribes from subordinate employees to keep their jobs.[102] Ten employees refused to pay what they called extorted gifts to superiors, and they were fired. The investigators' conclusion—that the allegations were "not confirmed"—seems flimsy at best.

Yet another variant of corruption in the Soviet economic behemoth featured the giving of gifts to employees of the national or republic-level economic ministries by the personnel of enterprises subordinate to them. In an April 1950 investigation, again involving the bread industry, the Party Control Commission laid bare a series of long-running relationships in the RSFSR Ministry of Food.[103] Between 1946 and 1949, Dvorianchikov, the director of the city of Kuibeshev's Bread Factory No. 9, provided valuable gifts to key employees in the Food Ministry, including the chief engineer of the Main Committee (*Glavka*) and the chief of the supply department. On April 20, 1947, Dvorianchikov and an associate traveled to Moscow, bringing packages containing flour, butter, jam, sugar, and 200 kilograms of sausage to distribute to several top officials at the main bread trust of the Russian Republic (*Rosglavkhleb*). According to the KPK investigator, the first time they went to Moscow to present these "gifts," Dvorianchikov and his associate panicked when someone at the Kazan' railroad station started to check their luggage. Fearing difficult questions if the horde of foodstuffs were discovered, they simply ran away, abandoning the packages in the station. They later resumed their trip to Moscow with another cache of presents. This time they successfully delivered their valuable presents to the sister of a high-ranking food ministry employee.

The alcohol industry is another example of a leading—and natural—location for entrenched networks of high-level gift giving. Managers in the alcohol industry were well prepared to distribute desirable and well-placed gifts to local power elites. Regional party secretaries were often the beneficiaries of this largesse. The authorities issued various laws in the postwar years prohibiting the giving of valuable presents by the employees of economic ministries to the staff of local party organizations (and their families) charged with supervising them, indicating that this was a major problem.[104] Party leaders apparently believed that the receipt of such gifts would damage the independence (or the loyalty) of local political leaders. A 1949 investigation into an epidemic of theft in the Ul'ianovsk oblast' alcohol industry uncovered relationships between employees of the Ul'ianovsk alcohol trust and staff at various levels of the provincial government administration.[105] When discovered, the culprits tried to bribe investigators with alcohol. One inspector undertaking an investigation of an alcohol factory said that he woke up in his hotel room to find that 2.5 liters of alcohol from that very factory had been delivered to his room. Before he left the city, he said, another twenty liters mysteriously "appeared" in his room. In 1947, a second inspector received 10,000 rubles from the head of an alcohol factory, and several auditors accepted well-placed bribes.[106]

Judging by one major investigation, the fish industry enjoyed its own unique and creative brand of podnoshenie. In January 1951, the Party Control Commission reviewed a case in which subordinate employees in the Ministry of the Fish Industry allegedly distributed expensive and improper gifts to the higher-ups.[107] Investigators accused the minister of the fish industry and his deputy of abusing their offices by accepting eight sealskins and several silver fox pelts, valued at 3,200 rubles, from their underling, the chief of the Main Sakhalin Fish Industry. The chief sent these gifts to the Moscow office of the minister (at government expense). For his part, the deputy minister was accused of accepting three sets of chess pieces carved from mammoth bones from the director of the Yakutsk fish trust. In 1944, the deputy minister went to Moscow to present the minister with two of the chess sets, which were valued at about 2,000 rubles each. These men, "using their official positions, accepted free gifts from subordinate employees and [this] created an environment of obsequiousness and servility in the Ministry."[108] The minister received a violin as a gift, sent to him from Germany by his deputy. He admitted accepting the instrument but, as he protested in his own defense, "It was no Stradivarius."

The case of the Fish Ministry illustrates two important points. First, the long-established practice of podnoshenie still had its place in Soviet times as the directors of enterprises and their subordinates continued to distribute gifts up the economic-administrative hierarchy. Second, top officials apparently blithely accepted these valuables from their subordinates, as if this were the natural order of things. After an investigation, the two received nothing more than a warning. These examples also serve to illustrate the tangled nature of the official and unofficial economies. Bribe, reward, gift, or favor? Legal, illegal, or semi-legal? At times, it was difficult for the participants and prosecutors (and for us) to make these distinctions.

Another variety of payment at the workplace was that offered "in the interest of production" by managers attempting to obtain materials or break through bottlenecks to meet plan targets. In these cases, the main purpose of the deal typically was not personal profit. Deals were intended to enable factories, farms, and, indeed, entire branches of industry to operate according to plan.[109] Prosecutors generally understood that payments made "in the interests of production" (to fulfill plan quotas) were not done for personal gain, and they therefore treated such payments differently than a deal motivated by self-interst.[110] Of course, a person could still benefit indirectly from such arrangements, because, for instance, the payer could earn a larger bonus if their enterprise met plan targets. For this category of transaction, however, individual benefit was not the leading reason for the payment.

Concerns about meeting production targets on collective farms, for example, inspired rural officials to make deals. The head of the Pushkin regional section of the Moscow Oblast' Energy Trust (Mosoblenergo) and an engineer were said to have taken bribes from collective farms in 1946 to speed work on the electrification of the farms.[111] They accepted bribes of cash and several tons of vegetables, which they likely sold on the black market. Similarly, in 1950, party supervisors sanctioned a collective farm chairman in Tadzhikistan for paying bribes to obtain greatly needed fertilizer, which he could not acquire through the normal procedures thanks to bottlenecks.[112] The chairman had sent representatives around to various chemical factories in the region to obtain the fertilizer, bypassing the normal planning bodies. Unable to obtain the fertilizer legally, they spent 150,000 rubles of the farm's funds, buying it at high prices. This expenditure was hidden on the books of the collective farm, it was said, by understating the revenues from sales of dried fruit. It is important to note that there was no evidence that (in the words of the report) the "honest" chairman took any money for himself, or that he had "greedy" or "mercenary" motives. That the collective farm was well run, annually improved its harvest of cotton, and fulfilled all its obligations to the state worked in the chairman's favor. He received only a "strict reprimand."[113]

Reliable transportation was critical to the success of any economic enterprise. Railway officials often demanded that enterprises pay extra fees. The planned economy and rapid industrialization of the 1930s gave the railroads extraordinary power. Enterprise managers sometimes cut deals with railway managers to guarantee delivery of scarce raw materials, or to break the supply bottlenecks so common to the planned economy. Those involved sometimes disguised these payments as "commissions" or "rewards" to employees of the railways, and paid them out of enterprise funds.

CONCLUSIONS: DIVERSITY AND OPPORTUNITY

There is a remarkable diversity in the varieties of bribery in the late Stalinist economy and society. Many of the cases described here are a product of their time, embedded in the postwar Stalinist years, as the effects of the war reverberated throughout the period and impacted every aspect of Soviet life. Informal relationships blossomed as people tried to navigate a system shaped by the war and its consequences in the following years. For Soviet citizens, offering a bribe was one option (albeit a very risky one) in an economy in which markets were suppressed, shortages of all manner of goods and services were epidemic, and bureaucracies were characterized by inefficiency and incompetence.

By the final years of postwar Stalinism, bribery was not merely the province of people desperately short of necessities who were trying to stabilize their lives in a period of crisis. It had become a tool to improve living standards for a population that still faced hardships but that was rising above the poverty level. Among the gradually growing middle class, and for the elites themselves, the desire for newly available consumer goods, furniture, and individual (rather than communal) apartments—all of which often could only be obtained through illicit channels—fueled demands to cut through red tape and rise to the top of long waiting lists. Bribery and shadow markets enabled an inflexible system to operate. One could argue that officials who broke the rules to get things done aided the country's recovery from the wartime catastrophes.

At the same time, anger about official corruption was intertwined with resentment at the appearance of a "new class" of bureaucrats, a privileged and entrenched elite that acted as though it "owned" its offices and sought to collect "rents" from them. Functionaries who accepted bribes seemed to regard themselves as above the law, and personified an increasingly inflexible and bureaucratized Soviet system. The massive postwar reconstruction of the country provided officialdom with ever more opportunities. The burgeoning bureaucracy, and especially the higher levels (*nomenklatura*), seems to have felt increasingly invulnerable, as officials solidified their positions in a post-purge USSR. It was not just the nomenklatura that was becoming larger and feeling more secure from prosecution, often protected by their superiors in the party and state administrations. The petty bureaucracy—poorly paid, with little professional ethos—continued to grow rapidly as well. To many of them, bribery seemed like a viable option to supplement their incomes.[114] The evidence points to a substantial degree of continuity between corruption in the late Stalin period and the corruption endemic in the Brezhnev period. Far from indicating a sharp break between the Stalin years and later periods, these examples show that certain continuities prevailed.

These conditions tend to confirm Katherine Verdery's contention about one of the peculiarities of postwar socialism in the Soviet space.[115] The state promised to guarantee people's dignity by satisfying their basic needs, a right enshrined in the Constitution. After the great victory in the war, having to pay bribes to government bureaucrats—whether to get a decent place to live, or to get a train ticket, or to get a job, or to secure medical treatment, or obtain a passport—deprived people of that dignity. Resentment grew as Soviet subjects had to make payoffs to get what they believed the state had promised to provide them.

Perhaps the gravest news, however, was that the legal agencies themselves were infected, as is further explored in the following chapter.

2 "Pick the Flowers while They're in Bloom"

The Contours of Bribery in the Agencies of Law Enforcement and Criminal Justice

IN 1942, a certain A. A. Praushkina, a judge in the Moscow City Court, warned her colleague and fellow jurist Valentina A. Chursina that if she was not careful, colleagues might notice her behavior—Chursina had been having suspicious meetings with petitioners in the conference rooms at the courthouse, and she went out to meals with people who had business before the court. Instead of heeding the warning, Chursina scoffed, offering her junior colleague some advice on how to earn extra money on the job: "Use your head. Pick the flowers while they're in bloom." Exploit the opportunities when they present themselves![1] Both judges were later convicted of accepting dozens of bribes from people with cases assigned to their courtrooms.

The late Stalinist USSR was full of occasions to "pick the flowers" in many areas of life and work. Circumstances presented a wide array of possibilities for plucking extra income with the help of one's official position. The agencies of justice and law enforcement were no exception. Indeed, for often-unexpected reasons, they provided some of the greatest temptations of all. Bribery in criminal justice and law enforcement agencies developed into one of the most common and most lucrative varieties, remaining so until the collapse of the Soviet Union in 1991 (and beyond).

Bribes were paid by members of the public who were in trouble with the law and accepted by judges, prosecutors, and police.[2] While the previous chapter surveyed the overall landscape of illegal payments made to officials and the functions these bribes served in Stalinist society and economy, this chapter probes an essentially unknown side of the agencies of law enforcement, and provides a comprehensive examination of the particular varieties of bribery engaged in by criminal justice and police personnel.

This study by no means intends to imply that all—or even most—agents of the law took bribes, of course. It is impossible to know exactly how many entered into illegal deals with citizens, or how often such transactions occurred. Rather, it outlines the context and explores the reasons for the bribery that did occur.

The agencies of law and justice serve as an excellent forum for investigating the factors that lured (or even compelled) many people into offering or soliciting gifts. In particular, the mass arrests that were a central feature of the Stalinist system combined with complicated legal procedures to place great stresses on the legal system, and led to many varieties of corruption among legal officials. For their part, police officers, judges and other court staff, and procuracy employees had fulsome opportunities to pad their incomes "on the side." While many people resisted these opportunities, some risked taking advantage of them.

One of the key factors spurring bribery in the agencies of law enforcement was the state's enthusiastic repression of most types of "unofficial" economic activity. This repression was closely related to the regime's obsession with protecting "state" or "socialist" property. At the same time, the extreme challenges to supply and production led to an increase in cases of "speculation"—the reselling of goods above their official price.[3] A crackdown on crimes by officials and on speculation resulted in hundreds of thousands of arrests in the wartime and postwar period. Adding to the burden on agencies of law enforcement, this crackdown coincided with the period of the monetary reform, which led to a round of prosecutions of people alleged to have profited from currency speculation.[4] The volume of convictions rose and the length of sentences grew.[5] But the exceptionally harsh laws targeting the theft of state property were the single most important factor in the spread of illicit deals in the legal system. Citizens attempted to negotiate to evade severe punishments for pilfering from the workplace, embezzling funds or valuables from the office, or stealing produce from collective farms.

This chapter also provides context for understanding an extraordinary bribery scandal that occurred in several of Moscow's high courts between 1947 and 1951, to be discussed in chapters 7 and 8. (Several other important causes of bribery among law enforcement personnel, including poor pay, low status, and weak professionalization, will be examined in depth in chapter 5.)

A FLOOD OF ARRESTS AND CONVICTIONS

What conditions spurred the forging of informal ties between law enforcement personnel and petitioners in the postwar period? A key element was the mass arrests that targeted certain types of criminals. The postwar years saw a sharp decline in the number of people accused of political crimes, such as domestic "traitors," "counterrevolutionaries," and other "enemies" (leaving aside, for the moment, Ukraine and the newly integrated western borderlands).[6] In fact, between 1946 and 1952, fewer than 10 percent of the approximately five million people given prison sentences were convicted of political crimes.[7] At the same time, however, there were huge numbers of arrests for so-called crimes against the socialist economy, crimes against state and personal property, and white-collar crimes. These "nonpolitical" crimes were tried in the regular courts.

The most important single factor in the rush of cases of nonpolitical crimes into the courts was arrests resulting from the increasingly draconian laws regarding the theft of state and personal property, including the theft law of August 1932 and, much more important, the decrees of June 4, 1947. These and other similar laws led to the convictions of over 2.1 million people between 1944 and 1952.[8] Indeed, in 1940 the proportion of the Gulag population that had been convicted of theft stood at only 1.9 percent; just before Stalin's death in January 1953, that number had leapt to an extraordinary 49.3 percent (over 1.2 million prisoners), as the June 4, 1947 laws took their toll.[9] (Another 66,000 prisoners had been convicted for speculation.) For most people accused of crimes after the war, the way stations between civilian life and the Gulag were the regular courts.

The declassified records of the Communist Party, the procuracy, and the legal system show that beginning in the summer of 1947 judges and procuracy staff were placed in the path of a veritable juridical tsunami.

Рис. Ю. ГАНФА

— Итак, голубчик, подашите нам икорки, балычка, водочки, заморозьте бутылочку шампанского, дайте фруктов! А пока что принесите сегодняшнюю газету.

Эй, послушайте! Всё отменяется! Подайте воблу и пару пива.

Figure 2.1. "Appetite Spoiled"

1. "Listen, buddy, bring us some caviar, sturgeon, vodka, and a bottle of cold champagne. And give us some fruit. And bring today's newspaper while you're at it!"

2. [Newspaper headline says:] "A Decree of the Presidium of the USSR Supreme Soviet on Theft of State Property . . ."

3. "Hold on! Take all this away! Bring us *vobla* [dried fish] and a couple of beers!"
Krokodil, June 30, 1947.

A huge number of cases (and, soon enough, appeals and formal legal complaints about the convictions) threatened to overwhelm the procuracy and the courts. During the time period from June 1947 to December 1952, between 162,000 and 387,000 people were convicted each year under the June 4 decree on the theft of state property alone, with convictions peaking in the second half of 1947. Nearly all of these people convicted of theft of state property, even of the pettiest variety, were given extremely long sentences.[10] By June 1947, the average sentence for theft of state property was 8.7 years. Judges were under pressure from the highest levels of the party, and mandatory sentences ranged between seven and ten years in the Gulag; about 10 percent of those convicted were given even longer sentences, between eleven and twenty years.[11] For theft of personal property, the average sentence went from 1.5 years in prison in the period between 1937 and 1940, to 6.2 years between June 1947 and December 1952.

The accused were by no means professional thieves; more than 90 percent of those found guilty of theft of state property in 1950, for example, had no prior criminal record.[12] Laws against speculation also contributed to the rising tide of arrests and lengthy sentences for nonpolitical crimes. As late as 1946, 38 percent of sentences were one year or shorter. But by June 1947, about half of all convictions resulted in sentences of six years or longer.[13]

BRIBERY AMONG POLICE

As in all modern societies, police officers in the USSR, as grassroots "first responders," were in a powerful position to demand illegal payments from people who found themselves on the wrong side of the law. Indeed, central authorities expressed concern about pervasive police corruption. In the words of a 1948 survey of crimes by police officials, "Among other crimes committed by employees of the police, bribery has a widespread character and acquires special significance if we keep in mind that this form of crime among police employees enables increased criminality among the population."[14]

Opportunities abounded for police to exploit frightened citizens. To create extra income on the side, some police officers cultivated the image that they were more powerful than they really were. According to a report produced for the USSR Supreme Court, a policeman in the Ministry of State Security (MGB) confessed to accepting 12,000 rubles from a prisoner to ensure that he would be imprisoned in Moscow oblast' rather than in a distant region far from his home.[15] Moreover, in March 1948 he took 4,800 rubles from a convict's wife on a promise to have the prisoner quickly released from a camp, something well beyond his powers. As frequently happened, the police officer's failure to live up to the deal was his undoing. The bribe was exposed when the convict's wife complained to the police that nothing had been done about her husband's case and she was furious that the officer had not returned her money.[16]

Some police officers took bribes to release people after arrest, or *not* to arrest a suspect in the first place. In Ternopol' oblast, Ukrainian SSR, thirty-three-year old Mikhail Sobchak was said to have offered two chickens and thirty-seven eggs to the head of the local police force to dismiss a criminal case against his wife, who was accused of brewing moonshine. (Sobchak was caught and received one year in prison.)[17] Prosecutors uncovered a major police scandal in 1952 in the city of Ivanovo. They charged nine police employees with soliciting bribes in exchange for arranging the release from custody of individuals accused of theft and speculation.[18]

In April 1947, a police officer extorted 3,500 rubles to release two men who had stolen hay from a collective farm.[19] The same police officer demanded 100 rubles from a man accused of stealing a calf. A 1952 party investigation of trade networks in the city of Kiev found that a number of police officers, as well as procuracy employees and judges, had been bought off as part of a cover-up of huge amounts of theft from retail trade organizations.[20]

At times, police officers shook down people who were under the threat of arrest, or extorted bribes from their relatives. In December 1951, a certain B. L. Krikun wrote a letter to the Moscow city procuracy reporting that after the arrest of his father, an unknown citizen had come to his apartment and, claiming to be a policeman, tried to extort a cash payment.[21] The procuracy arrested two people in the scheme. The first, Ikonnikov, was an employee of OBKhSS, the department of the Ministry of Internal Affairs responsible for undercover police work. Ikonnikov took advantage of his access to information to extort money from relatives of the accused. With the incriminating information in hand, his partner went to people's apartments and demanded bribes from the families to throw out the cases. He had solicited payments from three separate families, mistakenly assuming that the victims would not report the shakedown. In fact, the intended targets refused to pay, and one of them turned the officers in.[22]

A variation on this kind of operation occurred in Moscow in 1950 when two police inspectors extorted hush money from retail trade employees by confronting them with evidence of their alleged profiteering in scarce products. In the course of one day, the inspectors went to three stores and, discovering that salespeople were selling goods at inflated prices and pocketing the difference, demanded bribes to keep the activity quiet. For 600 rubles and a bottle of cognac, the two inspectors agreed to destroy their arrest report.[23]

The officers who worked as traffic police (and their supervisors) in the State Automobile Inspectorate (GAI) demonstrate the persistence of both podnoshenie (the offering of gifts) and otkormlenie ("feeding from" the population) in the Soviet context. Poorly paid throughout the Soviet period, GAI officers were (and still are) infamous for asking for under-the-table payments from drivers whom they stopped for having broken tail-lights, driving without a driver's license, being involved in minor accidents, or committing other (usually) minor infractions on the roads. By accepting payments from drivers to bypass the regular courts, GAI officers "fed from" the automobile-driving population. In Rostov oblast', for example, a senior automobile inspector demanded 5,000 rubles from the relatives of a chauffeur who had caused an accident; in exchange, the auto inspector covered up the fact that the chauffeur had violated traffic laws. Two weeks later, the inspector returned the chauffeur's driver's license in exchange for two lengths of fabric for a dress. Investigators found that the inspector had been enriching himself illegally for several years, and had spent 100,000 rubles to build himself a dacha.[24]

As was the case in many Soviet administrations, relationships in GAI agencies built on bribery went well beyond the malfeasance of individual officers, taking on a systematic character that pervaded multiple levels of the organization. An anonymous letter received by the Party Control Commission in 1947 alleged that a number of GAI officials in

Moscow oblast' were abusing their positions. A secret investigation into these accusations launched by the Party Control Commission revealed details of a complete "food chain." At the lowest level of the organization, rank-and-file traffic inspectors demanded bribes from drivers, who paid them in order to stave off further unpleasantness, or to reduce the inconvenience of getting tangled up in the courts or paying fines.[25] This was a classic example of "feeding," as the bureaucracy fleeced a population it was, in theory, serving. Indeed, the investigators' report used the word *otkormit'* (to feed from) to describe the actions of GAI officers. In July 1946, the MVD had issued a directive that forbade inspectors from collecting cash fines on the highways, the leading source of bribes for the inspectors. Yet as a result, the report went on, rather than collect a fine, the police would now seize the offenders' driver's licenses pending payment, providing drivers with another incentive to offer a bribe, and giving inspectors another way to "feed from" automobile owners. Traffic police defended themselves by arguing that drivers *wanted* to pay them, preferring to offer cash as a convenience, to avoid having to go to the GAI offices to pick up their licenses.

The second dimension of the food chain, podnoshenie, was also visible in all its glory in the ranks of the Moscow traffic inspectorate. From the top of the organization, the chief of the Moscow GAI, Maksimov, demanded "gifts" from his subordinates if they wanted to keep their jobs. The investigation revealed that inspectors indeed provided him with a veritable cornucopia of presents. The head inspector for Lenin region supplied his boss with vegetables and berries two or three times a week; Inspector Dugin brought him milk and vegetables; another "fed" him with pork; Inspector Volchenkov dropped off potatoes and vegetables at his apartment. One inspector fixed the boss's suit, others bought him a radio receiver and theater tickets, and yet another devoted three days to making repairs in his apartment.[26] The report describes GAI as a classic food chain, one that most likely would have been perfectly recognizable to most Russian bureaucrats (and subjects) in the nineteenth century. Investigators simplistically blamed Maksimov alone, as the chief of the Moscow GAI, rather than highlighting the system-wide incentives and pressures for drivers to offer gifts, inspectors to accept them, and lower-level officials to pass kickbacks up the ladder to superiors.

BRIBERY IN THE COURTS IN WARTIME AND AFTER

A variety of bribery that prevailed during this period involved judges charging illicit fees to intervene illegally in civil cases. As the previous chapter illustrated, judges had the ability to issue documents verifying identities, to rule in housing disputes, to exempt people from paying taxes, and to take other civil actions. Some took payments to fulfill or expedite these tasks. One party in a case could pay a judge in order to get a favorable ruling in matters such as divorces, housing disputes, or disagreements between neighbors. In other cases, judges would issue valuable documents and permits pertaining to work, residence, and social benefits.

Judging by the types of bribery cases that were prosecuted, however, the most common and lucrative opportunities for judicial officials lay in *criminal* cases. Soviet state and party archives document numerous instances of legal professionals providing illegal assistance in exchange for money or gifts in cases involving the theft of state property, "speculation," abuse of office, and violations of the severe labor laws.

The wartime cases involving judges highlight the desperation of the population, to be sure. Yet they often underscore individual ingenuity as well.[27] In late 1944, when the war was still ongoing, a notable series of cases came to trial in the Komintern and Sokolniki regions of Moscow. Procurators accused several judges of taking bribes in exchange for lenient sentences and decisions. Beginning in early 1943, according to prosecutors, workers at a milk factory who had been arrested for stealing offered judges bribes, including clothing and thousands of rubles, in exchange for acquittals. In one instance, a judge accepted one piece of wool cloth and some women's shoes from the accused. In a second case from September 1944, staff members of Bania (Bathhouse) No. 4 in the Komintern district of the city were arrested for stealing and illegally reselling bath soap. The director of the bathhouse contacted a court cleaning woman to act as an intermediary between the bathhouse staff and the judge. Through the cleaning woman the accused paid 6,000 rubles to the judge in exchange for light sentences; each received a reduced sentence of only one year of forced labor rather than the usual two years. One of the convicted bathhouse employees was still dissatisfied with the reduced sentence, however. She approached the same cleaning woman and negotiated to reduce the sentence further—to six months of corrective labor.[28]

Indeed, clerical workers commonly acted as go-betweens, exploiting this potentially profitable gatekeeper position between a judge and the public. A secretary who served in the military tribunal for the city of Moscow, Ol'ga V. Sprimon, had access both to case files and to the military tribunal's official stamp. Sprimon regularly created, and then sent to Gulag camps and colonies, fake copies of decisions declaring that the tribunal had commuted prisoners' sentences. Between June 1943 and the end of 1944, according to a Ministry of Justice official, she arranged for eleven people to be released from jail.[29] For this service, she accepted payments both from the relatives of the prisoners and from the convicts themselves. Payments were often in cash, but they also took the form of food, manufactured goods, and valuables. Over the course of eighteen months, according to investigators, Sprimon received at least 200,000 rubles' worth of bribes.

Bribery involving petty crimes during wartime had its place in the rural courts as well. Judge A. N. Starikova, a party member with only six years of education, was just twenty-four years old in March 1944 when she became a people's court judge in the Zav'ianlovskii raion of the Udmurt Autonomous Republic, one of the female judges quickly appointed to fill the positions vacated by men called to the front.[30] According to a report by the Ministry of Justice, she regularly accepted personal payments from people requesting leniency, sometimes in cash and sometimes in kind. In 1944, she allowed a convicted speculator to avoid prison in exchange for 1,500 rubles and twenty eggs. Similarly, in return for 1,100 rubles and a coveted wristwatch, Judge Starikova sentenced two women convicted of petty theft of state property to workplace labor rather than prison. After accepting sixteen kilograms of mutton and three kilograms of *salo* (pork fat), she spared a certain Chukavin from prison, assigning him nothing more than probation for violating the June 26, 1940 decree on labor discipline.[31] A mix of accused black marketeers, petty thieves, and labor shirkers—classic targets of Stalinist repression—found their way into Starikova's rural courtroom, and then sought common ground with the judge for negotiating reduced sentences.

Pressure on the courts to convict and to assign unforgiving sentences remained intense for years. In August 1949, Deputy Minister of Justice P. A. Kudriavtsev attacked judges for failing to take the June 4 decree on theft of state property seriously enough. He alleged that too many judges were still overly "liberal" in their approach, assigning minimum rather than maximum sentences for the theft of state property and other "serious crimes."[32] Some judges were even groundlessly acquitting thieves of state property, even though "the main work of all courts is the battle with theft." Kudriavtsev charged that many judges incorrectly differentiated between crimes against state property and political crimes. He inquired sarcastically:

> Why is it that, when a judge rules on a case of a counterrevolutionary crime, the judge's hands do not shake as he signs a sentence assigning twenty-five years [in prison]? But when he decides a case about thieves and swindlers—they are also enemies of the people, after all—then the judge resorts to assigning the minimum sanction, and the full force of the law is not applied.[33]

Political authorities pressed for maximum sentences, urging judges to show no leniency towards defendants simply because their crimes were not counterrevolutionary in nature.[34]

Mass repression for nonpolitical crimes (and the very long sentences associated with some of them) gave rise to an unintended consequence: a growing market inside the legal system for buyers and sellers to arrange deals, as people attempted to purchase mercy for defendants who had received extremely harsh sentences.[35] Although it may seem counterintuitive, arbitrary mass arrests and outrageously long sentences for nonpolitical crimes thus created tremendous opportunities for officials working in the agencies of law enforcement.[36] Some police, prosecutors, judges, and lawyers (but by no means all) took advantage and lined their own pockets.[37] Law enforcement officials who were willing to take the risk of accepting illicit gifts or payments enjoyed a brief but golden age of opportunity to profit in the late Stalinist courts.

Not only were there abundant opportunities for bribe taking, but the demand for the mitigation of sentences from the population was also tremendous. Who, in the main, was offering bribes to judges? According to official and anecdotal evidence, most of the people who resorted to bribery during the wartime and postwar years did so to overturn the conviction—or secure the release from prison—of a family member. The regime unintentionally created a large cohort of potential bribe givers among the *families* of hundreds of thousands of prisoners accused of being "thieves" and "speculators." Interestingly, because it was mostly men who were being arrested, it was mainly the wives (together with the children and parents) of convicts who offered bribes for their release.[38] One can assert without exaggeration that families of people sentenced to the Gulag for crimes against the economy or state property comprised a large proportion of those who offered bribes to judges and procurators.

The huge numbers of arrests and long sentences for petty crimes also fueled the (often correct) impression that many of those accused had been wrongly arrested and imprisoned.[39] This perception extended to judges reviewing cases, defense lawyers, and some of the general population. Some of the aggrieved parties were inspired to resolve these perceived injustices by offering bribes to legal officials. In many cases they had tried legal channels first, to no avail. The wounded veteran Solov'ev said about his own case, "I considered myself to have been convicted incorrectly and, having a large family, I searched for a way out from under the misfortune that had befallen me. That is why I made the approach" to bribe a judge.[40] The fact that many bribes were given to judges with the intention of producing correct and legal sentences (rather than overturning proper decisions) is further indication that the distortions of Stalinist justice were one of the prime causes of illegal payments in the courts, if an inadvertent one. During their bribery trials, many accused judges attempted to defend their actions by claiming that they had not taken bribes, but rather had accepted "tokens of appreciation" after correcting mistakes made at lower levels by incompetent courts.

As several leaders of the legal agencies noted, the long, mandatory sentences for theft and economic crimes confused many citizens, and this confusion may have made people more willing to seek informal redress of their convictions. On June 19, 1948, General Procurator of the USSR Safonov wrote to Central Committee Secretary Zhdanov on the subject of the sentences mandated by the theft decrees issued the previous year. "Sometimes such sentences are not entirely understandable to citizens and they create an impression of incongruity between the severity of the crime and the sentence, since the punishments for other serious crimes are much less than the punishment for theft."[41]

Moreover, some defendants and their families simply could not decipher the legal system. One Georgian man accused of offering a bribe told the court that the former procurator of his region told him that the court had improperly convicted and sentenced his sister. He stated that he did not know that his payment to the lawyer handling his sister's case "violated the legal procedure for complaining about a sentence." "I myself did not know how to write an appeal, since I don't know Russian, and I am not familiar with juridical questions."[42]

At a closed forum in February 1948, Supreme Court Chairman Goliakov affirmed the notion that there was popular confusion about the theft laws. As he told a meeting of the leadership of the Ministries of Justice and State Control, neither local judges nor average citizens properly understood the June 4, 1947 decrees and their severe penalties. In fact, good Soviet people sympathized with the criminals. He argued that it was up to judges to do a better job of explaining the law to the masses:

> Until the broad masses of the people understand our legal and penal policy—it will be difficult to fight crime. We increased the penalties but the quantity of crimes is not dropping. . . . Where are the results of our work? We must act not only upon the criminal, but also on the masses, that is, so that a legal consciousness grows among the masses (*rosla pravosoznanie*), a respect for the law and an intolerance for crime. . . . Comrade Stalin has said that we must declare a [moral] boycott of all criminals, so that the masses themselves express hatred for these criminals, *but we handle cases in a way that the people now only have sympathy for criminals.* The court must act in the name of the masses and the people, but they [the judges] do not understand this and the collective farmers write that this fellow or that woman was convicted for nothing [emphasis added].[43]

In this notable comment, Goliakov argues that penal policy is backfiring by creating popular compassion for those convicted of breaking the law. Judges, he says, were not sufficiently explaining the rationale and purpose of the June 4 decrees. In fact, some judges themselves did not understand the law or did not fully comprehend its significance.

A remarkable November 1948 letter sent by a prisoner in a Gulag camp to Beria at the Council of Ministers encapsulates many of the enormous (and unanticipated) consequences of the June 4, 1947 decrees— their consequences for the Stalinist system of law and punishment, for the Soviet population, and for popular faith in the courts.[44] The author of the eight-page letter was prisoner Timofei Z. Saraev, the former chief of the *Oktiabrskii* regional party committee in Cheliabinsk oblast'. Saraev's letter testifies to a deep sense that the June 4 decrees had unfairly punished vast numbers of honest and loyal Soviet citizens. The letter is notable in several ways: the leadership position the author held in the party (as the head of a regional party committee in a major province); his clear, continuing dedication to party ideals; the breadth of his vision and experience; his acute observations about the consequences for the country of the unjust convictions of so many nonpolitical prisoners (Saraev was convicted for theft, not for a political crime); and his observations about the innocent people imprisoned in the Gulag.

In his letter, Saraev (who had been imprisoned in the camp for eighteen months) immediately professes his love for, and dedication to, Joseph Stalin, the party, the revolution, and the motherland. He is no dissident.[45] Saraev writes that the cruel postwar decrees against theft of state and personal property were absolutely necessary. He applauds the Soviet government's fierce battle against thieves, bandits, and all the enemies of the Soviet state in the wake of the war and the failed harvest of 1946. "From this [situation of widespread crime] it followed that the government completely correctly and in a timely manner published the June 4, 1947 decrees protecting state property and the personal property of citizens." The legal agencies must protect socialist property and the state apparatus from both the internal *and* external enemies of Soviet power, all of whom must be exposed and crushed.

Having acknowledged that dangerous "criminal elements" lurk in Soviet society, the letter changes direction sharply. Saraev warns that certain employees of the courts and procuracy are prosecuting and convicting *innocent* people. They are making serious errors reminiscent of the mistakes of the high point of the Great Purges, "analogous, more or less, to the errors of 1937." Further, "with their incorrect methods of work, they harm our government, create animosity among the people, and artificially inflate [the amount of] criminality and the [number of] enemies of the people in the country." In fact, mistaken convictions by procuracy investigators aid the cause of the "Anglo-American imperialists" because they embitter the Soviet people against their leaders.

Turning to his own experience in the Gulag, Saraev notes that many of the thousands of prisoners who have passed through the camp where he is located had fought against fascism for the entire four years of the war. "They courageously fought for Moscow, for Stalingrad, for Kursk, and so on. They have state medals and repeated thanks from Joseph Vissarionovich Stalin." Yet, "very, very many of them were charged and convicted incorrectly." Procuracy investigators have artificially created cases against them, or inflated the severity of their crimes. "Everyone is lumped together—a person who accidentally makes some insignificant mistake at work, a recidivist thief, and an inveterate enemy of Soviet power" are all treated the same—as dangerous criminals. Saraev cites the cases of several people he met in the camps who were wrongly convicted and given long sentences; each involved convictions for theft of state property. Party members whose underlings embezzled funds were convicted and sentenced to long terms even though the supervisors had no knowledge of the crimes. In still other cases, "simple, uneducated" people that he met in the camps were serving outlandishly long sentences for petty crimes. He recounts the case of a certain G. A. Barkhatov, a deaf and illiterate man who worked as a mechanic in a garage. One day, his cigarette lighter ran out of fluid, so he filled it with two tablespoons of gasoline, valued at eighteen kopecks. "The investigator compiled the material for the indictment in a threatening spirit, and the judge gave [Barkhatov] eight years in prison. . . . Do the employees of the procuracy really consider this sentence correct?"

The author lamented, "It would be possible to send you scores and even hundreds of examples of cases in which the courts have deprived people of freedom for ten or twenty years for petty crimes, for [the theft of] five or six kilograms of potatoes, for 750 grams of flour, for seven kilograms of salt, and so on." Saraev calls for a special commission to investigate the procuracy and judicial agencies, and to free all innocent people from prison. This, he claims, would "reduce criminality in the country by 60–70 percent." In other words, he believes that up to 70 percent of prisoners have been convicted or sentenced incorrectly. Yet, he points out, when the convicted people or their relatives file appeals about unjust convictions, nearly all of them are immediately rejected.[46] He sums up, "Only my faith in the government, in the Central Committee of the Party, and personally in Joseph Vissarionovich Stalin, has given me the strength to appeal for freedom from imprisonment and restoration to the ranks of the Communist Party."

Saraev's letter highlights a sense among some people that the wave of arrests for theft of state property was an indication that the agencies of criminal justice simply were not working, raising doubts about the convictions of huge numbers of innocent people for petty crimes. Many of these people, together with their families, sought informal ways to address the perceived injustice. Negotiating deals based on illicit gifts was one of those ways.

NO DEALS FOR "COUNTERREVOLUTIONARIES"

It is important to note that there appear to have been limits on the kinds of cases for which judges would take bribes. Even bribe-taking judges, one could argue, operated within a certain moral universe. In nearly all the documented cases that I have seen, judges who accepted illegal payments offered leniency only for economic or property crimes (not political or violent crimes). This was the case for several reasons. First, judges appear to have believed that there was less risk in taking a bribe in the case of an economic crime or a property crime than a political or violent crime; second, the disproportionate punishment for petty economic activity or pilfering inspired family members to try to free the accused; third, intermediaries were also more reluctant to get involved in transactions that involved political or violent crimes; and finally, most judges seem to have regarded it as morally wrong to release violent criminals or "enemies of the state." In the case of nonpolitical crimes, however, many appear to have rationalized their actions on the grounds that they were, to some degree, correcting an injustice.

Judging by the available evidence, intervention on behalf of a person charged with a *political* or a *violent* offense could be purchased only very rarely. Very few examples have surfaced of prosecutors or judges who accepted a bribe in exchange for special consideration in cases of people charged with counterrevolutionary crimes under Article 58.[47] The Supreme Court judge Shevchenko testified that, when asked to intercede (for a price) in the case of Chachiashvili, he refused because the latter had been arrested for a "counterrevolutionary crime."[48] Similarly, there are only a small handful of instances of documented cases where a defendant who had committed a violent crime was helped by a judge in exchange for a bribe.[49] It is unclear whether judges refused to get involved in such cases because of ethical qualms or because they were unwilling to risk the more serious penalties of discovery.[50]

Thus, although some judges were willing—for a fee—to release people convicted of property, economic, or official crimes that they considered to lie under a certain invisible threshold, they were unwilling to cross the line on behalf of "dangerous" criminals. It appears that there was a certain range on the spectrum of criminal cases for which judges and procurators would be willing to put themselves at risk. The convicts in these cases were not career criminals. They were mainly small-scale embezzlers, petty thieves, employees stealing at work, peasants pilfering food from stocks or fields, or profiteers working in the shadow economy. Generally, judges (and, most likely, procurators and police) apparently did not consider such criminals to be "dangerous," and were able to justify to themselves overturning a conviction. In contrast, judges considered political criminals to be threats to society, as they did murderers, violent thugs, and armed thieves.

As we have seen, the number of cases that lay along this spectrum, within this zone of "acceptable" bribery, grew quickly with the crackdown on thieves and economic criminals in 1945–1949. The mass convictions for nonpolitical crimes created an enormous reservoir of people seeking special consideration. These were just the type of "criminals" with whom certain judges were most willing to deal.

Judges were not typical Soviet bribe takers. They were not providing access to the usual scarce goods and services that were in extremely high demand, and worth paying for—apartments, food, documents, exemption from labor or military service, and relief from burdensome state obligations. Instead, judges sold access to the justice that Soviet people had been promised was their birthright in a socialist society (and that the Stalin Constitution of 1936 had guaranteed, if only on paper), but that many believed had been denied to them.

"WE TOOK BUDAPEST": LAWYERS AND THE PHENOMENON OF *MIKST*

Another important professional group that was especially well-placed to take advantage of the opportunities provided by the rush of arrests and court cases were defense lawyers (*advokaty*). Lawyers play a leading role in any discussion of corruption in the Soviet courts (as in any courts), since they served as intermediaries in many informal deals between petitioners and judges.

Starting in the middle of the war and accelerating quickly afterwards, defense lawyers found themselves in the middle of a controversy regarding the extra "fees for service" that they sometimes demanded. It became a common practice in wartime and postwar courts for lawyers to charge clients an additional fee beyond the standard, very modest official rates set by the state for legal services.[51] (These standard rates had been set in 1932, when the government outlawed the provision of legal services by private parties.) Among themselves, defense attorneys had a rather sarcastic name for this extra fee: *mikst,* an acronym for *Maksimal'noe ispol'zovanie klientov sverkh tarifa,* or "the maximum use of clients above the regular fee."

Mikst is perhaps most accurately regarded as an extra fee for service. Such a fee technically was not a bribe, though lawyers themselves often referred to it as a violation of the rules of the defense bar (*advokatura*). Nevertheless, the acceptance of mikst resulted in prosecutors' unfairly leveling allegations of bribery against many lawyers, when those lawyers were more likely simply committing an ethical breach by overcharging their clients.

It is clear that many defense lawyers considered mikst to be well-deserved compensation for extra travel or paperwork, or for an especially complex case or appeal. By all accounts, mikst was a pervasive and revealing phenomenon in the Stalinist (and post-Stalinist) legal system beginning in the late 1930s or early 1940s. (There has been no original historical research on the topic of mikst during the wartime or late Stalin periods.)[52] Several lawyers testified that mikst was common during and immediately after the war. As one lawyer put it to investigators in 1951 (describing the period between 1941 and 1947), likely with some exaggeration, "I affirm that in this period in Moscow literally all lawyers took large sums of money from clients, the so-called 'mikst,' and I remember lawyers who took a sum of 25,000 rubles from clients—they were not charged with a crime, but [instead] they were expelled from the Moscow collegium of defense lawyers." It was a "normal phenomenon."[53] Judging by the testimony of defense attorneys, the official salary scale for lawyers was not enough to provide much of a living. One lawyer, a certain Kniazeva, told an acquaintance that in 1945 she was discharged from the army, worked as a lawyer and "lived poorly." Kniazeva asked her acquaintance, who worked for the Ministry of Justice, to help "find clients for her" to represent in court cases, "since it was necessary, as she expressed it, to 'earn some money.'"[54]

Demand for lawyers' help in negotiating the legal system was enormous. In the year 1945 alone, clients used the services of defense lawyers attached to the courts of Moscow over 170,000 times. According to Ministry of Justice statistics provided to the Central Committee, just in the first half of 1950 more than 700,000 people throughout the USSR came to members of the defense bar with questions or requests for services; defense attorneys handled 191,000 criminal cases and more than 50,000 civil cases.[55] In the city of Moscow, the standard fee set by the *iuriskonsul'tant* (legal consultancy) department of the courts for hiring a lawyer to draw up a simple appeal was fifty or 100 rubles.[56] Flouting the rules, lawyers often asked for five or ten times this rate.

At times, defense lawyers told clients—or at least implied to them—that they would not work as hard on the client's behalf if no extra payments were made. In 1945, for example, a certain Golikov, the head of a consumer cooperative union (*potrebsoiuz*) in Moscow oblast', was accused of theft of state property. The defense lawyer assigned to him by the court, who was supposed to charge the official rate of 1,000 rubles to represent him, demanded a total of 9,000 rubles from his wife. The lawyer told her that he needed the additional 8,000 rubles for "expenses," though he did not specify the exact services involved. According to Golikov's wife, "He urged me to tell no one and asked that I bring the money only to his apartment [rather than to the courthouse]. I asked him, 'What will you spend this money on? You don't have any children or a wife.' Lugovskoi answered me: 'It is needed for the government [tax].' I believed him, thinking that he really was going to use this money legally for expenditures connected with the case of my husband." (This same lawyer also demanded extra fees in other cases.)[57]

Lawyers often implied to clients that a judge had demanded extra money to grant a favorable ruling. Lawyers would ask the client for several thousand rubles above the normal rate, hinting that a part of this "fee" would be passed on to the judge to guarantee success. Investigations showed that the client sometimes believed that the lawyer had passed a bribe to a judge, even if he had not. On occasion, a lawyer might even promise a money-back guarantee: if the defendants did not receive the desired result, the lawyer would return the client's money.[58] In fact, lawyers often simply kept the money.[59] At a 1951 trial held in Moscow, the court found several lawyers guilty of soliciting bribes from clients in 1945–1947. The lawyers had bragged to petitioners of their excellent informal relationships with judges. In the words of the sentence, they "ignored their duty to help carry out Soviet justice." Instead, they "spread rumors among those who came to them for legal help about their personal friendships and connections with judicial employees."[60] Rather than passing the bribes along to the judges, they pocketed the money.

Defense lawyers sometimes acted like middlemen, expecting a "commission" after the fact, when a successful result was achieved. As part of their "deal" with the client, they would ask for a bonus if they achieved an acquittal or a reduced sentence through their efforts as an intermediary. In a case involving a "gang" of nine speculators in wool cloth, reported in November 1951 to Malenkov by the MGB, a certain Leningrad lawyer, B. L. Liatskii, received a "reward" of 3,000 rubles for acting as intermediary in a payment to a judge. Defense lawyers quite often acted as intermediaries in transactions between convicted people (or their family members) and judges, as they were well placed to undertake these negotiations. (Secretaries, consultants, clerks, and other court personnel who enjoyed contact with both judges and petitioners also frequently served as intermediaries.) In the Liatskii case, the payment came from the daughter of one of the accused speculators.[61] The bribe was allegedly uncovered when a police informant told the Leningrad police that, when the case was dismissed, the judge, the lawyer, and one of the defendants had gone to a restaurant to celebrate together. As one apparently remorseful lawyer remarked at his trial, "I did not join the defense bar with the goal of making money [by crooked means], but you have every opportunity to give and receive bribes there."[62]

Evidently it was a common perception that access to skilled practitioners who could help navigate one or another bureaucratic maze (such as lawyers, or doctors in the case of health care) would either cost extra or require personal contacts. Lacking the requisite connections (colloquially known as *blat*), many people believed that they needed to hire a well-connected lawyer simply to have their case heard and decided fairly. As for the value of those connections, one person charged with paying a bribe defended himself by arguing that the low-cost state-provided legal services employed only "evening students, who were therefore inexperienced people." Another defendant stated that he understood perfectly when his wife paid a lawyer 2,000 rubles, quite a bit more than the official rate, because "it was completely clear to me that no one would do anything without getting paid." A lawyer from Khar'kov went so far as to claim that if she did *not* charge extra fees for her services, clients would not hire her because they assumed she would be ineffective.[63]

Officials willing to accept under-the-table payments could exploit this view that the state-provided services were inadequate. One accused bribe giver disparaged the defense bar at his trial, reflecting a common attitude: "I wanted to give the case of Tsypeniuk to a defense lawyer, but I assumed that the lawyer would handle it in a superficial way and would not devote his entire effort to help me in this case."[64] The Procurator General Safonov himself alleged that one lawyer, a certain Senderov, boasted to clients about the fact that he was once an assistant to the Minister of Justice, in order to demonstrate "his excellent connections with court employees in his activities as a lawyer. . . . Senderov always bragged that he supposedly had close personal connections with employees of the Ministry of Justice and the USSR Supreme Court."[65] The desperation of families, and the confusion of legal procedures, helped persuade them that extra money paid to lawyers was the only way to get results, and if they failed to pay, the outcome would likely be disappointing. As one woman who sold her cow to raise money to pay her lawyer wrote, "I needed someone to help my son, who, in my opinion was convicted incorrectly." She contended that she did not pay a bribe; rather she paid a lawyer for his help. "I was sure that I was obliged to make a good and orderly person out of my son, and I decided to give this money [to the lawyer] to help me in the case of my son."[66]

The July 1949 trial of a defense lawyer, Berta Radchik, highlights several elements of the mechanism of mikst. The court asked Radchik, who had confessed to acting as an intermediary in several bribes, about the large sums of cash that the police found in her apartment when she was arrested. "I can explain the origin of my thousands of rubles by the fact that in my last years as a defense lawyer I enthusiastically accepted so-called 'mikst,' which I began to solicit only during my joint work with the lawyer Kommodov in the city of Chkalov [the temporarily renamed city of Orenburg]. At the time, I was in a difficult material situation. Upon learning that I never took mikst from clients, Kommodov called me an idiot and persuaded me to regularly accept mikst from clients." Radchik described how profitable the extra payments were: "I began to take mikst in 1943. In one month in Chkalov I handled no less than fifteen cases, and for each case I took 2,000, 3,000, [or] 5,000 rubles of mikst."[67]

For most people, these sums represented very large amounts of money, and the willingness to pay indicates how anxious people were to achieve positive results in the courts. In her testimony before the court, the defense attorney Radchik went on to denounce mikst as unethical and harmful to correct sentencing and the proper functioning of the court in general:

> "Mikst" will give birth to extremely harmful consequences for the interests of justice. Because when a lawyer takes mikst he enters into a personal relationship with the client, and this wipes out the impartial relationship to the case. On the other hand, when the lawyer enters a personal relationship with members of the court then this naturally has an influence on the issuance of an unjust sentence.

She says that while she worked in Chkalov she lost her "conscience" and her "honor" as a Soviet citizen: "I confess my guilt, and with my actions I did damage to Soviet justice, although mikst wasn't against the law." Radchik confesses her errors, while still hedging her bets.[68]

Some lawyers defended the practice of accepting an extra fee by arguing that their clients insisted that they take a gift for a job well done. In one case, a lawyer said that as a voluntarily offered "token of gratitude alongside everything else, clients always give me gifts—money in amounts of 300, 500, 1,000 or more rubles." These personal "bonuses" were given in addition to the official fees paid to the court.[69] This example highlights the fact that most lawyers likely did not think of mikst as a bribe, but rather as the (perhaps unethical, but not criminal) acceptance of extra fees voluntarily offered in exchange for extra service.[70]

In the spring of 1948, the question of mikst came to the attention of the Minister of State Control, Lev Z. Mekhlis, at a meeting with leading officials in the Ministry of Justice, which had supervisory responsibility for the defense bar. Mekhlis, who pushed to criminalize the giving and acceptance of mikst as bribery, expressed his complete frustration, indeed disgust, with the situation among lawyers. He contrasts the might of the Red Army with the weakness of the Ministry of Justice in its efforts to control the fees that lawyers demanded:

> We took Budapest, we took Prague, we took Warsaw, but we cannot defeat the gang that sits there [lawyers in the Moscow *advokatura*]. What kind of ministry is this and what kind of deputy ministers and deputy in charge of cadres are they, who cannot change the situation in

the Moscow *advokatura?* This is outrageous. There is not a single ministry like the Ministry of Justice.[71]

One can reasonably interpret the target of Mekhlis's contempt as something well beyond lawyers' unofficial fees—the general inability of the party to control the illicit activities of court and law enforcement employees throughout the entire state apparatus. The USSR had defeated the fascists but could not wipe out crime among its own civil servants, even in Moscow. The fact that Mekhlis makes a verbal connection between lawyers and Nazi Germany strengthens his condemnation of them as "enemies."[72] In the view of Mekhlis and other party leaders, the court system—a key weapon of the revolutionary state and the enforcer of socialist legality—was being manipulated from the inside by defense lawyers, who weakened it with their greed and moral laxity. The case of mikst further highlights the official view that bribery posed a serious ideological problem.[73]

DEALS INVOLVING EMPLOYEES OF THE PROCURACY

For many of the same reasons that judges and lawyers could benefit from their positions, procuracy employees had myriad opportunities to solicit illegal payments both during and after the war. The procuracy played a critical role in the Soviet government as the agency that ensured that the regime's laws were being consistently enforced throughout the country. As Lenin wrote in his 1922 article "On 'Dual Subordination' and Legality":

> The procurator has the right and the obligation to do only one thing: to watch over the establishment of an effective, uniform understanding of legality in all the republics, ignoring all local differences and in spite of any kind of local influences. . . . The procurator is responsible for seeing that not a single decision of a single local authority diverges from the law, and only from that point of view must the procurator protest any illegal decisions.[74]

The regime policies that targeted crimes against the Soviet economy and socialist property brought procurators into close contact with a large number of alleged criminals. In the Soviet system, as in most of the continental European legal systems, procuracy investigators (*sledovateli* and *prokurory*) rather than the police led criminal investigations, and were responsible for interrogating the accused and witnesses.[75] In one case during the war, a deputy procurator and three investigators in the city of Kuibeshev were convicted of accepting bribes in cash and in kind to throw out the cases of workers who had "deserted" from enterprises involved in the militarized industries. These workers were liable to receive five to eight years in a labor camp under the December 1941 law against desertion from key defense industries. Upon accepting payments from the accused, the procurators declined to pursue their cases, claiming that the investigation had produced insufficient evidence. Following their own convictions in 1946, these four procuracy employees were sentenced to eight to ten years in prison for bribery.[76] Other procurators accepted "gifts" in exchange for help. A military procurator, I. S. Razno, accepted two gold watches, a gold ring, and a metal chain from the wife of the accused suspect. Three days later, Razno saw to it that the accused was released on probation. Razno was later convicted of taking bribes and sentenced to five years in a penal camp.[77]

State and party archives contain many examples of employees of collective farms who paid off procuracy investigators to avoid arrest or prosecution for stealing or damaging state property. In one case from 1946, the chief of a field brigade at the collective farm "The Call of Il'ich" accidentally started a fire that destroyed stored grain.[78] Afraid of being charged with a crime, he paid an investigator one hundred kilograms of grain, through an intermediary, to look the other way. The investigator improperly suspended the case, a fact that was discovered when some of the collective farmers overheard the brigadier bragging about the deal. The giver of the bribe received two years in prison; the investigator got five years.[79]

Prosecutors were also in a position to extort bribes by threatening uncooperative suspects with negative consequences, such as arrest, additional criminal charges, or longer sentences. Violations of labor discipline in war-related industries inspired attempts to extort money. In a case described in an early 1947 procuracy report, Azhdar Ragimov, an assistant procurator for the Lenin region of the city of Baku, investigated accusations that a group of teenagers had deserted from the factory to which they had been mobilized for wartime labor.[80] Ragimov called the teenagers to his office and demanded 2,000 rubles from each of the boys, promising that if they cooperated, they would be released from jail and the charges against them would be limited to the relatively minor crime of "shirking" under the decree of June 26, 1940 (rather than the more serious charge of "labor desertion"). After paying Ragimov 500 rubles apiece, the teens immediately went back to their factory and told the head of the party organization about the blackmail. Ragimov received seven years in prison for extorting a bribe.

Those accused of theft of state property were especially eager to strike deals with prosecutors. In a case from 1949, an investigator in the procurator's office in the Stalinisk region of the city of Ivanovo was said to have extorted 1,000 rubles from a certain Ponzhina, who had been accused of stealing 419 rubles.[81] According to the KPK report, the same investigator later extorted a bribe from an employee of a bread factory who had been accused of stealing. He also suspended two cases of hooliganism after being treated to meals and vodka by the defendants and their father. The investigator later was convicted and sentenced to ten years in prison.[82]

Investigators responsible for looking into criminal activities in certain industrial enterprises were also well positioned to extort bribes. Managers in the food and alcohol industries would give procuracy employees sumptuous gifts to keep them from arresting employees for illegal speculation on the black market or other economic crimes. Managers subsidized the local officials with scarce food and liquor, and also unofficially supplied their parties. A certain M. S. Lobanov, a senior inspector in the Saratov city procurator's office, who was responsible for investigating allegations of wrongdoing in the local alcohol and tobacco industries, was said to have accepted gifts to throw out criminal cases.[83] An investigation concluded in May 1949 reported that, in the course of his investigations, he "received cigarettes at the cigarette factory [and] beer at the beer factory." Investigators alleged that local police or procurators who came to investigate discrepancies at economic enterprises could often be silenced with "tokens of appreciation," typically gifts of free produce or alcohol.

Indeed, many procurators were in an excellent position to receive such "gifts" from the managers of industries located in their regions. In April 1950, the Party Control Commission examined a case in which a deputy procurator for Krasnoiarsk krai, V. S. Babenko, was accused of accepting gifts of meat products and alcohol from suspects who had themselves been accused of theft of state property.[84] According to the investigation, "a group of criminals" from the meat trust, including the head of the trust, the main engineer, the bookkeeper, and a supply attendant, sold stolen meat and alcohol on the black market. To cover up their crimes, they gave procuracy staff gifts. Indeed, the employees of the meat trust passed out gifts to many of the leading cadres of the region, including high-ranking officials in the procuracy and the Ministry of State Security, the chief of the railroad, and the deputy chair of the cadres department in the regional party committee. Moreover, the procuracy employees received gifts of alcohol from the Krasnoiarsk vodka and liquor trust—"allegedly for technical purposes"—and sold 780 liters on the side for "their personal benefit." All these employees used their access to valuable goods in scarce supply to buy off the power elites in the region. For example, meat was passed out to a wide circle of soviet and party workers for the October 1946 holidays. In February 1946, staff from the vodka and liquor trust distributed forty liters of alcohol to the members of a delegation traveling to Moscow to represent Krasnoiarsk krai at a session of the Supreme Soviet. The prosecutor then allegedly halted an investigation into this malfeasance in exchange for gifts of alcohol. An investigation by the Party Control Commission investigation concluded that much of the krai leadership (including the party leadership, the head of the police, and the chair of the soviet executive committee) knew about the situation but did nothing, sometimes remaining silent in exchange for gifts. For his part in this scheme, the deputy procurer, Babenko, received only a strict reprimand in April 1950, probably because he was well connected in the local political structure.[85]

Indeed, the drive for stronger punishments for bribery at the end of the war came in part because provincial prosecutors and other local officials were so easily bought off by small inducements.[86] According to a detailed investigation of bribery in the Ukrainian Republic in 1949, most bribes offered to (and accepted by) the police, judges, and procuracy employees were very small, between fifty and 200 rubles. In rural Western Ukraine, food products were the most popular bribe.[87] Clearly, the authorities were concerned that local procurators' acceptance of modest gifts in exchange for looking the other way could diminish the state's ability to enforce its laws, thus limiting the reach of central power. As these examples indicate, in the years immediately after the war, and especially in rural areas, bribes were often offered in kind rather than in cash, or sometimes as a combination of the two. In a shortage economy, even bribes could be de-monetized. (It also was easier for participants to disguise a bribe if it was not offered as cash; bribes in the form of food or other goods could more easily be disguised by traditions of gift giving.)[88] In one case that came before the Party Control Commission, a Russian prosecutor admitted taking gifts of money and food "in small amounts" from the relatives of the accused. In 1946, the relative of a person accused of stealing ten kilos of leather came to her apartment and gave her a present of 500 rubles, a piece of salo, and 900 grams of sausage. Another bribe consisted of (among other things) two and a half meters of silk fabric, two pieces of bacon fat, 400 grams of butter, forty-five eggs, a duck, a chicken, and 500 grams of sour cream.[89] Such small payments-in-kind were a common feature of the landscape of gifts to officials, meant to seal deals.

CONCLUSION: FORMAL CHANNELS AND INFORMAL RELATIONSHIPS

What do these findings tell us about the anatomy of the bribe in the late Stalinist agencies of law enforcement and criminal justice? Historians naturally have devoted much effort to describing the mass arrests and harsh penalties of the Stalin period, which serve as the framework for analyzing bribery in the postwar legal system. The question of how and why police, judges, and prosecutors could profit from their positions, however, has not been explored in detail. In general, corruption occurs under conditions where people believe that the reward will outweigh the risks inherent to the action. After the war, sentences for "counterrevolutionary" crimes were relatively rare compared to in the 1930s. Much more common were seven- to twenty-five-year sentences doled out by the regular courts. Yet the fierce postwar repressions of nonpolitical crimes against state property and the economy gave birth to an unexpected consequence—appeals aimed at annulling or reducing outrageous sentences. Hundreds of thousands of cases poured into the courts, often fueled by righteous indignation.

In the Soviet Union, bribery had both enabling and disabling functions. At times bribery allowed the Stalinist legal system to work through major obstacles, in a speedier fashion. As Yoram Gorlizki and Peter Solomon have pointed out, the June 4 decrees closed the loopholes that judges had been able to employ to moderate mandatory sentences, or to dismiss cases in light of mitigating factors or extraordinary circumstances.[90] This weakening of judicial discretion within an inflexible Stalinist legal system made sub-rosa resolutions to seemingly intractable problems even more appealing. Moreover, power relations meant that punishments were unevenly distributed, depending on connections, party membership, and other "subjective" factors. The perception that the well-connected had an advantage in their interactions with the bureaucracy reinforced the sense of injustice. Elites, naturally, had a major advantage when they engaged in corrupt activities, assuming they did not find themselves caught up in a political campaign, a factional struggle, or a personal vendetta. People who lacked influential connections were tempted to purchase the special attention that they would not otherwise be given. In the short term, a successful bribe could give an ordinary person access to the same privileged consideration that people with connections enjoyed. A gift to a person well placed in the legal system could temporarily level the playing field.

Bribery could also allow people to circumvent opaque or irrational legal procedures. It was difficult for individuals to obtain reliable information about how to gain redress in the legal system. In her study of gift giving in early modern France, Natalie Zemon Davis notes that lawyers were quite frequently given gifts of food because they could help common people navigate the complicated and alien-seeming legal system.[91] One could say the same about the capricious Stalinist legal maze in which many people found themselves unwittingly trapped and demoralized. Under-the-table deals involving law enforcement officials were essentially a rational response both by Soviet people facing arbitrary arrests on a mass scale, and by the beleaguered police, procuracy, and judicial authorities attempting to process them. In this light, bribery in the legal system can be seen as a logical reaction to a party-state structure with little respect for the courts, legal procedures, or the rights of individuals before the law.[92] That petitioners found many court, police, and procuracy employees willing to negotiate, and no shortage of go-betweens willing to broker those deals, only increased incentives to make shadow arrangements. Corruption in the legal system, one could argue, minimized the damage done both by draconian laws and by the pressure on judges and procurators to convict at all costs. One could also argue that bribery, like gift giving to officials before the revolution, offset to some degree the low pay for officialdom, and therefore served a kind of positive economic function at a time when much of the civil service lived at a subsistence level.[93] (The same could be said of mikst for defense lawyers.)

Overall, however, bribes in the courts in some senses exacerbated the problems they aspired to solve. They added to frustration over the unfair distribution of justice, which was based not on the merits of the case, but on the intervention of powerful (and paid) extralegal "contacts." The consequent sense of injustice further discredited the entire legal system, and led to a growing distance between "society" and "rulers," between "us" and "them." Rumors circulated to the effect that palms needed to be greased in a certain region, town, or courtroom, which encouraged more people to resort to paying bribes. Corruption, in effect, was both the problem and the solution. To get around a corrupt officialdom, one of the few options is to pay illegally. As is often the case, corruption begat corruption in a spiraling, self-reinforcing pattern.

The attitude toward agencies of criminal justice and law enforcement in the postwar Stalin period reveals a widespread popular belief that the official channels simply were not effective or fair. The demand for back-door solutions to legal problems was fueled by desperation: the arrest of people for crimes that condemned them to long sentences, insufficient personnel to meet the need for services, impenetrable and confusing red tape, and a sense that it was futile to petition the cumbersome and unresponsive administration through official means. Thus many people were motivated to seek out informal, personalized resolutions to their problems. The system of low-paid, court-appointed defense lawyers was poorly equipped to represent defendants' interests and rights, but well positioned to facilitate the establishment of informal relationships with judges (for a price). Many clients believed that they either had to pay extra fees to defense lawyers to encourage them to devote sufficient attention to their case, or (sometimes simultaneously) to make other extralegal arrangements, such as bribing a judge.

Stalinist repression could not eliminate such shadow relationships, of course. In fact, these relationships acted as critical mechanisms within the Soviet bureaucracy.[94] As the party-state struggled to regain its grip on society after the war, cultures of reciprocity—which sometimes morphed into bribery—were one way that people maneuvered to endure or gain advantage. In the case of law enforcement, bribery was something of a "cash for amnesty" program. The paying of bribes could be seen as society's natural reaction to Soviet officials who were seen to abuse their offices with impunity.

The Soviet state claimed to be committed to transforming the culture of petty bribery that infected the bureaucracy. The regime endeavored to understand—and then sought to control, if not destroy—the crime of bribery. Nevertheless, despite heated rhetoric, several factors hindered a serious crackdown on bribery. One of Stalin's most important postwar priorities—to defend the economic bases of Soviet socialism, including state property, at all costs—created opportunities for those involved in the enforcement of the punitive laws. Through its policies and actions, then, the regime helped to create the conditions that fed the corruption that it was attempting to crush.

The phenomena discussed in this chapter shed new light on the state of a desperate Soviet society, petitioning a compromised legal system to protect it from an arbitrarily repressive party-state that regularly demonstrated its contempt for the rule of law. Indeed, the laws and legal system described here illustrate yet another way in which the state essentially compelled many of its subjects to act outside the law, to find alternative ways to achieve justice.

As the next chapter will explore, in the game of deal-making in the Soviet Union, the bribe had its own unwritten rules.

II

3 "The Word 'Bribe' Was Never Mentioned"
Everyday Practice and the
Art of the Bribe

BRIBERY WAS AN EVERYDAY PHENOMENON in the late Stalinist USSR. This chapter examines the risky interactions between ordinary people and the state officials who accepted payments for services that were either in violation of existing laws or that were supposed to be provided free of charge. This study has argued that the bribe is a mode of negotiation—one that sometimes involved elements of coercion—most often occurring between petitioners and officeholders, between the buyers and sellers of services. In the Soviet Union, such negotiations had their own subculture with shared language, rituals, attitudes, and practices.

In the late Stalin period, bribery, as a type of deal-making involving people from across the social spectrum, was situated at the intersection of state, the law, the shadow economy, and criminality. Of course, state and society were not completely separate spheres. Officials who accepted a bribe to discharge a function on one day may have themselves paid a bribe to arrange a different service the next day. Indeed, one of the advantages of the approach taken in this book is that it examines the vast middle ground of (mainly) petty graft. Bribery was a participatory exercise that included people from all walks of Soviet life. Officials with access to scarce goods or resources might be tempted to sell the fruits of that access. Professionals and administrators accepted bribes;

secretaries, clerks, lawyers, and people with no other means of support whatsoever acted as intermediaries between petitioners and officials. And bribes were *offered* by all types of people—from collective farmers to workers, engineers, and pensioners—who needed apartments, jobs, documents, or other commodities in short supply, or whose family members had encountered problems with the legal system.

How did ordinary Soviet people interact with officials in positions of power in the time of Stalin? The bribe was one of the many unofficial practices that we think of as "corruption." It can be regarded as a particular form of informal relationship that enabled many individuals, both officials and ordinary people, to get things done. Bribery was one type of unofficial exchange between the representatives of state power and the population. Blat, or reciprocal favors based on acquaintanceship, was another. The sociologist Alena Ledeneva notes the distinction between blat, which is not illegal and is based on a degree of trust and friendly relations without the immediate expectation of anything in return; and bribery, which does not necessarily derive from personal relations, involves a payment and an expectation of quid pro quo, and is a criminal violation.[1] A bribe is a one-time payment, in cash or other valuables, in the absence of an ongoing relationship, while blat implies an ongoing reciprocal relationship based on acquaintanceship and mutual favors, and not on cash or other one-off gifts.

Such interactions between officials and the general population illuminate those formal parts of the system that failed to work according to plan, and underscore the large gap between "consumer" demand and the extremely limited supply of essential goods and services. Yet they also allow us to explore the experience of ordinary individuals, and the drama of the complex choices they had to make in a time of great uncertainty. In examining these choices, we will not indulge in moralizing, which is both ahistorical and presumptuous. According to Western standards, bribery is deviant. The condemnation of bribery that one finds in most writing by journalists and observers (and by some academics), however, rarely if ever takes into account political or cultural traditions. This book argues that in many cases, for the participants, bribery was not deviant. Transactions criminalized as bribery were sometimes actions that many people thought of as consistent with human needs and values.

Normally, bribery is thought of either as a crime (in a purely legalistic or criminological approach) or as a personal transgression (a morally condemned wrong). Most commonly, perhaps, states understand bribery both as a crime against society *and* as a kind of individual vice. The Soviet regime, like most others, shared this view, condemning bribery both as a form of serious professional malfeasance and as a violation of core "Soviet values." I would propose that deal-making involving bribes also can be usefully regarded as a type of "art," a practice we can understand as a type of negotiation shaped by cultural contexts and attitudes, rather than simply as a socially dangerous crime or as a moral evil.

Although the late Stalin years were a period of transition, certain consistent factors shaped this stage of Soviet history. As we have seen, the exigencies of postwar reconstruction amid scarcities of food, housing, and other essentials provided both a tremendous demand for goods and services and bountiful opportunities for officials in a position to acquire and offer them illegally. Party officials struggled, with mixed success, to combat such abuses of office. Not surprisingly, long-standing traditions of what Catriona Kelly has called "self-interested giving" proved impossible to eliminate.[2]

POPULAR UNDERSTANDINGS OF THE BRIBE

The state succeeded in inculcating the idea that Soviet subjects were entitled to certain services guaranteed in the Soviet Constitution of 1936 (known as the Stalin Constitution). By the late Stalin period, the idea that the state was not fulfilling its obligations to the population, at least in certain respects, appears to have been a commonly held view, as evidenced by the enormous amount of petitioning to the courts and other agencies for things like apartments and appeals of "unjust" sentences. To some degree, the need to pay bribes reinforced resentment of the state's failure to provide. The historian Elena Zubkova has emphasized that in this period the population tended to perceive the national government and its authorities as an abstract and immutable force that an individual could only rarely influence. At the same time, both higher authorities and the population focused their criticisms on the incompetence or malfeasance of *local* officials, or "proximate power."[3] Resentment of abuses by local bureaucrats was rife. In light of this attitude, one can imagine that many people perceived the offering of bribes as a necessity, not a crime, believing that they were entitled to employ any means at their disposal to get what they were owed from a state whose dishonest or inept bureaucrats frustrated them. From that perspective, they most likely believed that offering bribes to state officials did not warrant punishment, since it was not possible for an individual to "damage" this impersonal state with its often-corrupt local administrations.

In light of the extremely difficult conditions during and after the war, many individuals felt an increased sense of entitlement after their wartime sacrifices.[4] Nevertheless, because of insufficient production, compounded by an inequitable and inefficient distribution of goods and services, the regime was unable to convince people that the state was *theirs,* and that stealing from the state somehow involved cheating *themselves.* Small-scale bribery (together with the petty theft of state property and profiteering) was often seen as part of a necessary survival strategy.[5] In court, bribe givers emphasized their desperate material situation. Many people believed that paying a bribe could be a morally justifiable decision within the bounds of what was needed to get by or to achieve some semblance of justice.

One frequently encounters Soviet citizens making moral distinctions between the acts of *offering* a bribe and *accepting* a bribe. Authorities understandably expressed concern about such an attitude. Many individuals appear to have believed that bribe *taking* by an official was a heinous crime that deserved punishment. Bribe takers were referred to as "blood suckers" or "leeches" (*krovosos*), among other choice epithets.[6] Bribe *givers,* on the other hand, were regarded as innocent victims who were compelled to give up scarce money or other assets to make the system work properly or to make life bearable. As Caroline Humphrey has pointed out, the Russian word for bribe, *vziatka* (from the word *vziat'*—to take), itself puts the onus on the *taking* official and hints at a degree of extortion. This meaning stands in contrast to the English word *bribe,* which implies that the giver is just as much the initiator (and manipulator) in the arrangement.[7] (The French words for bribery, like the English, imply that the "buyer" is most instrumental in the relationship: *acheter* [to buy], *soudoyer* [to give or offer something to influence a person], or to offer gifts of *pots de vin.*) Evidence drawn from Soviet court cases, petitions, and letters indicates that these two sides of the coin—that officials who accepted bribes were devious criminals whom Soviet power must punish mercilessly, while those who offered payments were innocents justifiably attempting to soften their plight—coexisted in the minds of many Soviet people.[8]

This dual understanding explains how a certain Vol'skii, who had just offered a 5,000-ruble bribe to a court employee, could almost simultaneously address a signed complaint to the Central Committee, despairing that "people charged with a crime more and more rarely visit the court's legal consultants [iuridkonsultatsiia] for advice, and more and more often knock on the back doors of court offices."[9] He paid the bribe with one hand, even as he wrote and signed a letter complaining about the need to do so with the other. Not surprisingly, this letter was used against him at trial—he was convicted and sentenced to five years in a labor camp.

This impression that there was a degree of tolerance for those who gave payments to officials is reinforced by a 1949 observation made by the USSR Supreme Court, that local judges often simply dismissed charges against bribe givers. In some cases, judges even went so far as to return to bribe givers the money or other valuables they had offered to officials.[10] Such actions by judges may have reflected (and reinforced) an impression that bribe givers were often the blameless victims of unscrupulous officials, and that the giving of bribes should not always be considered a crime. An example of sympathy for bribe givers is found in an anonymous letter sent from Alma Ata to Minister of Justice Rychkov, and dated June 5, 1947. The author complains that officials convicted of taking bribes were being punished lightly and given the minimum sentence of two years, while at the same time "the bribe givers—dark, illiterate collective farmers—were judged more harshly."[11] Sometimes those who accepted bribes conceded as much. As one lawyer who confessed to offering bribes put it: "I consider the initiator of a bribe in every case to be the person taking the bribe, otherwise the bribe giver could too easily land in prison."[12] Morally, in this view, it was "better to give than to receive," since corrupt state functionaries forced people to offer bribes. This double standard allowed ordinary people to imagine a moral disconnect between the two parties to a bribe, even though both were engaged in the same transaction.

The case of Naumov, a war veteran, is a striking example of the belief that it was morally acceptable to offer a bribe in the extraordinary postwar years. Naumov confessed at trial that he had attempted to pay a bribe for the release of his only son, who had been arrested at the end of 1946 and sentenced to one year in prison plus five years' exile from Moscow. In his final statement at trial, Naumov told the court: "It was easier to go on the attack at the front during the War for the Fatherland than it is to stand here in front of the court. . . . But I fulfilled the civic duty [*grazhdanskii dolg*] of a father, trying somehow to make the fate of my son easier."[13] One can imagine that such sentiments from a serviceman, declaring that it was his "civic duty" to pay a bribe on behalf of his imprisoned son, would have concerned legal and party authorities.

Many judges seem to have shared this perspective. During this period the sentences given to bribe givers were typically shorter than those assigned for accepting them, even though the law mandated the opposite. During the war many convicted bribe givers did not even receive jail terms. Did the shorter sentences of bribe givers send a message that what they had done was only a minor infraction, especially in times of crisis? Almost certainly the more severe punishment of bribe takers sent the message that accepting bribes was morally worse than giving them. While people charged with taking bribes occasionally pled guilty in court, people accused of offering them almost never did. They frequently simply did not believe that they had committed a crime. Legal publications tried to discourage judges and prosecutors from being softer on the givers of bribes, because offering and receiving bribes were *both* serious crimes. An article in the journal *Socialist Legality* made this point: "Despite the fact that taking bribes and receiving bribes are in different articles [of the criminal code], both acts are inseparably connected with each other. And although they are committed by different people and are expressed in different actions, they nevertheless represent one two-sided crime: giving–accepting a bribe (*dacha–poluchenie vziatki*)."[14]

In late 1945 and 1946, the popular satirical magazine *Krokodil* published cartoons that reinforce the impression that party authorities wanted to challenge the social acceptability of giving bribes. *Krokodil*'s simple depictions of bribery seem to be attempting to contradict a common belief that those forced to offer bribes would (or at least *should*) remain unpunished. The thrust of the cartoons is to instruct readers that not only the acceptors of bribes, but also those who offered them, would be arrested and imprisoned. One cartoon, entitled "Irregular [literally, Incorrect] Verb" takes the form of a grammar lesson, making fun of one man's misconception that "I give [a bribe], you take [the

Figure 3.1. "Nepravil'nyi glagol" [Irregular Verb] ("I Give. You Take. He Sits [in Prison]"). *Krokodil,* November 10, 1945.

bribe], he sits [in prison]." The official who *accepted* the bribe will have to do time, not he, the cartoon's hapless bribe giver tells us. This use of the verbs is "incorrect," since they will *both* "sit" in prison. Two more *Krokodil* cartoons that appeared around the same time repeat the theme of the clueless bribe giver who believes himself innocent and is surprised to find out that he must go to prison. They depict citizens passing on cash to bureaucrats in the first frame, only to be led away by police or thrown in jail in the next frame (see figures 2 and 3).[15] These cartoons emphasize the consequences of the transaction—punishment will be meted out to *both* the recipient *and* the giver of bribes.

The evidence indicates that, in fact, legal authorities were sending mixed messages to the population. The law declared that it was illegal to give a gift even if it was after the fact; that food could be a bribe; that small gifts—"tokens of appreciation"—could be bribes; and that a gift passed through an intermediary could be a bribe. Nevertheless, according to accepted practices none of these things were considered out of the ordinary, much less criminal behavior on the part of the giver.[16] A newspaper article sarcastically noted that in Kiev, for example, it was considered "unconscionable" *not* to give a token of thanks to (that is, not to bribe) service personnel.[17] Some judges ruled that a small gift

Figure 3.2. "Zhestokii romans" [Cruel Romance] ("Let's hand each other something [cash]/ and then we'll be off on a long road for many years"). This cartoon plays on the lyrics of a popular song. Rather than friends shaking hands and wishing each other goodbye 'til they see each other many years from now, a bribe giver and bribe taker exchange cash from hand to hand and are sentenced to long years in prison. *Krokodil,* November 30, 1945.

should not be considered a bribe, as long as the official who accepted it did nothing that broke the law in exchange for it.

Although *Krokodil* published cartoons warning the population of the consequences of participating in bribery, in each cartoon the bribe is in the form of cash. So petitioners who gave gifts—food or valuables, or theater tickets, or repairs to apartments or other services—in some cases might understand that since no money changed hands, *they* were not bribe givers. In addition, in every case, the cartoon shows the bribe giver and the bribe taker together, passing the bribe from hand to hand, when in fact many gifts were passed through intermediaries. A person might assume that sending a gift through a go-between absolved them of guilt. According to these cartoons, a bribe involved a face-to-face and consensual (if apparently underhanded) deal involving cash.

Рис. М. Черемных

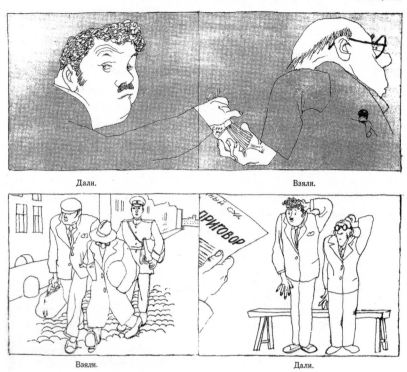

Дали.   Взяли.

Взяли.   Дали.

Figure 3.3. "Dali. Vziali. Vziali. Dali" ("They gave. They took. They were taken [arrested]. They were given [sentences in prison]"). *Krokodil*, August 20, 1946.

The notion that a bribe could be regarded as acceptable, efficient, and often absolutely necessary for cutting through bureaucratic red tape was encouraged by a number of enduring traditional *poslovitsy* (proverbs): *Ruka daiushchego ne oskudeet* (The giving hand shall never go wanting); *Nado zh dat', ili nado zhdat'* (You have to give, or you have to wait); *Ruka moet ruku, a obe khotiat byt' bely* (One hand washes the other, and both want to be clean). Another, *Sukhaia lozhka rot deret* (a dry spoon grates the mouth), points out that gifts must be given to make bureaucracy more effective. To "grease" the wheels or someone's palms (*podmazat'*) was another common metaphor that conveyed the need to unstick the otherwise jammed gears of the bureaucratic machinery with a well-placed offering.[18]

Obtaining confessions in cases of bribery posed a problem for the authorities. People seldom confessed to bribing officials, or to accepting bribes, and they only very rarely described their own activity as "bribery," even in the face of overwhelming evidence.[19] An example of this reluctance is seen in a statement by I. M. Lebedev, an investigator for the Moscow oblast' procuracy who was accused of acting as an intermediary in forwarding a bribe to a judge. He continued to deny the charges against him, despite reliable testimony. Referring to his own unpersuasive denials of the charges at his hearing, he declared, "To sum up everything I have said: I must admit that all my explanations are completely unconvincing, especially to myself, as an experienced procuracy employee."[20] People commonly described their actions as "helping out" friends or acquaintances, or as "gifts" to officials as thanks for their assistance.[21] In one case, for example, a Ukrainian woman on trial for offering a bribe said that she had simply offered a "little present" (*podarochek*) of 10,000 rubles and a woman's wristwatch to anyone who could help minimize her husband's long prison sentence.[22]

In contrast, the apparently genuine remorse expressed at trial by some defendants who confessed to taking bribes illustrates that the shame popularly associated with the act was often internalized. Several defendants described their actions as "sinful." One woman who confessed told the court, "I will serve out my punishment with a feeling of relief that I have left no sins behind, that I have hidden nothing." She added that she had confessed to her own transgressions and testified about the bribery of others "so that I can die an honest person after all my crimes."[23] The acceptance of bribes was frequently described by defendants as "dark," "dirty," or "unclean."[24] An anonymous letter accused an intermediary of behaving like a "filthy spider," crawling over her victims.[25] One accused judge said that he greatly regretted that he had been "dragged into this dirty affair."[26] A court employee confessed: "I understand that one ought not to have lived such a criminal, confused, dark life, but I did not have the strength to say this myself before they arrested me."[27] Using the language of decay that often underlay discourses around bribery, the judge Shevchenko lamented, "I was dragged into the swamp of bribery."[28] The sense of guilt that some felt in accepting a bribe, meanwhile, can be seen in a private conversation between a judge and a secretary, both of whom intervened in cases in exchange for illegal payments: "It is terrible to be paid for this," one said to the other.[29] (Both parties confirmed the conversation.)

Indeed, participants normally hid exchanges in the language of gift giving, loans, or "treating." Petitioners did not mention money but would instead tell the official "I will pay you back," or "I will not remain in your debt," or "You will not be offended." The person offering the gift might promise that, "You will not be forgotten" or "You will be taken care of."[30] One accused lawyer spoke of approaching a judge in his office about his client's case. He offered the judge 1,500 rubles and urged him to review the case "just a little more carefully" (*povnimatel'nee*).[31]

In one very revealing instance, a woman convicted of offering a bribe claimed that in fact she had given a judge a "gift" of 1,800 rubles. "But this was no bribe. It was simply a gift for his children since I was at his apartment many times and saw the cramped material situation of his family." In her defense she insisted, "The word 'bribe' was never mentioned between us." Yet as the judge who accepted this "gift" himself quite correctly pointed out, bribery was frequently disguised with a variety of more neutral, but perfectly understood, terms. "I confirm that we never had a conversation about a bribe, as such. But only rarely, at any time, or in any place, would the word 'bribe' itself be mentioned between people. This word is usually replaced with the words 'to treat' (*ugostit'*), 'to have a drink,' 'to thank,' 'to give a gift,' and so on." He went on ruefully, "I recognize that in this admission lies my own destruction, but the evidence is a stubborn thing and one shouldn't close one's eyes to it."[32]

When they accepted prohibited gifts, officials often did everything they could to rationalize it to themselves (and, later, to prosecutors and judges). Some officials excused themselves by saying that they only took "rewards" or "commissions" (not bribes); only *after the fact;* never through *extortion;* and only after carrying out an action that was *legal* or that *reversed an incorrect decision.* Although such rewards could violate professional ethics in some cases, they said, they were traditional tokens of appreciation, not criminal actions. The judge Kumekhov testified that he would only accept money to overturn an *incorrect* sentence, and, he insisted, such an action was not illegal. (He was mistaken in the eyes of the law, as the Supreme Court had determined in 1946.)[33] Such rewards given after an action was taken were sometimes referred to as *mzda* (or even the Persian word *baksheesh*), which connoted gifts of thanks accepted by officials after the fact and only after they had done their duties properly. In this view, accepting mzda was not corruption, and one who accepted it should not be accused of breaking any laws; it was, rather, a longstanding tradition cementing a relationship between official and petitioner.[34]

Sometimes, officials (often, but not always, from the Caucasus) defended their gift giving to officials by deploying the concept of *magarych,* the idea that one should give a meal or drinks to an official who provided assistance. Like mzda, magarych referred only to something done after the fact, as a gesture of thanks after an official had corrected an injustice or reversed an incorrect decision. For example, upon telling a woman from Dagestan that her husband's sentence would be reduced, one lawyer asked her for money that he would present to the judge as magarych—a token of thanks to be given to the person who made this decision. She answered, "There will be magarych—[but only] after my husband is freed."[35] Investigators, however, did not regard this exchange as a convivial regional custom; all involved were convicted of bribery.

Although Soviet legislation simply rejected such justifications, tsarist law in fact had encoded many of the distinctions that defendants made when claiming they had taken a token of appreciation rather than a bribe. In Imperial Russia, the law recognized both legal and illegal varieties of gift giving between subjects and officials. There was a legal distinction—as well as a difference in popular sensibilities—between the *giving* and *receipt* of bribes, enshrined in the laws and shared in public opinion. An 1802 law made this distinction concrete by separating the two acts—the offering and acceptance of bribes—into two different articles of the criminal code.[36] (The distinction between the two would be codified throughout the Soviet period.) Until the collapse of the Romanov dynasty in 1917, laws clearly placed the onus of a bribery transaction on the official who *took* the bribe, so that officials (rather than the payer of the bribe) shouldered the burden of the guilt. Bribe givers were rarely punished in the 1845 criminal code. An 1866 act decriminalized the giving of bribes in all cases except for the most extreme: payments to an official to enable the counterfeiting of documents or kidnapping. A major 1903 revision of the code (which, though never published, was imitated in some respects by the drafters of early Soviet law codes) anticipated restoring criminal sanctions for bribe givers, but it was never put into effect. It was not until 1916, in an emergency wartime measure, that bribe givers were punished by the law.[37]

The Empire's bribery laws on the acceptance of bribes (contained in the 1845 criminal code in the section that addressed crimes by officials) made several more crucial distinctions. The most important article distinguished among several types of prohibited gifts.[38] The acceptance of a gift by an official simply to do something that they were supposed to do anyway, that is an encouragement to do something legal that fell within the purview of their duties, was called *mzdoimstvo*. (The illicit gift itself was called mzda). As would be the case in Soviet criminal codes, a bribe could be any gift of value, no matter how small, and not only money.

The law described two categories of mzdoimstvo. Was the gift to an official given *before* or *after* the official's action? The criminal code considered a gift offered *after* the fact, as a type of "reward" for doing something, to be an ethical offense, but not a crime, as long as the action for which the official was rewarded was a *legal* one. The law regarded such after-the-fact rewards (the first type of forbidden gift) as a common practice, more as "tokens of appreciation" to officials for carrying out their duties in a timely and correct manner. As a very mild punishment, an official who had accepted such a gift had to pay a fine equivalent to its value (and to return the gift). Clearly, Imperial law was relatively tolerant of this type of "gift of gratitude."

Somewhat more serious, and forbidden by the Imperial criminal code, was a second kind of mzdoimstvo—the official who accepted a gift *before the fact* to fulfill his duty. The acceptance of such a gift, even if the subsequent action or service was not illegal, was still treated by the criminal code as an inducement that could distort an official's judgment. In this kind of case, the offending official had to pay a fine equal to double the value of the gift, still a fairly mild rebuke.

The third and much more serious type of bribe described in the Imperial code was when an official accepted a gift—whether before or after the fact—as an inducement to do something that *violated the law*. The penal code called such an act *likhoimstvo*. If convicted of likhoimstvo, an official would be sentenced to a much harsher punishment—one to three years of exile in the Siberian provinces of Tomsk or Tobol'sk and the loss of all personal property.

Soviet law, in contrast, wholly rejected these distinctions. In an attempt to send a message about the widespread acceptance of such small, non-cash "tokens of appreciation," the USSR Supreme Court in

1948 made a critical determination. It upheld the notion that any gift to an official, however small, should be considered a bribe. The Supreme Court's decision stemmed from a case in Lithuania in which an official accepted a gift of half a liter of vodka. The local court found both the giver and the taker of the vodka guilty of bribery. The Lithuanian Supreme Court then overturned this verdict, stating that the half bottle of vodka did not qualify as a bribe because it was "insignificant" in value. Upon review, however, the USSR Supreme Court reversed the Lithuanian Supreme Court's decision, stating that there was no such thing as an "insignificant" bribe.[39] The Supreme Court declared that a bottle of alcohol and other small gifts should be treated as bribes that could distort an official's judgment; both givers and acceptors of such minor tokens of appreciation should be prosecuted.

And, indeed, payments or gifts to officials could take on an enormous variety of forms. Soviet life provided prolific opportunities for money, gifts, and prizes to change hands legally; it was but a small step secretly to incorporate an illegal payment into these exchanges. Pretending to lose a bet, buying something from one's boss, awarding an undeserving employee a prize—each of these transactions could hide a bribe. Legal authorities had a term for such covert payments that were not an obvious trade of cash for favors: the "masked bribe." Although some were executed rather clumsily, masked bribes often involved a high degree of creativity.[40] The "disguising" of bribes was one factor that made it difficult for law enforcement to prove that the participants had committed a crime.

A comprehensive July 1947 report prepared by the head of the *Ugolovno-sudebnyi* (criminal court) department of the USSR Procuracy's office adds another dimension to popular understandings of bribery.[41] According to the report, bribery was most often uncovered when the giver believed that the payment constituted a type of "contract" that the bribe-taking official later had broken. In such cases, the bribe giver would not be deterred by a sense of shame or fear in reporting the agreement to authorities. Though law enforcement officials urged citizens to report when they witnessed the solicitation of a bribe, the low numbers of convictions resulting from such informants would indicate that they rarely did so. Instead, people entered into deals, believing them either necessary or beneficial in other ways. The bribe, then, was a form of reciprocity that was most likely to be condemned by the bribe giver when the person with whom they were dealing was unusually greedy or demanding, or when the terms of the deal were not kept. In one rather extreme example, according to testimony at trial, a person paid 15,000 rubles to a lawyer to arrange to get his mother-in-law out of jail. The court, however, rejected the appeal that the lawyer submitted. When the lawyer offered to return the money, the bribe giver screamed "I don't want my money, I want my mother-in-law!" He then demanded, "Give me back my money or I'll kill you!" As the lawyer told the court, "Wishing to avoid a scandal, I sold my things . . . and returned his 15,000."[42] For the recipient of a bribe, a disappointed bribe giver often represented the greatest threat of exposure.

All criminal codes recognize that bribes come in nearly infinite varieties and certainly are not limited to money. Depending on local custom, as we have seen, illicit gifts to officials can take myriad forms, from cash, to food, to clothing and household items, to jewelry or other valuables. Not surprisingly, in a space like the postwar Soviet Union, whose economy was less monetized than the capitalist economies of the West, one encounters many kinds of non-cash bribes, as well as many other transactions based on barter, trade, or favors that were not technically illegal. Nevertheless, the stereotype that money had little value in the Soviet Union is clearly incorrect. There certainly was a place for cash. Certain items found in illegal or semi-legal markets, such as scarce medicines, household goods in large demand, motorcycles, and automobiles, often could be obtained only with money. And the reality that desirable goods were often available to most people only on the black market gave officials incentive to sell favors and access for cash.

THE ART OF THE BRIBE

Determining who would accept a bribe, and then getting it into the right hands, were skills mastered by many in the Soviet Union. A certain Tsagareishvili testified that he could immediately identify officials who took bribes by observing their clothing and attitude: "Usually, he would be well-dressed, very lively, and presumptuous."[43] Tsagareishvili was quite surprised when a "modestly dressed" person who "made a pleasant impression" turned out to be a bribe taker. In a story called "Precise Proof," *Krokodil* spoofed a favorite pastime of some Soviet citizens—privately speculating about which officials were corrupt. One vignette told of three men who tried to figure out whether their bosses were taking bribes.[44] How could they tell? Was it the look in their eyes? Was it the way their hands shake? Or was it that their wives go around in expensive clothes? One of the men rejects each of these methods. He had spent a whole month trying to figure out whether his boss took bribes. All the signs pointed to the fact that he did, but how could he be sure? One day the man went to his boss's office, but he was not at his desk. The man asked the office staff:

—Where is the boss?
—They put him in jail yesterday!
—For what?
—For [taking] bribes!

"Here," the man concludes, "is the most precise proof [that the boss takes bribes]!" The official lesson of the *Krokodil* tale? All bribe takers will be arrested.

One person interviewed in the early 1950s noted that conspicuous consumption could raise suspicions that an individual was taking bribes.[45] He observed, for example, that people who ate in restaurants could raise eyebrows. "Nearly every big institution and enterprise has its own dining room [so] restaurants are not used very much. They are mostly used by people who are traveling for work. A man who uses a restaurant is considered corrupt, so that only those who have to, use them. . . . The restaurants are very expensive, so who are the people who can use them? Only those who get a lot of money from somewhere. If a man uses a restaurant frequently, he will be suspected of engaging in graft, and people will wonder where he gets his income from." A court employee who had confessed to accepting bribes testified that she suspected that her husband had also been a bribe taker, because he often used to go out with a certain judge: "They would drink a lot, and you cannot pay for that on your own salary."[46]

Judging by court and procuracy records, many Soviet people understood that the official who was in need of money would be the most receptive to a well-placed bribe. When privately attempting to account for the causes of malfeasance, procuracy and judicial authorities focused on the issues of salary and professional ethics. During the war, many professions, including bureaucrats serving in economic and government administrations, were decimated. Replacements were typically inexperienced, were poorly trained and paid, and lacked a well-developed sense of professional ethics. A USSR Procuracy commission charged with researching the causes of bribery among prosecutors listed material deprivation as the most important single factor leading to the acceptance of bribes. In hearings, professionals often cited financial hardship as the principal reason for having taken illegal gifts. Asked what led him on the path of taking bribes, the Moscow people's court judge Timofei R. Morozov told investigators: "I swear to you, a difficult material situation and shortcomings. My family is large: three children and a wife, but only my daughter and I work and it's not enough to live on."[47] Employees in other governmental and economic agencies, of course, faced similar economic hardships (and lack of professional training).

The procuracy commission further noted that many people were cognizant of—and exploited—the penury of local authorities. They calculated that impoverished officials would be the most susceptible to bribes. In the midst of the postwar famine, a law of September 27, 1946, which denied food rations to the dependents of white-collar officials and workers, likely made bureaucrats even more motivated to accept "gifts" of cash and food.[48] For example, a certain Rogozin, a procuracy investigator in Leningrad, was found to have taken a bribe of 700 rubles (about one month's salary) and been treated to several meals (worth 216 rubles) in November 1946.[49] Prosecutors alleged that Rogozin would visit the apartment of the accused bribe giver. Once there, he would complain that his family was in desperate financial straits. Rogozin explained that he had five children and a mother-in-law with no ration card. He lacked enough money even to buy bread, he insisted. Rogozin demanded that the accused deliver milk and food to his office, and he would eat during the interrogation. Convicted of taking bribes, he was sentenced to four years of corrective labor. Although the abolition of rationing in 1947 led to more food in the stores, it also caused price increases for numerous items, putting them out of reach for many people and rendering them excellent currency for bribes.[50]

In an internal report devoted to the "techniques" of bribe givers, a USSR Procuracy specialist analyzed dozens of cases, describing how bribe givers found their targets. The report was intended as a warning to prosecutors and court employees to be on the lookout for people who might exploit officials' weaknesses. As the report explained: "[The offer of a bribe] is usually preceded by studying the procuracy employee, his character and temperament, his 'weak sides,' his inclinations, material situation, and so on. That is, he is sized up in every respect with the aim of discovering the best opportunities for negotiating with him, for 'buying' him."[51]

Through such "study," informed by a lifetime of experience with petty officialdom, individuals developed a sense of who might be sympathetic to their overtures. People tried to ascertain which officials would listen to their pleas and could be coaxed to drop their official front. This talent was a critical dimension of the "art of the bribe." To offer a bribe to an official prematurely greatly increased the danger, and was less likely to succeed. As the report put it, citizens would try to "get to know" officials, try to guess who would break the rules, probe their defenses, and figure out what would tempt them and how they could best be approached.[52] According to this report, the tone of the face-to-face conversation would change at some point. The official would drop his façade and might even begin to commiserate or show a hint of compassion. Petitioners could then feel confident that they had an ally, and they could "move to the attack." This stage, the author goes on to explain, could entail an immediate offer of money or it could lead to "a suggestion to go to the apartment of the employee, to an invitation to sit and talk at their own apartment, or to go to a restaurant to have a drink, and so on."[53] Many ordinary people learned to probe the defenses of officials to determine who would (and who would not) enter an illegal deal. The term courtship, even seduction, seems appropriate to describe this process of negotiation.[54]

The author of the procuracy report notes that, in any given location, bribe givers could draw on a veritable intelligence network of people who had observed and gathered valuable information about the employees at various workplaces.[55] A virtual army of petitioners, complainants, janitors, housekeepers, secretaries, and others who had interacted with officials in some way (mostly informally) quietly compiled information about potential targets. One could collect such local knowledge from seemingly innocent conversations, learning more and more about a given official.

And, in fact, many Soviet people developed a sixth sense as to which individuals would be amenable to accepting a payment or gift, or to acting as a go-between in the transaction. Such a talent was an essential prerequisite to proposing a deal, of course, since the consequences of an offer to the wrong person could be disastrous. One man told a hearing before the USSR Supreme Court, "Why did I so easily approach Morozov about a bribe? There was no particular reason, but I somehow instinctively felt that he would go for a bribe."[56] This instinct may have also been shaped by his observation of Morozov's habits: "Besides that, I knew that Morozov loves to drink." Banquets were often held at work. During these occasions, the staff socialized together, getting to know one another on a personal level, and enabling "criminal relationships" to bloom.

During an interrogation in another case, a certain A. M. Shestopalov offered an Odessa regional investigator, M. S. Solov'ev, a cherry. The investigator accepted it, "relaxing the official tension in the relationship between the investigator and the accused." Shestopalov instantly intuited that Solov'ev would also accept a bribe.[57] Shestopalov's wife, who had been standing in the corridor during the investigation, mentioned to the investigator that her family had some cherry trees, which produced a lot of fruit: "They're not expensive, and if you'd like I can bring some over to your apartment and make some jam." The investigator agreed. She showed up that evening at Solov'ev's flat armed with 12 kilograms of cherries and 3,000 rubles in cash. The deal to release her husband was sealed.[58]

"GIFTS CAN JUST BE GIFTS"

Interviews of Soviet émigrés concerning life in the USSR conducted by Harvard University researchers, primarily in Munich and New York in the years 1950–1951, are a very valuable source for historians of Stalinist society. They provide evidence regarding popular attitudes toward the bribe. Most respondents had left the USSR between 1942 and 1945, and their interviews illuminate aspects of Soviet life during the 1930s and the first years of the 1940s. The project's American directors were interested in exploring what they called the "informal mechanisms at the workplace and in daily life," including bribery and blat. In particular, they asked about the ways that people got things done outside the formal rules. One set of questions posed by interviewers inquired whether a bribe could help people switch jobs (or prevent them from being transferred), advance in their career, or cut through red tape. Another set of questions queried doctors about the practice of accepting gifts from patients. The answers provide some information about attitudes toward these types of deals.

Responses to interviewers' questions varied widely, as would be expected. Some respondents claimed that bribery was completely unknown in the Soviet Union.[59] Others said that they had heard of instances of bribery by friends or co-workers but that they were too afraid to engage in the practice themselves. Still others spoke of bribery as if it were a veritable plague that infected all of Soviet society. One fifty-one-year-old male Russian who came from a rural area and had only an elementary education made bold claims about the unique power of a gift of alcohol: "With a liter of vodka anything can be done. A liter of vodka can do anything."[60] Such sweeping statements are not helpful for determining the scale and scope of the phenomenon, but do highlight the myth that Soviet officialdom was wholly corrupt, a venal "them" in opposition to a suffering and victimized "us."

The provision of medical services—and the relationship between doctor and patient—perhaps best reflects the complexity of establishing the fine line between gifts and bribes. Although they experienced quite a bit of anxiety about the inherent risks, some medical professionals reported receiving payments or gifts from patients. In many cases, prosecutors could have construed certain gifts to doctors as bribes, and participants were aware of this. In interviews, they reflected in some detail on the customs surrounding gift exchanges between patients and physicians. A patient might give a doctor a present as thanks for putting them at the head of the line, or for providing better care. Many people believed that the free, state-provided clinical services were inferior, so there was good reason to pay under the table for a competent doctor. As one doctor put it: "First of all, you must understand that free medical care did not always please the people. In general, they felt that if they paid, they would receive better medical care, but on the other side they did not have enough money to pay for private medical care."[61] This concern about quality of service was similar to the concerns regarding legal help, which often resulted in the payment of the extra fees, known as mikst, to defense lawyers (as was discussed in chapter 2).

One doctor from St. Petersburg who was interviewed in the Harvard project thoughtfully discussed this complex situation, and his testimony (even if self-serving) emphasizes several telling points. First, he argued, "peasant traditions" dictated that patients offer their doctor a gift. As a matter of custom, he said, patients insisted on giving "tokens of grat-itude" to people in positions of authority who helped them with a diffi-cult situation. He told his interviewers that it was extremely difficult for doctors to refuse these small gifts. His observations again underscore the often murky distinction between a bribe, a gift, and a fee:

> The patient feels that he must, somehow, repay you [for your help]. Or let us say that you are in a clinic, and you want a doctor whom you trust to operate on you. Then again, this question of the gratitude of the patient comes in. The patient will always try to pay you, although you cannot ask for anything, at least I did not ask for any payment because I felt that if a patient paid me, let's say, twenty rubles, he and his family might starve for a few days. Or the patient would send you something by mail, thanking you and asking you to accept his modest gift as a token of gratitude. Then the question arose in my mind, did I have the moral right to return this gift? I tried to return them, but it wasn't very successful. What they had sent was not enough, and I wanted them to send more, they thought. Or some might come to see you and waste your valuable time trying to make you accept the gift, or some were simply insulted.

Or, he expands: "Here is a woman who is at the hospital. I have oper-ated on her. She previously did not make any arrangements with me. I operated on her free of charge, as it was my duty. Then I would get a letter from her with fifty or a hundred rubles, an expression of sentimen-tal gratitude." He felt that returning this gift, given after the fact, would be an insulting gesture. "Let us take another example. There is another woman who I operated on who is poor. She sends me a necktie and a note saying, 'I am poor, please accept this as a token of gratitude.'"[62]

This doctor's observations underscore several elements integral to the practice of gift giving to officials in the Stalin period. Quite often, the recipient could make a detailed justification for the acceptance of gifts as traditional "tokens of gratitude." This doctor does not state how he can discern the distinction between a "bribe" and a "gift of grati-tude," but he is quite certain that he understands this difference. He defends these gifts as part of the age-old relationship between the pa-tient and the caregiver, expressing this bond in the language of psychol-ogy. As he put it, "All of these examples [of patients offering tokens of gratitude to doctors] are given to you in order to show that there must be a psychological bond between the doctor and the patient, and that this psychological bond plays a role of great importance. . . . Thus, the psychological connection between the doctor and the patient is primordial [and must be reinforced by gifts from patient to doctor]. We still know very little about the workings of the human mind."[63] Thus, somewhat condescendingly citing an ancient impulse among his peasant patients, this doctor denies that he accepted bribes or illegal fees. Rather, he was simply holding up his end of a bond between patient and doctor, cemented after the fact, that transcends money. Refusing to accept the gift would have been offensive.

Another physician took a less psychological approach, while still placing the giving of gifts to a service provider in the context of entrenched peasant cultural practices: "The taking of fees from patients is forbidden, but the custom of gifts, particularly among the peasantry, is still fairly prevalent and in some respects gifts of food are better than salaries. Authorities try to fight against these old customs."[64]

A third doctor described the rituals involved, as doctors initially had to pretend to refuse gifts, which could never be openly solicited and which had to be offered after the fact:

> The rule was anyway, Do not ask anything from the patient, but if he gives it to you, you could accept it. ([Question]: Was there any danger of its being looked upon as a bribe?) A doctor will never accept a gift in a dispensary, he will always refuse it. If he sees a patient at home, he might get it on his way out. Or if I go on an emergency call, when I have finished, someone can give me something and I do not refuse. In a dispensary you might be accused of accepting a bribe in order to give a day off [from work]. ([Question:] What about house calls?) It is free; you must not pay the doctor anything. Moreover, you must never offer the doctor anything before the consultation, only after, when he is going away. [The doctor] must refuse for the [sake of] form, and you must be able to say "I was forced into accepting it; it was very difficult for me to refuse it."[65]

This culture of the post-facto "token of appreciation" persisted until well after the war. Though it was couched in the language and rituals of giving gifts, officials understood that such an exchange outside the normal channels could be regarded as a bribe by police, prosecutors, and judges. Still, they justified, or rationalized, the acceptance of these gifts, by considering it to be a cultural practice that was nearly impossible to resist, that maintained a kind of social peace between authorities and citizens, and that was in no way morally wrong.

Along these lines, one person emphasized that money was very infrequently exchanged between enterprises.[66] Instead, enterprises exchanged "gifts" they needed—a swap of pencils for rubber, for example. The danger inherent in not fulfilling plan targets outweighed the risk of being caught in these bartering practices. Asking for (and paying) money was dangerous, but an exchange of gifts could be disguised more easily. As he put it: "Usually it is done through gifts, and much more rarely by money. Money is a pure bribe, but gifts may just be gifts."

This story and others like it highlight two important points. First, it was believed that it was much more difficult for prosecutors to prove that exchanges of non-cash "gifts" involved quid pro quo. And second, the interviews provide further evidence that ordinary people were quite aware that gifts to officials could be disguised bribes—whether extorted by bureaucrats or voluntarily given with the expectation of a favorable result.

THE GO-BETWEENS

Go-betweens figured prominently in the landscape of Soviet bribery. Enterprising individuals created what were essentially small businesses as intermediaries. They moved back and forth between those seeking assistance to accomplish a difficult task and those willing to accept illegal payments to provide that help. Often this process involved a good deal of negotiating until the parties struck a satisfactory deal. Intermediaries normally kept a portion of the payment for themselves as a fee. Go-betweens could be professionals, secretaries, janitors, or others who had relationships with officials in a position to help. Their role was to transfer bribes from petitioners to officials. The most successful intermediaries had a contact or, better yet, a network of contacts, inside the relevant institution. Like people who speculated in scarce goods, intermediaries were motivated purely by financial considerations; they were in it solely for the money. They played both sides, both taking and giving bribes. In the eyes of prosecutors, an intermediary was a heinous creature in the world of graft. The intermediary was a capitalist two times over, buying *and* selling illegal favors, who accelerated the corruption of officials and common people alike, while profiting handsomely from the transactions.[67]

In one instance, a certain Anisimova traveled to Moscow from Dagestan in December 1945, carrying 30,000 rubles in cash to be used as a bribe to free her husband from prison. She also brought personal belongings, including a rug, to sell for additional cash. For two months, she searched for the best person to help her pass the bribe to the right judge, until she finally found a moonlighting middleman in February 1946. This intermediary offered to pass a bribe of 50,000 rubles to an employee in the Military Collegium of the USSR Supreme Court. As a result of the bribe, the judge reduced the charges against Anisimova's husband from theft of state property, governed under the severe August 1932 law, to the much less serious crime of abuse of office. The court reduced the sentence to three years' imprisonment. Both parties were ultimately convicted of engaging in bribery, however. The intermediary was sentenced to ten years in a labor camp, and Anisimova received five years.[68]

The role of intermediaries reminds us that bribery always involves at least two very different actors, and that both givers and takers of bribes took large risks. This danger explains in part why many transactions involved a third critical actor—the intermediary who served as a conduit to pass the payment from the giver to the acceptor. This separation between the two parties could reduce risk in one sense. But by increasing the number of people involved in the transaction it could also increase the chances of exposure.

Intermediaries (whom investigators derisively called "brokers" [maklery]—an unmistakably capitalist term) passed on money, valuables, and other goods to officials in position to help. Go-betweens were much reviled by legal experts, for they were a "social danger" as the "initiators" of bribes. At times, they demanded "advances" for their services.[69] In some cases, two or more intermediaries teamed up in a kind of chain of graft: a lawyer might take money intended as a bribe from the family member of an accused person, and then pass that money on to a partner intermediary who worked in the court, who would finally pass it on to the judge or prosecutor (or both). Each intermediary would extract a portion of the payment as a commission.

The actions of these intermediaries further support the argument that there existed a kind of "bribery market"—yet another Soviet shadow economy, where buyers sought out sellers (and vice versa), sometimes with the help of well-connected middlemen. In these conditions, intermediaries often had to be fast on their feet to protect their "business" and turf. In one example from 1947, A. V. Vol'skii, a lawyer acting on behalf of a man who had been imprisoned in Kazan' for speculation, negotiated with two different intermediaries, seeking the best contacts and the optimal deal. Each promised access to someone who could provide a favorable decision in the stalled appeal Vol'skii had filed with the USSR Supreme Court. Of course, the larger the number of people involved in a deal, the more likely it is to be exposed, and this was one cause of the scheme's demise.

If they could not achieve the promised result, go-betweens sometimes returned their advance.[70] One disappointed person found fault with an intermediary when he could achieve only a reduction of her husband's sentence, not his freedom.[71] She quite logically demanded a discount, offering the middleman half of the originally agreed-upon sum.

CONCLUSIONS

According to the official narrative, bribery was on the verge of extinction in the late Stalin period. It was a sputtering, if embarrassing, relic of capitalism, limited to a few pathetic scoundrels. Based on materials from the archives, however, a picture emerges of vibrant, productive, and often creative informal relationships between officials and Soviet subjects. As long as it served a purpose and demand remained strong, bribery and the rituals surrounding it would persist. As we have seen, the postwar wave of repression, characterized by profound shortages, bureaucratic chaos, and mass arrests for theft of state property, petty economic crime, and labor infractions, served to foster markets for under-the-table favors, as opportunities for officials and intermediaries alike burgeoned.

The evidence presented underscores the many ways that Soviet people devised to circumvent disaster or improve their lives, taking initiative at many levels, and creating effective informal, if sometimes criminal, relationships. Intermediaries filled an important niche by connecting givers and takers of gifts, and profiting from the service. While the legal system aimed to uproot and prosecute the moral and professional failings of officials, efforts to track down acts of bribery also exposed the flaws of the Soviet state, the extraordinary challenges of everyday survival, and the distance between the state's promises and daily reality. This shadowy universe of unofficial and complex relationships reveals but one dimension of what one might call the "drama of everyday crime" in the period of postwar recovery and reconstruction.

An analysis of these practices and culture highlights not only public perceptions of bribery but public *participation* in bribery. We should not exclude the general population by concluding that people had no choice but to accede to the extortion of corrupt bureaucrats. Looking at bribery from the participants' vantage point, it is clear that people were not exclusively victims of official corruption (though they frequently were, of course). Often, they participated willingly, making deals to their own advantage. Evidence provided by party and state archives illuminates a landscape in which many Soviet people learned to finesse "the art of the bribe." At least a part of the Soviet population was not passive in its relationship with unresponsive state officials. On the contrary, individuals faced with arbitrary authorities often took the initiative as they attempted to adapt to difficult circumstances. Paying bribes was a skill, honed through experience, practiced by individuals who studied, negotiated, targeted, bartered with, and even "bought," state officials. Soviet people used this skill to make the state work for them, albeit at great risk and substantial cost. Although many of the examples in this chapter come from justice and law enforcement venues, evidence presented earlier shows that multiple government administrations—housing, medical, transportation, educational, and food procurement, to take several major examples—were subject to these types of negotiations in similarly configured unofficial transactions.

The emphasis here on the actions of ordinary people is not to say that they had the upper hand in relationships with state officials; of course, they did not. An official who refused to accept a bribe could destroy the petitioner's life by reporting the offer to the police. Officials could accept the money and refuse to follow through, with full knowledge that the petitioner would be confessing to the serious crime of offering a bribe if he complained to the authorities. One must not romanticize or underestimate the inequality inherent in relationships between petitioners and officials. Yet the evidence complicates the conventional picture of bribery as a phenomenon by which an extortionate state exclusively victimized the powerless; instead, it also approaches the bribe as a tool in the arsenal of the individual in Soviet society.

The historians Golfo Alexopoulos and Sheila Fitzpatrick have both provided accounts of the adventures of "con artists" as they traveled across the Soviet landscape, duping state bureaucrats into providing them with cash, essential documents, and favors.[72] As both authors point out, the figure of the con artist has enjoyed a long history in Russia. Fitzpatrick, in her 2002 article subtitled "Soviet Confidence Men in the Stalin Period," ventures into the postwar period examined in this book, investigating what she calls Soviet tricksterism or Soviet conmanship. She is interested in how these conmen flimflammed hapless, "softheaded as well as softhearted" functionaries in a vulnerable and, one gets the impression, dense bureaucracy.[73]

When discussing the relationship between official and petitioners in the Stalin era, I would suggest supplementing Fitzpatrick's and Alexopoulos's model of "the con" with one revolving around "the art of the bribe," a process of negotiation with unwritten rules, occurring in shadow markets. The art of the bribe was practiced in many workplaces and offices every day, participated in fully by officials and Soviet subjects alike. Bribe givers and bribe takers bargained and made deals (sometimes with the help of intermediaries), seeking the optimal partners, the best possible terms, and the least possible danger. "Artists," in other words, were to be found on both sides of the desk. Corruption in the postwar period, then, developed inside a system that served both to abet illegal relationships and to cover them up, a system whereby both officials and average people strove to improve their lot. The art of the bribe was a response to conditions of extreme shortage and profound dislocation, combined with widespread perceptions of grave social and legal injustice. The metaphor of "the deal" is rooted in time-honored traditions of gift giving, and especially "self-interested giving." The functionary angling to make something extra on the side, willing to profit by selling his services when the balance of risk and reward was favorable, was likely a much more recognizable "type" to the average Soviet person than the prototypical professional trickster or easily conned bureaucrat.

The next chapter traces the extraordinary story of one Soviet judge whose arrest and secret trial for bribery vividly illustrate this complex postwar world of gifts, reciprocal obligations, and "the art of the bribe," as his social relationships and ambiguous choices in a nearly impossible situation came under intense scrutiny.

4 "Greetings from Sunny Georgia!"
Cultural Brokers and the Bribe Trail

THE SOVIET VICTORY over the Nazi aggressors in World War II was an extraordinary triumph that seemed to prove the success of the Soviet system. Yet as the USSR began its recovery from wartime devastation, corruption among state officials surged. Attempting to elude the reach of the state, people sought out informal contacts with officials, sometimes purchasing their illicit assistance. For their part, officials could demand under-the-table payments either to perform their assigned duties, or to exploit their offices to carry out illegal actions. As the following two chapters will show in detail, Stalin's regime struggled to curb these "unofficial" criminal contacts, which seemed to have taken on a dangerous new vitality during and after the war.

This chapter investigates a revealing case of accusations of bribery that took place in the most important Soviet appeals court in the years after the end of World War II—one of the scores of cases of bribe taking by judges that were prosecuted each year in the late Stalinist period. In late 1949, a Georgian judge on the Soviet Supreme Court, Levan Kirillovich Chichua, was accused of accepting numerous bribes during his tenure on the court. The allegations against Judge Chichua highlight the conflict between a consciously "rationalizing" and modernizing Soviet legal culture and many of the diverse regional or ethnic cultures across the Soviet space—cultures that were governed more by "familial" codes of conduct.

This chapter focuses on, among other things, the cultural dimension of gifts to officials and bribery. How did the sense of mutual obligation and social bonds, influenced by outlooks, values, and traditions, conflict in practice with "Soviet" norms of legal behavior? A study of bribery and gift giving to officials enables an investigation of relationships operating in the shadows of daily life—in the grey areas between tradition and law, between official duty and official crime, between office holder and subject. Indeed, a fascinating and overlooked dynamic in the study of bribery is that it often involves rituals rooted in traditional customs and practices of gift giving. Anthropologists are interested in gift giving as a revealing social act, but few examine the bribe as a variant of gift giving. Our task here is to take a historical perspective on a particular type of gift—the bribe—in a specific cultural context.

Although the examples included in this chapter primarily involve people who hailed from the Soviet republic of Georgia (located in the southern borderlands of the USSR in the Caucasus Mountains), the phenomena described apply to many cultures within the borders of the Soviet Union. Georgia is but one region where clientelistic and kinship relations were important in social life; therefore this study should not be taken as a discussion of a feature particular to only one part of the country or one ethnic group.[1]

This chapter also explores the role of what I refer to as "cultural brokers" in the courts. Cultural brokers were those individuals who acted as intermediaries between two cultures, or between two institutional and traditional arrangements: the set of assumptions that dominated on the Soviet periphery, and a very different set of legal procedures and norms in Moscow.

THE BRIBE TRAIL: A JUDGE'S STORY

In her insightful study of gift giving in sixteenth-century France, Natalie Zemon Davis writes that, in order to discover the meaning and functions of gift giving in that society, she aspires "to follow the gift trail." Davis traces not only the status of gifts in the culture, but the paths those gifts took as they moved, in a certain political and sociocultural context, from the offer of the gift, to the acceptance by the recipient, to the result of the action. Davis explores the varieties of gifts and the reasons for offering them, the customs and traditions surrounding gift giving, the types of reciprocity they engendered, and the sensitive processes of negotiation in early modern France.[2] Like nearly all scholars who study gift giving, Davis explores *legal* and *socially accepted* gifts. The present study, on the other hand, examines exchanges that legal authorities alleged violated the law and sanctioned heavily.

As Davis follows "the gift trail" in early modern France, this chapter follows what I call "the bribe trail" in one interesting late Stalin-era case: the allegations against Judge Chichua. This trail begins with the accused bribe givers and the reasons they felt compelled to make offers; moves to the go-betweens who played a part negotiating the deals; examines the venue where petitioners and the judge met; reflects on the offerings that were made; includes the investigation by the prosecutors; and, finally, moves to the verdict of the court that decided Chichua's fate.

What was at the center of this case? Four years after the end of World War II, prosecutors accused the Supreme Court justice representing the Soviet Socialist Republic of Georgia of accepting multiple bribes in the course of his duties. This Georgian judge, Levan K. Chichua, had served in the agencies of the court and procuracy for twenty-nine years, and in the Soviet Supreme Court for about a year and a half.[3] He had been appointed in June 1947, the sole Georgian on the country's highest appeals court. In these years, the USSR Supreme Court functioned not as a constitutional court, but rather as the highest court of appeals for both criminal and civil cases.[4] Judge Chichua's assignment was to review all appeals coming from the Georgian republic. He was to consider requests for re-examination of convictions, protests about procedures, and, in particular, the appeals of Georgians who claimed that they had been improperly convicted and sentenced in the Georgian courts.[5]

After a lengthy investigation into his actions, prosecutors charged Judge Chichua with several counts of taking bribes and other abuses of his office. The indictment alleged that Chichua had frequently accepted bribes from the relatives of convicted people, including meals, alcoholic drinks, and cash. Investigators claimed that Chichua routinely met in secret with petitioners who wanted his assistance with the appeals process, thus compromising his integrity as a judge. He did illegal favors for Georgian petitioners, it was charged, intervening to help them with appeals before the Supreme Court. It is important to note that, among all the charges lodged against Chichua, prosecutors cited only one instance in which money allegedly changed hands. In the indictment's other counts, Chichua was accused of accepting bribes of food and drink in exchange for improperly assisting with appeals. Chichua was arrested in late 1949, and he remained in prison for over two years until his trial in March 1952.[6]

Ultimately, a puzzle lies at the heart of this case. Considering the obvious and quite serious risks at this level, why would a judge serving on the Soviet Supreme Court accept a bribe—or even risk giving the *appearance* of doing so—in the time of Stalin?

The records of the Communist Party, the procuracy, and the courts show that Judge Chichua, like many appeals court judges in this period, was placed in the path of a virtual juridical tidal wave when he was appointed to the Soviet Supreme Court in June 1947. The timing of his hiring could not have been worse for a judge, especially a judge on the USSR Supreme Court. Chichua assumed his post in Moscow just a few weeks after the issuance of the draconian June 4, 1947 edicts on the theft of state and personal property. Laws on "speculation" (profiteering in scarce goods) and other "economic crimes" were also strengthened, and penalties increased, at this time.[7] The family members of those convicted under these June 4, 1947 edicts quickly began to flood the courts with a huge number of appeals. Thus mid-1947 was a very difficult time for Chichua—who was by his own account poorly educated, and who was still being tutored in the Russian language—to begin a stint in the country's highest and most overburdened court of appeals.[8]

Chichua quickly became a magnet for residents of Georgia seeking any kind of assistance with the legal system. According to the "zone principle," the Supreme Court distributed cases for review to its judges by geographical "zone." Chichua, for example, was responsible for appeals in which the appellant was convicted on the territory of the Georgian Republic. Although he was a member of the USSR Supreme Court for only eighteen months in all, he reviewed about a thousand appeals of criminal convictions. In particular, Chichua reviewed the appeals of hundreds of very stiff sentences for theft of state property and speculation, as well as white-collar crimes such as negligence.[9] Those convicted, or their family members, had every incentive to try to persuade Judge Chichua to assist them in appealing the severe sentences.

"GREETINGS FROM SUNNY GEORGIA!"
THE INTERMEDIARIES

What triggered the bribery charges against Chichua? The key bribe that he was said to have accepted was a package containing thirty kilos of pork, delivered to his home in Tbilisi (the capital city of the Georgian Republic) in October 1948.[10] The pork was allegedly sent to Chichua through an intermediary, Andronika S. Eremadze, a long-time acquaintance of Chichua. (Eremadze claimed that Judge Chichua was not at home when the meat was delivered. Chichua's wife categorically denied receiving the pork, and testified that Eremadze was lying.) Investigators estimated the meat to be worth 300 rubles. The purported instigator of the bribe was Indiko V. Bukiia, who was seeking the judge's help to appeal his sister's conviction. Bukiia's sister had been sentenced to ten years in the Gulag on July 11, 1948, for violating the June 4 decree on theft of state property. "Her conviction was a heavy blow to the family," Bukiia stated later. Believing that the conviction of his sister was incorrect and that she had been improperly sentenced, Bukiia allegedly paid Eremadze several thousand rubles to contact Judge Chichua for help with her case.[11] Prosecutors also claimed that Chichua accepted a second bribe, a meal at the home of Eremadze's brother-in-law.

As highlighted in the last chapter, intermediaries were important figures in many bribery transactions. I would suggest that many of the intermediaries who represented Georgian clients in the courts of Moscow should be regarded as a Soviet variety of "cultural broker." From its inception, the Soviet Union absorbed and tried to assimilate hundreds of regional and local cultures, leading to widespread cultural conflict and confusion. Some people, such as these intermediaries in the courts, became quite adept at moving back and forth between two milieux: from selected areas of the periphery to the established Soviet bureaucratic agencies, and back again. Brokers developed connections in the Russian courts, became acquainted with various legal cultures, negotiated deals between petitioners and court employees, and of course charged people for these specialized services. If they got results and kept their clients satisfied, their businesses would expand as their reputations spread by word of mouth. Many defense lawyers, in particular, were well positioned to play this role. Entrepreneurial intermediaries understood the needs of petitioners—usually to get the sentences of relatives reduced or annulled. They also understood what court employees required—both a guarantee of absolute secrecy and a material incentive to compensate them for the substantial risk they took in accepting a bribe. Brokers convinced petitioners of their valuable connections in Moscow, their expertise, and their knowledge of the ways of the courts in the capital. Thanks to the enormous and multinational character of the Soviet empire, there was a great deal of room for—and demand for—these cultural brokers in many spheres of social and economic life.

Judging by the courts of Moscow in this period, it seems that, in addition to Georgians, many other ethnic groups, including Bashkir, Jewish, North Ossetian, Dagestani, and other communities, had similar networks of intermediaries on which they could rely when they needed help with the legal system. These go-betweens understood the ways both of the homeland and of the Soviet courtrooms, and had credibility in both arenas.[12]

Most intermediaries who worked with Georgian petitioners in Moscow were themselves Georgian. Some quietly established relationships in the courts. Others were quite bold and demonstrative in their actions, practicing what Erik R. Scott has called "the performative aspect of Georgian economic activity."[13] One Georgian lawyer who acted as a middleman had success dropping in to the Supreme Court bearing gifts for court employees in one hand and petitioners' appeals in the other. As a court secretary testified, "A lawyer named Melik-Nubarov, who behaved himself in an overly familiar manner in the offices of the Supreme Court, came from Georgia. Once, he called me on the telephone and told me that he brought greetings from Georgia, [and that he had] a crate of lemons and a packet of complaints [appealing sentences]. I was offended at the words of Melik-Nubarov. He said, 'Why are you so offended? I gave Makarov [a different court employee] a crate of lemons and he accepted them!'"[14] Another member of the court staff complained about a lawyer who would show up in the reception area of the USSR Supreme Court with a handful of petitions to be passed to judges, loudly declaring "Greetings from sunny Georgia!"[15]

This lawyer likely was trying to capitalize on a common perception in the court—that Georgian clients were willing to give gifts, or to pay, or to pursue nearly any available avenue to get their relatives released from jail. Thanks to Georgia's geographic location, Georgians had abundant access to rare and desirable commodities such as citrus fruits, teas, and wines. Georgia was well known, even "branded" in the minds of Soviet consumers, for the exotic food products that grew in its warm and wonderful climate.[16] The lawyer's message clearly implied that there would be more tropical "fruit" for court employees willing to play along.

The stereotyped preconceptions of Georgians may also explain why at least two lawyers implicated in acting as intermediaries in Moscow courts went so far as to adopt Georgian surnames, adding the common Georgian suffix "-vili" to their actual last names. A certain Mushailov was known in the Supreme Court building as Muradashvili, while the lawyer Mesarkov went by the name Mesarkishvili.[17] Because court employees did not verify the identities of people who said they were lawyers, it was not difficult to pose as a person of another nationality. According to court employees, Mushailov would come to the court every two or three months, carrying petitions about various cases. "Mushailov presented himself as a Georgian, saying that he was from Georgia, and that his name was Muradashvili, [and] he loved to talk about Georgia."[18] He even went out of his way to dress in traditional Georgian clothing.

It is not wholly clear why these lawyers adopted false Georgian identities. When confronted about his pseudonym, Mushailov chose a "friendship of peoples" approach, disingenuously telling an interrogator: "All nations are the same to me."[19] A much more likely explanation is that they hoped that the pseudonyms would advertise to potential Georgian clients that they were approachable and knew how to represent their clients' interests in Moscow courts. Indeed, Mushailov falsely bragged to clients that he was a "Kremlin lawyer," perhaps trying to encourage the idea that he had contacts with Stalin, the Georgian in the Kremlin.[20] On the other side of the transaction, court employees may have seen an outgoing, demonstrably Georgian lawyer as more willing to "deal" on behalf of his clients.

THIRTY KILOS OF PORK: GIFTS, MEALS, AND BRIBES

In the Soviet Union, as in many other societies, the bribe trail was frequently paved with gifts and meals. Prosecutors accused Judge Chichua of accepting multiple bribes, usually "disguised" in the form of fruit, alcohol, or meals, which distorted his professional judgment to the benefit of the giver. A crucial piece of evidence against Chichua was that he accepted a meal at the home of an intermediary's relative. To counter allegations that the meal was a bribe, the accused intermediary, Eremadze, referred to Chichua as his "*zemliak* [a person from the same locality] whom I have known for more than fifteen years and who lived in a neighboring area."[21] They had met in the city of Batumi, when Eremadze worked as an instructor for the regional party committee's youth league (Komsomol) and Chichua served as a judge. At the hearing, Eremadze took pains to show that he and the judge were friends; they had treated each other to food and drink many times over the years. His point was that although he feted Chichua at his brother-in-law's home and spent 300 rubles on food and drink, the two men had an ongoing relationship. The meal was nothing more than a meal: a sign of friendship, not an attempt to influence Chichua's judgment. (In any case, Eremadze pointed out, Chichua was ill at the time and only had one glass of beer.) For his part, Chichua said that he had "no material interest" in the case that Eremadze wanted to discuss. Rather, "I agreed to the invitation of Eremadze to go visit his brother-in-law. As a Georgian, I could not refuse. This was my weakness and this is also our Georgian tradition."[22] For the prosecutors in this case, such acknowledgements that he "could not refuse" must have been telling, cementing their sense that Georgians could not deny one another.

As the anthropologist Marcel Mauss has noted about gifts, "The thing given is not inactive. Invested with life, often possessing individuality, it seeks to return to what Hertz called its 'place of origin' or to produce, on behalf of the clan and the native soil from which it sprang, an equivalent to replace it."[23] Indeed, in these cases Georgians did not give each other typical gifts of cash, jewelry, or clothing (the most common bribes in Soviet courts in this period), but rather gifts of fruit, wine, meat, and other things that came from the land. Moreover, these exchanges were *required*. Not only did tradition mandate that the giver *offer* gifts, but the recipient was obliged to *accept* them. As will be explored, this sense of obligation made Judge Chichua highly uncomfortable as he straddled the two incompatible cultures, because he knew enough of Soviet legal mores to realize that accepting such gifts from petitioners might appear to be illegal.[24] However, within the Georgian cultural world it would be contemptuous to refuse to meet with fellow Georgians or not to accept the gifts they offered. It would have been a violation of traditional social relations; it would have been akin to social suicide. Accepting gifts, on the other hand, could be professional suicide. For Georgians, fruit and wine made for wonderful gifts, coming from the homeland. In the eyes of Moscow law enforcement, however, these rare delicacies were bribes, a way to "buy" an official, to both expedite and disguise an illegal deal.[25] These different ways of understanding gift giving and bribery lay at the heart of Judge Chichua's troubles.

One of the most complicated questions that prosecutors and judges had to address was how to determine this line—to some degree culturally constructed—between a "gift" and a "bribe." When following the bribe trail, prosecutors had to prove quid pro quo, and this was no easy task. In many cultures, for example, petitioners would bring a gift of fruit or other food to a judge as a sign of gratitude if a case were decided to their satisfaction.[26] Thus in several cases of alleged bribery tried in Soviet courts at this time, judges ruled that small gifts to court or procuracy employees given by a party after the case was decided should not be construed as bribes. In August 1948, for example, a woman with three small children in the Ukrainian Republic gave fifty rubles to a regional procurator after her husband was acquitted. The prosecutor refused to charge her with bribery, deciding that this was not a bribe. Rather "her action should be regarded as a tradition rooted among people to thank them for completely lawful actions." The Ukrainian Supreme Court justices evaluating this case, however, determined that this merciful reading of the law was completely incorrect, and that the woman should indeed be charged with offering a bribe.[27]

At his trial, Chichua argued that, as a Georgian, he was obliged to be courteous to other Georgians and to lawfully help them when possible. He repeatedly emphasized to the court that this traditional hospitality did not oblige him to break the law, nor did it have any influence whatsoever on his decisions as an "honest Soviet judge" (a term by which he frequently referred to himself with pride).

THE VENUE: THE HOTEL "EVROPA"

Where did Chichua and Georgian petitioners come together to talk, whether legally or illicitly? The next step on the bribe trail is the venue where most of the alleged bribes were passed to Judge Chichua. At his trial, Chichua argued that the living circumstances provided to him by the Supreme Court posed extreme challenges for a public official trying to maintain impartiality as he exercised the substantial power that attached to his position. Indeed, living and working conditions for many Supreme Court judges were precarious and allowed dubious contact with petitioners. In a June 27, 1947 letter to Stalin, Gusev, the party Secretary of the Supreme Court, complained about the lamentable housing situation of some Supreme Court judges and employees.[28] Gusev pointed out that several judges new to the Supreme Court in 1947 (including Chichua) had moved to Moscow from distant union republics, but no apartments had been provided for them. "They live in hotels, for which they are not in a position to pay and for which the USSR Supreme Court has no funds."[29] The hotel administrations were even making noises about evicting the judges for lack of payment. Private apartments, in buildings complete with security personnel to limit the number of spontaneous visitors, would have been a much more desirable location for prominent judges.

Chichua was one of those judges who had no private living space. Citing a shortage of apartments, Moscow housing authorities assigned him to room 312 at the Hotel Evropa (the Hotel Europe) in Moscow. The fact that Chichua received petitioners in his hotel room—and he certainly did not deny this—featured prominently in the charges against him. Chichua testified that he repeatedly asked the chairman of the Supreme Court, I. T. Goliakov, for help finding an apartment, which would have allowed him much more privacy and greatly limited opportunities for petitioners to drop in unannounced.[30] Yet Moscow housing agencies did not come through with an apartment for him, leaving him in the hotel in the middle of Moscow, a magnet for hundreds of desperate Georgian people who had traveled to the capital to appeal unjust convictions. Judge Chichua lamented to the court, "My weakness is that I received people and offered assistance to them. If I had had an apartment and not lived in a hotel, this would not have happened."[31]

Chichua testified that many dozens of Georgians came to his hotel at various times and brought him all kinds of petitions, requests, and inquiries, typically accompanied by traditional gifts. Chichua described to the court a typical interaction in his hotel room: "Often it went like this: Some person knocks on my door. He enters and begins to explain his case or the case of a relative. I say that I am not a lawyer and there is nothing I can do. He informs me, 'You are a Georgian, and why can't you tell me where to go and whom to see?'" He summed up the ludi-crous situation: "I lived in a hotel, and *everyone* could drop in on me, even the hotel maid. And *even the maid* herself would comment that a lot of people were constantly coming to see me" (emphasis added). Georgian traditions of hospitality prevented him from refusing to meet with petitioners, he said. "I couldn't throw visitors out on their faces."[32]

One incident stands out: on New Year's Eve in 1947, Judge Chichua collapsed in his room at the Hotel Evropa. Suffering with a fever of 102 degrees, Chichua took to his bed, his lungs filled with fluid. His cousin, who happened also to be staying in the hotel, found him in this terrible state and called the hotel's front desk. Because the ailing judge was a justice on the Supreme Court, the hotel immediately called the Kremlin clinic. The cousin, understanding that it would take some time before the Kremlin nurse showed up, ran down the hall and fetched a Geor-gian acquaintance, a doctor who was also staying at the hotel. Suspect-ing pneumonia, the 27-year-old doctor used a traditional remedy com-mon in the treatment of respiratory ailments—he heated several glass jars and placed them upside down on the ailing judge's chest. When the Georgian doctor heard that a nurse from the Second Kremlin Hospital was on her way, he became very curious about his patient. "Who is this man?" the doctor asked his friend. "He's a judge on the Supreme Court."

On hearing this news, what did the doctor do? With five or six peo-ple in the room as witnesses, the doctor took this opportunity to in-form the judge, who was flat on his back with hot glass jars covering his chest, shaking with fever and soaked with sweat, that his father had been "improperly" arrested for theft of state property and had been sentenced to seven years in prison. He asked Chichua (in Georgian) how to file an appeal that would get his father's sentence overturned. Equally surprisingly, the judge, who would seem to have been fully within his rights to silence the doctor, instead queried the doctor about his father's case and instructed him how to write a letter of complaint. Even with the judge sprawled out in bed with pneumonia, a Georgian petitioner still felt that he could ask him for assistance, and the judge felt obli-gated to respond. Nearly five years later, both the doctor and the judge were on trial, forced to explain their brief and labored conversation in the Hotel Evropa on New Year's Eve, 1947.[33]

This incident in the hotel supports the impression that Georgian petitioners believed they had the right to request Judge Chichua's legal assistance, anywhere, at any time. For his part, Chichua simply could not find the vocabulary to decline meetings with Georgian visitors. Indeed, within the first few minutes of his testimony at trial, he brought up the difficulties imposed on him by this Georgian "cult of hospitality."[34] Subsequently Chichua himself provided several additional examples when, he said, he was bound by Georgian tradition. These meetings, he acknowledged, had given the false impression of a conflict of interest. As he put it (using the double negative), "I couldn't *not* receive them, but I swear that I did nothing for them. . . ."[35]

The case of one defendant accused of offering Chichua a bribe is telling. N. S. Chkuaseli, the director of a fruit and vegetable store, had been accused of negligence involving the spoilage of some potatoes (a serious economic crime for a store manager). He contacted Chichua to help get the sentence annulled. Chkuaseli arrived unannounced at Chichua's hotel room at ten o'clock in the morning to discuss his case.[36] "I could not chase the Georgian Chkuaseli from my [hotel] room, since I am myself Georgian. We have such customs [*obychai*]." (As Tsagareishvili, a defendant in another case, stated at trial, "Among us Georgians it is accepted that you offer each other help.")[37] For his part, the defendant Chkuaseli claimed, "I approached Chichua not as a member of the Supreme Court, but as a Georgian."[38] Chichua said that he tried to do his duty as an officer of the court, but he nevertheless blamed himself in retrospect for not insisting that the petitioner leave: "I told him that his case will be reviewed according to the law. My weakness consisted of the fact that I did not chase Chkuaseli from my room."

Chichua complained that streams of Georgian petitioners, both ordinary people and well-known elites, came to his hotel to implore him to help with their legal problems. Among the petitioners were high-ranking party officials, including the deputy secretary of the Communist Party of Georgia, the chair of the Council of Ministers of the Adzharskaia Autonomous Republic, numerous secretaries of regional party committees (*raikomy*), and many others. At least two Georgian generals asked for help. A number of famous artists stopped by. The son of the famous screen actor Kiril Macharadze approached him on behalf of a friend who had gotten into trouble. Chichua also received a visit from the well-known actor Alexander Zhozholani, who appeared in thirty films between 1926 and 1970. Zhozholani had accidentally left some costumes on a train, and he had been fined 15,000 rubles. He swung by the Hotel Evropa to ask Chichua for help with the appeals process. "To get rid of him, I took his statement," Chichua testified, though he said that he never followed up on it.[39]

One prominent Georgian who never dropped in to ask Chichua for help, of course, was Josef Stalin. Remarkably, however, the man who *played Stalin* in the movies—the beloved Georgian screen actor Mikhail Gelovani—did come by the Hotel Evropa to request a favor.[40] Stalin loved the way that the tall and handsome actor portrayed him, and he ordered Gelovani to play him in every film. Gelovani performed the role of Stalin in at least fourteen enormously popular films between 1938 and 1952. Perhaps Gelovani's most acclaimed film was the over-the-top 1949 paean to Stalin's brilliant and humane wartime leadership, *Padenie Berlina (The Fall of Berlin)*, which became a staple of the Stalin cult. Even the fantastically famous Gelovani knew to turn to Judge Chichua on behalf of Georgian relatives or acquaintances who faced problems with the law.

It was not only Judge Chichua whom Georgians approached for help negotiating the maze of Moscow's legal bureaucracies. According to trial testimony, the family members of the accused also frequently asked prominent Georgian defense lawyers for "unofficial" assistance. Lawyers who were thought to be well connected in the courts would constantly be approached by relatives, friends, friends of relatives, and relatives of friends, even distant relatives and barely-known acquaintances. High-ranking officers in the military similarly found themselves in high demand. The renowned Georgian General M. G. Kiknadze, who had commanded an artillery division in the North Caucasus during World War II, testified that he was burdened by endless requests as a result of his prominence. He testified that he did whatever he could to dodge the visits of his fellow Georgians: "Very many of my fellow native Georgians come to me, barraging me with various kinds of requests. In order to avoid this I am compelled to stay outside the city on my unit's military base, since it is unacceptable [*ne priniato*] to refuse these requests." The general admitted that agreeing to bring forward a petition to the Supreme Court on behalf of one of his Georgian soldiers had been an enormous mistake. "I affirm that . . . I have become conscious of the error of this act. I have been the commander of a[n artillery] division for eleven years, but I have never experienced the kind of unpleasantness that I am going through now."[41]

At his trial Chichua blamed both the petitioners who came to see him without regard for his need to maintain some professional distance, and the court itself for not giving him the secure living space needed to preserve his privacy and impartiality. Nevertheless, he also found fault with his own actions. He admitted: "Accepting citizens in my room at the Hotel Evropa, of course, I discredited myself as a member of the Supreme Court of the USSR and I confess my guilt in this." Ultimately, Chichua admitted to the *appearance* of misusing his office, but denied that he actually did so. He refused to confess to any crime, despite intense pressure from prosecutors. The evidence presented in the trials supported Chichua's position. Multiple counts of bribery against him were dismissed because prosecutors did not demonstrate quid pro quo. Chichua repeatedly confessed to poor judgment, while denying that he ever acted illegally. He understood that his "culture defense" would not succeed if prosecutors could prove that he had violated the law.

IN THE HANDS OF THE PROSECUTORS

As the cases described here show once again, it was often very difficult to distinguish bribes from expressions of hospitality, gifts to friends, or tokens of appreciation. It was difficult for investigators, difficult for judges, and sometimes even for the participants themselves to tell when a basket of apples, thirty kilos of pork, or a shared dinner and wine were merely selfless signs of gratitude, and when they were payoffs intended to buy a favor or corrupt the judgment of an official. Gifts and bribes often traveled along the same trail. For prosecutors the distinction between a legal gift and an illicit bribe was more than a purely academic one; prosecutors' decisions about whether to press charges, and judges' decision to convict, meant the difference between prison and freedom.

For their part, Georgian defendants claimed that the giving of gifts and generous hospitality were integral parts of their culture—merely acts of friendship and solidarity. And many officials regularly argued that refusing to accept small gifts would be insulting, and that accepting such offerings did not affect their judgment. A saying cited in Dal's dictionary of familiar Russian quotations, published in the early 1880s, is apropos here: "We do not take bribes, but we do accept tokens of gratitude" (*"Vziatok ne berem, a blagodarnosti prinimaem."*)[42] Meanwhile, prosecutors regarded the personal relationships between judges and petitioners based on ethnic and kinship bonds with a large degree of suspicion. Indictments made it clear that legal authorities suspected that bribery was involved when a decision was rendered after any exchange involving food or drink. Furthermore, gifts (including food or drink) given *after* a judge made a decision also came under scrutiny.

When it came to their investigations of corruption in the courts, prosecutors regarded the ways of many cultures—including, but not limited to, Georgian culture—as highly suspect and often criminal. For people serving in the Soviet legal agencies, pork, fruit, and wine were not just standard presents, but luxurious and rare delicacies. These classically Georgian products were extremely scarce in Moscow and most of the Russian Republic. To a Georgian judge living far from home, these bounteous gifts would serve as a reminder of the traditions of their homeland and the people they left behind. Indeed, when Chichua's wife visited the judge in Moscow, she always brought fruit and cheese from Georgia.[43] Yet investigators searching for evidence of bribery, sensitive to bribes that were "disguised" as gifts or friendly social exchanges, were always wary when they discovered that Georgians were treating each other with these goods. They were also highly suspicious of judges dining with common citizens, no matter the explanation. To Soviet prosecutors, a petitioner's gift of wine or fruit from his native land looked like a bribe, no different in principle or purpose from a gold watch or an envelope stuffed with cash.[44] Investigators regarded these luxuries as currency, and also believed that "hosting" or "entertaining" was often a cover for illicit activity. In Chichua's case, prosecutors assumed this flurry of meetings and gifts to be bribery.

Certain stereotypes about Georgians—and even open hostility to them—frequently surfaced in testimony by Russian defendants and witnesses as well as among the prosecutors. Georgians were seen as "backward," clannish, and inclined to form criminal associations. Several investigators told Georgian defendants and witnesses that they were eager to "cleanse Moscow of Georgians." During preliminary questioning of the accused in a separate case of alleged judicial corruption, an investigator repeated a rumor that the Georgians who managed the famous Aragvi restaurant in Moscow threw drunken orgies in which the patrons participated.[45] Such accusations reinforced the stereotype that Georgians were morally depraved, prone to acting outside the law, and highly protective of one another. Soviet prosecutors also seemed to characterize Georgians' behavior as particularly corrupt and reprehensible.

The historian Ronald Suny cites the "reliance on close familial and personal ties in all aspects of life and the reluctance to betray one's relatives and comrades" as factors contributing to Georgia's reputation as a haven for corruption. The economist Gregory Grossman has made a similar observation.[46] Gerald Mars and Yochanan Altman argue that in Georgia "all relationships are personalized . . . and formal organizational structures are bent, modified and adapted to serve personal and familial needs." "Social networks binding individuals and families together" are extremely powerful.[47] In such a context, gift giving between citizens and persons holding official positions could be highly ambiguous. While many of these behaviors deviated from the ideals of Soviet law or communist morality, of course, they maintained a kind of logic within their own cultural universes.

The Georgian cases described in this chapter were not unique, of course. They were variations on a theme. The Soviet state could no more wipe out the practice of gift giving between public officials and the population than it could abolish religious faith or traditional music. All over the country, people asked officials to intervene for their friends and relatives, sometimes for a price. They often found it difficult to refuse. Russian peasant traditions of gift exchange and entertaining certainly come to mind here, and it is notable that bribes in the countryside most often were "in-kind," taking the form of food (eggs, flour, chickens) or drink (vodka and homebrew). Traditions of obligation and expectations of reciprocity are not peculiar to one culture, and many cultures with similar characteristics could be found inside the borders of the Russian Republic (and in many other societies). The Russian judge Shevchenko, for example, testified in a different case that a certain Semashko treated him to vodka and food (*zakuski*) and, as he understood it, "this was a masked bribe—*zakuski* and drinks—after which I could not refuse his request."[48]

It is clear that between 1946 and 1953 there was tremendous pressure from central party agencies to find and prosecute bribe-taking judges, especially in the country's highest appeals courts. In the bribery cases exposed in the late 1940s, prosecutors seem to have been working from a sort of master bribery narrative (as will be discussed in chapter 8). One plotline implicated Georgians and their networks for their clannishness, prioritizing of mutual obligations, and willingness to "buy" court employees. In the view of the prosecutors, Georgians had a type of ingrained, permanent, and partially disguised bribe culture, corrupted by gifts, drinks, and fruit, and their "tribal" obligations to lend assistance to each other. To win convictions, prosecutors were not only *following* bribe trails, they were sometimes *creating* them, reframing innocent or ambiguous meetings and exchanges of meals and presents as criminal conspiracies.

THE VERDICT

Chichua always categorically denied that he was guilty of bribery, despite the endless imploring of petitioners. Chichua argued that rogue prosecutors had greatly exaggerated the extent of his alleged crimes in their indictment. "Not one witness in court said what was written in the preliminary investigation. The investigator Golenkov wanted to make me into a bribe taker. Call me what you want, but I am not a bribe taker." He noted that multiple investigators turned over every stone in their attempts to find someone who had given him a bribe, but they could not find anyone.[49] In support of his innocence, Chichua declared that he had no need for citizens' gratuitous gifts of meat and wine because his wife, daughter, and son-in-law all had jobs. He did not live beyond his means; his family back in Tbilisi still lived in a communal apartment.[50] What is more, taking a bribe, he said, would have been disgraceful.[51] "I tried to preserve the honor of a member of the Supreme Court," Chichua insisted. I decided cases "according to my conscience as a judge [*po sudeiskoi sovesti*]."[52]

Chichua was tried in a closed session presided over by three members of the Soviet Supreme Court. At the conclusion of the trial in March 1952, the court found Chichua guilty of two counts of abuse of office and one count of bribery. He was sentenced to seven years in prison and expelled from the Communist Party. Chichua vehemently protested his conviction, claiming that it was the product of a huge misunderstanding. Although one cannot know definitively from this historical distance, the testimony and evidence presented at trial and in subsequent appeals support Chichua's denial. Indeed, the judges cleared him of multiple accusations of bribery, with one exception: the incident involving the thirty kilos of pork (an incident that later testimony showed was likely fabricated) and an alleged dinner with the supposed intermediary, Eremadze. (The latter received a sentence of four years in prison, and Bukiia, who supposedly offered the bribe to free his sister, received two years in prison.)[53]

CONCLUSIONS

This chapter has portrayed important informal relationships common to the postwar period in a new light. In highlighting personal initiative and the building of personal and ethnic networks, the research challenges stereotypes of a cowed and paralyzed postwar Soviet society, and also questions the popular caricature of the prototypically corrupt Soviet bureaucrat.

Earlier, we discussed Georgian intermediaries in the Moscow courts as Soviet "cultural brokers" who moved between two sets of legal and cultural norms and practices. Judge Chichua is an example of a second type of cultural broker, one who struggled to uphold "Soviet" legal standards in the face of countless requests by petitioners to bend the rules. Part of Chichua's job was to explain Soviet law and legal procedures to the Georgians who came to Moscow to appeal, to elucidate the "higher," impersonal Soviet legal culture to people who were supposedly at a lower cultural level, and who had not yet fully internalized "Soviet consciousness." Not all petitioners understood, for example, that their private requests for help and gestures of appreciation were regarded by Soviet authorities as illegal or improper, and therefore entailed the risk of prosecution. Chichua, for his part, understood perfectly that actions acceptable in one culture could give the appearance of a conflict of interest—even of bribery—in another. He made extraordinary efforts to avoid violating the norms of either culture.

Chichua found himself in an extremely difficult position, expected to uphold the law against the pleadings of acquaintances, kin, and unknown fellow Georgians. Not only did the judge have to enforce the rules for appeals, he also had to resist the supplications of people who believed that he had an obligation to help them, not simply as Georgians, but as Georgians who had treated him to meals or given him gifts.

Chichua was caught between conflicting expectations, trapped in an untenable position. At some essential level, he had to shed, or at least temper, important elements of his Georgian identity. But he could not leave that identity behind completely. In practice, Georgian customs and the webs of relationships they created strongly challenged Chichua's adopted Soviet legal culture. And, paradoxically, the party leadership that appointed him to this position inadvertently reinforced these ties, by requiring him to deal exclusively with appeals from Georgia.

Chichua resisted requests to abuse his office or otherwise violate the law, despite the persistent requests of people who invested their hopes in him, yet had little faith in "the state" in the abstract. Nevertheless, his situation further illustrates the tenuous hold of "Soviet values," both among some officials and throughout much of the population, in spite of efforts to transform the population culturally. The Soviet regime was attempting to create a new social and economic system. To organize and run that system, it also aimed to create a "New Soviet Person," wholly dedicated to unselfishly upholding its collective values.[54] But like Judge Chichua, many people moved back and forth, between those elements of the Soviet system that they found appealing and their own traditions and values, never fully embracing either.

III

5 "A Grave Evil and Danger"
Postwar "Campaigns" against Bribery

UPON TAKING POWER in October 1917, the new Soviet government vowed to eradicate the scourge of bribery from the lands of the Russian Empire forever, as the Bolsheviks dreamed of a government and society without corruption. For a number of reasons, this vision failed, and spectacularly. After World War II, the party quickly launched a "campaign" against bribery. Thanks to declassified documents from state archives, it is now possible to trace the course of this unsuccessful but revealing campaign. The 1946–1947 attack against bribery represents what can be called a "campaign spasm," a brief and intense attempt by the party-state to eliminate some sort of negative phenomenon afflicting Soviet society. As the scholars Heyman and Smart have pointed out, most states strive to make "the cultural fabric" of their society resistant "to the use of public office for private gain."[1] At the same time, though, in the Soviet Union, as in other societies, informal deal-making between bureaucrats and citizens was a practice closely enmeshed with (and sometimes disguised by) cultures of gift giving and reciprocity, and surrounded by incentives to keep it quiet.

From the outset, the "campaign" against bribery was hardly a full-fledged attack on the root causes of the phenomenon—the hyper-centralized planning and bloated bureaucracy of the Soviet command-administrative system; the insufficient income, poor prestige, and inadequate professional preparation and legal consciousness of officials; the acute shortages of goods and services; poor access to housing; the lack of justice in the legal system; and a party leadership that was less than enthusiastic about prosecuting official malfeasance among party members and (especially) elites in a serious way. As we have seen, all of these conditions provided abundant opportunities for officials to profit in the shadows of Stalinist society. Despite a good deal of bluster, there was important opposition among key agencies to serious measures to curtail malfeasance. By the postwar Stalin period, the informal relationships that linked state functionaries and the general population had become fundamental to the functioning of the state and economy.[2] The campaign's reach was limited by the regime's obsession with secrecy, an unwillingness to discuss the real parameters of the problem in the press, a fixation on the wrong targets, and great concern with the Soviet Union's image abroad during the early years of the Cold War.

It has been said that the late Imperial Russian government energetically tried to uproot bribery with one hand, while with the other hand it equally energetically, if inadvertently, cultivated the conditions that produced a new generation of bribe takers.[3] This observation remained true in the 1940s, 1950s, and 1960s and beyond. Even as the regime clumsily swatted at bribery, it simultaneously fortified the conditions that enabled the practice to thrive.

THE LETTER THAT LAUNCHED A CAMPAIGN

On May 3, 1946, P. I. Minin, a Communist Party member working in the Political Administration of the Baku Military District, addressed a desperate letter to Joseph V. Stalin. (At that time, Baku was the capital city of the Azerbaizhani SSR.) Minin sent the letter to the Special Sector (*Osobyi sektor*) of the Central Committee, perhaps hoping that, through this channel, the letter would come to the attention of Stalin himself. In his letter, Minin described an "epidemic" of bribery and its debilitating effects.[4] In five paragraphs, Minin claimed that bribery was contaminating all walks of Soviet life. With a tone of anger and frustration, Minin's letter, now preserved in the archive of the USSR Ministry of Justice, vividly expresses his disappointment about what he sees as the breakdown of social norms, formal state mechanisms, and morality during and after the Great Patriotic War. This letter ultimately launched a postwar "campaign" against bribery.

Minin did not mention the bartering, shadow-market exchanges "in the interests of production," blat, and other types of informal relationships that were common among managers in industrial enterprises and collective farms who were scrambling to obtain materials and fulfill ambitious plans. He instead referred to a tidal wave of everyday graft, as bureaucrats took bribes from Soviet people trying to acquire every manner of scarce goods and services. Bribery, he wrote, was endured by a population that was desperate to make ends meet, but forced to deal with state functionaries who demanded payments for needed services.

Because of the upheavals experienced during the war, Minin writes, "bribery has now become an extremely widespread phenomenon." Since 1943–1944, he notes, there has been an upswing in this kind of crime among state bureaucrats, many of whom have become greatly emboldened. Bribes "are given and accepted by people of the most varied professions and in the most varied forms." Focusing on the omnipresent role of the bribe in everyday life, Minin laments that mail carriers take a "reward" for delivering mail and telegrams, and if one refuses to pay, one's correspondence would be "lost," or delivered only after a long delay. Pipe fitters insist on payments to connect individuals to the municipal gas and water networks. Railroad employees demand extra "fees" to allow passengers to ride or to claim packages. Teachers and professors take bribes to admit students into institutes or to allow them to pass exams. In sum, Minin writes, bribery "has become a grave evil and danger against which we must lead a decisive battle."

One of Minin's sharpest complaints was the disturbing degree to which local officials in positions of power either tolerated or actively participated in bribery: "Unfortunately, certain staff in positions of authority have no qualms about bribery, because most often it takes the form of a gift, podnoshenie offered either in kind or as money." (Minin uses the word *podnoshenie*—expressed with a large dose of disgust, to be sure—referring to the traditional practice of gift giving to officials.) Minin makes the critical observation that officials believed that accepting a "gift" in exchange for a favor was something less than a bribe, and certainly nothing to get excited about. In Minin's view, this tolerant attitude was a perilous sign indicating that officials had become inured to the stigma that should accompany bribery. Like Minin, the courts and procuracy often described bribery as an "epidemic," similar to a contagious disease. Yet it was a disease against which many officials felt no need to fight.[5]

In Minin's mind, these two factors taken together—the "epidemic" nature of bribery in combination with the high level of tolerance for bribery among responsible officials and society at large—created a very dangerous situation. He recognized that the social controls and internal discipline that should have been in place were largely absent. Those engaged in bribery had no sense of shame. Even eyewitnesses felt no moral outrage about such crimes, and therefore, numbed by apathy, did not report them. Indeed, in law enforcement records, one frequently sees confirmation of what Minin refers to as troubling "conspiracies of silence" (or *krugovaia poruka,* as it was known). Groups of people in courts, warehouses, housing offices, and other workplaces created criminal collectives that protected each other. If just one person in the workplace had informed the authorities about a criminal group instead of turning their backs (or even participating), the group could have been broken up.

Having noted the demoralizing effect of the need to give bribes, Minin argues that graft causes even further damage. Bribes "corrupt both the giver and the receiver, corrupt the work of government institutions and enterprises, become a serious obstacle in our construction, [and] provoke legitimate dissatisfaction and indignation among the laboring masses." Illicit deals between officials and petitioners had grave ramifications both for the regime and for the population's attitudes toward the state. In Minin's opinion, the fact that officials who accepted bribes were rarely prosecuted created hostility toward the state and opened a rift between the government and the population. The inaction of the courts gave birth to feelings of impunity among corrupt officials, according to Minin. Officials were certain that they would not be caught, and that if they were apprehended they would not be punished. Minin relates the case of a group of Baku doctors who were tried in March 1946. Prosecutors had charged them with accepting bribes to exempt men from military service. One of the doctor's bookkeepers was convicted of receiving a whopping 1.5 million rubles. Minin alleged in his letter that the citizens of Baku, made cynical by widespread corruption, predicted that nothing would happen to this bookkeeper: "Well, they'll sentence him to be shot," they said, "but then they'll change the [sentence from] execution to ten years in prison, and then with the help of money and his friends he'll be free in two or three years." And, indeed, the court did sentence the bookkeeper to death, but then reduced the punishment to ten years. (Whether he was freed "in two or three years" is unknown.)

Although crime statistics were not published in the Stalin period, secret reports available in Ministry of Justice archives suggest that throughout the late Stalin years, law enforcement agencies only infrequently arrested people for bribery. Material further indicates that most bribery went unreported and unpunished, and that the legal agencies were well aware of this fact.[6] The largest number of convictions for bribery in any year between 1937 and 1956 was about 5,600 (in 1947). Such small numbers suggest a huge gap between the actual level of bribery and the way the phenomenon was reflected in the statistics.[7]

It is not wholly clear why P. I. Minin's letter in particular drew the attention that it did, and eventually inspired a campaign against bribery. The letter was an idealistic attempt to mobilize the state's energy and resources to combat what he regarded as a grave crime and moral ill.[8] To be sure, Minin's was not the first communication sent to the party leadership containing such allegations; since 1943, the procuracy and the Ministry of Justice had been reporting an increase in cases of bribery. Certainly, the letter's heartfelt, anguished description of a cascade of bribery through all levels of society, even among Communist Party members, captured the interest of someone in the highest reaches of the party. Minin's fears that the existence of unfettered bribery could challenge the state's legitimacy most likely resonated. It was Andrei Zhdanov, a Central Committee Secretary and the person in charge of ideological matters in the Central Committee's Department of Agitation and Propaganda, who demanded that the heads of the legal agencies respond to Minin's charges.[9]

Doubtless, the author's position as a high-ranking party member in the Baku Military District caught Zhdanov's attention. The letter was signed ("With communist greetings—Minin"), unlike the innumerable anonymous denunciations that poured into central offices every month, and whose accuracy was very difficult for overstretched party control agencies to verify. The fact that Minin made allegations without mentioning names, describing instead a general phenomenon, may have assured Zhdanov that he was not motivated by a personal grudge—a common reason for false or exaggerated accusations of corruption (and other criminal activity) after the war.[10] Apparently, the letter also eventually caught the attention of Stalin, without whose approval such a campaign almost certainly could not have proceeded, based on our knowledge of the postwar Stalinist political system.[11]

The sometimes contentious internal discussions surrounding the "battle against bribery" that was launched in 1946 provide insight into many aspects of late Stalinist political and social life, including the causes for a burgeoning of informal practices; official attitudes toward bribery and the conflicts they produced among the leaders of the legal agencies; and hesitation by state officials to press forward with aggressive measures to address the problem. These discussions also shed light on how the postwar campaign was formulated and launched; how institutional interests shaped the parameters of the campaign; and the reasons for its disappointing results.[12]

The Central Committee put judicial and procuracy agencies in charge of researching the causes of bribery and creating the campaign against it. This made sense, since these agencies were deeply involved in the investigation and prosecution of all criminal cases. Yet bribery also infected the legal agencies in a disproportionate way. As we have seen, the courts could dispense an extremely valuable commodity in the late Stalin period—the mitigation of punishments, including freedom from prison. Individual procurators, judges, and other personnel in the legal agencies could profit handsomely from illicitly carrying out this service. The courts and procuracy were therefore at the center of anticorruption campaigns—in an uncomfortable, dual position both as key institutions for carrying out the campaign, and as one of its main targets.

"THE FINAL CARD OF THE COUNTERREVOLUTION!": FIGHTING BRIBERY DURING THE NEW ECONOMIC POLICY

This postwar campaign was not the first state-coordinated assault on bribery in the Soviet period. In the first years after the revolution, the Bolshevik impulse to cleanse society of bribery expressed itself in a major series of trials that peaked in 1922–1923. As Red Army soldiers battled the White armies during the Civil War (1917–1921), the Bolsheviks also vilified another enemy—the bribe-taking official. Launching a bitter campaign against bribery, official instructions used the martial language so typical of the times, declaring "the opening of a new front—the bribery front."[13] But progress was slow. In the fourth year of the revolution, Lenin was still decrying bribery as one of the "three main enemies" of the revolution (together with illiteracy and the high-handed "arrogance" of party officials).[14]

Indeed, bribery appears to have experienced something of a renaissance at the beginning of the 1920s. In the wake of the Red victory in the Civil War, the New Economic Policy (NEP), introduced in March of 1921, had legalized trade and established the right to lease state property for small-scale business activities. The financial relationships forged between political and civilian actors under NEP paved the way for illicit payments to officials. Leading Bolsheviks complained about lax ethics among party members. In the year 1921 alone, for example, seventeen thousand party members were expelled from the Communist Party for bribery, abuse of office, extortion, and other malfeasance.[15]

Concurrently, the revolutionary regime's assault on what they regarded as an increasingly disruptive crime gained steam, with the launch of the first major antibribery campaign. The NEP saw the appearance of the "Nepman," the proto-capitalist villain and potential corrupter of party officials. Most so-called Nepmen were private entrepreneurs who operated various types of small businesses. Others were intermediaries who brokered deals between state and private entities, especially in manufacturing, supply, and trade. They faced accusations that they had "bought off" state officials to guarantee their own profit from these arrangements.

The heated rhetoric that the party used to describe such deal-making after the revolution emphasized that bribery was being undertaken by class enemies who were eager to undercut socialism. An order issued by the GPU (the successor to the Cheka) on October 12, 1922, made it clear that, while widespread bribery under the Old Regime had been a "natural" element of that rotting system, such crimes in the Soviet era were abnormal, practiced only by those who intended to subvert the new socialist order.

> The level that bribery has reached in all areas of the Republic's economic life is well known to all of us. . . . We should understand very clearly that bribery has a deeply class character, that it is a manifestation

Figure 5.1. "Death to the Bribe!" (Artist unknown, ca. 1923). The poster reads:
"Who is the most threatening enemy of the Revolution right now?
  —The Bribe taker.
Who is the most dangerous, hidden thief of the people's economy right now?
  —The Bribe taker.
Who is the most dangerous counter-revolutionary right now?
  —The Bribe taker."
The Sergo Grigorian Collection

of petty-bourgeois, private-capital anarchy (*stikhiia*), directed against the very foundations of the existing [socialist] structure. . . . A bribe stands in [opposition to] the very essence of the proletarian state and is aimed against it. It is a tool intended to completely disorganize the state economic apparatus, to transfer the real material resources of the worker-peasant treasury into the "private" pockets of the capitalists.[16]

It was holdover capitalists, then, who were fully responsible for the ugly phenomenon of bribery, and they were using it as a tool to ruin the socialist economy and government.

In the summer of 1922, declaring that bribery was nearly omnipresent, while labeling its survival as an abomination, the Bolshevik state launched a loud, well-publicized campaign to uproot it.[17] On August 24, 1922, the Politburo established a commission to investigate party members who took bribes or were complicit in hiding the crime.[18] At the same time, the people's commissariats and other major agencies organized their own committees to fight it. GPU leaders pursued their mission with zeal, even recalling retired Cheka agents to assist.[19] As part of the investigations, the GPU created networks of secret informants to expose bribery in government offices. Originally active in uncovering political opponents of the regime, the police informants now had an expanded mission: to root out economic crime. Locked boxes for signed complaints were placed in highly visible locations in the offices of agencies under investigation, as well as in railway stations and other public places. (Anonymous denunciations were to be ignored.) The boxes were labeled with a sign that read, "Here accepting complaints about bribe takers in positions of authority in administration, the police, investigative agencies, and the department of communal housing."[20] The GPU tried to stir up anger towards corrupt officials in every agency of government.[21]

At the heart of the campaign was a wave of public trials that lasted from October 1922 to February 1923.[22] The People's Commissariat of Justice instructed all courts in the country to set aside other business between October 10 and November 10, 1922, and focus exclusively on bribery cases. The Commissariat of Justice was in charge of the trials, which were to be short and to the point. Trials were held in theaters, workers' clubs, and trade union auditoriums, and were said to be very well attended.[23] Those who were convicted were sent to the country's harshest labor camp, in Archangelsk. During the trials, the press took an active role, describing for the public the dramatic testimony playing out before them. The local press provided colorful sketches of bribe-taking officials to shame them and warn others. Newspapers published barbed slogans, emphasizing that bribery was a tool of the bourgeois enemies of the revolution, and that the defendants were vile creatures: "The bribe is the final card of the counterrevolution. It must be smashed no matter what!" And the pithy, rhyming couplet, addressed to a venal bureaucrat: "Tell me, you reptile/ How much [money] was given to you?" (*Ty, skazhi-ka, gadina, skol'ko tebe dadeno?*)[24] A typical broadsheet distributed in the city of Blagoveshchensk in 1923 urged people to report on suspected corruption in their workplaces: "Comrades and Citizens: Bribery is a great evil. It destroys our young state organism, undermining the authority of Soviet institutions. Although this evil was tolerated by the monarchy with indifference and silence, it cannot and must not exist in the country where power is in the hands of the workers and peasants."[25]

According to Soviet sources, bribery was dealt a serious blow by the campaigns of 1922–1923. In the words of one author, "In the main, bribery as a mass phenomenon was finished."[26] The legal press and the Great Soviet Encyclopedia repeated this conclusion.[27] Still, the published statistics were incomplete. There is no reason to think that instances of bribery were truly on the decline. Indeed, police data that were unpublished at the time show increasing numbers of arrests over the course of the 1920s; by 1926, arrests for bribery had again reached precampaign levels.[28]

The campaign against bribery in the 1920s—the regime's first—was an early indication that the party's efforts were directed at the wrong causes. The class-based assumptions of the regime during NEP—that capitalism was the root of all evil and, in this case, the root of all corruption—overlooked the fact that for centuries in Russia (as in other countries), bureaucrats with no ties to business had capitalized on making deals with (or "feeding from") local populations. The trials and anticorruption efforts in this period indicate that party leaders saw corruption as a "relic of capitalism" rather than as a problem rooted in power, scarcity, disrespect for law, long-standing bureaucratic practice, insufficient salaries, greed, and opportunity, with strong structural dimensions. This worldview made the efforts to wipe out traditional forms of reciprocity between citizens and officials all the more frantic and tinged with desperation. The assumption that bribery would disappear along with the final remnants of capitalism likely hampered efforts to control it, by focusing undue attention on the subversive activities of "class enemies."

THE VIEW FROM THE STATE: THE RISKS OF PERSISTENT CORRUPTION

There was a sharp increase in concern about bribery among Soviet law enforcement and party authorities at the national level beginning around mid-1943 and continuing the following year.[29] The regime's concern about malfeasance by its own officials in this period was rooted in several factors, including the postwar crises of production and distribution, an ideology that greatly valued the defense of "socialist property," and the special role of the Soviet functionary as the point of contact between regime and populace.

Lenin had denounced bribery as a vile crime as early as 1918. He had believed, however, that it was intrinsic to capitalism and would disappear as socialist construction progressed. This sentiment that the stain of bribery was "the birthmark of capitalism" survived the war.[30] More than thirty years after the revolution, legal officials and scholars still labeled crime—including bribery—one of "the most shameful relics of the capitalist past." According to the official narrative, although crime in the Soviet Union was dying out, criminality still lingered because, even though the exploiting classes had been eliminated, the bourgeois "environment" and its "ideology," attitudes, and habits, had not yet been fully eradicated. The notoriously corrupt mores of tsarist bureaucrats had purportedly infected Soviet functionaries across the revolutionary divide. Shadows of "alien" ways of thinking still lurked among some officials. In this view, bribery was a rare and fading remnant of the ideology of private capital, persisting only in a small number of the "most backward," self-serving Soviet citizens.[31] The demise of corruption would be inevitable as standards of living rose and as the "consciousness" and cultural level of the population rapidly developed.[32]

The stubborn persistence of bribery after the great victory over fascism presented an ideological dilemma that would underlie any efforts to combat it. A full generation after the revolution brought the Bolsheviks to power, the continued presence of bribery could be regarded as sullying the Soviet Union's carefully crafted image abroad. Any implication that bribery still played an important part in Soviet life would tarnish the image of the new superpower, so eager to act as an economic and moral model for the world. The newly socialist "people's democracies" of Eastern Europe, or the third world countries that the USSR was trying to persuade to join the socialist camp, could see corruption (as well as other crime and negative social phenomena) as a major flaw in the socialist promise. In the propaganda war with the United States and Western Europe, corruption could tarnish the Soviet Union's official representation of itself. In fact, the perception prevailed after the war that Soviet involvement on the European front had temporarily removed the carefully guarded walls between capitalism and Soviet socialism, and that dangerous ideological influences had infiltrated the USSR from the West. In the words of the historian Aleksandr Nekrich: "The war had broken down borders and torn down barriers which had so reliably protected the soul of the Soviet people from 'contamination' by capitalist infection."[33]

Indeed, concern arose that corruption in government offices would erode the legitimacy of state institutions and the party itself in the eyes of the population. Soviet legal scholars made a distinction in theory between the *state* and its *officials*. The law was a tool of the state; it did not serve to protect individuals from the state or its policies, since in a socialist society the state by definition served the interests of all Soviet people. Instead, the law guaranteed citizens protection against the wrongdoing of individual state officials.[34] As Soviet leaders came to understand, however, ordinary citizens did not always make such a distinction, often regarding the corrupt local official as the face of the state itself. Popular resentment toward individual bureaucrats could morph into a questioning of the state's authority. As Minin's letter emphasized, if the party were perceived to tolerate bribery it could create significant dissatisfaction among the population and a loss of faith in the institutions of Soviet power. Moreover, corruption threatened the regime's monopoly on distribution and production, and at the same time challenged the regime's image as a "paternal state" that adequately provided for every individual (an ideal that, Katherine Verdery has argued, formed the bedrock of communist regimes' legitimacy).[35]

In the immediate postwar years, the party leadership aspired to reclaim control over its own state functionaries. As John Barber and Mark Harrison point out, the state had allowed power in many areas of the wartime economy and administration to devolve to local authorities, who were presumably better in tune with the situation on the ground.[36] In the cities and villages of the Soviet Union, individuals maneuvered to elude or minimize arbitrary or repressive laws and other rules. The temporary loosening of strict party controls over the economy and social life raised expectations for liberalization after the sacrifices of wartime. But as party leaders launched reconstruction efforts, they tried to reassert their hold over the bureaucracy, the economy, the courts, and the social infrastructure, including the collective farms, housing, and the trade and distribution networks.[37] The party sought to regain both practical control over institutions and ideological control over the moral and political lives of officialdom; to reclaim and buttress both the political allegiance and the moral world of the "New Soviet Man." Fighting bribery was conceived of as an important step in this process.

The regime's ongoing obsession with halting the widespread theft of public property also contributed to heightened focus on bribery, since theft often occurred in tandem with liberally distributed bribes. Payoffs to auditors, inspectors, and managers by thieving employees, the investigators understood, often greased the wheels to facilitate, and then cover up, the pilfering of state resources. In the wake of the war, the wave of concern about "defending public property" reached new heights, accelerated by the famine of 1946–1947 and culminating with the June 4, 1947 decree on theft of state property. The defense of state property lay at the very center of Stalinist ideology. The 1936 Constitution of the USSR stated, "It is the duty of every citizen of the USSR to safeguard and strengthen public, socialist property as the sacred and inviolable foundation of the Soviet system." As a July 15, 1946 instruction (*prikaz*) of the USSR Ministry of Justice, Ministry of Internal Affairs, and Procuracy General warned, "Bribery in all its forms corrupts workers of the government and economic apparatuses, enables the theft and resale of socialist property and every kind of illegality."[38]

Internal procuracy reports in the late Stalin years went further, lamenting the insidious nature of graft. The reports noted that an officialdom susceptible to bribery is, in fact, a gateway to anarchy, as weak-willed, "bought-off" civil servants would suspend their vigilance, fail to uphold social norms, and open the door to crime and chaos. When the conscience of a morally weak official can be purchased, the consequences are grave. Bureaucrats on the take could even aid the enemies of Soviet power, weakening national security. In this vein, the procuracy accused local procurators and judges of underestimating the "social danger" of bribery.[39] First, officials become morally corrupted and second, the state's interests are "damaged" as the state is robbed. This language, which asserted that corruption was both dangerous to the social fabric *and* harmful to state interests, was pervasive in public discourse, as well as in internal discussions.[40]

A private letter written on March 8, 1948 by Procurator General of the USSR Safonov added his righteous indignation at the bribe-taking official. Safonov had been informed that a procurator by the name of Tolcheev had accepted three bribes totaling 20,000 rubles. Safonov's rhetoric is heated: "If the review of our cadres goes like this everywhere, I can only imagine how many of our people suffer, and how the state suffers, at the hands of all those who want to fill their own pockets and build up their own well-being at the expense of the sweat and blood of millions of working people."[41]

THE VIEW FROM THE LEGAL AGENCIES

From the regime's perspective, one of the simplest—yet most unsettling—of questions was, "How could it be that corruption still exists in the socialist USSR?" In his pointed 1946 letter, Minin did not offer any reasons why bribery was so widespread. But the party ideologists and legal specialists who were asked to respond to his keen observations certainly did.

As we have seen, ideologists offered one major cause for the persistence of corruption. They blamed undesirable social phenomena on the remnants of a prerevolutionary mentality that lingered in the minds of some people. Lazy and selfish "parasites" had this outlook. They refused honest labor; these few bribe-taking Soviet officials were greedy people who lusted for comfort and ease at the expense of the interests of the state and their fellow citizens. Press coverage of bribery, limited as it was, reflected this perspective, emphasizing that bosses chose cadres poorly.[42] They based their decisions not on the moral or political qualities of the person, but on friendships or unverified recommendations. Officially, then, a few bad apples clung to the discredited morality of the past. It is clear, however, that by the 1940s nearly all corrupt officials, many of whom were party members, indisputably were creations of the Soviet system.[43]

A very different package of explanations for the persistence of bribery was presented in certain internal reports and correspondence by legal officials themselves. When attempting to explain corruption among their own personnel, procuracy and judicial authorities typically focused on the issues of training and professional ethics, respect for the law, poor pay, difficult working conditions, and status. Abstract notions of "capitalist mentalities" were rarely raised in internal reports.

Cadres' low level of education was a major reason cited by legal officials for the persistence of official malfeasance. With incomplete education and flawed supervision on the job, officials failed to internalize the mores necessary to serve the Soviet public. To take the case of judges, more specifically, a number of factors were in play. At the end of the war, judges, like professionals in many branches of economy and administration, were inexperienced and poorly trained.[44] There was huge staff turnover during the war due to conscription, death, injury, illness, and relocation of personnel, as Minister of Justice N. M. Rychkov pointed out in a letter to Stalin. By war's end, the majority of judicial officials in place were new, often quite young, and without juridical training or a well-developed professional ethic.[45] In many places, "it was necessary to build the entire judicial apparatus all over again from scratch." This was the case in Ukraine, Belorussia, Lithuania, Latvia, Estonia, Moldavia, Karelo-Finlandia, and in the formerly occupied parts of the Russian Republic. As late as 1948, barely 10 percent of judges had higher legal education.[46] A resolution of the Central Committee, "On Expanding and Improving Juridical Education in the Country," issued on October 5, 1946, called for training a new cohort of legal specialists, who should be given middle or higher legal education.[47] A number of schools began offering courses to train new judges and to retrain sitting ones.

In August 1948, Procurator General Safonov echoed these concerns about untrained officials in a letter to Molotov. He said that the poor qualifications of procuracy investigators was one reason why many cases brought by investigators lacked viable evidence and were eventually dismissed or resulted in acquittals.[48] Safonov noted that the drop in qualifications was in large part due to the mass conscription of senior investigators during the war: "They had to be replaced by youths, who have insufficient experience." "In fact, the overwhelming majority" were trained with nothing more than a three-month course in the law. In August 1948, he wrote, 75 percent of the 7,855 investigators had less than three years' experience, and 35 percent had served less than one year. He compared the situation in the Soviet Union unfavorably not only with tsarist Russia, but with the United States, France, Spain, Holland, Latvia, and even Brazil.

Officials' pay remained very low during and after the war, making them more amenable to accepting under-the-table payments.[49] A deputy minister of justice reported that the average pay of judges in the city of Moscow was only about 960 rubles per month. Court secretaries received just 400–600 rubles per month. These low salaries were all the more insufficient considering the high cost of living in Moscow.[50] Salaries were not high enough to attract and keep highly trained personnel. According to urgent letters by the minister of justice to Stalin, Shvernik, and Molotov throughout 1948, stagnant salaries were contributing to the tremendous turnover of judges: nearly one of every five judges left the judiciary in 1947. Many were leaving provincial courts and procuracy agencies for better-paid positions in industrial administrations and other bureaucracies. At the end of 1948, the minister of justice wrote to Stalin asking that salaries for court employees be raised by an average of 47 percent.[51] Requests for pay raises continued throughout the late Stalin period.

Legal officials brought attention to a related factor leading to a weak professional ethos among judges and procurators: the perception that their professional status was low.[52] One proposed solution was to give legal professionals awards for long service, which would bring them respect from the population (and, one assumes, greater self-respect). Between 1945 and 1948, the procuracy and Ministry of Justice repeatedly recommended that awards and medals be given to judicial and procuracy employees for meritorious long-term service. These medals would be based on those awarded to officers in the military and in the NKVD. Procuracy employees who had served for ten years would receive a medal called "For Valor in Labor"; for twenty years of service employees would be given the "Order of the Laboring Red Banner";

and for twenty-five years, they would be awarded the "Order of Lenin." The heads of the legal agencies also suggested introducing uniforms for the employees.[53] As early as 1945, detailed descriptions of judges' proposed uniforms were drawn up.[54] These gestures were intended to keep trained employees on the job and instill a sense of professionalism at a time when concerns about combating corruption became paramount.[55] The introduction of named decorations and special attire was an inexpensive way of compensating cadres at a time when the state was not willing to raise their salaries. These proposals can be thought of as anticorruption measures on the cheap.

A procuracy commission created to investigate why its employees accepted illegal gifts also explored why the phenomenon persisted. Although the commission's report was produced in 1947–1948, its conclusions can be applied to the entire late Stalin period. And while the commission focused on bribery inside the procuracy itself, its observations are also relevant for understanding the causes of corruption among other state employees. The commission noted that procuracy employees frequently had minimal ethical training. New staff (and not only the new) too often failed to understand the concept of conflict of interest, which would prohibit accepting "gifts" from petitioners.[56] Indeed, despite the government's admonishment to civil servants to use their offices only to serve the public good, many people saw no clear-cut distinction between public and private life. To the giver, rewarding a public official for a job well done could be seen as the equivalent of giving a gift to a friend. For their part, many officials expected such tokens of gratitude and saw no problem in accepting them. There simply was no hard and fast line between the *official* and the *office*. The commission report argued that such misconceptions should be countered, in part, by the publication of articles dedicated to reinforcing notions of professional integrity in the procuracy's monthly journal, *Sotsialisticheskaia zakonnost'* (*Socialist Legality*). Articles were to emphasize such simple things as employees' obligation to recuse themselves from cases involving friends or family.

Sounding another theme in common with the judiciary reports, the procuracy commission argued that professional status was lacking. Procuracy employees, the commission argued, were underpaid not only in an absolute sense, but also relative to other professionals. As a result, turnover continued after the war, especially among those with higher education, as Procurator General Safonov had noted in a letter to

E. E. Andreev at the Central Committee's Department of Administrative Organs.[57] Especially in light of legal agencies' "high ideological and political level and service to the interests of the people and the state," the commission argued, improvements must be made to the "intolerable" material conditions of procuracy personnel. The lack of prestige, reflected in low pay and the absence of perks, eased officials' decisions to supplement their income illegally. Local procurators often "ended up in direct material dependence on local traders and cooperative organizations, as a result of which the ground is laid for procuracy employees to mingle with the employees of these organizations." Especially in the provinces, such relationships were based on "mutual concessions and favors."[58] In these murky circumstances, "hustlers" operating in the shadows of the official economy did favors for law enforcement officials, swapping food or scarce manufactures (and the occasional cash payment) for assistance solving legal problems.

A related point made by the procuracy commission was arguably the most critical. The commission noted that the state could certainly increase penalties, strengthen procedures, and shame wrongdoers in the press and in trials. But as long as segments of the Soviet population (including officialdom) felt aggrieved and lacking in money, food, and access to justice, poorly paid officials would continue to solicit illegal payments for their services, and the population would continue to pay. Indeed, this combination of factors—underpaid officials who lacked status; shortages; lax, inconsistent, and overwhelmed law enforcement; an undeveloped legal consciousness; popular desperation and enormous, unmet demand; and traditions of reciprocity—was a recipe for corruption in many areas of Soviet life.

It was against this backdrop of wartime and postwar crises in the spring of 1946 that Minin wrote his impassioned letter to Stalin demanding action against the types of bribery he saw all around him. And as we have seen, Minin's distressed observations were essentially confirmed in the reports of law enforcement.

"ORDINARY AND EVERYDAY"

In his letter to Stalin deploring the highly corrosive effects of the widespread bribery he witnessed, Minin had argued that only a determined national campaign, including strict new laws, could begin "to uproot bribery and everything connected with it." He insisted that the party must deploy all possible resources of government action and public opinion (*obshchestvennost'*) in the crackdown. Minin believed that the cornerstone of the battle should be either a public resolution of the Council of Ministers or a severe new edict (ukaz) of the Supreme Soviet.

To be sure, law enforcement faced a number of challenges in prosecuting bribery. A bribe leaves no obvious trace. There was usually no missing stock or products, no falsified account books or empty cashier's drawers. Unless one of the parties turned in the other, the arrangement nearly always remained hidden.[59] Generally, the authorities discovered the existence of such transactions only when participants became dissatisfied with the deal that had been struck, feeling that they had been "deceived" or that "their money vanished in vain." One procuracy document marveled over the bold protestations of bribe givers if they did not receive what they had expected: "Without fearing threat of punishment for offering a bribe, they [bribe givers] informed various organizations and demanded the return of their money."[60] In other cases, one of the actors panicked or experienced a sudden twinge of conscience. Sources agree that the proportion of bribes that were somehow discovered *and* reported to the authorities *and* prosecuted reflected only the very tip of the iceberg. As is the case in all societies, most Soviet bribe givers and takers led quiet lives, undiscovered and unpunished.

Minin's observations caused a major stir with at least one prominent party leader. On May 15, 1946, Andrei Zhdanov forwarded copies of Minin's letter to the USSR Ministry of Justice and the USSR Supreme Court. Zhdanov demanded immediate action from the country's most important legal agencies. In his capacity as a Central Committee Secretary, he requested that the head of each agency respond to Minin's letter, including "their opinion and evaluation of the situation concerning bribery."[61] The fact that it was Zhdanov who made the request made it clear that the initiative came from the highest reaches of the party, not from the legal agencies themselves.[62]

The legal agencies jumped to reply to Zhdanov's request. Yet, what is most remarkable about their responses is that they became more and more tepid with time. Originally, they endorsed Minin's pointed allegations, affirming that bribery was a major problem at all levels in Soviet society and in the party itself, one that needed immediate and serious attention—including strong new laws. Ultimately, however, for several reasons, they (together with the Central Committee) chose not to acknowledge the severity of the problem, either publicly or in available private correspondence, downplaying its effects and refusing to take serious action.

Minister of Justice Rychkov wrote to Zhdanov with his first reaction to Minin's stinging observations on May 23, 1946.[63] Rychkov concluded that Minin was right, for the most part. Although "the author of the letter, perhaps, generalizes about the evidence of bribery too much," Rychkov still confirmed that "lately, especially during the war, it [bribery] has acquired a widespread character." He conceded, "It is also doubtless the case that the struggle against it has been undertaken with extreme hesitancy." In a separate letter to Central Committee Secretary N. S. Patolichev, Rychkov echoed several of Minin's laments, agreeing that Minin was "completely correct." Rychkov stated that "in many organizations, primarily those connected with serving the population and with supply (railways, housing organs, apartment administration, bases for supplying food and manufactured goods, etc.), bribery has become an almost ordinary, everyday phenomenon."[64]

Such explicit language describing bribery as "ordinary" and "everyday" is startling indeed. Rychkov went further, candidly implicating the employees of the legal system itself: "Even the organs of the court, the procuracy, and the police are frequently infected with bribery." Minin's metaphor of corruption as a contagious disease is repeated here, conveying how bribery "infects" the very agencies that are responsible for eradicating it. Indeed, bribery was described by legal officials and party watchdogs as symptomatic of a perilous variety of moral rot which, like other forms of vice, was seen as highly contagious. Corrupt officials could contaminate those with weak characters, luring them into criminal activity.

Rychkov argues that to fight bribery it is also necessary "to overcome party members' conciliatory attitude to this disgraceful phenomenon."[65] Many party members, made aware of cases of bribery, remain silent rather than report the crime to the authorities.[66] According to Rychkov, the party, the Komsomol, and the trade unions have failed to do the educational work necessary to change this tolerant approach. There are even instances when leading party workers leap to the defense of bribe-taking colleagues. "We have to finish off this tolerant attitude towards bribery and the passivity of party organizations and party members in the struggle against bribery." To combat toleration of the practice among party members, Minister of Justice Rychkov called on the Central Committee to issue a decree on "the struggle with bribery," a draft of which he appended. He further argued that one reason for pervasive bribery during and after the war was that the courts were not punishing people severely enough, if at all. Rychkov had been arguing for several years that too many judges had done a poor job, failing to imprison a significant proportion of those convicted.[67]

And indeed, a revealing feature of the postwar prosecutions was the discrepancy in punishments for bribe takers versus bribe givers. As chapter 3 noted, Ministry of Justice statistics show that average punishments for bribe givers became significantly lighter during the war, and that those who *offered* bribes were punished significantly less severely than those who *accepted* bribes, even though the law mandated that bribe givers be punished more severely.[68] According to several sources, bribe givers and intermediaries often were not charged at all, even if prosecuting authorities knew their identities.[69] It is possible to conclude that judges were sympathetic to the plight of ordinary people forced to give illicit payments during the war and in its wake. Judges might have often believed either that instances of bribe giving simply did not rise to the level of a crime, or that the givers could be excused considering their dire circumstances.

Nevertheless, in a bit of institutional defensiveness that anticipates important conflicts over the fate of the campaign, Minister of Justice Rychkov attempted to deflect blame from the judiciary wherever possible. Instead, he laid the bulk of the responsibility at the feet of police and procuracy investigators for their failure to find guilty parties and properly investigate their crimes. While acknowledging the possible role of lenient sentencing, Rychkov took every opportunity to highlight the shortcomings of procurators and police in the struggle. "The amount of evidence that is uncovered about bribery is insignificant . . . *The organs of the procuracy and police wage the struggle against these crimes very weakly*" (emphasis in original). Procuracy investigators gathered evidence haphazardly, and the police failed to follow up on information supplied by informants and to make arrests.[70] While Rychkov conceded the difficulty of exposing guilty parties in cases of bribery, he insisted that criminals could be tracked down if investigations (by the procuracy) were carried out with care, aided by good undercover work (by the police). He judged the efforts of the procuracy since the beginning of 1945 to have been ineffective. "There is no noticeable strengthening in the struggle against bribery" and "this creates an atmosphere of impunity" among those who engage in it.[71]

WEAKENING THE CAMPAIGN'S LANGUAGE

Minister of Justice Rychkov's response makes it clear that the legal agencies were scrambling both to protect their institutional interests and to defend the prestige of the party and the state, even if these goals conflicted with a serious antibribery campaign.[72] These documents reveal a growing divergence between the procuracy and Ministry of Justice's pointed *private* discussions about the causes and extent of bribery (mentioned above), and the *official language* they eventually used in public statements. Many of the leadership's candid, private observations— that local procurators and judges were overly tolerant of graft, especially in their own ranks; that some lacked a keen sense of ethics and professionalism; and that they were underpaid and tempted to make deals—were certainly correct. It is important to note, however, that such observations did not become part of the vocabulary of the antibribery effort. Instead, the language that framed the campaign was watered down, falling victim to self-censorship and inter-agency competition.

On July 6, 1946, Minister of Justice Rychkov's office forwarded drafts of several documents outlining a proposed campaign against bribery to the office of Procurator General K. P. Gorshenin. These drafts already had weakened the stinging language of earlier correspondence. The procuracy's response to the documents took the form of quite substantial editing that significantly muted their thrust. An examination of some of these redactions enables us to reconstruct the Procuracy and Justice leaders' objections to certain wording. A comparison of the edited versions with the originals indicates the approach that these leaders did— and did not—want to take toward the highly sensitive questions surrounding the problem of bribery.

One of the documents that the Ministry of Justice sent to the procuracy for review was a draft Central Committee resolution, entitled "On the Struggle with Bribery," dated July 4, 1946. This version contains major shifts in content and emphasis from earlier correspondence between the Ministry of Justice and the Central Committee. The draft begins: "Recently, numerous reports and information from the population about the growth of bribery have poured into the Central Committee. Exploiting the difficulties of wartime and the postwar period, criminal and morally unstable elements in the state apparatus have taken the path of accepting and extorting bribes." In its correspondence, then, the Ministry of Justice had already shifted away from the notion that bribery had become an "almost ordinary, everyday phenomenon" (as it had written in the letter to Zhdanov in May). The Ministry now asserted that it was only the "morally unstable and criminal elements" who took bribes.[73]

The procuracy leadership revised the harsh language in the formative documents of the antibribery campaign even further. Rychkov's original letter to the Central Committee stated that bribery "corrupts the state apparatus, paralyzes its normal work, and prepares the soil for every possible kind of illegality." The procuracy's editing dropped this sweeping language, instead blaming just a few bad apples, stating that "certain employees in the state and economic apparatuses" were corrupt. The explosive statement that bribery had "paralyzed" the operations of government was also excised. Elsewhere, the procuracy editors excised the original phrase "The number of people charged with accepting and offering bribes is insignificant," which would have been an affront to the procuracy's own efforts, while highlighting that only a small fraction of instances of bribery were ever discovered. Redactions also minimized the scope of the phenomenon by changing the incendiary assertion that bribery had reached "epidemic" proportions to the banal statement that bribery is "alien by nature to the Soviet government." In another significant change, the version edited by the procuracy implicated lower-level employees as the main culprits, thereby removing the accent on party members or even "employees in position of authority."[74] The final version acknowledged, but no longer emphasized, that party members were enabling bribery—but now it was mostly through their passive tolerance rather than their active participation.

And perhaps most striking of all, the final version of the instruction launching the campaign conveniently eliminates any reference to cor-

ruption *inside* the legal agencies themselves. Although both the Ministry of Justice and the procuracy had initially acknowledged that bribery had "infected" their own personnel, no mention of this corruption
was made in the final instruction. Rather, the instruction noted that
bribery was widespread "especially on transport, [and] in trade, supply,
and distribution organizations," omitting any mention of the procuracy, the police, and the courts.

In these evolving versions of the formative document of the campaign,
then, one sees two competing narratives about the causes and extent of
bribery during the postwar years. In the original narrative, which is
much more accurate and blunt, bribery is described as a significant—if
frequently ignored or tolerated—problem that deeply affects state administration and the economy. The party is fully implicated, as are the
legal agencies themselves. In the final, sanitized version, bribery is not
seen to be systemic; rather, it is a crime committed by individual rogue
officials who, in relatively rare instances, have become corrupted. Party
members are, at worst, passive observers, not participants. The legal
agencies, far from being "contaminated" with bribery, are not mentioned at all. After all this editing, the final version implies that while
Minin's original frustrated and despondent letter of complaint may
have identified an important, albeit isolated, phenomenon, he greatly
exaggerated its extent and its threat to the postwar Soviet world and
the party's legitimacy.

TO GO PUBLIC?

The impulse among many political actors to downplay—indeed to
cover up—the seriousness of postwar corruption is further revealed in
the discussion of whether or not to issue a public decree (ukaz) calling
for an intensified battle against bribery. The internal debate within the
party and the legal agencies over how to manage the problem also included a discussion about the extent to which the issue should be aired
publicly. A public decree would have been issued outside the regular
criminal code, but it would have the force of law and would be widely
distributed. Such a decree demanding tougher penalties, stronger enforcement, and greater media attention to the crime would have been
published in national and local newspapers, and would have brought
much greater attention to the campaign against graft.

A public decree would also have pressured procurators to demand longer sentences for bribery (beyond what the criminal code called for), and forced judges to assign them.[75] The decree would have sounded a warning about the growing threat of officials' corrupt interactions with ordinary people. A draft version of just such a public decree, dated July 4, 1946 (and likely produced by the Ministry of Internal Affairs), was circulated to the minister of justice and the chairman of the Supreme Court. This draft provided for a significant increase in penalties for the receipt and rendering of bribes. For the acceptance of a bribe by any person in a position of authority (*dolzhnostnoe litso*) it called for a five-year minimum prison term and the confiscation of property. In particularly aggravating circumstances, the receipt of bribes could be punished by execution before a firing squad. Offering bribes or acting as an intermediary would result in a term of no fewer than three years plus the confiscation of property. This represented a significant strengthening of punishments for bribe giving, with the previous minimum prison term of six months (and a two-year maximum) increased to a three- to five-year minimum term.[76]

Ultimately, however, the legal agencies opposed the publication of a special decree toughening penalties. The Ministry of Justice argued that a new law was not necessary.[77] The criminal code was strong enough, Rychkov argued, for it stipulated that any person who accepted a bribe would be punished with at least two years in prison. If an official of the state were involved or if extortion took place, the sentence could be increased to ten years with confiscation of property.[78] In Rychkov's opinion, the criminal code's current punishments were severe enough (although he provided no indication of the reasoning behind his conclusion).

The Supreme Court's response to Minin's letter offered a different series of objections to the proposal to issue a public decree. Addressed to Zhdanov at the Central Committee, the memorandum was written by Ivan T. Goliakov, the chair of the Supreme Court. Like the heads of the procuracy and the Justice Ministry, Goliakov argued that the current criminal statutes were sufficient for dealing with the bribery wave. The police, procuracy, and courts simply needed to enforce the present laws "correctly, reasonably, and with consequences."[79]

Goliakov offered a robust, if defensive and largely unconvincing, denial of Minin's picture of pervasive corruption. According to Justice Goliakov, the war had inspired among most people "a great upsurge of patriotism, directed toward overcoming obstacles and defeating the enemy." At the same time, unfortunately, the war had "corrupted the unstable and mercenary elements" of the population. In Goliakov's view, Minin had overstated the problem, painting the situation "with overly gloomy colors, considering bribery in our time to be an extremely widespread phenomenon that practically takes the form of a natural disaster." He found Minin's claim that "everyone takes bribes" to be exaggerated and not credible. Of course, Minin had never alleged that "everyone takes bribes." Rather, he much more persuasively argued that the problem was pervasive enough to corrupt many institutions and economic agencies and to raise "legitimate grievances in Soviet society." Unchecked bribery, Minin had argued, could threaten the authority of the regime in the eyes of the population.

Beyond the assertion that Minin had distorted the real situation, Supreme Court Chairman Goliakov introduced a new argument against the issuance of a decree to kick off a national drive against bribery. Minin's allegations, he writes, amount to "slander directed against Soviet society." A public decree would be embarrassing—and even harmful—to the regime. "The publication and wide promulgation of such a law could create a false, distorted picture, both in our country and especially abroad, about the moral character of Soviet society, and could be used by hostile elements with anti-Soviet aims." Goliakov worried about the possibility of dangerous negative reactions both of Soviet citizens and of "hostile elements" outside the borders of the USSR.

Goliakov's objection to a public decree is further confirmation that the existence of bribery posed an ideological problem for the regime. According to Soviet ideology, corruption was a defining characteristic of *capitalism* and *fascism*. A public decree decrying the stubborn persistence of bribery and calling for an intensive war against it would amount to an admission that thirty years after the revolution, socialism had not penetrated as deeply into the consciousness and "moral character" of the Soviet people as the regime claimed. The existence of widespread graft after the noble war that destroyed Nazism contradicted the regime's principles.[80] Indeed, with the regime having declared bribery all but extinct in the 1930s, a public lament about the return of bribery could seem like a major setback. Goliakov pressed for secrecy. Stalin (and other party leaders) likely agreed.

Among party leaders, there was a great deal of sensitivity about the standing of the USSR in the world and about the reputation of the Soviet experiment abroad. For example, Goliakov wrote to the Central Committee on July 3, 1945 that the condition of the building housing the offices of the Supreme Court was so decrepit and cramped that it was awkward when delegations of foreign jurists visited the court. As he put it, "One must take into account that the Soviet Union's ever-strengthening international ties, which attract foreign interest in all our activities, including our judicial activities, can encourage foreign legal activists and scholars to visit the Supreme Court building in Moscow. Considering the condition of the Supreme Court [building] at present, such visits can make an extremely unpleasant impression and damage the prestige of the Soviet Union abroad."[81] Considering itself an example to the world, the regime did not want foreigners, either in Eastern Europe or in the "new democracies" undergoing decolonization in the third world, to associate the Soviet government with corruption. After the war, the Soviet social, economic, and political systems were being exported wholesale to Eastern Europe. Would these populations assume that corruption would also be exported? Historians have suggested that both the 1945 amnesty of Gulag prisoners and the 1947 decree abolishing the death penalty were carried out in part to impress international audiences.[82] A system in which the party and the protectors of justice seem to accept bribes from a demoralized society (or that failed to prosecute bribe-taking officials) could be attacked by anti-Soviet propagandists in the West.

Ultimately, such reasoning won the day. Neither a public decree nor a resolution of the Council of Ministers was ever published. Rather, an *internal* and *secret* instruction (prikaz) was issued jointly by the Ministry of Justice, the procuracy, and the Ministry of Internal Affairs. This instruction was accompanied by an internal and secret resolution (*postanovlenie*) of the Central Committee.[83]

Moreover, the press "campaign" called for by party and legal authorities turned out to be quite muted. A key theme in discussions was that the press must "mobilize society" to fight bribery. The legal agencies called for placing articles in newspapers about bribery trials and the harsh sentences that resulted. Yet despite the promises of a major press campaign, in the end the results were rather minimal.[84] According to a Ministry of Justice complaint, only twenty-three articles about bribery trials appeared in newspapers throughout the country during the second half of 1946. A review of the press indicates that after an initial upsurge in the number of articles in central newspapers in the final six months of 1946, the volume quickly tapered off. Likely with the goal of protecting the country's international reputation, the press published very few articles mentioning bribery cases during the period between 1945 and 1953, either in the regular newspapers or in the specialized legal journals.[85] Moreover, after 1946 the type of cartoons mocking the bribe-taking bureaucrat disappeared from the pages of popular magazines like Krokodil.[86]

"FOR A FREE BOTTLE OF ALCOHOL": NEW LIFE FOR THE CAMPAIGN?

The bureaucratic logjam that hindered the 1946 initiatives was temporarily broken by the shocking arrests of dozens of high court and regional judges (and other judicial employees) for bribery in 1948 (to be explored in detail in chapter 8). This scandal resulted in a quick, if temporary, about face, inspiring a new push to fortify punishments for bribery. Proposing stiffer penalties, Procurator General Safonov and the new Minister of Justice Gorshenin both wrote to Stalin on May 14, 1948, reversing their earlier position that bribery in the country was not a serious problem. Safonov wrote, "The significant spread of bribery demands a strengthening of the struggle against these crimes, especially in instances of bribery committed by persons in a position of authority (judges, procurators, employees of the Ministry of Internal Affairs, employees of local Soviet organs, etc.)." He called for an all-Union law that would assure consistency in legislation in the various republics, which assigned widely divergent sentences. Moreover, he compared the relatively weak penalties for bribery—only one year in prison in certain circumstances—with the mandatory minimum sentence of seven years of prison for petty theft of state property.[87] As Gorshenin put it: "Despite the widespread existence of a phenomenon such as bribery that is dangerous and impermissible in the Soviet state, the struggle with it is waged extremely weakly."[88] One of the reasons, he wrote, was that penalties were too soft. In response, the procuracy and Ministry of

Justice drafted a decree that called for the acceptance of bribes to be punishable by six to ten years in prison in normal circumstances, and ten to fifteen years in aggravating circumstances (bribery by persons in positions of authority, or by persons who committed the crime more than once or had prior convictions for bribery). Bribe givers were to receive terms in a labor camp of two to five years, or between five and ten years for repeat offenders.[89]

Yet the 1948 proposal to raise penalties was tabled by the Bureau of the Council of Ministers on May 12, 1949. The legal expert who reviewed the proposal stated in his decision that it should be set aside because a commission was drafting a new criminal code which, it was presumed, would include new punishments.[90] This pattern would later repeat itself; a major, long-discussed revision of the criminal code which again proposed raising penalties for bribery was drafted in 1952, but this project also was not carried through to fruition before Stalin's death.[91] There were several attempts to introduce stronger sentences into the criminal code in the late Stalin period, but no changes to the law were made.

Just as stronger punishments for bribery were not adopted, so the working conditions of judges, procurators, and investigators, which contributed to under-the-table deal-making in the legal agencies, failed to improve. Anecdotal evidence continued to pour into Moscow about very difficult conditions outside the city. An anonymous letter addressed to the chair of the Council of Ministers and the Central Committee, from a person who identified himself only as a rural procuracy employee, provides graphic evidence that poor pay made investigators vulnerable to bribes.[92] The letter complained that even though poorly educated employees of the police forces had received salary increases two years earlier, the procuracy employees in the region languished with inadequate income. This situation, the author claimed, leads to the undermining of local justice. It also incites turnover in the procuracy, as its employees can find higher paying positions in the MVD, the local soviets, and other agencies.

> What kind of procurator am I if I receive less [pay] than everyone and I am [financially] dependent on everyone? It is no accident that in the organs of the procuracy and courts very qualified jurists themselves still end up on the defendants' bench [in court, charged with] taking bribes, since this is caused by the material side [of life]. It is no accident

that serious criminals sometimes remain unpunished in the organs of justice, because this material side has an influence on them.

To fight this influence, he asks for salaries of employees of the procuracy and courts to be brought even with employees of the police. The government and the honest people "will win" and "only the criminal element will lose." Safonov added a brief note to this anonymous letter, writing that he "agreed in principle" with its contents.

Indeed, in an extraordinary plea in July 1949, Safonov wrote to Stalin urging him to approve increased salaries for procuracy employees. Especially outside the big cities, these employees were mostly young, poorly qualified, and tempted to accept illicit gifts. "The organs of the procuracy can only be of really great use to the government when they are truly independent of local influences and when they have authority and cannot be bought off (*nepodkuplennyi*)."[93] Safonov went on: "It is worth keeping in mind that criminal elements, with the goal of getting themselves out of legal trouble . . . try to find the weak link in the apparatus and buy off certain unstable employees. . . . Sometimes they succeed, and this influences the authority of the procuracy in the most pernicious way." Safonov noted that, "In many instances procurators lose their authority and independence, profiting from some kind of 'tip' from various farmers and from collective farms, in the form of food that they can purchase at low prices, or some free hay-making land, or someone cuts them some hay for their personal cattle, etc." "Finding politically and morally steady cadres, who are responsive to all necessary demands, meets serious difficulties as a result of the low levels of their salaries compared to that of many other specialties, including ordinary defense lawyers."[94] Thanks to the inadequate pay, many qualified people left the ranks of the procuracy between 1946 and 1948; nearly a quarter of procuracy employees in the country left their jobs in 1948 alone.

In a personal and quite remarkable note written to Beria the same day as this letter to Stalin (July 2, 1949), Safonov expressed himself even more bluntly. Asking Beria to back his request to increase salaries of procuracy employees, Safonov pleaded: "I am asking you urgently to support this request, Lavrentii Pavlovich. The possibility of fortifying the procuracy's personnel with honorable employees depends on the positive resolution of this question. [Cadres must be] able to understand their work in a politically correct way, to resist local influences and various temptations, such as a free bottle of alcohol (*spirt*) or discounted food purchased at the collective farm."[95] In sum, the nation's lead prosecutor was writing to Stalin and Beria to boldly state that the country's rank-and-file legal officials could too often be easily bribed with a bottle of alcohol or some cheap food.

It was not only procuracy officials who highlighted the risks of insufficient salaries. Judicial authorities were still requesting higher salaries for local judges as late as 1952, an indication that at least one root cause of bribery, in their view, had not been addressed. Judges and other court employees continued to link their own low pay, insufficient training and status, and poor education (the scourge of local administration for centuries, of course) with the problem of bribery. An anonymous July 10, 1952 letter to Molotov, signed "a people's judge from a rural area in the Urals," decried the poor prestige, grossly inadequate salaries, and highly challenging material situation of employees of the judicial administration.[96] The judge assures Molotov that he is not motivated simply by a desire to improve his own living standards, but by a concern about the corrupting influence of judges' low pay. He arrives at his central point: why it is so harmful for judges to be paid so poorly? He addresses Molotov: "Do not think, Viacheslav Mikhailovich, that the author of this letter is a careerist or a narrow-minded pedant. I am informing you of the facts, and such facts pertain not only to me. In general, the material support of judges is very low and it raises questions about reviewing it from the perspective of preserving judges' independence, to eliminate any temptation stemming from insufficient material support." In other words, judges feel pressed to take advantage of every opportunity to supplement their miserly salaries, even if it compromises their integrity.

To be sure, the legal agencies also tried to use campaigns against corruption—and the stinging descriptions of instances of graft among its own employees—as an opportunity to lobby for greater pay and heightened status. And throughout the period, procuracy and justice officials continued to complain about a lack of respect afforded them and their work.[97]

"COMPLETELY PASSIVE": CAMPAIGNS AND REALITY

Ultimately, the campaign to eradicate bribery achieved very little in the opinion of those who argued that it corrupted institutions, tarnished the authority of the law enforcement and other important institutions of Soviet power, and had a detrimental impact on the everyday lives of the Soviet citizens who had sacrificed so much during the war. The campaign's weaknesses—and the reasons for them—highlight significant features of the late Stalinist state and its interactions with a society struggling to recover from the wartime catastrophe.[98]

The antibribery campaigns of postwar Stalinism do seem to have had certain modest short-term results.[99] According to Ministry of Justice statistics, judges did assign marginally more severe punishments to people convicted of bribery after the prikaz (instruction) was issued in 1946 than previously. The proportion of people sentenced to prison for accepting bribes rose from 74 percent in 1946 to 88 percent in 1947. The proportion of those convicted for *giving* bribes who were sentenced to prison rose slightly from 67 percent in 1946 to 75 percent in 1947.[100] Nevertheless, in 1947 nearly a quarter of people convicted of rendering a bribe received no jail time.

Party agencies expressed disappointment at the outcome of the campaign. A February 14, 1947 letter signed by Nikitin, the deputy of the Central Committee's Cadres Administration, alleged that neither the minister of justice nor the procurator general had taken the prikaz seriously enough; they had failed to design and carry out the necessary measures. Worst of all, judges and procurators were still taking bribes, and they were not seriously disciplined.[101] "Large quantities" of denunciations claiming knowledge of bribery in judicial and procuracy agencies, as well as in numerous other organizations and enterprises, still poured in.

Internal Ministry of Justice data indicate that relatively small numbers of people were arrested for bribery throughout the late Stalin years. Statistics show a rise in the total number of convictions for bribery in 1946 and 1947, followed by a gradual decline beginning in 1948. In the long run, the campaign did not result in increased convictions.[102] This trend followed the general pattern of Soviet campaigns—a sharp initial upsurge in arrests and convictions, followed by a decline back to, or even below, the initial levels.

Within two years of its launch, the campaign had clearly deflated. By October 1950 a procuracy report noted that "procuracy agencies have weakened the attention they direct toward working on the struggle against bribery, this most serious form of crime."[103] Eighty-two people were charged with giving or receiving bribes in the city of Moscow in the first half of 1950. Yet procurators in seven of the city's regions brought no charges whatsoever. In the second half of the same year, procurators in eight of Moscow's regions pursued no cases of bribery.[104] In the entire year 1951, procuracy investigators in Moscow oblast' sent only thirty-one cases of bribe taking, involving a total of fifty people, to the courts.[105] The total number of people charged with offering bribes was only thirty-five.[106]

Internal correspondence shows that legal authorities were well aware that these official statistics did not reflect real rates of crime. For its part, the procuracy did not claim that this decline in convictions illustrated the effectiveness of the antibribery measures, or that it reflected some inevitable decline in criminality as Soviet society progressed toward a bright communist future. To the contrary, their reports indicated that bribery continued to be pervasive but was still rarely detected or prosecuted. The procurator general wrote in April 1952, "The reduction in the number of fully investigated cases and the [small] quantity of persons charged in bribery cases is explained to a significant degree by the fact that the struggle against this crime by the agencies of the procuracy is still insufficient."[107] There were still entire Soviet republics where bribery went essentially unnoticed, uninvestigated and unpunished. In the Armenian Republic, for example, prosecutors brought only four cases of bribe taking in all of 1952; only ten cases were brought for offering bribes.[108]

In a report later in 1952, Aleksandrov, the chief of the Investigation Administration of the USSR Procuracy, expressed dismay that the numbers of cases of bribery brought by the procuracy had dropped so sharply over the years.[109] Aleksandrov asked, "Do these data reflect the state of criminality? Is this crime really declining, and is substantiated evidence of bribery rare?" He answers his own question: "Cases that have been investigated show that there is evidence of bribery in a great variety of organizations, institutions, and enterprises." "In many cases, skilled and persistent scrutiny has uncovered a[n] organized system of bribery," especially in trade, food supply, requisitioning, and financial organizations. "Similar evidence testifies to the fact that the comparatively rare prosecution of bribery cases is explained not because cases of bribery are infrequent, but because they are rarely uncovered, thanks to a struggle against bribery that is clearly unsatisfactory."

Aleksandrov here makes a highly damning statement: "In this regard, it is typical that in general the number of cases involving the offering of bribes is falling by a large percentage *because bribes are being given to the employees of those very agencies that are responsible for the fight against bribery and for exposing evidence of bribery, namely the organs of the police, the courts, and the procuracy*" (emphasis added). He notes that in the major cities, about a third of the bribes offered (and discovered) were given to police and procuracy personnel. In other words, many instances of bribery are not exposed because some law enforcement officials responsible for rooting it out are themselves on the take. Aleksandrov claims that investigators expect to be handed a bribe before they open a criminal case, and they often will do nothing if they do not receive one. "In this way, the judicial and investigative organs open cases [only] when bribes are offered to employees of these organs. As concerns instances of bribery in other organizations, the position of employees of the investigative organs is completely passive."[110]

CONCLUSION: A CAMPAIGN SPASM

In the final analysis, the postwar campaign against bribery was created without conviction and carried out without enthusiasm. As the proposed campaign was discussed by the legal agencies over time, both the seriousness and the scope of the problem were played down, and the campaign became unfocused and muted. Agencies were willing to engage in a limited amount of *samokritika* (self-criticism) in private forums or in closed letters to the Central Committee, but they hesitated to do so publicly. A subdued campaign protected institutional interests. Sparring and defensiveness on the part of the legal agencies was a major reason for the absence of a public campaign. Agencies wanted to protect themselves, as they tried to deflect the blame for bribery—and other crimes—onto other agencies. A discussion out of the public eye also protected the Soviet state from embarrassment, since an open debate about the reality of (in the original words of the campaign's foundational documents) "ordinary," "everyday," "infectious," and "tolerated" corruption undermined the positive image the Soviet Union was trying to project to its own citizens and to the rest of the world.

Entering deals based on illicit gifts was by no means a form of popular "resistance" to the Soviet state, Stalinism, or anything else. People did not have political resistance or protest on their minds when they gave or accepted bribes. Rather, their goals were eluding punishment, cutting bureaucratic red tape, or improving their standard of living. It was the Soviet government, beginning in 1918, that defined bribery as a "counterrevolutionary" act, the last refuge of capitalist villains attempting to destroy the foundations of socialism. Although this language persisted after the war in some public discourse, it was rarely used by procurators or judges. They seem, in practice, to have given up on this explanation by 1945 at the latest. When Minin despaired at the bribery all around him, he never claimed that it was a deadly threat to Soviet power, to the Communist Party, or to socialism. Rather, he said that graft was a major obstacle for the legitimacy of the party-state, for Soviet construction, for the morality of the Soviet people, and for popular trust in this government. He hoped that a campaign against bribery could contribute to a moral revival. He did not state, nor did he imply, that those taking or giving bribes were in any way consciously attempting to weaken the government. Indeed, in a stark reminder of how much the atmosphere had changed since the highly publicized trials of the early 1920s, Supreme Court Chair Goliakov claimed that Minin's *allegations* of widespread bribery were themselves anti-Soviet. This type of reasoning reveals a double standard common to the battle against corruption in many states. Officials rationalize that public discussion of pervasive government corruption will create resentment against the state and damage confidence in the criminal justice system. By quashing debate over the causes and true extent of corruption, they thereby protect the system—and their own positions and advantages in it—while derailing open critique of systemic flaws. This environment favored postwar stability over a true crackdown on corruption.

The campaign against bribery highlighted anxieties about the "defects" of postwar Soviet officialdom that remained deeply troubling to the ruling party. As is often the case, conversations about corruption served as a proxy for broader political and social issues, including crime and social disobedience. Discussions about bribery highlighted numerous concerns of the regime: that the country and its bureaucracy remained "uncultured," even "backward," and potentially disloyal to the goals of the party leadership; that a "new class" of officials was forming—a separate, privileged caste of self-serving bureaucrats who were using their positions to enrich themselves in violation of public trust; that officials were creating informal, underground relationships with Soviet subjects, subverting established patterns of authority and power; that state property must be urgently protected; that the law was not serving its proper function as a tool of the revolutionary party for fighting crime and enforcing socialist legality; that information about domestic problems could embarrass the USSR abroad; and finally, that the postwar courts would be unreliable when the regime needed them to carry out critical central initiatives. All of these anxieties found resonance in the observation that illegal arrangements between officials and ordinary Soviet people were not dying out, but, rather, were on the rise after the war. These concerns would survive the death of Stalin, and they would again be highlighted in the periodic—if ultimately ineffective— anticorruption campaigns in the Khrushchev and Brezhnev eras.

6 Informers and the State

WRITING A FEW MONTHS after Stalin's death in March 1953, a top police official reflected on what the previous eight years had taught him about the challenges that law enforcement faced in catching dangerous criminals who paid or accepted bribes. Colonel D. Lebin was the chief of OBKhSS, the police agency charged with managing the network of secret informants tasked with exposing bribery, the theft of state property, and speculation. He urged all supervisors to instruct their informants to be vigilant for an almost infinite variety of "masked bribes."[1] Sometimes, for example, an uneven sale between an official and a citizen actually hid a bribe. Lebin cautioned agents to be on the lookout for "the purchase by the bribe taker of expensive things for next to nothing or, conversely, the sale of a worthless trinket for a high price." In other cases, Lebin warned, bosses could abuse the system whereby prizes were given for outstanding work, hiding an under-the-table payment. A bribe could also be disguised as a loan. Even more cleverly, some individuals were masking payoffs by pretending to lose to an official at cards.[2] Bribe givers could even attempt to hide their illegal gift by fixing an important person's suit, getting them a job, or arranging a relaxing trip to a sanatorium.

Indeed, OBKhSS had an explicit mandate to train its informant network in how to uncover incidents of bribery, and bring the perpetrators to justice. Yet Lebin's letter once again underscores both how difficult it was to expose bribery (as well as other forms of corruption) and the rather clever lengths to which people would go to hide it. Because it was so hard to uncover the crime through normal auditing or investigative measures, and thanks to the critical role a well-placed bribe could play in schemes dedicated to stealing state property, the police deployed informants to try to find people engaged in bribery, among other crimes, with only mixed success.

The historian Robert Gellately has noted, "No police force in modern European history has been able to function without the cooperation or participation of the population in its efforts."[3] In the Soviet Union during and after the Great Patriotic War, the Stalinist regime considered marshalling that popular cooperation to be critical, if not without its challenges. In the years between the start of the war and the death of Stalin, the regime used informant networks in its effort to eradicate what they described as a veritable epidemic of bribery, crimes against state property, and economic crimes such as profiteering in scarce goods (or speculation). Ordinary Soviet people were recruited and deployed as informants to expose or prevent a variety of nonpolitical crimes. Since the collapse of communism and the partial opening of police records in the former Soviet Bloc, scholars have become increasingly interested in practices of denunciation. Yet, little is known about the informant network charged with unearthing these transgressions during and after World War II. Historians have not yet assessed the way that the nationalization of the economy, together with an ideology that viewed state property as "the people's wealth," created the need for a large informant network.

Information provided by citizen informers was a critical part of the Stalinist law enforcement system after the war. Apart from regular police work, the primary tool for uncovering crimes by officials and crimes against state property was the deployment of secret informants (*osvedomiteli, rezidenty,* and *agenty,* known collectively as *agentura*). After examining police strategies for using informants, this chapter explores what police leaders regarded as the strengths and weaknesses of this network, and examines their explanations for its limitations. Finally, we ask why the system of informants was less effective than its organizers intended, and why its actions provoked certain unexpected outcomes. The limitations of the network provide insight into the deepening patterns of "everyday corruption" that remained an entrenched part of the country's social, legal, and political systems through the collapse of the USSR.

The network of informants has not yet been analyzed in detail largely because records describing its activities have not been available. Due to the (understandable) lack of memoirs by admitted informants, and the reluctance of the Soviet regime to acknowledge the existence of this army of informants, the historian is dependent upon the often rich materials produced by the Ministry of Internal Affairs (MVD) and the police. The present chapter uses materials produced by OBKhSS (*Otdel bor'by s khishcheniem sotsialisticheskoi sobstvennosti i spekuliatsiei*), the Ministry of Internal Affairs' "Department for Combating the Theft of Socialist Property and Speculation," which was a division of the regular police force (GUM). This MVD agency was charged with unearthing crimes against socialist property and white-collar crimes. Access to some archival documentation, including all files of individual informants and the files devoted to particular cases, is still restricted. We do have, however, multiple internal reports discussing the benefits and weaknesses of the networks, as well as summaries of a number of cases in this critical period. Taken together, this material offers a unique opportunity to study the functioning of an informant network involved in the postwar campaign to expose crimes by officials and protect state property against theft.

Previous scholarship on informants in Soviet history has focused largely on those who provided information in cases of "political," "counterrevolutionary," or "anti-Soviet crimes,"[4] activities supposedly aimed at undermining the foundations of Soviet authority or its institutions. This chapter, by contrast, focuses on the network of informers charged with uncovering "nonpolitical" offenses, which were tried in regular courts.[5] After the war, political crimes were not prosecuted as vigorously as they had been in the 1930s—those convicted under Article 58 accounted for only a small proportion of all criminals. Instead, in the immediate postwar years, the protection of state property re-emerged as a central theme in official ideology, leading to increased focus on it by the police. According to statistics compiled by the Supreme Soviet, for example, about 120,000 people were convicted in 1946 for "counterrevolutionary crimes" by the special courts (military tribunals, transport courts, and labor camp courts) and the regular courts; while 527,000 were convicted for the theft of state or personal property. After 1946—with the exception of 1949—at least five times as many people were convicted of property crimes as were convicted of "counterrevolutionary" crimes each year until 1953.[6] The role of informants in exposing these nonpolitical crimes became proportionally much more pronounced than previously.

The present chapter does not examine spontaneous denunciations, typically made by letter, such as those discussed in studies by Vladimir A. Kozlov and Sheila Fitzpatrick.[7] The authors of those denunciations (sometimes known as "signals from below") often put forth elaborate ideological, patriotic, or personal justifications for turning in some "enemy" of the state or people. Such one-time informants usually wrote to authorities about a particular incident that they had witnessed, or to warn authorities about something that could soon happen.[8] Nor does this chapter examine the people who informed the regime about the "mood" of a given population, typically by passing on tidbits overheard in public places or at work. In the case of information-gathering about the population's morale or their opinion about a certain policy, police authorities usually did not follow up with criminal investigations. The discussion here, on the other hand, concerns information usually passed orally by a more-or-less permanent network of informers during face-to-face meetings with police supervisors. The information that these informants passed on to authorities typically was not offered spontaneously.[9] Rather, the police harvested information in regular, secret meetings.[10] One might argue that this variety of informing was less dramatic than many of the unsolicited denunciations that historians have previously analyzed. Yet considering the growing proportion of cases of nonpolitical crime in relation to the number of cases of "political offenses" (about which most denunciations were lodged) in the late Stalin period, informing likely played a role in law enforcement equal to or greater than that of denunciations.

On November 17, 1938, a famous instruction was issued by Sovnarkom and the Central Committee that called a halt to the "mass operations" and mass denunciations from below, and subsequently the role of informers in regular policing grew.[11] The instruction ordered the NKVD and the procuracy to identify criminals on the basis of evidence that they had committed a crime, rather than simply presuming guilt by association. In this environment, the role of informers expanded sharply in the 1940s and 1950s, as evidence collected and verified by the police and procuracy investigators became more important in prosecuting violations of the criminal statutes.

This chapter also begins to explore an intriguing dimension of the Soviet system that has not yet been investigated: those informants who, while officially counted as part of the network, simply did not provide information as expected. The emphasis by scholars on denunciations (the unsolicited and enthusiastic offering of damaging information) perhaps minimizes the frequency with which people who witnessed "crimes" apparently chose, for a variety of reasons, to remain silent, or in other ways failed to live up to the expectations of their police supervisors.

THE MISSION

The Department for Combating the Theft of Socialist Property and Speculation (OBKhSS) was charged with rooting out crimes that resulted in "material or financial damage to state interests." Such crimes were prosecuted primarily under two categories of the criminal code, or under special *ukazy* (decrees). One type of crime that OBKhSS was to expose was what the criminal code labeled "crimes by officials" (*dolzhnostnye prestupleniia*, sometimes translated as "professional" or "white-collar" crimes), which included the giving and accepting of bribes. Convictions for white-collar crimes rose sharply during and immediately after the war.[12] The stillborn campaign against bribery described in the previous chapter, launched in 1946, specifically ordered OBKhSS to use its informant network to expose bribery (as well as other types of official malfeasance). Two secret orders created a mandate to use the informant networks to locate bribe givers and takers. OBKhSS was specifically charged with "organizing informant work to uncover bribery" by Instruction No. 036/0210/126s of the Ministry of Justice, the Ministry of Internal Affairs, and the General Procurator's Office, and which was issued on July 15, 1946. A USSR Council of Ministers Instruction No. 2062-852s of September 13, 1946, called for "strengthening the struggle against all forms of speculation, theft of socialist property, and bribery."[13] These secret instructions stayed in effect until Stalin's death (and beyond).

A separate, but obviously quite closely related, responsibility of OBKhSS was to uncover "theft of socialist and societal property" (*raskhi-shchenie sotsialisticheskoi i obshchestvennoi sobstvennosti*), most typically the theft of state property. Law enforcement regarded bribery as a crime that enabled embezzlement and other varieties of corruption and looting of state resources, covered under the section of the criminal code labeled "crimes against state property." As noted earlier, important types of corruption, including all cases of theft of state property, embezzlement and misappropriation, were subsumed under the draconian decree of June 4, 1947.[14]

Using the media, workplace agitation and propaganda, and education, the regime after the war urged the Soviet population to be "vigilant" against crime of all types, and to inform the authorities whenever they witnessed it. Social condemnation of the informer was widespread in the Soviet Union, as in many societies, and the Soviet law enforcement system had to overcome the population's mistrust of informers. While in the 1930s the regime had incited subjects to report "wreckers," fascist spies, and other "counterrevolutionaries," in the late Stalin years nonpolitical criminals in all their guises became a central target. Embezzlers, pilferers, speculators, and their protectors in the bureaucracy were singled out as particularly nefarious criminals. The 1936 Constitution's blunt statement that state property was "sacred and inviolable" (language borrowed from the August 1932 edict on the theft of state property) took on new meaning after the mass destruction of the war. Party authorities attempted to create a public environment in which average people would not only respect state property as "the people's wealth," but would actively defend it from those who threatened to abscond with it or enable its theft. Individuals, the press trumpeted, should report anyone witnessed stealing state property or taking bribes to enable such activity.[15] As the legal scholar B. A. Kurinov wrote, "Every Soviet citizen has the moral duty to inform the organs of power about all known instances of the theft of state and socialist property."[16] The USSR Minister of Justice, K. P. Gorshenin, encouraged informing about the theft of state property in 1948: "Such a struggle must be the business of all Soviet people. Comrade Stalin teaches us this." This task demands "the creation of an atmosphere of contempt and hate by all of society toward all thieves of the people's property."[17] The regime made clear that those who reported crimes to the police would contribute to the preservation of the people's wealth, protect social stability, improve living standards for ordinary people, and ultimately accelerate society's transition from socialism to communism.

In this context, "the failure to inform" (*nedonesenie*) became a serious crime. Article 5 of the June 4, 1947 decree on theft of state property established penalties of two to three years in prison or five to seven years' banishment to distant areas for failing to report theft or turn in people preparing to commit theft. This article of the decree effectively criminalized a sizable proportion of the population—those who had witnessed theft of food on a collective farm or pilfering at work, but chose not to report it.[18] The fact that the regime attempted to mandate informing, and then severely punished the failure to inform, indicates that many people were not reporting on actions that the government considered to be crimes.

THE ORGANIZATION OF THE INFORMANT NETWORK

Created in March 1937, OBKhSS played the primary role in exposing individuals involved in bribery, embezzlement, theft of socialist property, and speculation. OBKhSS was under the jurisdiction of the regular militia, which was in charge of curbing social disorder and nonpolitical crime.[19]

Both the Ministry of Internal Affairs and procuracy leadership trumpeted the organization of effective networks of secret informants as crucial for rooting out crime or, better yet, preventing it altogether. Every annual report of OBKhSS between 1943 and 1953 emphasized the need to expand the work of the informant network. When OBKhSS leaders planned their war on crime, they looked to the informant network first. This deployment of informants to thwart crime or, failing that, to uncover the deeds after the fact, was called *operativno-profilakticheskaia rabota* or *agenturno-operativnaia rabota*.

The structure of the informant network that OBKhSS mobilized resembled other informant networks, such as those reporting information about the intelligentsia and those suspected of political crimes. There were two levels to the permanent informant network.[20] At the lowest level were the so-called osvedomiteli, or informants. These people reported information to the police in the course of their regular lives. Operating at the grassroots, this group comprised by far the largest total of the three levels. Osvedomiteli provided the police with what was called "primary evidence." Based on this information, police investigators created dossiers (*delo-formuliary*).

This pool of informants seems to have represented a cross section of the general population. They included white-collar personnel such as bookkeepers, accountants, and managers, as well as unskilled or semi-skilled labor such as cleaning personnel, clerks, waiters, chauffeurs, and night watch staff. (Demographic data on the sex or age of informants has not been made available.) Informants in this disparate cohort were linked by their ability to undertake surveillance of people who might be tempted to steal, take bribes, or otherwise take advantage of their positions. Located at thousands of workplaces in every part of the country, informers ultimately comprised something of a social subgroup that cut across class, professional, and occupational boundaries.

The second tier of the network, the so-called rezidenty, were drafted from among the "most active" and "reliable" osvedomiteli. In the late Stalin period, the total number of osvedomiteli stood at approximately eighteen to thirty times the number of rezidenty.[21] Rezidenty cooperated with the MVD while simultaneously keeping their regular jobs. The rezidenty worked as intermediaries between the operations staff of the police and the osvedomiteli themselves; in principle, no police employee associated directly with the osvedomiteli. Each informant was tied to a certain rezident, and the MVD received information from the informants through that rezident.

A parallel informant network was the agentura. This was a roaming network of undercover police "agents" who were mobilized for a temporary assignment, usually after the police received a tip, to investigate a certain enterprise, or an entire industry, or a branch of the economy in a specific area. This system operated without rezidenty. An agent worked undercover inside a certain workplace or agency. The agent reported to an OBKhSS supervisor (*operupolnomochennyi* or *operativnyi rabotnik*), usually in the operations department (*operativnoe upravlenie*) or investigations department (*rozysk*) of OBKhSS. Agents in the agentura network were supposed to recruit undercover informants inside the workplace. These local networks would work to uncover a certain scheme, or to clean out criminals from a particular enterprise or branch of industry, and then disband. In all informant networks, agents and residents were responsible for ensuring that trustworthy informants were located, recruited, and groomed, and that they actively provided useful information to the police.

A brief description of one agentura operation that involved bribery, theft, and abuse of office offers some insight into the actions of the informant network. According to a 1953 report from the MVD's Main Administration of the Police (GUM), in January MVD officials received information concerning a suspected criminal operation in the Main Circus Administration (*Glavnoe upravlenie tsirkami*).[22] Moscow instructed the local police forces in several locales visited by the traveling circus (including Krasnoiar, Krasnodar, and Rostov oblast') to investigate, but they came up empty-handed.

Normal auditing procedures had failed to uncover the scheme. So the police sent in an *agenturnaia set'*, a group of agents charged with recruiting informants, whose job was to penetrate the criminal groups and report back to the police. An investigation had determined that between 1948 and 1952, circus employees had been operating an elaborate scam. The perpetrators illegally obtained blank tickets from movie theaters by bribing theater managers or bookkeepers. They stamped the tickets with the name of the circus and hid them for safekeeping in the elephant's cage. When the box office opened each evening, they retrieved the fake tickets, mixed them in together with the genuine ones, and sold them to the audience. Preliminary data revealed that the fraud netted more than 1.5 million rubles. The ring of thieves divided the proceeds from the sale of the phony tickets among themselves, reserving a portion of this money to pay bribes to officials in the Main Circus Administration and its local branches. These payoffs guaranteed the traveling circus the most popular routes and venues. Bribes also secured the best animals. The exotic beasts and choice locations secured through bribes ensured the circus's success on its tour, guaranteed big, enthusiastic audiences, secured the highest possible ticket sales, and thus maximized the perpetrators' illicit gains. According to the arrested suspects, this type of operation was also common in many other circuses and traveling zoos around the Soviet Union. In the city of Dnepropetrovsk alone, a similar scheme resulted in the arrest of eleven people for grand theft and bribery, including bookkeepers, a cashier, and printers. Once the perpetrators were arrested, the police dissolved this group of informants.

AN EXPANDING NETWORK

To be sure, the statistics reported in OBKhSS reports, like all statistics produced by the Soviet bureaucracy, must be viewed with some caution. Data on the number of active informants, for example, which OBKhSS reported to superiors in the Ministry of Internal Affairs, may have been inflated, as local police forces reacted to pressure from above to meet quotas by recruiting more informants. One finds the occasional complaint in the reports that the police were recruiting people based on "quantity, not quality."[23] There are, nevertheless, reasons to believe that the figures are generally accurate, primarily because the MVD's preoccupation with the informant network and high levels of property, economic, and white-collar crime led to increased scrutiny and pressure on lower levels to report more precisely. Multiple sources and channels of information enabled those towards the top of the hierarchy to interpret the statistics that local agents or police supervisors may have exaggerated. Moreover, periodic audits of local police informant rolls led to the annual removal of tens of thousands of informants who no longer contributed information. Thus, although the figures should be used with care, there is reason to believe that the figures approach some semblance of accuracy and that the general size of the network can be tracked over time.

During the first months of the German invasion, the Soviet informant network nearly evaporated. Tens of thousands of informants and rezidenty were drafted into the army, died at the hands of the Germans, or were evacuated to the east. Subsequently the police had to regenerate the network almost from scratch, beginning in the second half of 1941. As one OBKhSS official wrote, "In fact, at that time the informant apparatus had to be completely created anew." According to OBKhSS documents, the authorities achieved this reconstruction very quickly. On January 1, 1942, about 42,000 informants were listed as part of the network. Massive recruitment took place in the second half of 1942 and 1943. Indeed, by January 1944 the informant network had grown to over 140,000 people, more than tripling in the course of two years.[24]

What explains the quick rebirth and accelerated growth of the informant network during the war? Clearly, part of the answer is that previous informants again became active in reoccupied lands as the Red Army drove out the Germans.[25] Yet, reoccupation by itself does not fully explain the rapid growth. Amid the wartime crime wave, in February and July 1943 NKVD USSR called for the expansion of a "mass" informant network for fighting property crimes, economic crimes, and crimes by officials in the bureaucracy, greatly increasing both its size and scope.[26] These orders represent a major turning point in the evolution of the network. Before 1943, OBKhSS had been responsible for the ambitious, but still relatively limited, missions of fighting bribery, speculation and counterfeiting, and combating theft in trade agencies, industrial cooperatives, banks, and food collection organizations. During the war, the theft, counterfeiting, and misuse of ration cards and the mass resale of goods—aided by bribery—had become prevalent, especially on military bases, in stores, and in dining halls. Speculation and theft, covered up by bribery, also became rampant in consumer cooperatives, warehouses, industrial cooperatives, food enterprises, and collective farms. The OBKhSS mandate included orders to reduce crime in all these areas.

The new orders issued in 1943, however, vastly expanded the duties of OBKhSS, making it responsible for detecting and preventing crime in every economic enterprise in the country. OBKhSS was now given several additional, highly ambitious tasks, including the exposure of criminal activity in all supply, trade, construction, and industrial enterprises in the Soviet Union—taking a key role, together with the procuracy, in safeguarding state property throughout the entire Soviet economy. The informant network was to be the leading weapon of the police in the struggle.[27] According to OBKhSS, informants provided information that led to 98,400 criminal investigations in 1943.[28]

The rapid expansion of the OBKhSS informant network during and immediately after the war can be seen as a legacy of the wartime conditions that have served as the social and economic context for much of this book. Profound and lingering shortages created opportunities for those who would offer scarce services or deal in shadow markets. In the immediate postwar years, persistent scarcity and vast reconstruction projects continued to fuel pilfering and bribery.

The experience of the network during the war highlights a central quandary inherent in the regime's dependence upon informants drawn from among the population. The Stalinist informant network ultimately was subject to the same seismic demographic shifts and catastrophes that affected the general population. When the regime evacuated pop-

ulations or drafted people into the army during the war, police informants were also drafted or evacuated, and they were, at least temporarily, of little or no use. When thousands died in the famine of 1946–1947,
a portion of the informant network died with them. And when over
600,000 prisoners were amnestied from the Gulag after the conclusion
of the war in 1945 (and in 1953, when about 1.5 million inmates were
released), tens of thousands of prison informants were also swept out
of the penal camps and colonies, much to the chagrin of the camp authorities who had relied on their information about the activities of the
camp population and staff.[29] Authorities had to adjust to the fact that
the same powerful forces that shaped Soviet life also buffeted the informant network.

According to Ministry of Internal Affairs reports, over 200,000 informants operated under OBKhSS supervision by 1945. Amid the wave
of theft, profiteering, and bribery that accompanied the postwar famine, that number jumped to 286,000 by the beginning of 1946. This
total does not include informants involved in uncovering counterrevolutionary offenses, or crimes in the military, or crimes against persons. (No figures are available for informants involved in these areas
of policing. It is possible, of course, that there was some overlap among
these cohorts.) OBKhSS supervisors, however, were not satisfied with
these totals. One noted in 1945, "The quantity of the current informant
network still cannot be considered sufficient."[30] He urged that the police deploy more people in venues where the risk of crime was greatest,
including retail stores, dining halls, warehouses, trade agencies, auditing bureaus, and supply organizations.

By September 1951, the total number of OBKhSS informants had
nearly doubled from the level at war's end, to more than 380,000. This
figure represented an explosive nine-fold increase since 1942. Even
after the campaign that accompanied the June 1947 decree on theft of
socialist property had ended, and arrests associated with the campaign
had dropped back to pre–June 1947 levels, the number of informants
continued to increase in each of the four years between 1948 and 1951
(the last year for which data are available). Moreover, figures describing
(and lamenting) the high levels of turnover among informants demonstrate that, during the course of a given year, many more people were
part of the network than the figure for any one date would indicate.
If one includes the approximately 80,000 informants culled from the

network over the course of 1950, for example, the total number of informants on the rolls at some point during that year would exceed 450,000, rather than the nearly 377,000 officially on OBKhSS lists on December 1, 1950. Thus, between 1942 and 1951, the size of the network grew each year; every informant excluded from the rolls was replaced, and then some.

Why did the number of informants continue to grow until at least 1951, even after arrests declined following the campaign accompanying the June 1947 decree? Comments recorded in 1951 provide part of the answer. According to OBKhSS officials, there were not enough informants to keep up with the "enormous growth of the economy."[31] One consequence of the postwar reconstruction was an upsurge in opportunities for theft of state property and white-collar crimes. An OBKhSS leader neatly summed up the problem: the crime rate was growing together with the economy. The police simply could not hope to control crime without a massive influx of informants into the new enterprises that were springing up around the country (and into the sprawling state administrations that managed them). Reports indicate that by the late 1940s police were becoming convinced that the amount of large-scale, well-organized criminal activity was, if not growing, then holding steady amid conditions ripe for crime to prosper. It was especially difficult for the informants to catch bribe givers and takers. A 1949 report noted that "groups of thieves and speculators operate for an extended time without being punished; in the majority of instances, those committing the major crimes are revealed only after significant material damage has already been done to the state. The prevention of large and organized crimes has not been assured. The underworld of speculators has been also uncovered poorly. As for bribery, the situation is even worse."[32]

STRENGTHS AND LIMITATIONS

Catching people engaged in bribery or theft of state property was not easy under any circumstances, even with the help of a massive informant network. Throughout the postwar period OBKhSS and MVD authorities complained about shortcomings in the network. Nevertheless, law enforcement clearly valued the network for its role in exposing crime. Its contributions are reflected in the large number of criminal cases initiated by OBKhSS as a result of informants' tips. According to data reported to the Ministry of Internal Affairs, for example, OBKhSS initiated more than 301,000 cases union-wide in 1946. Approximately 353,000 people were "brought to responsibility" (*privlecheny k otvet-stvennosti*), and subjected to criminal charges, indictments, or fines. The majority of these cases were brought on the basis of "official data," meaning regular police work rather than information reported by informants. Nevertheless, about 28 percent of these 1946 cases initiated union-wide, or about 84,000 cases, were based on tips from informants. Cases generated by the informant network resulted in nearly 100,000 people being "brought to responsibility" in 1946.[33] In 1948, 34 percent of OBKhSS cases, or more than 125,000 cases, were launched because of reports from informants.[34] Between 1945 and 1948, OBKhSS initiated at least 360,000 cases on the basis of informants' tips.

Despite these hundreds of thousands of arrests, OBKhSS leaders consistently noted a number of telling flaws in the system. They frequently lamented that the informant network was ineffective in critical ways.[35] The Ministry of Internal Affairs was dissatisfied both with certain aspects of the informant network itself and with the OBKhSS leaders who supervised it. First, there was concern that many informants were, in fact, not producing useful information. As audits indicated, individuals were often still listed as active informants on official rolls when in fact they had fallen out of touch with their supervisors. One complaint about the Leningrad oblast' informant network stated, "The overwhelming majority either provides nothing at all or they provide useless material."[36] A 1947 audit in Krasnoiarsk krai noted that, of 256 agents and informers, 46 percent had reported no information whatsoever during the previous three months. Thirty percent of agents and informants in Stalingrad oblast' were "inert."[37] Elsewhere, the proportion of what was called *ballast* was even larger. During the first half of 1948, only twelve of 117 informants in one region in Gorkii oblast' had delivered information that led the police to lodge charges.[38]

Each year, OBKhSS removed approximately 20 to 40 percent of the informers in the network from the lists because they were not providing useful information.[39] In 1940, 38 percent of all informants were culled as dead weight.[40] In 1948, over 64,000 informants and rezidenty were struck from the lists. OBKhSS lamented this "enormous turnover."[41] Some informants would lose touch with handlers for understandable reasons, of course. They died, were drafted, retired, switched jobs, moved, or fell ill. It is also likely that some OBKhSS employees, under pressure to fulfill quotas, simply added names to their lists more or less at random. Some people officially on lists apparently never agreed to be informants in the first place.

In other cases, police handlers were blamed for failing to "cultivate" their informants. The assumption was that informants were eager to assist authorities, but that their handlers failed to draw out information or to use it correctly. Ministry of Internal Affairs chiefs often blamed OBKhSS officials for failing to maintain good relations with informants, or for neglecting and even showing contempt toward them.[42] Moreover, blame for the poor quality of informants often fell directly on the OBKhSS recruiters, who were accused of drafting weak, incompetent, or untrustworthy informers. As one report put it in 1948: "Many operational employees of OBKhSS and chiefs of police organs approach the recruitment of new informants without thinking, and even irresponsibly, as a result of which the agent-informant network is swollen with people who are incapable of fulfilling the tasks they are given and people who cannot be trusted."[43]

In other instances, however, informants simply failed to report useful information. Frequently, informants did not share what they knew with their supervisors when asked to do so. They chose to remain out of touch with supervisors, rarely if ever passing along incriminating information about criminal activity that they witnessed. Others frustrated their OBKhSS supervisors by providing false information. Interestingly, there is no evidence that the authorities in any way punished uncooperative informants, nor is there any discussion of contingencies for doing so. OBKhSS appears simply to have deleted such informants from the rolls.[44]

In internal reports, while OBKhSS credited tips from informants for catching tens of thousands of criminals, investigators were nevertheless highly critical of informants for failing to provide information that would expose the larger criminal groups. Complaints were rife that informants were primarily reporting people who had committed petty theft and malfeasance of office; such small-scale crime was a lower priority for the police.[45] Meanwhile, most major crimes went undetected. White-collar criminals were netting tens or hundreds of thousands of rubles in complex schemes that often involved bribery, embezzlement, and theft. Yet OBKhSS authorities emphasized the great difficulties involved in infiltrating the most damaging groups of criminals. One OBKhSS chief protested that such organized crime came to the attention of the police only when it had already done significant damage. By that time, special informants were no longer necessary to uncover it.[46] Pressure to uncover large "criminal conspiracies" expressed an ongoing, paramount concern in this period: to defend state property from wholesale plundering, by exposing thieves and the bribe-taking officials who protected them or otherwise conspired with them.

By 1947, the conviction that the most ambitious criminals had become more skilled than the police who were trying to track them down was pervasive in MVD discussions. OBKhSS leaders observed that the postwar crackdowns had actually forced criminals to become more adept at concealing their activities. In the words of one OBKhSS report, after the June 1947 decree on theft of socialist property imposed harsh penalties, "thieves, bribe takers, and speculators act more carefully [and] assume more clever methods of stealing socialist property and covering the tracks of their crimes."[47] Some police officials grew frustrated that criminals were able to adapt to changing circumstances more adroitly than the police themselves. As the OBKhSS annual report for 1948 states, although police methods had changed for the better, "the methods of stealing and speculation have also changed. Even as we have strengthened repression and improved our methods of struggle, criminals have adopted more clever techniques of theft and speculation, and have moved into the deep underground (*glubokoe podpol'e*), which has complicated the struggle against them to a significant degree."[48] Criminals organized themselves "defensively" in such a way that the police could not infiltrate their groups. Another report noted that many OBKhSS officials were not up to the challenge of cracking sophisticated underground groups: "A preponderance of OBKhSS cadres . . . are not prepared to penetrate the criminal designs of thieves and speculators in a timely fashion, in order to uncover all the criminals' tricks and frustrate their skillful designs."[49]

HARNESSING THE "CRIMINAL ELEMENT"

From the available documents, it is impossible in most cases to discern what motivated an individual to become a police informant.[50] The police did not record the reasons why informants chose to report suspicious activity. So with rare exceptions, these records provide very little insight into *why* people cooperated with the police.[51] One motive is clear, however: the police essentially blackmailed many people into becoming informants after taking them into custody. In exchange for freedom or favorable consideration in connection with a pending criminal charge, the police sent detainees back to their workplaces as informants, charged with reporting suspicious behavior or providing information about the activities of groups with which they had been involved.[52] The Ministry of Internal Affairs urged police to recruit more informants on the basis of "compromising material," reasoning that they would agree to snitch on their partners in crime in order to stay out of prison themselves. In a stark example of this principle, a 1946 report complained that in the Ivanovo municipal OBKhSS department, only twenty-nine of the 197 secret informants "were recruited on the basis of compromising materials." The report went on to criticize the fact that several agents working undercover as accountants were recruited not because they had been caught associating with criminals but "merely" because of their qualifications as bookkeepers.[53]

To detect the more tenacious conspiracies, authorities decided to accelerate recruiting efforts among the "criminal element," a strategy that intensified during the war. Observing that information about the major criminal schemes rarely came from more "orthodox" sources, central OBKhSS leaders urged police supervisors to draw informants from among actual white-collar criminals, bribe takers, and thieves of state property. Amid postwar crackdowns on crime, OBKhSS leaders urged agents energetically to recruit informants from criminal circles in order to infiltrate groups that often included other officials. Indeed, one "honest" bookkeeper at Dining Room No. 5 in Voronezh was reported to be worthless as an informant because his "honesty and uprightness meet with unfriendly relations on the part of many co-workers who serve above him."[54] Another report called agents "cowardly" for failing to venture into the criminal underworld. Correspondence from 1947 noted that "police organs and, in particular, OBKhSS agencies, still do not have a sufficient quantity of qualified agents capable of uncovering the deep criminal underground."[55]

Concerns developed, however, about this practice of depending on coerced informants with suspect pasts. Not surprisingly, such informants often turned out to be untrustworthy. Reports state that many informants were "double dealers" who only provided "disinformation" to the authorities and were "merging with the criminal element."[56] Moreover, OBKhSS officials observed by 1948 that informants were often using their relationship with the police as protection in pursuing new illegal activities. One report noted, "In a series of cases, thieves, bribe takers, and speculators comprising the informant network of OBKhSS are sheltered by their connections with the police organs, have been committing crimes without being punished, and thus discredit the police organs."[57] By 1953, the MVD was taking steps—albeit small ones— to address this concern. In a burst of wishful thinking, the MVD issued an order allowing the recruitment of criminals as informants only if they had "completely confessed the crimes they had committed and renounced all criminal ties."[58] Judging by the complaints of supervisors, such pledges hardly guaranteed responsible behavior. In other cases, according to OBKhSS chiefs, informants with criminal backgrounds frequently came under the influence of the very people they were supposed to be exposing, "slipping back onto the criminal path."[59] A surreal situation then resulted whereby the police had to recruit a new layer of informers to inform on the existing informers.

The Ministry of Internal Affairs expressed concern about the failure of OBKhSS employees to "maintain the conspiracy," that is, to protect informants' identities. Informants were subject to many types of risks, including social ostracism, job loss, or even violence. Yet, authorities cited numerous ways in which handlers compromised their informants' confidentiality. One police supervisor summoned agents and informants to secret meetings using uncoded, open postcards, which he sent to informants' apartments and workplaces. At other times, police supervisors would meet an informant (or discuss them by name) in a public place such as a park or a restaurant, making no effort to disguise their police affiliation. The MVD had a term for such blunders: "*raskonspiratsiia*"—the conspiracy falls apart.[60]

Ultimately, this adoption of the language of conspiracy by law enforcement officials reveals their perspective on fighting crimes like bribery: it is the struggle of one conspiracy—the police, together with their imperfect allies, the informants—against an almost infinite number of others—these relatively small, yet often impenetrable and highly damaging, criminal conspiracies. One occasionally gets the sense that the regime feared it was losing this struggle.

"FAILURE TO INFORM"

The state depended on informants drawn from the general population for information about damage done to state interests, including the malfeasance of its own officials. As we have seen, this complex relationship posed certain problems. Of course, many people did inform reliably, and they did so for a variety of reasons described above. Yet, it is worthwhile speculating that other variables were also at work, and that these complicated the regime's quest for reliable information. In that context, it is worth discussing a related but almost wholly ignored group of people: those who did *not* inform, who maintained their silence, who chose *not* to blow the whistle.

Several factors help explain why informers sometimes chose to withhold information from the authorities. As noted above, some may have feared that police incompetence would somehow ruin the "conspiracy" protecting their identity.[61] Other potential informants chose to remain silent because they believed that the possible consequences of disclosing information—harassment or losing one's job—outweighed the potential gains.[62] Informing, after all, often involved great risks. An informer who reported on his employer had to continue to work in that enterprise or bureaucracy and might face reprisals, including being reported in turn for some infraction. J. M. Montias and Susan Rose-Ackerman have observed: "When everyone depends in a complex way on everyone else, no one may be willing to expose others for fear that he will only end up harming himself. This is particularly likely to be true for corrupt behavior where there are no impartial observers, and the only witnesses to the breaking of rules are the briber and the bribee."[63] As Joseph Berliner pointed out, many forms of enterprise-level impropriety undertaken by managers to fulfill plans implicated almost all employees of that enterprise.[64] Turning in a manager who paid bribes to obtain scarce materials through (or around) a cumbersome bureaucracy could damage the informant's chances of receiving a share of the enterprise's bonus for fulfilling the plan. Thanks to the gift-giving practices of *podnoshenie,* many potential informants were also in a position to obtain valuables as a result of the illegal activities of co-workers. When an OBKhSS informant turned in the director of the Moscow restaurant Uzbekistan, who had shaken down his staff for more than 17,000 rubles in bribes in 1950, it is certainly possible that many of the employees nevertheless rued their loss of job security and the increased scrutiny from police after their boss's arrest.[65]

The degree to which employees were obligated to each other on a "moral" or "friendly" basis also may have discouraged them from reporting their co-workers' dubious actions to authorities.[66] This sense of obligation clearly applied to many party members, who were bound together by privilege or a shared community of belief. A 1952 report of the Party Control Commission lamented that when party members *were* caught in misdeeds, it was rarely because a fellow party member had turned them in. Rather they were typically nabbed as a result of criminal investigations undertaken by the procuracy and the civilian courts.[67] A procuracy report on bribery schemes related to the distribution of apartments pointed out drily, "It is interesting to note that not in a single case of bribery in the housing system was there an example when an employee of the housing administration informed investigators about a bribe attempt, even when he had refused the offer [of a bribe]."[68] Even officials who declined a bribe usually failed to turn in the people who made the offer.

In some instances, informants may have simply believed that the behavior they witnessed, though labeled a crime, did not rise to the level of criminal activity that deserved punishment. Potential informants may have considered what they witnessed to be simple blat transactions, not crimes but favors based on a web of friendly, personal relationships that harmed no one. As this study has argued, the boundaries between "gifts," "favors," "tips," and "bribes" is quite porous in many cultures and communities.[69] Other potential informants may have felt that some so-called "crimes" should carry no stigma or penalty when they were undertaken only for the purpose of survival in the face of a powerful state—a state that reserved privileges for a small, closed elite, and that had not yet fulfilled its oft-repeated promise to provide abundance to all Soviet subjects.[70] As R. W. Davies has pointed out, "Throughout the Stalin years, nearly all dissidents, party and nonparty, criticized the regime not because it failed to emulate Western capitalism, but because it failed to live up to socialist ideals."[71] Thus petty economic crimes could be regarded as normal forms of coping, enabling ordinary people to address difficult problems in an environment of poverty and frequent injustice. Similarly, many informants might have shared what, by most accounts, was a common sentiment that, while theft from an individual was reprehensible, there was nothing wrong with taking from the state. A popular saying of the time is appropriate in this context: "If you don't steal from the state, you're stealing from your own family."[72] Thus, while some witnesses chose to denounce people "in the name of justice" (as Vladimir A. Kozlov has observed),[73] others chose to remain silent "in the name of justice."

CONCLUSIONS

Like denunciations, the activities of informers occupied "a kind of intermediate space between the society 'below' and the state or the authorities 'above.'"[74] This network of informants for nonpolitical crimes represents a case study in the interaction between the regime— dependent on the population to advance one of the critical elements of postwar ideology, the protection of state property—and the Soviet population, whose view of officialdom and notions of state property were, at the very least, complex. These uneasy interactions between the representatives of state power and the ordinary people who were asked to help protect "the people's wealth" are a central issue for historians of the Soviet experience.[75]

By the final years of Stalin's reign, OBKhSS reports reveal a growing frustration with the informant network. This attitude highlights some of the dilemmas inherent in a system of governance that was at least partly dependent upon a vast, if unreliable, network of ordinary people to expose the corrupt activities endemic to its own bureaucracy.

Even after the 1947 campaign had subsided, and convictions for theft of state property and crimes by officials had dropped by about two-thirds, the informant network continued to grow. Although we must exercise caution when discussing the absolute number of informants, it is clear that in relative terms the network grew exponentially between the start of the war and late 1951. This expansion indicates that, despite its flaws, the regime regarded the system of informants as a critical feature of law enforcement. The growth of the network must be understood in the postwar conditions of a quickly expanding economy, an apparent epidemic of theft of state property (and other self-enriching crimes by officials), and concern about the failure to inculcate Soviet subjects with respect for "socialist property." At the same time, police supervisors concluded that a significant proportion of the network was either dead wood or "double-dealers" who did not provide accurate information (or who simply disappeared from sight).

For a whole range of reasons, many people chose not to inform the police about improper or illegal activities they witnessed. However, the unwillingness or reluctance of some of the Soviet population to inform on their neighbors should not be confused with a conscious, active or passive "resistance" to socialism, the Soviet state, Stalin's leadership, or anything else. It seems clear that many Soviet subjects could simultaneously support the promise of Soviet socialism *and* pilfer government property or engage in petty bribery, without compunction or guilt. Others might offer or accept bribes in the interest of achieving social justice or gaining access to scarce goods, yet still believe in the brilliance of Stalin's guidance or in socialism's superiority to capitalism. We can argue, however, that for all its apparent success in convincing Soviet subjects of the moral, social, and economic advantages of socialism, the regime failed—in the case of its subjects and officials alike—to convince Soviet people that respect for state property should be equivalent to respect for one's own belongings. This fact represents a fundamental failure of the Soviet system. "Socialist property" never translated into "our property"; the state was never seen as belonging to all the people. In this understanding of "the state" and "its" property, we recognize attitudes that foreshadow the extralegal economic activity and official corruption that blossomed in the Khrushchev and Brezhnev periods.

7 Military Justice at the Intersection of Counterrevolution and Corruption

IN THE BIZARRE PUBLIC CHARADES that exemplified Stalinist political justice during the Great Terror, Judge Vasilii V. Ul'rikh played a central—and often very visible—role. The chairman of the Military Collegium of the USSR Supreme Court, Ul'rikh served as the presiding judge at the three infamous Moscow show trials of 1936–1938. His somber, surly, and mostly silent presence was overshadowed by the flamboyantly bloodthirsty prosecutor, Andrei Vyshinskii. The journalist Eugene Lyons, who covered the show trials for United Press International (UPI), mocked Ul'rikh's appearance: "In his round face the gods had modeled a mask of impish, gloating cruelty. His flushed, overstuffed features were twisted continually into a grimace of brutal sarcasm. . . . That melon-face, hovering over the trial, sneering and jeering, was a caricature of the very idea of justice."[1] Ul'rikh loyally oversaw the closed trials of the disgraced NKVD chiefs Genrikh G. Yagoda and Nikolai I. Yezhov (both of whom were shot after judges quickly handed down death sentences) and the secret trials of Marshal Mikhail N. Tukhachevskii and other leading officers when Stalin ruthlessly purged the armed forces in 1937–1938.

Charged with dispensing justice in cases of extraordinary military and political importance, the Military Collegium at the height of the purges unflinchingly condemned tens of thousands of traitors and other

Figure 7.1. Vasilii V. Ul'rikh, chair of the USSR Military Collegium. Russian State Archive of Photographic and Cinematic Documents at Krasnogorsk (RGAKFD).

"counterrevolutionaries" to death for invented "terroristic" crimes, after closed, secret, and brief trials lasting only a few minutes; many thousands more were sentenced to long prison terms.[2] Between February 1937 and September 1938, the secret police created lists—all signed by Stalin—of over 44,000 people to be given death sentences or lengthy stints in the Gulag, whom the Military Collegium obligingly sentenced.[3] Ul'rikh's Military Collegium was rewarded with a spacious new building, away from the cramped structure in central Moscow that housed the Supreme Court.[4] For his work convicting "enemies of the people," Ul'rikh was given the rank of "Colonel-General of Justice"; other justices of the Collegium also received military ranks. Ul'rikh proudly wore a military uniform for the rest of his life.

Yet remarkably, in the spring of 1948 the Cadres Directorate of the Central Committee claimed that Ul'rikh had in some way condoned the acceptance of bribes by people close to him in several sensitive political cases. Ul'rikh himself was not accused of being a counterrevolutionary, as so many of the country's most important judges had been in 1937–1938 before they were shot as "enemies of the people." Rather, he was smeared with the allegation that he both tolerated corruption and associated closely with bribe takers. Eventually, several of his colleagues from the Military Collegium were also tainted with the accusation that they accepted bribes or cast a blind eye on bribery in their midst.

The fact that several high-ranking judges in the country's most important military court found themselves embroiled in a postwar *bribery* scandal—of all things—is a puzzle worth exploring. In fact, the personnel of several Moscow agencies of military justice, from the low-level military tribunals to the Military Collegium of the USSR Supreme Court, the country's highest military appeals court, were reported to be dealing in bribes. Not coincidentally, these allegations surfaced just as the regime was making extensive efforts to locate and punish wartime criminals, including Soviet citizens who had collaborated with the Nazis.

An exploration of these bribery allegations in Moscow's military courts provides essential background for an even larger scandal that rocked the Soviet high courts between 1948 and 1952, an affair that ultimately became one of the most striking corruption cases in the history of the Soviet Union. Through the Military Collegium, investigators would follow a trail of alleged judicial corruption to other high courts in Moscow and, eventually, to high-level courts around the USSR. That extraordinary and unknown affair is the subject of the next chapter.

Several intriguing questions arise from the Ul'rikh affair. Why at this moment would Stalin endorse an attack on the Military Collegium of the Supreme Court, and ultimately on the reliable "hanging judge" Ul'rikh, using accusations of corruption as the basis? How did the Soviet agencies of military justice become embroiled in a bribery scandal at this time? What features of the Stalinist political and legal system might have driven these unusual charges of corruption in the military courts?

This scandal in the military courts has never been explored in detail in scholarly literature or in the popular press. Yet, we would argue, a close study of these cases can shed light on critical elements of the late Stalinist state and the peculiarities of its anticorruption drives, and can contribute to a deeper knowledge of aspects of high politics in the post-war years.[5] These cases provide insight into how accusations of corruption were used to discipline institutions and individuals and to exert central control over the legal system. As many observers have noted, the state's attacks on corruption, wherever they may occur, often have political aims that go well beyond the mere eradication of graft by functionaries.[6]

Major postwar political, legal, and ideological concerns shaped the drives against corruption in the courts. The regime's obsession with exposing counterrevolutionaries, wartime collaborators, and others guilty of "crimes against the state" was the driving force behind a no-holds-barred barrage aimed at any hint of corruption in the military courts. From the perspective of the party leadership, it was imperative to eliminate illicit deals between court employees and petitioners that might minimize punishments for counterrevolutionaries and wartime traitors.[7] Furthermore, the prosecutors in these cases, surely empowered by Stalin to attack the military courts, used aggressive methods to obtain compromising evidence and confessions. As was common in Stalinist political practice, party and procuracy investigators detected conspiracies nearly everywhere they looked. (These patterns of forceful—and often suspect—prosecution would repeat themselves, though in a different fashion, during the investigations of scandals in the high courts, detailed in chapter 8.) And, finally, this chapter provides a case study in how *accusations* of bribery (and other types of corruption) came to be used by party leaders as an effective, nonviolent political tool in late Stalinism, one whose use continued into later periods. This evolution of accusations of corruption into a political tool is one reason why the postwar Stalin period represents a transitional moment in the history of Soviet anticorruption efforts.

A precondition for the bribery case in the military courts was the "campaign" against bribery launched in the summer of 1946 (discussed in chapter 5). That drive had already lost steam by early 1947. Judging by the small number of arrests and convictions, the campaign's efforts were largely ineffective and unenthusiastically carried out. The drive stalled thanks in no small part to the foot-dragging and finger-pointing of the legal agencies themselves, which were aware of the illegal relationships that were present to some extent in the agencies of law enforcement. The procuracy and Ministry of Justice hesitated to draw attention to the corruption among their own cadres and within their institutions, and were reluctant to expose their own weak efforts at fighting it. Some party leaders expressed frustration at the snail's pace and sparse results of the campaign. Nevertheless, the 1946 drive sensitized party leaders, the courts, and the procuracy to the problem of bribery, while sending a warning to the bureaucracy that any hint of shady dealing could be scrutinized.

The campaign against bribery achieved one other thing that fueled later accusations: it pushed individuals to provide incriminating information about judges, procuracy employees, and other legal personnel that party authorities could deploy as needed. The Stalinist system constantly pressured Soviet people to denounce colleagues, co-workers, and others, and to provide compromising information about them. (Such bits of incriminating information were called "signals.") The huge informant network, flawed as it was in some ways, demonstrated the regime's commitment to extracting denunciations and confidential tips about all kinds of criminal (and moral) wrongdoing. In some instances, the details of alleged crimes by officials that flowed into party and law enforcement agencies served as political ammunition to be used against people who had fallen out of favor. Party authorities decided to take action against the accused in some of these cases. But since almost none of these investigations turned into major scandals, it is worth asking why party leaders decided to act so swiftly and forcefully when cases of alleged bribery in the military courts came to their attention in 1947.

THE SPARK: THE CASE OF LIEUTENANT BAKANOV AND THE MOSCOW MILITARY TRIBUNALS

Surprisingly, the trail that would eventually lead all the way to the country's most prominent military jurists seems to have begun with the secret dealings of a midlevel employee in a relatively minor military court in Moscow. The first hint of the coming scandal can be found in a letter sent to Central Committee Secretary Aleksei A. Kuznetsov by his deputies, on February 14, 1947, informing him that a criminal investigation into allegations of bribery in the judicial and procuratorial agencies of the Soviet armed forces had been initiated in November 1946.[8] The party's handling of this case lit the fuse that eventually would lead to explosive allegations regarding the Military Collegium of the USSR Supreme Court.

An important department of the Central Committee, the Cadres Directorate (*Upravlenie kadrov*), played a key role in this case, closely monitoring and framing the investigations. The Cadres Directorate, which was under the "general supervision" of Kuznetsov, was involved from the start of the scandal. It had responsibility for appointing officials to positions throughout the government and economy, as well as for monitoring the political reliability and moral transgressions of all party members. One of its roles was to gather compromising information about party members.[9]

The Cadres Directorate launched the investigation into the military courts upon the receipt of a denunciatory statement with an inflammatory claim—that bribery was widespread in several Moscow military tribunals. (The file does not state whether the denunciation was signed, and there is no information about its author.)[10] The Cadres Directorate report stated that investigators in the Main Military Procuracy of the Armed Forces had uncovered "proof" that employees in several of the military's legal agencies had accepted—or passed along as intermediaries—bribes from people with cases before the court. (The Military Procuracy reported to the USSR Procurator General.)[11] Nearly all these instances of bribery involved military courts in Moscow—both the lower-level military tribunals, and the intermediate-level military courts where convictions could be appealed. (It is worth noting that the quality of justice in the military tribunals was deemed by jurists to be of higher quality than the regular courts. Allegations of corruption in the military courts would have been regarded as especially shocking.) The report described motives, methods, and opportunities that are by now familiar. Petitioners with pending appeals allegedly paid cash or valuables to court employees, sometimes through go-betweens, in order to get favorable rulings.

The pivotal figure in this opening chapter of the scandal was a midlevel official, Senior Lieutenant of Justice Aleksei G. Bakanov, a twenty-eight-year-old senior secretary in the military tribunal of the Moscow Military District. Bakanov had served in that capacity since January 1946. (Between July 1941 and January 1946, he had been a senior secretary in the military tribunal of the Moscow Military Garrison, a lower-level military court.) Before his arrest on December 3, 1946, Bakanov allegedly took advantage of his positions in these military tribunals to solicit dozens of bribes.

In February 1947, investigators informed the Cadres Directorate that Bakanov had taken bribes in more than forty cases over the previous three years, stretching back to the middle of the war. He had purportedly pocketed about 150,000 rubles since October 1943, and spent much of his ill-gained money on drinking parties and gifts for performers in the well-known "Romen" gypsy theater in Moscow. When petitioners came to the court, "he promised to offer 'assistance' by speeding up the review of complaints, the reconsideration of court cases, and the release from custody of arrested and convicted individuals" in exchange for illegal payments.[12] Capitalizing on his access to members of the military tribunal of the Moscow Military District (an appeals court), he promised the family members of those convicted that the appeals court would annul or reduce the sentences assigned by lower-level tribunals.[13] With his unscrupulous actions, according to the Cadres Directorate, Bakanov had "undermined the authority and honor of the Soviet judiciary."

For employees of the military courts to have displayed leniency toward serious political criminals was egregious; to have done so in exchange for bribes was especially heinous. Bakanov was alleged to have accepted 1,300 rubles from one woman to help in the case of her sister, who had been convicted in 1942 of anti-Soviet agitation, a counterrevolutionary crime under Article 58–10. Another person allegedly gave Bakanov 3,000 rubles and some vodka in 1945, with the goal of having his son's conviction for desertion reversed. In a case from early 1946, a certain Arapova approached Bakanov and gave him 2,400 rubles for help in the case of her brother, who had been convicted by a military tribunal. (Bakanov had told her that there would be "some expenses connected with freeing her brother.") In still another instance, Bakanov took 5,600 rubles after promising the fathers of two men convicted by military tribunals that he would arrange for the reversal of their sons' sentences. (It is not clear what the sons were convicted of, and, in any case, Bakanov seems to have never followed through on his promise. Nevertheless, according to Soviet law, a bribe did not have to be successful to be considered a crime.) The indictment contains many similar instances in which the wives, husbands, parents, and children of people convicted by military tribunals allegedly approached Bakanov, either in person or through intermediaries, and paid him for assistance.[14]

During the Military Procuracy's preliminary investigations, Bakanov confessed to numerous instances of taking money and other gifts from the relatives of people who had been convicted by military tribunals in exchange for illegally softening their sentences or dismissing the charges against them. And although it is impossible to know definitively based on the available evidence, it does seem quite likely that some of the charges against Bakanov were grounded in reality.

In these cases, investigators concluded, bribes were usually offered via the conduit of well-placed court employees or defense lawyers. What was extraordinary about these accusations at the time was that the alleged bribes were nearly all related to cases involving *political* crimes such as counterrevolution or collaboration. As noted earlier, the acceptance of bribes in cases of political crimes seems to have been extremely rare in this period. Shockingly, investigators concluded that scores of illegal payments also had been accepted by several other employees of the Moscow military courts. Implicated in particular were staff of the military tribunal and the Military Procuracy of the Moscow Garrison (at the grassroots), and, at the intermediate appeal level, the military tribunal of the Moscow Military District (*okrug*).[15] Importantly, then, prosecutors were alleging that bribery in the agencies of military justice had occurred both in a lower-level Moscow military tribunal and, more important, in the intermediate-level court that heard appeals of these cases.

THE MILITARY TRIBUNALS

What were these military tribunals, whose personnel were now implicated, and what was their role? The NKVD *dvoiki* and *troiki* (two-person and three-person tribunals) established in 1937 had conducted perfunctory trials of "enemies of the people" and other political criminals. When these were abolished in November 1938, the military tribunals assumed responsibility for handling most of these counterrevolutionary cases, including "treason, espionage, terrorism, explosions, arson, and other forms of sabotage."[16] (The military tribunals handled many ordinary nonpolitical cases as well as these more sensitive cases.) During the war, the military tribunals heard cases of crimes related to the state of war, including spreading false rumors, creating undue alarm among the population, and voluntarily abandoning ("deserting from") one's job in a war-related industry. The Moscow Military Tribunal, headed by Aleksandr Vasnev, was created in October 1941, and it was especially active in the first months of the war.[17] Army bases and garrisons had their own tribunals, and units at the front established them as well. During the period of German occupation, nearly all regular courts in the country were reorganized into military tribunals.

Military tribunals tried thousands of alleged Soviet traitors and others accused of counterrevolutionary crimes, including, by early 1942, those alleged to have collaborated with the Nazis.[18] (The military tribunals also tried many people who were not accused of military crimes, including thieves, speculators, and hooligans.) In 1942, military tribunals tried over 16,000 Soviet citizens as "betrayers of the homeland" (*izmeniki rodiny*). The first major public trial staged by a military tribunal occurred in the Northern Caucasus city of Krasnodar in July 1943.[19] The trial, which ended with the public hanging of eight collaborators in front of a crowd of as many as 30,000 people, received enormous media coverage. (Nearly all other tribunals were held in secret.) Tribunals remained active for several years after the war. Between 1945 and 1953, tens of thousands of Soviet citizens were arrested and charged every year with treason or collusion with the Nazis.[20] Thousands were condemned to death by military tribunals, until the abolition of the death penalty in May 1947.[21] Others were sentenced to terms of imprisonment, typically from seven to twenty-five years. Many of those convicted appealed their sentences to higher military courts; it was allegations of illicit deal-making over these appeals that lay at the heart of this scandal.

The Military Collegium of the USSR Supreme Court supervised this large network of military tribunals which were busy processing—and putting on trial—hundreds of thousands of Soviet citizens accused of counterrevolutionary crimes, including wartime collaboration with the Nazis, under Article 58 of the Criminal Code. As the highest court of appeals for those convicted of crimes by the military tribunals, the Military Collegium made final determinations about the sentences handed down by grassroots tribunals in cases of alleged collaboration and other treasonous acts. Structurally, the Military Collegium was one of five collegiums within the USSR Supreme Court, each of which heard certain types of cases. (By the Stalin period, the USSR Supreme Court itself functioned not as a constitutional court—it had lost that responsibility in 1929—but rather as the country's highest court of appeals.)[22]

Many types of activity[23] from active support for the Nazis, to performing menial jobs such as cooking or cleaning for German forces in occupied territory (often under the threat of death), to the highly nebulous "treasonous intentions" and "hostile attitudes" toward Soviet power, were tried as counterrevolutionary crimes under Article 58.[24] The legal situation in the USSR was quite different from the postwar atmosphere in Europe (notably in France and Belgium), where courts dismissed or sharply reduced charges for certain acts of collaboration as "legitimate, albeit undesirable, efforts to survive." Mass amnesties followed.[25] In the Soviet Union, the courts' dominant approach was to support harsh retribution even toward passive bystanders or those for whom resistance to Nazi orders would have meant execution at the hands of the occupiers.

DENUNCIATIONS AND THE MILITARY COLLEGIUM

Taken by itself, the bribery case of Lieutenant Bakanov was unusual but not extremely so. It was certainly atypical to find allegations that military court personnel took bribes, but these allegations were originally confined to a few lower- and midlevel courts in Moscow. What is critical, however, is that the Bakanov case appears to have been used by Stalin as a pretext to target the Military Collegium of the Supreme Court with corruption charges.

A February 1947 Central Committee instruction provides evidence that pressure was being applied on the procuracy to push the Bakanov case much further, and to spare no effort to expose more bribe takers in the military-legal agencies of the capital. The instruction ordered the Main Military Procuror of the Armed Forces, N. P. Afanas'ev, to "personally supervise the investigation into cases of bribery in the military-procuratorial organs of the city of Moscow, ensuring its timely execution."[26]

Bakanov incriminated dozens of people in various Moscow military-legal agencies while in custody, with the result that these cases metamorphosed into a major scandal. Bakanov implicated dozens of employees at various levels of military justice for accepting bribes (not including more than twenty people who he claimed gave him bribes). Altogether, Bakanov incriminated as many as three dozen people with whom he had worked, including numerous military judges who, he said, took money to annul or reduce sentences. Those arrested included three judges from the military tribunal of the Moscow Military District; four judges and three secretaries who served on the military tribunal of the Moscow Garrison (plus two former members of that tribunal); a secretary for the chairman of the Moscow City Court; and a military investigator and an adjutant who served in the Main Military Procuracy of the USSR.[27] Eventually, the procuracy would accuse sixty-one people of involvement in bribery, with nearly all of the charges based on the denunciations of one person—Lieutenant of Justice Aleksei Bakanov.[28]

The Bakanov bribery affair might well have remained an isolated, if alarming, example of corruption at the lower levels of military justice in Moscow. Yet, judging by the course of the investigation, this case came to the attention of Stalin himself. The Cadres Directorate under Kuznetsov pursued the matter with exceptional diligence, and may have been instrumental in pushing the case forward. Crucially, the Cadres Directorate claimed that Bakanov had provided investigators evidence that some employees in the country's highest court of appeals for cases involving military crimes—the Military Collegium of the USSR Supreme Court—were taking bribes. As evidence of this, investigators stated that, after reviewing appeals, the judges of the Military Collegium in some cases minimized—or even dismissed—the sentences imposed by subordinate military courts.

"I WILL NOT SLANDER": THE PECULIAR TRIAL OF BAKANOV

Investigators alleged that Bakanov told petitioners he had powerful connections inside the Military Collegium itself. People willing to give bribes could expect positive results from Bakanov because he would take their cases to certain "helpful" members of the Military Collegium. During interrogations, Bakanov implicated at least two employees of the Military Collegium—Kevesh, an assistant secretary, and Borodavkin, an inspector. Bakanov's denunciations of staff in the Military Collegium helped to create a major scandal that would envelop several Soviet high courts for years.

In the midsummer of 1947, between July 17 and July 24, one of the most unusual bribery trials in the history of the Soviet Union took place in Moscow. It was a closed trial of twenty-five people allegedly involved in the Bakanov affair. Because these cases were considered to be of exceptional importance, they were tried by a special session of the Military Collegium of the Supreme Court itself. A three-judge panel comprising justices of the Military Collegium therefore had the exceedingly uncomfortable (and, one could argue, particularly Stalinist) task of presiding over a trial in which testimony implicated some of the Collegium's own employees.

At the conclusion of the trial, the judges convicted Aleksei Bakanov of accepting or acting as a conduit in bribes totaling nearly 100,000 rubles. Because many of these bribes involved cases of counterrevolutionary crimes, Bakanov was convicted under Article 58-7 of using a state agency for subversive activity (or "wrecking"), and under Article 16 for a "crime against the social order."[29] The Military Collegium sentenced Bakanov to twenty-five years in a labor camp, the maximum possible sentence. Bakanov's timing, inadvertently, was excellent; Stalin had abolished the death penalty just two months earlier.[30] The court convicted nineteen other defendants for giving bribes or acting as intermediaries, assigning them sentences ranging from two to five years in prison.

Yet, in spite of this predictable outcome, the case had many striking peculiarities. One quite noteworthy aspect is that many of the original charges were thrown out before the case even came to trial. During the preliminary investigation, the military prosecutors released thirty-four of the people they had originally charged. The dismissal of so many charges was highly atypical in Soviet legal practice.[31] And despite the fact that the Military Procuracy originally arrested more than a dozen people for taking bribes, judges convicted only one person, Aleksei Bakanov, of actually having accepted bribes.[32] Several judges from local military tribunals whom Bakanov had implicated were released. Moreover, five of the twenty-five people who eventually *were* put on trial were acquitted for lack of evidence by the presiding judge, Fedor F.

Karavaikov, another rare occurrence in Soviet judicial practice. Ultimately, the court convicted only twenty of the sixty-one people originally charged.

Why were so many of the defendants let go or acquitted? Two remarkable letters preserved in state archives help to answer this question. On August 18, 1947, three weeks after the Bakanov trial had concluded, Ul'rikh wrote a letter complaining bitterly about how the prosecution had conducted the investigation. In this "top secret" and "personal" letter to I. T. Goliakov, the chairman of the USSR Supreme Court, Ul'rikh condemned the methods used by the Military Procuracy in the Bakanov case.[33] He warned Goliakov that, under extraordinary pressure from prosecutors, the lead defendant Bakanov had slandered at least forty innocent people. According to Ul'rikh, the trial revealed that prosecutors had pressured Bakanov to invent stories portraying court and procuracy employees as corrupt. In an attempt to reduce his own sentence, Bakanov had falsely implicated dozens of colleagues, and even people he knew only in passing, none of whom had anything to do with Bakanov's schemes.[34]

Ul'rikh's allegation of prosecutorial wrongdoing is all the more striking because he understood that the Military Procuracy was subordinate to the USSR Procuracy's office; he did not openly state, but clearly implied, that the Military Procuracy could not have taken these actions without the approval of the Procurator General of the USSR. Still, it seems clear that Ul'rikh felt himself safe writing about prosecutor misconduct. Perhaps he believed that he had earned a degree of impunity thanks to his service as the always-reliable lead judge in the political trials of the 1930s. There is, of course, no small irony in the thought of Ul'rikh, who had over the course of many years blithely sentenced to death thousands of innocent people on invented charges of treason and espionage, complaining about the "unfair" tactics of investigators who had coerced witnesses.

A second angry letter, this one written in August 1947 by the presiding judge at the Bakanov trial, Military Collegium justice Fedor F. Karavaikov, added some rather stunning details. He claimed that procuracy investigators had compromised the case in multiple ways. Judge Karavaikov was so bold as to claim that the investigators, before they had even begun their investigation, had already decided to "find" a major bribery case in the courts of Moscow. "My review of the materials in the case of Bakanov et al. shows that [investigators'] preliminary investigation *began with* [*the goal of*] *exposing a major case of systematic bribery, organized by a group, in the court organs of the city of Moscow* . . ." (emphasis added). Karavaikov claimed that investigators coerced Bakanov into implicating dozens of innocent people who held positions in Moscow military courts, including several employees of the Military Collegium in which Karavaikov served. In effect, Karavaikov was claiming that the USSR Procuracy had used a few scattered instances of petty bribery to concoct an enormous, artificial scandal.

Karavaikov's contention that the Military Procuracy could have acted as a rogue force, inventing scandals that reached into the Military Collegium, was incorrect—or, perhaps only partially right. Similarly, although one could speculate that Kuznetsov himself decided to launch an attack on Ul'rikh, either for his own personal reasons or as part of a factional battle, this seems highly unlikely in the Stalinist system. It is more likely that the decision to use the Bakanov case to create false charges against judges in the Military Collegium ultimately had to have been sanctioned by Stalin himself, considering the stature and fame of the Collegium's judges. The procuracy was more than likely following orders from the highest level of the party. Although Kuznetsov, as the chief of the Cadres Directorate, might have supplied Stalin with compromising information about the alarming prevalence of bribery in the military courts as a way of challenging Ul'rikh politically, in the Stalinist political system it was essentially inconceivable that the procuracy (or the Cadres Directorate) could have moved against a figure so prominent without explicit clearance from the dictator himself.

In his letter, Judge Karavaikov went on to lay bare the investigators' methods. During the trial, Bakanov told Karavaikov and the court that investigators had demanded that he lie during their interrogations. According to Bakanov, "One investigator told me, 'You, Bakanov, accepted 10,000 rubles in this case and got Makarychev released from custody, but you couldn't have done it alone. Who are your co-conspirators? Confess, name people, and it will be easier for you.' . . . [So] I named people." Once Bakanov began falsely denouncing his co-workers, "the investigators not only failed to cut short the unacceptable behavior of Bakanov, who went so far as to groundlessly depict as a bribe taker almost every judicial employee that he knew personally. The people carrying on the investigation even actively urged on Bakanov toward this kind of behavior."[35] In one case, Bakanov was granted a meeting with his wife and the right to correspond only after he agreed to falsely accuse a member of the military tribunal of the Moscow Garrison.[36] Karavaikov cited numerous instances in the printed record where Bakanov told the court that investigators had coerced him into accusing people he knew to be innocent.

Moreover, evidence shows that prosecutors were particularly interested in prodding Bakanov to implicate "organized groups" of employees of the Military Collegium of the Supreme Court in major bribery schemes.[37] At his closed trial, Bakanov testified that he had falsely accused Kevesh, a secretary in the Military Collegium, whom he barely knew. "I slandered Kevesh. I slandered her because the investigator constantly was trying to extract testimony from me about which employees of the Military Collegium I was criminally associated with." During the trial, Bakanov told judges that he had tried to rescind his lies. But prosecutors told him that if he would stick to his previous (false) statements, they would reward him by moving him out of solitary confinement, which he had already endured for eight months. At the trial, Kevesh herself told the judges that investigators pressured her to confess to nonexistent illegal deals with Bakanov. They constantly demanded to know which employees of the Military Collegium she had bribed. She refused, however: "I received no money from Bakanov, and I will not slander the staff of the Military Collegium."

Several patterns central to the course of the Bakanov case in the military courts foreshadow the forthcoming investigations of corruption in the high courts (to be discussed in chapter 8). In light of the available evidence, one can conclude that investigators, undoubtedly under the guidance of the party leadership, decided what kinds of crimes they would find—and who would be involved—in advance of their investigation. These cases came to the attention of the Cadres Directorate of the Central Committee, which acted on them. Party leaders seem to have worked from a playbook that provided the framework for investigation into Bakanov's dealings in the military courts. As Judge Karavaikov's extraordinary letter highlights, procuracy investigators wanted to find (in the words of Judge Karavaikov) "major cases" of "organized groups" of judges and court staff, who "systematically" took "large-scale" bribes, acting in concert in a far-reaching criminal "conspiracy." And although investigators implicated many low-level court staff, prosecutors set their sights on employees—especially judges—in the Military Collegium of the USSR Supreme Court.

The Bakanov case is the first indication that top party officials in the Stalinist autocracy were intent on using allegations of bribery to smear and, in some cases, to prosecute judges and other employees in the Military Collegium. It is clear that investigators were willing to use coercive methods to gather evidence, tainted or not. Defendants told judges that prosecutors used physical and psychological pressure to extract confessions and denunciations. Justice Karavaikov's damning letter certainly supports those allegations.

"LIBERALISM" IN THE MILITARY COURTS

It remains to be asked why these particular cases in the Moscow military courts eventually would trigger the major bribery scandal of the late Stalin period. One can begin to answer this question by noting that the cases unfolded in the first half of 1947 against a certain political and legal backdrop, which contributed to a lightning response from the party leadership. Procuracy investigators and the Cadres Directorate claimed that military court employees had accepted illegal payments to mute punishments for certain *types* of crimes whose prosecution was an important political priority for the regime. The party's response can be understood, in part, as an attempt to intimidate the judges in key courts to intensify their prosecution of those accused of crimes the party leaders had chosen to punish most severely in the postwar years.

In 1947 and 1948 the Cadres Directorate declared that the Military Collegium was insufficiently rigorous in its prosecution of political and wartime crimes. In particular, the Central Committee Secretariat severely criticized the Military Collegium for being overly lenient in its treatment of people convicted of counterrevolutionary crimes under Article 58. Party leaders said that judges of the Military Collegium had frequently "reduced sentences without basis" in precisely these Article 58 crimes.[38] The Cadres Directorate expressed anger at this "careless" handling of wartime crimes on the part of the military court system. In this environment, legal personnel accused of accepting a bribe or otherwise interfering in sentencing in any Article 58 case would face the full wrath of the law.[39]

During the hostilities, military tribunals had actively applied the death penalty in convictions for collaboration and treason. After the war, however, judges of the Military Collegium reduced many severe sentences on appeal (including death sentences), believing that they had been wrongly imposed by local military tribunals that misunderstood the law.[40] Military Collegium judges considered themselves to be correcting the gross errors of overzealous local tribunals by moderating (or dismissing) their excessively harsh sentences, as the historians Sergey Kudryashov and Vanessa Voisin have shown. The Military Collegium complained that the local tribunals, staffed with inexperienced jurists, convicted without sufficient evidence, assigned penalties incorrectly, or applied the wrong law.[41] It sometimes even dismissed convictions altogether if there was not substantial, verifiable evidence of wrongdoing.[42]

Once the hostilities ended, though, such leniency among judges was labeled as a dangerous "political error" that demonstrated an unacceptable lack of vigilance. The military tribunals—and the Military Collegium that supervised them—were watering down the prosecution of counterrevolution and "betrayal of the homeland," incorrectly giving light sentences. At precisely the time that many Western European nations had begun to draft amnesty laws for convicted collaborators, the opposite was occurring in the Soviet Union, as pressure to punish them intensified.[43] After the death penalty was abolished in May 1947, some party leaders complained, many judges in tribunals became soft, too often failing to assign the maximum allowable sentence of twenty-five years imprisonment to the worst offenders, and instead imposing much lighter penalties in thousands of cases. Just in the third quarter of 1947, for example, the local tribunals assigned "sentences that were obviously too light" to more than two thousand soldiers convicted of "betrayal of the homeland" (74 percent of all those convicted).[44] The Cadres Directorate asserted that the Military Collegium should never have tolerated these mild punishments.[45] Party officials kept Stalin apprised of the number of sentences the Military Collegium "improperly" reduced. A November 1948 report sent to Stalin noted "a serious distortion of the judicial line," stating that the sentences of thousands of people convicted for political crimes, including treason against the homeland and "anti-Soviet agitation," had been improperly reduced in 1947 by the Military Collegium.[46]

Doubtless under pressure from top officials in the Central Committee, in a November 1947 letter Supreme Court Chair Goliakov chastised Ul'rikh because too many military tribunals were showing "impermissible liberalism," and the Military Collegium was failing to correct these mistakes. The Military Collegium had failed to treat counterrevolutionary crimes with sufficient gravity, according to Goliakov.[47] In one case Goliakov cited, a Red Army soldier who had been captured in late 1941, and then served in the German army when the Nazis retreated from Stavropol' region and escaped in November 1942, was given twenty-five years by a military tribunal in the Northern Caucasus. On appeal, the Military Collegium lowered the soldier's sentence to ten years, declaring that the original sentence was "too severe." Claims by the Military Collegium that the sentences of those convicted of "counterrevolutionary agitation" should be reduced because the guilty parties had only spread their harmful ideas "among a limited circle of people," or because they were first-time offenders, were met with scorn. Ul'rikh came in for harsh criticism for reducing the November 1941 sentence for "anti-Soviet agitation" (under Article 58–10) of a soldier who had been heard saying, "Hitler promised to get to the Urals, and he will get there." Ul'rikh had filed a protest in February 1948, arguing that the soldier's sentence should be lowered from seven to six years. All these actions were examples of a "politically harmful line on reducing punitive measures against people exposed in committing serious state crimes."[48]

The judges of the Military Collegium thus found themselves in the crosshairs of two major postwar party priorities that, at first glance, seem unconnected: the ruthless punishment of counterrevolutionaries, collaborators, and other "political criminals"; and the attack on the influence of bribery in the legal system, economy, and public administration. The party carried out these initiatives against a backdrop of heightened retribution against any person or institution perceived as showing disloyalty to the Soviet state. The upsurge in indiscipline among officials (both real and perceived) was a serious concern as the party-state struggled to regain control over its own cadres, even as it labored to punish collaborators.

TARGETING THE MILITARY COLLEGIUM

Archival documents show that procuracy investigators began to swarm around the Military Collegium in late 1947 and early 1948, seeking to expose staff compromised by corrupt dealings.[49] The party's Cadres Directorate worked closely with the procuracy as it prosecuted any Military Collegium staff tainted by bribery, many of whom had been denounced by Bakanov.

One employee of the Military Collegium who felt the full force of the drive to intimidate and punish the Military Collegium was the senior inspector Colonel Lev N. Kudriavtsev. Arrested on June 21, 1948, and charged with multiple counts of bribery (after being denounced in a related investigation), he was held for more than two years until his trial. He refused to confess to any crime. Investigators alleged that, over the course of nearly five years, Kudriavtsev had used his position improperly to intervene with judges, asking them to annul or reduce sentences in exchange for cash payments. Most egregiously, prosecutors alleged, he had accepted bribes for meddling in sentences of people involved in military and political crimes. It was said, for example, that he took a bribe from the father of a woman convicted in 1944 of "desertion" from a military factory and given eight years in prison.[50] Ultimately, Kudriavtsev was sentenced for violating Article 193-17(b) of the Criminal Code, which covered extreme abuse of office by a person in a position of authority in the armed forces.[51] Before the abolition of the death penalty in May 1947, individuals convicted under this article were subject to execution; Kudriavtsev received twenty-five years in a labor camp.[52]

It is clear from the archival material, however, that investigators were less interested in finding corrupt legal consultants, clerical personnel, or lawyers (though they did make some attempt to find and prosecute them). Instead, Central Committee and procuracy investigators most enthusiastically targeted individual judges. Investigators first set their sights on Fedor F. Karavaikov, the Military Collegium judge who had presided over the Bakanov trial in July 1947. It was Karavaikov who had dared to complain about investigators who, in his view, had used illegal methods to concoct a major scandal in the Moscow military courts. Investigators from the Central Committee Cadres Directorate now alleged that Karavaikov himself had handled cases of treason incorrectly. Karavaikov's "politically mistaken" actions were categorized as part of a pattern of illicit influences on judges in the Military Collegium. It was alleged that, in early 1948, "the Central Committee had to intervene" in the case of a certain Kopelev, an officer who was convicted by a local military tribunal for "anti-Soviet agitation" and sentenced only to three years in prison. In light of the defendant's previous "Trotskyist" sympathies and other "anti-Soviet activities," the tribunal raised Kopelev's sentence to ten years. Upon review, a three-judge panel of the Military Collegium, headed by the presiding judge Karavaikov, had then "improperly" lowered Kopelev's sentence from ten to six years.[53] In the wake of this incident, on April 24, 1948, the Central Committee Secretariat sanctioned Karavaikov's removal from the Military Collegium and his expulsion from the party, and referred the matter to the Politburo.[54] The Politburo heard the case at its meeting of May 3, 1948.[55]

The attack on judges serving in the Military Collegium continued in the summer of 1948. In July, the Central Committee's Cadres Directorate recommended that at least four more judges said to be "too soft" on traitors be removed from the Military Collegium bench.[56] Justice A. A. Dobrovol'skii, for example, had "systematically allowed groundless reductions of sentences for traitors" over the course of 1947 and the first three months of 1948. Implying that Dobrovol'skii had been influenced by payments to compromise his judgment, the Cadres Directorate reported that "he annulled twenty court decisions in cases that were argued before him in the Military Collegium, including ten decisions in which he lowered the punishments of traitors." Similarly, Judge Siul'din had incorrectly annulled thirteen sentences, while Mashkov had signed off on twenty-two overly lenient sentences assigned by the tribunals.[57] The strong implication was that members of the Military Collegium had been motivated by bribes or other "gifts" received from petitioners in exchange for these light sentences. (No evidence of actual bribery is contained in the accessible files.)

Remarkably, the Central Committee Cadres Directorate also made allegations of bribery against General Ioan T. Nikitchenko, an internationally prominent Military Collegium judge and a deputy chairman of the USSR Supreme Court. Between October 1945 and October 1946, Nikitchenko served as the lead Soviet judge in the Major War Crimes trials held at the International Military Tribunal in Nuremberg.[58] His

Figure 7.2. Ioan T. Nikitchenko. Russian State Archive of Photographic and Cinematic Documents at Krasnogorsk (RGAKFD).

international renown did not protect him from accusations of official and moral corruption at home. Nikitchenko's stature makes it almost certain that the move to tarnish him could only have come with Stalin's approval. It is possible that Stalin's frustration with the "leniency" shown by the final verdicts at Nuremberg, with several of the German defendants receiving life in prison or long terms of imprisonment rather than death sentences, contributed to the targeting of Judge Nikitchenko. More generally, the disappointing Nuremberg verdicts may simply have reinforced Stalin's determination to see Soviet courts severely punish any defendants who had participated in any way, no matter how small, in the Nazis' barbaric actions against the Soviet Union—and thus inflamed his growing impatience with any perceived leniency towards appeals reviewed by the Collegium.

Deposition and trial transcripts show that at least two of the witnesses who accused Nikitchenko of taking bribes were urged to so do by USSR Procuracy investigators while they were held in prison. Their testimony against Nikitchenko is suspect.[59] A third person who was pressured to implicate Nikitchenko was Lev N. Kudriavtsev, an accused bribe taker (discussed above) who had worked as a Senior Inspector in the Military Collegium. In a 1950 letter to the Procurator General Safonov, Kudriavtsev complained that investigators had demanded that he implicate Nikitchenko. He refused because, he said, he believed Nikitchenko to be innocent.[60]

There is no convincing evidence that Nikitchenko took bribes, but there is a good deal of evidence in depositions and trial transcripts that procuracy investigators strained to implicate him in corruption. Simultaneously, the Cadres Directorate claimed that Nikitchenko had serious political and moral failings. A July 8, 1948 report by the Directorate alleged that Nikitchenko had committed a "serious antiparty offense." According to the report, Nikitchenko had hidden from his superiors the fact that he had met in Germany with a female German acquaintance who had served as the director of a research institute in Khar'kov during the occupation of that city. The acquaintance and her husband fled to Germany before the Soviets retook Khar'kov.[61] Sealing Nikitchenko's disgrace, the Supreme Court reported to Stalin in October 1948 that Nikitchenko's son had been arrested a few weeks earlier and "accused of a counterrevolutionary crime." (The crime was not specified.)[62] The Council of Ministers removed Nikitchenko from his position in the Supreme Court on June 18, 1949.[63] Nikitchenko likely spent years expecting to be arrested, but he never was.

Investigators also targeted Military Collegium judge Colonel Vasilii Vasil'evich Bukanov. (Colonel Bukanov is not to be confused with Aleksei *Bakanov,* the lower military court senior secretary discussed earlier whose bribery case jump-started this scandal.) Born in the city of Kaluga, the son of an industrial worker, Colonel Bukanov fought in the Red Army during the Civil War. He worked in court and procuracy positions from 1925, serving as the procurator of the Ramenskii region of Moscow oblast' until 1937, when he became the chair of the Moscow oblast' court. In 1938, he became a member of the USSR Supreme Court. Bukanov served in the Military Collegium of the Supreme Court until 1946, at which time he was sent to the Soviet Military Administration in eastern Germany (SVAG), where he worked on the reorganization of the German court system.[64]

On October 6, 1948, the USSR Procuracy informed Central Committee Secretary Kuznetsov that investigators had information that Bukanov had illegally accepted gifts in exchange for help with cases that came before him in the Military Collegium. According to the procuracy, Bukanov began to accept bribes beginning in 1944, and since that time he had continued to participate in various schemes.[65] As a result of this accusation, Bukanov was removed from his position in Germany and brought back to Moscow. Procuracy investigators began asking him questions in February 1949, but he was not arrested until September 5, 1949. Following his arrest he remained in a cell, with no further interrogation, for nine months.[66] Over the course of several months, Bukanov was charged with accepting several bribes in various cases. He invariably denied all charges. More than a year elapsed from the time of Bukanov's arrest until his first trial, November 24–25, 1950, at which time the court found him guilty of accepting bribes.[67]

The case of Bukanov provides an example of the approach that procuracy officials would take to intimidate judges charged with bribery. In the case of Bukanov, investigators greatly exaggerated weak evidence, and used dubious methods to bias testimony and extract confessions from the accused. (Indeed, a notable consistency emerges in the complaints about the procuracy's coercive methods across multiple cases.) Prosecutors alleged that Bukanov and the RSFSR Supreme Court judge Pavel M. Shevchenko were involved in a major bribery scheme together. Yet, testifying at Bukanov's second trial, Shevchenko told the judges that he had provided incriminating evidence against Bukanov only under aggressive pressure from investigators. Shevchenko said that he was subjected to "all-night interrogations in difficult prison conditions," after which he felt—physically and mentally—that he had no choice but to agree with his interrogator's false accusations.[68] Saying that he had lied at the first trial, Shevchenko changed his testimony at the second trial, now insisting that Bukanov was innocent.[69]

Similarly, another witness in the Bukanov case, I. M. Lebedev (an investigator for the Moscow oblast' procuracy), testified about investigators' efforts to compel him to implicate Bukanov. Lebedev told the court that the lead investigator, Golinkov, had locked him in a punishment cell (*kartser*) for seven months to force him to confess to fictitious charges.[70] Golinkov wanted him to accuse one or more judges.[71] Explaining the prosecutors' attempt to coerce false testimony from him, Lebedev said that he believed that they were trying "to conjure up the figure of the grand bribe takers (*bol'shikh vziatochnikov*)."[72] Lebedev told the court that Golinkov had informed him that he was just a minor target; they were mainly in pursuit of the judges Shevchenko and Bukanov.[73]

At his second trial, Bukanov reminded the presiding judges that he was no "enemy." And certainly, Bukanov was certainly no liberal. As he told the court quite accurately, he had built his entire career on crushing the enemies of the revolution: "I have lived my whole life honestly and my conscience is clean. I was one of the most active participants in the Civil War and in the destruction of the Right-Trotskyist Bloc, and in the purge of the party. I am not guilty of anything, and I do not wish my legacy to be ruined."[74] He was eventually cleared of all charges, but not until he had endured nearly two years in prison, repeated interrogations by procuracy investigators, and two trials. Bukanov asked the judges, "I don't understand. For whom is my conviction necessary?"[75]

"OPEN THE GATES TO UL'RIKH"

Even as a number of employees of the Military Collegium were investigated, relieved of their duties, and in some cases arrested in the spring and summer of 1948, the leader of the Military Collegium, Vasilii V. Ul'rikh, managed to hold on to the position he had occupied for more than twenty years. Born in Riga on July 1, 1889, he joined the Bolsheviks in 1910 and the Cheka (the political police) in 1918. In 1926, he became chairman of the Military Collegium. In addition to his role as the lead judge in all the major political trials of the 1930s, he had headed the secret investigation into the murder of Leningrad party chief Sergei M. Kirov in 1934. For most of Stalin's rule, Ul'rikh was arguably the most famous judge in the Soviet Union. (The Nuremberg judge Nikitchenko and the Supreme Court chairman Goliakov would be the other contenders.)

Amid the snowballing investigation into the Military Collegium in 1947 and 1948, however, Ul'rikh's fortunes took a sharp turn for the worse. By the summer of 1948, the Cadres Directorate (certainly with Stalin's endorsement) had begun to attack Ul'rikh for serious "errors." Kuznetsov, the head of the Cadres Directorate, reported compromising information about Ul'rikh to Malenkov, alleging that he had crossed a very dangerous line: Ul'rikh had improperly intervened in political cases.[76] According to the report, Ul'rikh's wife, A. D. Kassel', had herself taken bribes and then tried to influence Ul'rikh in several cases heard by the Military Collegium including, most unforgivably, two cases involving people accused of counterrevolutionary crimes. In early 1947, the mother of a man who had been convicted of theft of state property under the law of August 7, 1932 (which was categorized as a "counterrevolutionary" crime) approached Ul'rikh's wife and asked her to use her relationship with Ul'rikh to help with the case of her son.[77] The mother then telephoned another member of the Military Collegium trying to secure his assistance. According to the Cadres Directorate, Ul'rikh intervened in the case, lodging a protest on behalf of the man and then chairing the panel that reduced his sentence to a mere three years of probation.

In addition to the accusations of serious breaches of professional and political standards, Ul'rikh was personally disgraced. The report alleged that Ul'rikh was an alcoholic who had a politically and morally compromised German mistress. This woman, a certain Litkens "with no permanent place of residence," was "a morally corrupt person, an alcoholic, and a morphine addict," with a questionable political past. "Her ex-husband was an officer in the tsarist army who had ties with Trotsky and [A. P.] Rozengol'ts [who had had been politically close to Trotsky for a time]. He met with Trotsky in Istanbul in 1929 after his exile from the USSR."[78] Ul'rikh's mistress, Litkens, "exerts enormous influence over him and enjoys his exclusive trust." Ul'rikh had illegally given her a permanent pass to the Military Collegium's building. She actually attended trials there, including the trial of "a convicted terrorist." Moreover, according to the report, Litkens met with the relatives of accused counterrevolutionaries who had cases before the Military Collegium and, in exchange for fees, allowed them to meet Ul'rikh. The report implied that Ul'rikh had known about a bribe given to his mistress by the wife of a man convicted for "counterrevolutionary activities" and sentenced to ten years in prison. (By the time the Cadres Directorate wrote the report, Litkens had already been arrested and charged.)[79] The allegations that Ul'rikh's wife and mistress had both traded on his position in cases of political crimes were no doubt especially dangerous for him. Such accusations of improper handling of the cases of counterrevolutionaries would have cost Ul'rikh his life in 1937–1938.

Ul'rikh apparently felt himself to be professionally endangered during the investigations into the actions of his fellow Military Collegium members in the spring of 1948. In May 1948, he began to denounce others in the Military Collegium in an attempt to save his own skin. Stalinist bureaucracies could place great pressure on individuals to denounce their colleagues in order to protect themselves. (The case of Minister of State Security Viktor Abakumov, denounced by his deputy Mikhail Riumin when Riumin came under suspicion, is an example of this phenomenon.)[80] Ul'rikh—like so many other party officials—turned on his co-workers. On May 24, he sent a letter of denunciation to the Cadres Directorate of the Central Committee. Feeling pressure from above, Ul'rikh wrote that a judge on the Military Collegium, A. A. Dobrovol'skii, had failed to disclose compromising information about his family background. In particular, Ul'rikh wrote, Dobrovol'skii's father had served one year in prison, charged with an Article 58 crime that was later downgraded to a charge of negligence. Moreover, Dobrovol'skii's sister was married to a man who at the beginning of 1945 was convicted of a counterrevolutionary crime under Article 58 and got five years in prison; that man's father had been executed in 1937.[81] As was common in the Stalinist system, at the same time as Ul'rikh was trying to protect himself by turning against his colleagues, his colleagues were facing demands to incriminate *him*.

On August 24, 1948, Ul'rikh was removed as chairman of the Military Collegium. The Central Committee simultaneously dismissed several other justices of the Military Collegium, including Dobrovol'skii, V. S. Maslov, A. M. Orlov, and G. I. Iurgen'ev. The Central Committee instruction ordering Ul'rikh's dismissal detailed the "political errors" committed by the Military Collegium in its treatment of appeals in cases of "crimes against the state" (*gosudarstvennye prestupleniia*). This instruction reiterated earlier charges that under Ul'rikh's watch the Military Collegium had groundlessly reduced the punishments of those convicted of very serious crimes, including counterrevolution and treason against the homeland. In a final failed attempt to demonstrate his loyalty and save his job, on the day of his removal Ul'rikh wrote a letter to Molotov on Supreme Court letterhead. Suggesting that lower-level staff were to blame for the Military Collegium's "political errors," Ul'rikh advised sending the personnel files of all the Supreme Court consultants, secretaries, and other technical personnel to the Ministry of State Security for detailed checks on their political reliability. Sounding desperate on the brink of his downfall, he urged a "decisive battle with all the enemies of the Homeland, traitors, spies, thieves, pilferers of socialist property, and bribe takers."[82]

Notably, for at least two years after his dismissal, USSR Procuracy investigators continued to seek evidence that Ul'rikh had accepted bribes. These ongoing efforts to paint Ul'rikh as a bribe taker are clear from the transcripts of trials and interrogations now available in state archives. One Supreme Court judge, Valentina Chursina, was prodded by investigators to say that she had heard that Ul'rikh took bribes.[83] A member of the Military Collegium, Colonel V. V. Bukanov (whose fate was discussed above), remarked at his own trial that as late as May 1950 procuracy investigators were still pressing him to implicate Ul'rikh in bribery. Colonel Bukanov testified that he was kept in solitary confinement for six and a half months to compel him to testify against Ul'rikh, but since he had no knowledge that Ul'rikh had taken bribes, he refused to do so. Investigators were aware that the two had quarreled in the past, and that Bukanov had even complained about Ul'rikh to the Central Committee. The investigators tried to exploit this personal animosity to obtain incriminating testimony—"to open the gates to Ul'rikh" in Bukanov's words.[84] This pressure on Bukanov as late as mid-1950 is further evidence that procuracy investigators, no doubt with instructions from the pinnacle of the party leadership, were intent on smearing Ul'rikh with accusations of bribery.

Despite these allegations and the USSR Procuracy's continuing efforts to find compromising material, Ul'rikh was never arrested. He died on May 10, 1951, and was buried in Moscow's Novodevichy cemetery, the final resting place of many political and cultural luminaries of the Soviet period.

CONCLUSIONS

In fact, there is very little evidence that anyone in the Military Collegium of the Supreme Court took bribes in the period under study here. Nevertheless, as this reconstruction of the chain of events in the military courts suggests, Stalin apparently decided to carry out a nonviolent purge, one that removed (and often disgraced) key figures in the Military Collegium through accusations not of counterrevolution, but of regular white-collar crimes.

The party leadership pushed an all-out assault on bribery in the military courts of Moscow, and then aimed at disgracing key judges in the Military Collegium, in part, I would argue, because Stalin believed that these actions reinforced crucial postwar political and legal priorities. The weak antibribery campaign launched in the summer of 1946 (discussed in chapter 5) finally gained traction—and with a vengeance—when allegations of bribery reached the agencies of military justice. A case of corruption in the military courts of Moscow, featuring an apparently quite entrepreneurial midlevel employee, served up a pretext for a sustained assault upon the Military Collegium. Prosecutors claimed that Military Collegium employees took payments to reduce sentences in cases of collaboration, treason, or other sensitive military crimes. One can imagine Stalin's rage at the notion that the Military Collegium of the Supreme Court, the country's final arbiter on the cases of collaboration and counterrevolution, harbored bribe takers, or tolerated bribery among its staff. Subsequently, a similar assault on bribery in several of the country's other major civilian appeals courts was unleashed in support of yet another urgent postwar priority—the protection of state property and the socialist economy, as chapter 8 will show.

According to Yoram Gorlizki and Oleg Khlevniuk, Stalin repeatedly resorted to a particular strategy: he targeted a figure whom he wished to disgrace or push aside, and then waited for an appropriate pretext to strike. The case of M. I. Baramiia, the second secretary of the Georgian Communist Party, is a good illustration. When Stalin wanted to eradicate alleged corruption among the leadership of the Georgian Republic in 1951, he used an otherwise mundane report on bribery in Georgian higher education as a reason to begin the attack. Stalin had already selected the target; he simply was waiting for the excuse. Baramiia was accused of using his patronage to defend bribe takers from among his own people. This was the beginning of what became known as the Mingrelian Affair, which resulted in the removal of the entire Georgian leadership and the undermining of Beria's patronage network.[85] Stalin's approach in that case appears to follow the same pattern as the campaign against the Military Collegium.

The attack on alleged corruption in the military courts highlights that the years between 1945 and 1948 represent an important transition in the history of corruption (and the drives against it) in the Soviet Union, bridging the indiscriminate violence against officials common to the 1930s and the nonviolent treatment of nearly all officials accused of crimes in the post-Stalin years.

One could argue that it was precisely in the period of postwar Stalinism that the party and procuracy began to perfect their use of accusations of corruption as a weapon, a political practice so common in later years.[86] As we have seen, in the decade following the October Revolution, the official narratives about bribery focused on the imminent threat of capitalist counterrevolution. Show trials of bribe-taking managers and middlemen in industry were intended to demonstrate that holdover capitalists and "Nepmen," in league with kulaks, were consciously trying to undermine the socialist economy. In the 1930s, after the kulaks had been eliminated and the economic bases of socialism had been solidified, the police linked all forms of abuse of office to Trotskyist and Bukharinist conspiracies, "wrecking" activities, or collusion with fascists and foreign intelligence services who were dedicated to betraying the Soviet Union to hostile forces abroad.[87] In the second half of the 1930s, the crime of bribery was largely ignored by the police and the procuracy, who instead tied deviance and criminality to nefarious and powerful enemies of the Soviet state. During these years, the few bribery charges that were lodged were typically folded into allegations of "antistate" activity.

Set against the memory of wholesale arrests of high court judges in the 1930s, the 1946–1947 accusations that the Moscow military-legal establishment showed a lack of vigilance in punishing "counterrevolutionaries" and "traitors" might have seemed to court staff to portend a new explosion of violence.[88] Yet, in a marked change, none of the judges removed from the Military Collegium after the war were accused of counterrevolutionary activity under Article 58 or purged as enemies of the people. Rather, in a modification of earlier practice (and in a link with the Khrushchev and Brezhnev periods), prosecutors charged them with regular white-collar crimes or simply labeled them as morally unreliable or incompetent.

In light of this changed state of affairs, accusations of corruption could now serve as a nonviolent tool of party discipline or as a proxy in political competitions. As was always the case in the Soviet Union, the law and the courts served both a political and a legal function; the law was a tool of state and served its goals. After the war, accusations of engaging in bribery—one of the mundane realities of Russian life for centuries—became one of the party's most effective methods for intimidating and removing members of the state bureaucracy and the party apparatus (and, in these cases, the courts) when they failed to respond to the leadership's priorities. Accusations alone served to disgrace the judges in these cases. Those judges who "incorrectly" reduced the sentences of counterrevolutionaries and others were not accused of treason, but they were accused of bribery or other forms of abuse of office. While some of them were imprisoned, in general the accusations were not accompanied by violence. These were witch-hunts, but nonviolent ones.

For several reasons, party watchdogs found that this approach served their purposes after the war. For one thing, corruption was a potent charge to level against the judiciary (among others in positions of authority). It was a very difficult accusation to defend oneself against, of course; it is a major challenge to prove that one is *not* corrupt. To be sure, a great deal of systemic corruption was not prosecuted, and many corrupt people eluded charges for many reasons, including their political connections. A major argument of this book is that, after the war and the purges ended, accusations of criminal corruption or white-collar abuse of office became more common. Stalin announced in 1939 that the Trotskyist opposition had been wiped out in the Terror; accusations of such ideological crimes and organized conspiracies had to vanish along with this claim. Now when the party and procuracy wished to undercut the authority of certain officials, they could charge them with corruption rather than a political crime. (Charges of corruption had never fully disappeared, of course, even during the purges.) This shift in descriptions of the "bad" official, from Trotskyist traitors and enemies of the people, to morally corrupt, "fallen" officials, can be regarded as something of an innovation of late Stalinism. Even in the 1930s, the police often smeared alleged "enemies of the people" with charges that they were somehow morally and professionally corrupt. But such allegations blossomed after the war (together with the material hardships that led many officials to resort to using their offices to earn income), while violence against officialdom nearly ended.

The investigations of corruption in the Moscow military courts in 1946–1948 form the backdrop to one of the largest bribery scandals in the history of the Soviet Union. Ultimately, evidence from those investigations would lead party and procuracy agencies into an extraordinary confrontation with the leading personnel of several of the country's most important courts. This "Affair of the High Courts" is the subject of chapter 8.

8 The Death of a Judge
Scandal and the Affair of the High Courts

PART I: THE AFFAIR OF THE HIGH COURTS

ON JUNE 4, 1948, the deputy chief justice of the Soviet Supreme Court, Andrei Petrovich Solodilov, shot himself in his Moscow apartment. Eleven months after Aleksei Bakanov was sentenced to twenty-five years in prison, convicted of accepting dozens of bribes in the Moscow military courts, this shocking incident rocked Moscow's judicial world. Forty-eight-year-old Judge Solodilov committed suicide in the midst of one of the largest bribery scandals in the history of the Soviet Union. Investigators had been closing in on Solodilov at the time of his death.[1] His funeral, witnesses said, was a somber event, marked by whispered speculation about the judge's early death.

Andrei Solodilov was a key figure in the Soviet judicial system at the time of his death, and an unlikely person to be caught in the web of a bribery scandal. In 1937–1938, he had served as chair of the RSFSR Supreme Court (the highest judicial body for the Russian Republic). Before his appointment to the all-Union Supreme Court in 1938, he had served on the Military Collegium of the Supreme Court. In his capacity as deputy chair of the USSR Supreme Court, Solodilov had oversight responsibility for a large proportion of criminal cases and all civil cases. Something of a legal scholar, Solodilov was the co-author of a textbook on inheritance law.[2] To his colleagues, he appeared to be very tense, with a skittish and volatile personality. His supervisor, the chairman of the USSR Supreme Court Ivan T. Goliakov, had described Solodilov as an essential jurist in the court, but also a "nervous, irritable, hot-tempered person" with a "serious heart condition" who "lacked tact."[3] A lawyer who knew Solodilov confirmed that he was an anxious man. During conversations in his office, Solodilov would jump out of his chair, tear up pieces of paper, and pace nervously about the room.[4]

And Solodilov had good reason to be nervous. He was a man with many secrets. At the time of his suicide in June 1948, procuracy investigators were preparing to charge him with soliciting dozens of bribes over the course of more than five years. And soon after Solodilov's death, the procuracy reported to Stalin and the top party leadership that the allegations of corruption against Solodilov were just the tip of the iceberg. Investigations reported that they had uncovered literally hundreds of instances of bribery, involving dozens of employees and multiple judges in many of the country's most prestigious courts. By mid-1949, Procurator General Safonov would claim that a minimum of twenty important judges had taken bribes from citizens in exchange for assigning lenient sentences, or had known that their colleagues were involved and had failed to report them. Recently declassified archives show that the scandal culminated with at least twenty-two secret trials involving more than three hundred defendants.[5]

This chapter examines the major bribery scandal of the Stalin period, what we will refer to as the "Affair of the High Courts." The scandal has never been studied in depth. It has been mentioned briefly in one academic study, and is essentially unknown to historians and nonspecialists alike.[6] Ultimately, the affair developed into one of the great corruption scandals of Soviet times.

The affair began in part with the troubling, if seemingly localized, cases of alleged bribery involving the agencies of military justice in Moscow—focusing on the transgressions of court secretary Alexei Bakanov—described in the previous chapter. Party and procuracy investigators followed trails that led from minor figures in peripheral courts to the country's most senior judges. From the Bakanov case in the Moscow military courts, the scandal branched out through multiple Moscow courts almost simultaneously. It first reached the Military Collegium of the USSR Supreme Court. Investigators then moved to

Figure 8.1. Clockwise from upper right: deputy chair of USSR Supreme Court A. P. Solodilov; chair of Military Collegium V. V. Ul'rikh; chair of USSR Supreme Court I. T. Goliakov; deputy chair of USSR Supreme Court I. T. Nikitchenko. Photo taken in 1938. Russian State Archive of Photographic and Cinematic Documents at Krasnogorsk (RGAKFD).

other major courts in Moscow, and eventually progressed to several republic-level and regional courts. (Although in most cases I have tried to ascertain whether the people accused were actually guilty of the bribery charges the procuracy lodged, that very difficult, retrospective task is not at the center of the chapter. While I have my suspicions—supported by the evidence—in many cases it is simply not possible to know definitively whether given individuals committed the actions the authorities ascribed to them.)

The scandal in the high courts is a revealing moment in the history of Stalinism, Soviet criminal justice, and the development and prosecution of corruption in the Soviet Union.[7] The first section of the chapter addresses several critical questions, some of which concern the location and timing of the affair. Questions about the investigations themselves also abound. How were these extremely sensitive and potentially embarrassing allegations investigated? What were the roles of leading party agencies and the procuracy as they reacted to claims of widespread criminality in the country's highest courts? What can the scandal tell us about postwar Stalinist high politics and the legal system? The second part of the chapter looks beyond the official accusations and narratives, asking why some high court judges and other court employees would make deals with petitioners and intermediaries in the first place, putting themselves at great risk.

Although from this distance we cannot be absolutely certain what transpired, it seems clear that certain judges in the high courts of Moscow did take bribes on occasion during the war and the postwar years. Bribe-taking judges and other employees were found almost simultaneously in several important high courts. Aggressive investigations were launched, and procuracy methods, which combined legitimate investigative work with coercion and denunciations, caught what seem to have been both innocent and guilty people in the net. In many cases, party and procuracy leaders likely did not themselves know who was guilty and who was innocent of the charges against them. While it would be simple to argue that high court judges were uniformly corrupt, or to argue that Stalin and his circle simply invented the scandal out of whole cloth, both of these extremes would be incorrect.

If the process of "bringing order" to the country's highest military court involved concocting false corruption charges against the staff of the Military Collegium (as described in the previous chapter), the matter became quite a bit more complicated as investigators began looking into the actions of employees in other key courts. Again, what we know about the political system Stalin designed leads us assume that any attack on the country's most senior and famous judges could only have been launched with Stalin's explicit approval, even if he was not himself immersed in the details of the investigations. If the model for the Military Collegium scandal was to target certain individuals, and then to use some of the many denunciations the system had produced to carry out an attack against them, then the High Courts affair bore certain similarities. Yet this affair also differed in essential ways. While Stalin clearly wished to discipline courts in Moscow, using allegations of corruption to do so, documents provide a good deal of evidence that investigators in fact exposed a troubling number of bribe takers in the courts. The course of the affair indicates that the scandal might have spread beyond what Stalin originally anticipated, and Stalin might have made efforts to put the brakes on a rapidly spreading scandal.

From the start of the affair, the Central Committee's Cadres Directorate (which existed until July, 1948) and its successor the Department of Administrative Organs (after its creation in July 1948) were closely involved in the investigations into corruption in the courts. They worked with and monitored the procuracy investigators working on the cases. Procurator General Safonov frequently provided progress reports to these Central Committee departments. During the series of cases that would come to make up this scandal, Central Committee departments—almost certainly with Stalin's approval—intervened at crucial moments, set the tone for the investigations, and made decisions about how to proceed with both investigations and trials. Documents give the impression that the Cadres Directorate essentially empowered the procuracy to pursue charges of corruption among court personnel with unalloyed enthusiasm, yet it also reined the investigation in at certain moments.

On July 10, 1948, the Politburo resolved to liquidate the Cadres Directorate and redistribute responsibility for personnel to several smaller departments (*otdely*), which were to be responsible for supervising the political actions and personnel of various branches of the economy and government.[8] With the disbanding of the Cadres Directorate, which had been headed by Central Committee Secretary Aleksei A. Kuznetsov, other Central Committee departments took on a more active role in appointing and monitoring party cadres in the organizations under their supervision. The department that would now have a huge role in the cases in the high courts was the new, blandly named, but extremely important, Department of Administrative Organs (*Administrativnyi otdel*). Kuznetsov had responsibility for "general supervision" of the new, split-off department. Despite its bureaucratic title, the Department of Administrative Organs was in fact charged with supervising the complex of legal and security agencies and their personnel, including the Ministry of State Security, but also the Supreme Court, the Ministry of Justice, and the procuracy.[9] Kuznetsov oversaw the party's monitoring of the investigations.

The Moscow City Court: Intoxicated with "the Easy and Happy Life"

As investigators pursued allegations of bribery in the Military Collegium in the spring of 1948, the scandal exploded and spread quickly throughout the judicial establishment in the city of Moscow. Correspondence demonstrates that investigations spread to several of the country's most important courts almost simultaneously—the Moscow City Court, the Supreme Court of the Russian Republic (RSFSR), and the USSR Supreme Court.

First, prosecutors followed the bribery trail from Moscow's military courts to an important appeals court, the Moscow City Court (*MosGorSud*). The Moscow City Court was created in 1932 to hear appeals coming from the lower-level people's courts in the Moscow region. By the spring of 1948, several employees of the Moscow City Court had been denounced by Aleksei Bakanov.[10] Bakanov implicated three people, including an assistant to the chairman of the Moscow City Court. They, in turn, implicated A. V. Vasnev, chairman of the Moscow City Court.[11]

If "counterrevolutionary" cases involving "betrayal of the homeland" were the driving force in investigations of bribery in the military courts, it was cases of "crimes against the socialist economy," especially theft of state property and, to a lesser degree, speculation in shortage goods, that were at the heart of the scandal in the Moscow City Court. Procuracy officials argued that, in exchange for under-the-table gifts and cash, judges had given excessively lenient sentences to thieves of state property and other "dangerous" criminals during and after the war.[12] In the postwar years, Stalin's drive to root out thieves of state property led to heightened scrutiny of appeals courts. Especially after the decree of June 4, 1947, Stalin exerted tremendous pressure on the courts and the procuracy to punish thieves of state property to the fullest extent of the law. During the immediate postwar years, the regime communicated to the courts very explicitly that judges had failed to understand the prosecution of theft of state property as an urgent state priority. The contours and scope of the scandal must be understood within the context of this campaign, which reached its apex in 1948, in the wake of the issuance of the June 4 decrees.

On May 8, 1948, Procurator General Safonov wrote to Central Committee Secretary Kuznetsov, claiming that its investigations had uncovered a "criminal group" of bribe-taking employees in the Moscow City Court.[13] The group included the judges V. V. Gutorkina, Vladimir V. Obukhov, and A. A. Praushkina, each of whom was alleged to have taken multiple bribes.[14] Two court secretaries were also arrested.

The Moscow City Court seems to have been something of a breeding ground for illegal deals between judges and petitioners. By August 1948, forty-nine people had been arrested in the investigations of the Moscow City Court. Eighteen were accused of paying bribes, seventeen were intermediaries, four were lawyers, and ten were former court employees, including five judges. The judge Gutorkina, for example, allegedly took payments from several people convicted of speculation, agreeing to overturn the five-year sentences they had been given.[15] Although one cannot be certain, of course, the judges Obukhov, Praushkina, and Gutorkina all appear actually to have accepted bribes during their time on the Moscow City Court between 1943 and 1948, based on the trial transcripts and supporting materials. Each confessed his or her guilt (at trials where many of the accused declared their innocence), and none seem to have appealed their convictions when they had the opportunity, even after Stalin's death, despite their close familiarity with the appeals process.

The most intriguing figure in the Moscow City Court case was the judge Valentina A. Chursina. On April 5, 1948, Chursina was arrested and charged with accepting bribes in exchange for reducing sentences in a multitude of cases.[16] Chursina would turn out to be a crucial figure and a catalyst for the spread of the scandal to other courts. Born in 1909, Chursina had served as a judge in the Moscow City Court between 1938 and 1946. She had been selected as a member of the USSR Supreme Court in 1946. For a time after Lenin's death in 1924, Chursina told investigators, she had been the personal secretary for Lenin's wife, Nadezhda Krupskaia.

According to the people who knew her, Chursina was, at minimum, a charismatic if eccentric person.[17] Some thought her to be a brilliant, straight-talking jurist; others found her bizarre and corrupt to the core. Upon her arrest in April 1948, Chursina confessed to accepting more than twenty bribes in cases before the Moscow City Court in the first half of the 1940s. Judging from her testimony and that of several of her colleagues, she was a masterful entrepreneur of the bribe. As Chursina told her interrogators, she developed an elaborate network of informal—and highly profitable—relationships throughout Moscow while she sat on the bench. She brought subordinate employees into her schemes, winning their trust—and ensuring their allegiance—by arranging to get them, for example, a doctor's treatment or medicine. One such employee said that she "felt herself bound by her hands and feet by Chursina's favors."[18] Chursina even invited potential bribe givers to her wedding. In exchange for favorable consideration of cases, they brought her fine gifts (and cash) and treated her to expensive meals in Moscow's best restaurants.

Procuracy documents and trial transcripts show that Chursina played a role in the high court scandals similar to the one that Bakanov had played in the military court cases in 1947. Chursina was representative of a certain "type" that was essential for Stalinist law enforcement—the highly placed official who both abused her office and, once caught, implicated her colleagues, often falsely, in an unsuccessful attempt to deflect blame and save her own skin. Once she had been arrested and come under pressure from investigators, Chursina became a liberal denouncer of dozens of people she knew. Procuracy investigators encouraged her to turn in other court employees, and especially her fellow judges.[19] Her main role in the procuracy's investigation was to act as the chief accuser of senior judges in the highest courts of Moscow. Investigators focused on uncovering the criminal relationships that Chursina said she had developed in order to provide evidence of intertwined conspiracies among employees of the capital's most important courts.

She cooperated with the prosecution, offering details about several allegedly corrupt judges and other participants in bribery deals. In a crucial distinction from the purging of the judiciary's leading figures in the 1930s, the judges in the High Courts affair were never themselves accused of being "counterrevolutionaries" or "enemies of the people." They were alleged to be morally degenerate lawbreakers who had sold their consciences and compromised their integrity, but not saboteurs or "wreckers."

When interrogators spoke to Chursina while she was in custody, it was clear that their main target in the Moscow City Court was A. V. Vasnev, its chairman. Mentioned as the fiery chairman of the military tribunal for the city of Moscow during World War II in Victor Kravchenko's famous memoir *I Chose Freedom,* Vasnev was one of the Soviet Union's most renowned judges.[20] Born in 1906, Vasnev had been a party member since 1930, when he graduated from the law department of Moscow State University. In 1938, he became a justice in the Moscow City Court, where he served for ten years; he chaired the court from 1941 until his arrest on July 14, 1948. Vasnev and his accuser, Chursina, had been lovers for a time when they served together on the court, according to both of them.

Chursina claimed that Vasnev had corrupted her morally and professionally, blaming her acceptance of bribes and her problems with alcohol on the "degenerate" Vasnev.[21] As Nazi armies besieged the city in the autumn of 1941, Vasnev had served as the chief of the military tribunal for the city of Moscow, sentencing to death or prison military deserters, suspected spies, and those who spread panic.[22] At war's end, he was one of the few jurists (together with USSR Supreme Court Chairman Goliakov and Minister of Justice Rychkov) to be awarded the Order of Lenin for his work to "strengthen revolutionary legality and preserve the interests of the state during the Great Fatherland War."[23]

On the basis of very thin evidence indeed, the procuracy alleged that over the course of many years Judge Vasnev had taken multiple bribes to overturn convictions or reduce sentences, especially in cases of theft of state property, speculation, and white-collar crime. Investigators claimed that several directors of stores and restaurants in the city of Moscow had approached Vasnev to intervene in criminal cases involving themselves or their relatives.[24] Investigators prodded Chursina to relate—or to invent—salacious details about the judges of the Moscow

City Court, and especially Vasnev. They clearly urged her to make claims about the moral degradation of judges, and to detail criminal conspiracies involving court employees and all varieties of suspect ethnic or professional groups.

Chursina's testimony about the Moscow City Court can be seen as the culmination of several themes that run through the allegations of bribery in the high courts in these years, including accusations of conspiracy among judges, sexual depredation and other serious moral transgressions, associations with criminally inclined ethnic groups, and the infection of subordinate employees by the court's leadership.

By the summer of 1948, procuracy correspondence had begun describing Vasnev as "the head of a criminal group of bribe takers in the Moscow City Court."[25] A ten-page report, written by Procurator General Safonov on February 16, 1949, and sent to the Central Committee's Department of Administrative Organs, summarizes the accusations against Vasnev.[26] It contains a number of hallmarks of the emerging stereotypes of the corrupted postwar Soviet official. The report accuses Vasnev of leading a "conspiracy" in the Moscow City Court that operated with the goal of releasing guilty people from prison in return for bribes. An "organized group of justices of the court, closely connected among themselves, systematically took bribes over many years to free criminals from punishment or to issue unjust sentences and decisions."[27] Vasnev had also allegedly corrupted his underlings. As Procurator General Safonov's letter put it, "Through his criminal activities, Vasnev enabled the moral dissipation of a significant group of employees of the Moscow City Court."[28]

Chursina told investigators that under Vasnev's devious influence she became enthralled with "the easy and happy life." The environment Vasnev created served to snare her into a life of crime. She came to delight in receiving gifts of free meals and stylish clothing from people who wanted to influence her. Chursina described the feelings of shame that, she said, she now felt: "Falling into these surroundings, into the atmosphere of 'the easy life,' having become accustomed to enjoying these favors and receiving gifts, I slid into the abyss, and I couldn't find a way to escape from it."[29]

The accusations went further. Chursina alleged that people with cases before the court often offered Vasnev gifts of food or treated him to meals in restaurants. Prosecutors claimed that Vasnev drank excessively with extended circles of people from whom he eventually accepted bribes. Chursina claimed that at least forty people, including the director of the Bol'shoi Theater, had given bribes to Vasnev. She told investigators that Vasnev even held drunken parties with his cronies at the Hotel Moscow (located just off Red Square) in the fall of 1941, when Nazi armies were attacking the outskirts of the city. Prosecutors thus characterized Vasnev as a coward who wholly lacked dedication to party ethics and the integrity of the Soviet state, and who ignored the sacrifices of Red Army soldiers.[30] Vasnev's absence of patriotism during the war, his partying, and his general moral collapse even as Soviet soldiers were dying just a few kilometers away were all key elements of a damning narrative.

Another central aspect of the accusations focused on Vasnev's suspicious circle of associates. The ethnic prejudices of investigators (and of the ordinary people who were asked to make denunciations) shine through here. The indictment against Vasnev stated that when he served as chairman of the court, the criminals with whom he made deals were frequently from ethnic minorities, including people who were Jewish or from the Caucasus (typically Georgian or Armenian), and heavily involved in the illegal economy.[31] Chursina alleged that Vasnev's cronies participated in subversive capitalist activities, saying that he took bribes from two people convicted of "speculating" in scarce food products, which they brought from the northern Caucasus and resold at high prices in the markets of Moscow.[32] The people from whom he allegedly took bribes often worked in retail trade networks, which were frequently said to be rife with corruption. The retail trade employees, including several store managers, used their access to steal scarce products—especially food and drink—and sell them for inflated prices on the black market. Prosecutors claimed that directors of stores, cafeterias, restaurants, and warehouses (many of whom had Jewish, Georgian, or Armenian-sounding names) sought out and befriended Judge Vasnev in order to buy their way out of convictions for crimes that they or their friends and family had committed. When asked about Vasnev's partners in crime, Chursina specifically named the managers of seven stores and five restaurants in Moscow, several of whom were Georgian or Armenian.

The evidence against Vasnev, however, was extremely thin, resting largely on Chursina's own testimony. Indeed, the available evidence supports Vasnev's position that Chursina lied about his activities.

In sum, the accusations against Judge Vasnev represent an amalgamated post-purge scenario featuring secret relationships, conspicuous consumption by elites, dangerous underground capitalism, wanton drunkenness, growing disloyalty, and the threats of Jewish and Caucasian criminal networks, all undergirded by a healthy dose of Great Russian chauvinism that tended to highlight the interethnic tensions that were becoming increasingly prominent in the postwar years. The Vasnev case, then, could be considered a prototype of the postwar Stalinist narrative of bribery, complete with a full cast of degraded supporting actors.

Engulfing the RSFSR Supreme Court

On May 10, 1948, just days after announcing that investigators had exposed a bribery scandal in the Moscow City Court, USSR Minister of Justice Gorshenin sent a dramatic letter to Kuznetsov at the Cadres Directorate. Gorshenin reported that evidence had been uncovered that implicated numerous employees of the RSFSR Supreme Court, including several judges, in "criminal malfeasance."[33] The letter was the first indication that the scandal had spread to another of the country's most prominent courts. The RSFSR (Russian Republican) Supreme Court was the country's second most important court, after the Supreme Court of the USSR. Safonov informed the Party Control Commission that bribery and abuse of office in the RSFSR Supreme Court were "extremely widespread."[34] The criminal patterns that the procuracy described are familiar: a large group of employees, including judges, clerks, secretaries, typists, and legal staff members who screened cases for review (*konsultanty*), had taken or arranged bribes "in an organized way," exploiting "an unhealthy atmosphere" in the court.

Safonov described the central position of intermediaries in the way that bribes changed hands in the RSFSR Supreme Court. Employees hatched schemes in which they would act as conduits between judges and petitioners bringing appeals to the court. "The criminal element," he noted, "seeking and finding ways to be freed from punishment, acted mainly through the intercession of defense lawyers and every kind of schemer, who functioned like middlemen in a type of business, using their close connections with certain judicial employees."[35] These intermediaries, often court secretaries and clerks, would strike deals with the relatives of the accused. As was the case in the Moscow City Court, nearly all the petitioners accused of offering bribes had been convicted of theft of state property or economic crimes. Under the phony pretext that they were representing their own relatives or acquaintances, intermediaries would approach judges and other top staff with requests to review a sentence. The intermediaries would write up the official appeals themselves. Once the court made a positive ruling, these go-betweens would bring the written ruling to the family. They would be rewarded with a fee that the parties had agreed upon beforehand.[36]

During the spring and summer of 1948, several judges who served on the RSFSR Supreme Court were arrested and charged with accepting bribes. Ultimately, at least five justices of the RSFSR Supreme Court were tried and convicted, including Pavel M. Shevchenko, Daniil Kh. Murzakhanov, and Bilial D. Kumekhov. In addition, a former deputy chair of the court, S. A. Pashutina, was arrested in 1950. (Discussion of Pashutina's case made it to the Politburo, though no detailed account is extant.)[37] Another deputy chair, N. V. Vasil'ev, was removed from his position as "not worthy of trust" on October 19, 1948, accused of knowing about corrupt activities but doing nothing.[38]

The chairman of the RSFSR Supreme Court, forty-three-year-old Aleksandr M. Nesterov, came in for sharp criticism, but he was never charged with a crime. On August 14, 1948, Kuznetsov's deputy Lopukhov called Nesterov to the Central Committee's Department of Administrative Organs and, in an undoubtedly testy meeting, "focused [Nesterov's] attention" on correcting the flaws of the court. Nesterov admitted shortcomings and promised to eliminate them.[39] On June 15, 1949, in spite of Nesterov's assurances, the Politburo removed him from his position for poor leadership and inadequate supervision of the court's employees.[40] He was accused of consciously overlooking evidence of ongoing bribery and moral degradation among members of the Supreme Court. Nesterov had also allegedly accepted a small gift of three bottles of alcohol from the head of an alcohol trust in 1945. Humiliated by his dismissal and denied another position in government despite repeated requests for a job as a jurist, Nesterov was excluded from the ranks of the Communist Party on July 28, 1949.[41]

Some of the procuracy's descriptions of bribe-taking employees in the RSFSR Supreme Court featured "debauchery," playing out in an environment that fostered dubious behavior and relationships.[42] Allegations against RSFSR employees emphasized pervasive drinking on the job among the staff. According to procuracy investigators, the leadership of the court—Chairman Nesterov and his deputies—"cultivated" drinking and banquets in the court's offices during work hours. Licentious behavior was widespread among the staff, feeding an atmosphere of recklessness. Many defendants in this case, such as the RSFSR Supreme Court senior consultant Popov, described their professional "fall" resulting from some personal vice that found fertile ground at the court. Popov testified that his descent into bribery resulted from his drunkenness.[43] Prosecutors alleged that "he never came to work sober over the course of many years, had ties with various people who had a personal interest in the outcome of cases, drank up their payments, and accepted bribes."[44]

Further accusations of moral degeneration surfaced as the investigations into the high courts proceeded in 1948–1949. In a mid-1948 report procuracy investigators highlighted the "corruption among female employees" of the RSFSR Supreme Court.[45] The forty-eight-year-old judge Maria G. Ivanova, who was arrested on August 24, 1948, was upbraided for her "immoral behavior."[46] The report condemned her private life: "Since 1935, Supreme Court Judge Ivanova had carried on abnormal sexual relations and cohabitated with S. A. Rostova, an employee of the Cadres Department of the RSFSR Supreme Court." The procuracy explained her professional corruption by pointing to her sexual "deviance." She was a morally depraved woman who also compromised her professional integrity, the report claimed. "On the basis of these abnormal relations," she was unable to refuse her lover's request to intervene in the case of a relative who had gotten into trouble. Under tremendous pressure at her trial, Ivanova told judges (in a closed-door meeting) that she had had sexual liaisons with women. Presiding judges required her to name all the women with whom she had had "intimate relations."[47] She was also forced to state that another justice on the RSFSR Supreme Court, N. P. Kiseleva (who still served on the court at the time of this trial), had had same-sex relations with women, and that Kiseleva had a lover (Smirnova) who was also an employee of the court. Even worse, according to investigators, "Kiseleva cohabitated not only with Smirnova, but with many other women who did not work in the Supreme Court."[48]

Similar allegations involving unseemly brews of sexual perversion, moral depravity, professional compromise, and unrestrained greed for private gain were at the center of many bribery narratives in the high courts of Moscow. When procuracy investigators wrote about bribery cases, they often relayed in lascivious detail the purported sins of their subjects. Investigators wasted no time forwarding such information to their supervisors in the Central Committee in their attempts to affirm that judges and lawyers who took bribes were both professionally and morally corrupt.[49]

Enterprising judges and court employees who profited from secret capitalist activities at work featured in another common accusation. In a stunning example of the alleged corrupting effect of "capitalist mentalities," prosecutors accused several judges and other staff at the RSFSR Supreme Court of an elaborate fraud that involved "speculating" in the fruit trade. In the late autumn, when fruit was scarcest in northern cities, a network of traders illegally transported apples to Moscow from the resort city of Sukhumi, located on the west coast of Georgia.[50] In 1945, thirteen and a half tons of apples were shipped by rail to Moscow with the help of Georgian middlemen. Most of the fruit was distributed to the staff of the court. But a group of employees siphoned off five tons of the apples for sale in private markets in Moscow. Still more were sold on the grounds of the court for a premium. The profits on the illegal sales were to be divided among a Supreme Court judge, other staff at the court, the middlemen, and the director of the Abkhazian collective farm that supplied the fruit. (The documents do not provide enough detail to fully understand what actually happened in this case. The procuracy likely embellished the situation, and, atypically, the files contain no rebuttal or explanation from court staff.) The employees involved were accused of succumbing to the temptation of a vile, illicit capitalism that took root on the grounds of the court, of all places. Similar narratives of greedy officials "falling" after being ensnared in the temptations of capitalism had great staying power throughout the entire Soviet period.

In a case that involved dozens of people working in Moscow, the RSFSR Supreme Court judge (and admitted recipient of multiple bribes) P. M. Shevchenko told the court that he fell into the grip of a Georgian criminal network in Moscow when he was desperate to obtain cash to repair his war-damaged apartment.[51] Shevchenko said that he was "bought" by several Georgians who gave him large cash bribes to intervene in criminal cases involving their friends and relatives who were accused of illegal underground trading.[52] In the fall of 1946, the Georgian manager of a Gorkii Street wine store who was trying to have his father's conviction for theft of state property overturned brought Shevchenko into contact with a group of his Georgian associates.[53] Having no money, Shevchenko borrowed several bottles of vodka from the store manager, Arkadii A. Rurua, to pay the people who were repairing his damaged roof. Henceforth, Shevchenko felt obligated to Rurua, who turned out to be a leader of a "network" of "criminal" Georgians.

Procuracy investigators alleged that Georgian retail trade workers and store managers, perfectly positioned to profiteer, used Shevchenko's help when they got in trouble for trafficking in scarce goods. They also blackmailed Shevchenko into fixing criminal cases involving people they knew. Shevchenko remained their puppet until his arrest in 1948.[54] Judge Shevchenko told the court that once he fell into the hands of these criminals he could not break free from them, fearing for his own safety and that of his family. The Georgians used intimidation and threats of violence to keep him compliant; Shevchenko even expressed relief to the police when he was arrested.[55] Again, these associations with Georgians trading in capitalism spelled disaster, according to the prosecutors.

Bribery in the USSR Supreme Court

As investigators continued to draw links among the cases in the Military Collegium, the Moscow City Court, and the RSFSR Supreme Court, a major new chapter of the affair opened. On May 14, 1948, just days after the procuracy had announced its investigation of the RSFSR Supreme Court, Procurator General Safonov wrote to the Central Committee, dramatically declaring that he had overwhelming evidence that the scourge of bribery had infected the country's highest judicial forum—the USSR Supreme Court.

The USSR Supreme Court was the country's highest court of appeals for both criminal and civil cases. (Interpreting the Constitution was officially the prerogative of the Presidium of the Supreme Soviet rather

Figure 8.2. I. T. Nikitchenko, center, and A. P. Solodilov, right. Russian State Archive of Photographic and Cinematic Documents at Krasnogorsk (RGAKFD).

than the Supreme Court.)[56] In order to fulfill its very broad case-review function, the USSR Supreme Court was quite large, comprising seventy justices by 1946, having grown from forty-six in the fall of 1938.

Procuracy archives show that by early 1948, Deputy Chairman of the USSR Supreme Court Andrei P. Solodilov (whose suicide opened this chapter) had been the target of intensive investigations for at least several months. It is impossible to know definitively whether Solodilov was guilty of all the charges leveled against him. There is, however, substantial documentary evidence and eyewitness testimony that Solodilov had taken advantage of opportunities to make illegal deals in multiple cases stretching back at least to 1943.

Yet the investigation in the Supreme Court went well beyond Solodilov. With the help of cooperating witnesses such as Judge Chursina, who denounced people nearly at random, investigators moved beyond cases of bribery that appeared to have strong evidentiary foundation to aggressively pursue numerous others that were supported by little or no evidence beyond denunciations. Moreover, procuracy and party supervisors seem to have assumed that if Solodilov took bribes, then other justices were doing the same.

Solodilov was born into a family of peasants in Shchigrovskii *uezd* in Kursk province in 1900. Solodilov took juridical courses for fifteen months in 1928–1929. After spending several years studying in an institute of foreign trade and doing party work in Western Siberia, he became a justice in the Civil Law Collegium of the USSR Supreme Court in July 1935. In October 1937, Solodilov succeeded the recently purged I. L. Bulat as the chair of the RSFSR Supreme Court. He served in that capacity for eleven months until September 1938, at which time he was transferred back to the USSR Supreme Court. He became the deputy chairman of the court with responsibility for civil cases.[57]

The criminal investigation into Solodilov's activities was triggered by an informant's tip claiming that Solodilov had illegally built a luxurious dacha in 1947 using money he accumulated by accepting bribes from petitioners who had appeals before the Supreme Court. Although it was not against the law in this period to build a dacha with one's own money, party control officials accused many people of embezzling funds and misappropriating building materials in order to construct dachas illegally.[58] Solodilov was called to the Central Committee building at the beginning of 1948 and asked by a deputy in the Department of Administrative Organs how he had managed to fund the suspicious dacha project.[59]

The inquiry into Solodilov's dacha soon merged with allegations that he had taken bribes.[60] Correspondence in Supreme Court archives produced well before the investigations of 1948 show that Supreme Court Chairman Goliakov had received complaints about Solodilov's suspicious activities as early as 1944.[61] In September 1946, the Central Committee Cadres Directorate forwarded a letter to Goliakov that included accusations that Solodilov had accepted bribes in several housing cases during 1945 and 1946.[62] The author detailed three instances in which he alleged that Solodilov had suspiciously intervened to reverse the decisions of lower courts in favor of parties with very weak claims. At trial, his co-worker told the courts that as a result of the mass of appeals flooding the Supreme Court, Solodilov was instructed to meet petitioners twice a month to help work through the backlog. Solodilov met with the public on other days as well, and he spoke to petitioners by telephone. It was during these personal meetings that Solodilov was said to have made illegal arrangements with complainants in both civil and criminal cases.[63]

The pace of the investigation quickened between January and May 1948. The new procurator general, Safonov, took a personal interest in Solodilov's case, even visiting Butyrsk prison to conduct interrogations himself.[64] On May 14, 1948, Safonov sent a seven-page summary of Solodilov's alleged crimes directly to Stalin and other top party leaders.[65] Full of sensational details, the report marks a major escalation of the scandal.[66] Safonov's report charges that Solodilov extorted bribes of sex from several petitioners. In his words, rumors had spread among Supreme Court employees about Solodilov's "indiscriminate, multiple connections with women." One witness told investigators, "Solodilov was a great lover of women. It was rare that Solodilov, having made the acquaintance of a woman, did not try to arrange a sexual liaison with her."[67]

Solodilov's alleged behavior was perhaps the most extreme scenario involving the kind of moral decrepitude that investigators claimed ran rampant in the high courts. According to investigators and the testimony of co-workers, Solodilov was a depraved person. The investigation found that for years Solodilov had exchanged official favors for sex (as well as for cash and building materials). He compelled numerous female complainants (or their family members) to sleep with him in exchange for his intervention in their cases. In one case, a pregnant woman, R., was forced by municipal authorities to leave her apartment in 1945.[68] Her doctor knew Solodilov and recommended that R. send a complaint to Solodilov's attention. Solodilov told the woman that he would consider her appeal, but only if she would spend the night with him. She testified that he forced her to sleep with him a second time when the case was being reviewed.[69] According to Vera N. Safronova, a senior legal consultant in the USSR Supreme Court, Solodilov used her apartment to have sex with no fewer than fifteen women, many of whom were petitioners with cases before the court. Others were court staff.[70]

As the historian David Hoffman points out, charges of moral degeneration were linked with suspicion of political unreliability throughout the 1920s and 1930s. Allegations of sexual misconduct, excessive drinking, a "degenerate lifestyle," and other immoral behaviors could be used against party members, and many communists were expelled from the party (and officials fired from their jobs) for such transgressions.[71] In the second half of the 1930s, "enemies" condemned for "lack of vigilance" or "wrecking" were also tainted with charges of personal corruption. As Hoffman notes, "In case after case of Party officials who were purged, charges of immorality were leveled alongside Trotskyism and sabotage."[72]

In the May 14 report to Stalin, Safonov recommended that Solodilov be removed from his post as deputy chair of the Supreme Court. Safonov insisted that the investigation into Solodilov's crimes must proceed in complete secrecy, however. "Considering the special position in the government that Solodilov occupies and, in connection with this, the need to maintain the strictest secrecy for the investigation," Solodilov must not be informed that the procuracy was looking into his criminal activity.[73]

On May 19, 1948, the Solodilov case reached the Politburo for discussion. The Politburo (which was fully under Stalin's personal control) resolved to remove Solodilov from the court for abusing his position.[74] The Politburo ordered the USSR Procuracy's office to open a criminal investigation into Solodilov's actions.[75] Following the procuracy's recommmendation of a few days earlier, the Politburo declared that Solodilov was not to be informed that an investigation had been launched, presumably so that he could not destroy evidence, try to silence potential witnesses, or go into hiding. According to testimony at the trial of his alleged co-conspirators, Solodilov somehow found out that his case had been referred for prosecution. According to the Cadres Directorate—and his colleagues at trial—Solodilov began to fear that his crimes had been exposed and he would be arrested. He shot himself on June 4, 1948.[76] Had Solodilov not taken his own life, he soon would have been charged with dozens of counts of bribery and abuse of office.[77]

Solodilov's suicide intensified the investigation into bribery in the USSR Supreme Court and other key courts. Investigators took his suicide as a confession that he was hopelessly entangled in a web of crime. Four other Supreme Court justices and dozens of court staff and lawyers who represented clients before the court were arrested in 1948–1949, charged with accepting bribes or acting as intermediaries in illegal transactions. Without direct evidence of Stalin's own reaction, we can only speculate that the suicide of a leading jurist suspected of flagrant corruption infuriated him. Stalin might have regarded this suicide as akin to treason, a coward's betrayal of the party and of himself personally.[78] It might also have confirmed any suspicions he had (based, perhaps, on information fed to him by Kuznetsov and Safonov) that corruption had become widespread in the high courts. Judging by the arrests of hundreds of court personnel in the months following Solodilov's death, Stalin likely ordered the Department of Administrative Organs to leave no stone unturned in investigating any hint of bribery in the courts of Moscow. At least initially, procuracy leaders and investigators seem to have believed that they had a mandate to use all means, and to take as long as necessary, to uncover corrupt actors. Indeed, one notices in the intensifying investigations in the spring and summer of 1948 a kind of reckless enthusiasm among procuracy investigators, who, it seems possible, went quite a bit further in these investigations than was initially planned in early 1948.

Over the course of 1948 and 1949, some party leaders followed the investigations closely. On July 8, 1948, one month after Solodilov's death, Kuznetsov, the head of the Cadres Directorate, sent Malenkov a scathing report entitled "On the Condition of Cadres and the Situation in the USSR Supreme Court."[79] The report describes numerous "political errors" among individual party members in the USSR Supreme Court and its Military Collegium. "Many members of the Supreme Court have made serious political errors in their work," and "many of the operational and technical workers of the apparatus have turned out to be politically dubious people."[80] Still, the letter evinces a certain degree of restraint—there was no attempt, for example, to paint the Supreme Court as a den of counterrevolutionaries or "enemies" of the revolution.

On August 24, 1948, the Politburo removed Goliakov as Supreme Court chairman at the same time that Ul'rikh was dismissed as head of the Military Collegium.[81] Under Goliakov's leadership, the Supreme Court was said to have "weakened the battle" against "betrayal of the homeland" and theft of state property.[82] The Central Committee appointed forty-five-year-old A. A. Volin to be the new chairman of the USSR Supreme Court. (A. A. Cheptsov became Volin's deputy, replacing Ul'rikh as chairman of the Military Collegium.)[83]

The "Conspiracy"

On August 31, 1948, seven days after Goliakov and Ul'rikh were removed from their positions, Procurator General Safonov made an announcement to the high party leadership, for the first time connecting the cases in all these major courts. He represented these bribery cases not as individual acts, but as an organized criminal conspiracy that ranged across multiple Soviet courts. Safonov sent an overview of hundreds of cases of alleged bribery to Stalin and fourteen others at the very top of the party hierarchy. The eleven-page report was based on information gathered in the interrogations that had been ongoing in Moscow's Butyrsk prison since the spring of 1948.[84] Safonov informed the party leaders that investigators had uncovered bribe takers in several of the country's most prestigious courts. Numerous regional courts also had staff deeply implicated in accepting bribes. Although these instances of bribery had been brought to the attention of the Central Committee in May 1948, it was not until this report, sent at the end of August, that the procuracy first claimed that the cases were in fact interconnected, linked together in a conspiracy.

"I am informing you," Safonov wrote, "that the USSR Procuracy has recently uncovered a great deal of evidence of bribery, abuse of office, improper association with the criminal element, and the issuance of incorrect sentences and decisions" in several of the country's major courts. Adopting a grave and angry tone, Safonov wrote that webs of conspiratorial relationships had flourished especially in the courts of Moscow, including the Moscow City Court, the RSFSR Supreme Court, and the USSR Supreme Court. Corrupt court staff had acted in concert. Safonov tried to draw links among the bribery schemes, detailing relationships and friendships among employees across the courts. "Individual court employees," he wrote, "committing these crimes at various rungs of the court system, were connected with each another, and in this manner they acted in an organized way."[85]

In light of the mass arrests of personnel of the high courts during the purge years, these accusations of major conspiracies in the Moscow courts must have been especially alarming. Nearly all the USSR Supreme Court's judges had been purged ten years earlier in 1937–1938.[86] In 1938 alone, 40 percent of all positions in republican and regional supreme courts turned over.

The procuracy leadership no doubt relished the opportunity to scour the appeals courts and find compromised judges, to cleanse the judiciary.[87] It certainly was in Safonov's professional interest to show that the procuracy had uncovered a major conspiracy. Inside the procuracy, these investigations into the high courts likely were seen as a huge success. While it is not clear whether this was his original intention, there are indications that, once the key judges had been exposed, Safonov might have pushed to indict, discredit, and convict even more, going beyond the Central Committee's original orders.

At the same time, evidence also supports the notion that Stalin seems to have taken steps to limit the expanding procuracy investigations, and that he wanted to wind up the investigations as soon as possible. In November 1948, the Department of Administrative Organs drafted an instruction ordering Safonov to pick up the pace of the procuracy's multiple investigations into corruption in the high courts, implying that they were dragging on too long. Likely apprehensive about the effects on the functioning and legitimacy of these visible courts, and the rumors swirling around continuing arrests, the instruction ordered "comrade Safonov to guarantee the speediest possible conclusion to the investigation into cases of bribery in the USSR Supreme Court, the RSFSR Supreme Court, the Moscow City Court, etc., without damaging the quality of the investigation."[88]

This may be an indication that Stalin wanted to rein in the investigations, which seemed to be spreading very quickly as procuracy investigators interrogated hundreds of defendants and witnesses in Butyrsk Prison during the summer and fall of 1948. We do know that in several cases Stalin punished leading party officials when they dared take initiative in legal matters without his permission, as Safonov may have done. In early 1948, for example, Stalin rebuked Kuznetsov and Abakumov for calling an honor court without permission to discipline two staff members in the Ministry of State Security. Both men were reprimanded by the Politburo.[89] In another case, the Department of Administrative Organs reproached Safonov for convening the All-Union Methodological Conference of the Best Investigators without permission in October 1948. The department scolded Safonov in particular for allowing Golinkov, one of the main investigators for the Supreme Court bribery cases, to give a talk at the conference.[90] In August, Golinkov had overseen the arrest of Judge Shevchenko (and the typist

Goleva) while the judge was working in his office at the RSFSR Supreme Court. This spectacle of arresting a high court judge at his place of work was seen as publically compromising the authority of the court, and the Soviet judiciary more generally.

Pursuing Justice Goliakov

Although USSR Supreme Court Chairman Goliakov strongly denied ever accepting a single bribe (and the evidence supports his claim), procuracy investigators continued harassing him until at least August 1951, fully three years after his dismissal in August 1948. They aggressively pursued incriminating evidence in order to persuade party agencies that the procuracy should charge Goliakov with taking bribes.[91] Safonov went so far as to ask the Central Committee for permission to arrest Goliakov in January 1951. Permission was not granted. Seven months later, on August 15, 1951, Volin wrote to Malenkov at the Central Committee describing new evidence against Goliakov. He informed Malenkov that a person convicted of acting as an intermediary in several deals, Ekaterina M. Velichko, had recently testified in a closed court session that she had passed bribes to Goliakov in three cases.[92] (Velichko was accused of perjury by several defendants, and her testimony cannot be considered reliable.) Velichko's dubious claim was the basis for the procuracy's request to reopen the case against Goliakov more than a year after the end of the trials of USSR court employees.[93] Nevertheless, in the end no charges were brought against Goliakov.

This harassment of Goliakov bears a strong similarity to that directed against the Military Collegium judges Ul'rikh and Nikitchenko. In all three cases, prosecutors continued to seek evidence that the accused judges had accepted bribes, even two or more years after they were removed from the court. None of them was ever charged with a crime. The fact that Ul'rikh, Nikitchenko, and Goliakov were *not* arrested despite procuracy requests is another indication that Safonov had been moving beyond what Stalin intended. One must assume that only Stalin could give permission to arrest judges as prominent and senior as these three, and permission was denied in each case. It is likely that in the course of these investigations between 1948 and 1951 the procuracy sometimes had to improvise, trying to guess what Stalin desired. They perhaps assumed that Stalin wanted them to do everything possible to purify the highest appeals courts, even if the evidence against the judges was slight. Stalin held them back in certain cases, including those of Goliakov and his deputies Ul'rikh and Nikitchenko (none of whom, in retrospect, appear to have been guilty of accepting bribes, judging by prosecutors' quite weak hearsay evidence).

Upon his dismissal from the Supreme Court in August 1948, Goliakov took a full-time academic post as director of the All-Union Institute of Juridical Sciences in Moscow, where he pursued scholarly work for the remainder of his life.

Spreading beyond Moscow

Even as procuracy and party investigators worked to expose crimes in key Moscow courts, they began to make claims that corruption abounded in courts outside the capital as well. By the late summer of 1948, the procuracy informed the Central Committee that the scandal extended to several republic-level and regional courts. Safonov announced that the procuracy had exposed long-running bribery schemes among groups of court employees in the Kiev oblast' court and the Krasnodar krai court (located in the Northern Caucasus region). By August 1948, twenty-nine people had been arrested in Kiev, including the former chairman of the Kiev oblast' court, twelve judges in people's courts, and several lawyers. Additionally, police had arrested fifteen people associated with the courts in Krasnodar (including the chair of the krai court and his deputy) who allegedly had been involved in another major scheme.[94]

And still, the scandal continued to spread like an epidemic. In January 1949, the RSFSR Procuracy announced that more than two dozen leading court and procuracy employees in the Bashkir Autonomous Soviet Socialist Republic had been arrested for either accepting or facilitating bribes.[95] An investigator reported that a "large circle of bribe-taking judges" had been discovered, including the deputy chairman of the Supreme Court of the republic, Amirkhanov, and two other justices on the court. In one case, Amirkhanov was accused of accepting an illegal payment of 1,500 rubles, half a liter of vodka, and a cooked goose.

Throughout 1949, the affair continued to extend its reach. In the summer of that year, investigators targeted the Georgian Republic. By August, six justices of the Georgian Supreme Court had been arrested for bribery.[96] The schemes were said to be very similar to the cases in the high courts of Moscow. They involved judges, intermediaries (often defense lawyers), the relatives of convicts (who had typically been found guilty of theft of state property or speculation), and payments both in cash and in kind.

And in 1949, after a long investigation, prosecutors announced that they had found bribe-taking judges in the Ukrainian Supreme Court. The USSR Procuracy's Office accused two of that court's judges—Dmitrii S. Suslo, the deputy chairman of the court between 1943 and 1946, and Supreme Court justice Aleksei K. Ishutin, of accepting bribes.[97] Many other court staff were also charged.[98]

Over the course of 1948 and 1949, the number of defendants grew steadily. As investigators obtained more incriminating evidence during interrogations, they made new arrests.[99] By the end of 1949, over 300 people had been arrested in the courts scandals, including judges and other court employees, intermediaries, and those alleged to have paid bribes.

"Who among Them Takes Bribes?" Judges as Targets and the Use of Coercion

It is clear that between 1948 and 1951 procuracy investigators aimed to implicate as many high court judges in bribery as they could. Investigators strained to label rather mundane instances of bribery and other improprieties as part of a coordinated "conspiracy" that involved high-level judges across several prominent judicial institutions. They accused judges and other court employees, stretching across multiple important courts, of making illicit deals with each other. It must be emphasized that investigators did not claim that these were the treasonous political conspiracies of the purge era, but rather portrayed them as more traditional criminal conspiracies. Nevertheless, by the summer of 1948, Politburo documents referred to the cases in the high courts as "organized groups" of employees engaged in bribery, though there was little or no substantial evidence that there were meaningful criminal ties among individuals in the various courts apart from normal professional or friendly relations.

In their investigations, the Department of Administrative Organs and procuracy investigators clearly were targeting the courts' leaderships—

the chief judges and their deputies. Goliakov and the deputy chairs of the USSR Supreme Court (Ul'rikh, Solodilov, and Nikitchenko) were implicated. At least three other USSR Supreme Court judges were also charged with accepting bribes. Deputy chairs of the RSFSR Supreme Court were also targeted (N. V. Vasil'ev, V. D. Bocharov, and S. A. Pashutina).[100] The RSFSR chairman, Nesterov, was forced out under a cloud of suspicion (though never arrested), as were five other judges (each of whom was convicted of bribery or abuse of office). Prosecutors charged the deputy chair of the Ukrainian Supreme Court, Suslo, with bribery, and Vasnev, chairman of the Moscow City Court, was arrested and convicted.

Apart from this pattern of arrest and prosecution of the leaders of the courts, there is further evidence that the Central Committee initially wished to implicate powerful and high-ranking conspirators, and especially judges. Investigators' desire to prove that judges were leading coordinated gangs elevated what was largely rather random petty bribe taking and gift giving to the level of an organized criminal enterprise involving major, synchronized schemes. The scandals in the high courts demonstrate how party authorities after the war still could choose to interpret petty malfeasance on the part of officials as a coordinated conspiracy headed by powerful figures.

The notion that investigators really wanted to convict the big fish is supported by a good deal of testimony and correspondence. During his June 1949 trial, for example, Shevchenko testified that investigators had told him during preliminary questioning that his fate was not important to them; their real targets were the highest-ranking judges: "[Member of the Military Collegium] Bukanov, [Chair of the RSFSR Supreme Court] Nesterov, [Chair of the USSR Supreme Court] Goliakov, . . . [Deputy Chair of the RSFSR Supreme Court] Vasil'ev. They stated directly: 'We need them, not you.'"[101] Another defendant made a similar claim to explain why so many judges were targeted. At a closed trial, a certain A. V. Iakushechkin, the former chief of administration (*Upravliaiushchii delami*) for the USSR Supreme Court, told judges that he had been framed by prosecutors. In the courtroom, he offered his explanation for why he had been arrested for bribery: to allow the procuracy to smear the judges of Goliakov's Supreme Court. Speaking about the lead investigator in his case, Iakushechkin claimed, "The case against me was invented by 'the Investigator in Especially Important

Cases' Bulaev. He wanted to blacken the previous cohort of the Supreme Court."[102]

Documents preserved in state and party archives leave little doubt that investigators sometimes used a variety of coercive methods to extract testimony from imprisoned defendants. People accused in these cases were sometimes imprisoned for a year or more without being charged, often without having access to the evidence used against them. The best source of information about the techniques of investigators is often the testimony at trial of the accused themselves. Defendants sometimes were granted a private meeting with the panel of presiding judges, separate from other defendants or prosecutors. Hoping that judges would be sympathetic to their stories of what they often called "illegal" investigator intimidation, they poured out a torrent of complaints about specific interrogators. In one of these private sessions with judges, the defendant F. P. Umanskaia (chief of the USSR Supreme Court's Department of Judicial Supervision) described how she was pressured to provide false accusations that Goliakov was a bribe taker:

> In September [1948], the investigator Tsatskin called me in and demanded that I "give" him two nice (*khoroshenkikh*) cases against Goliakov. I answered that I did not know of any crimes committed by Goliakov, but Tsatskin declared that I was concealing things about Goliakov, saying that "Safronova offered us such cases [of crimes by Goliakov] and we did something for her [that is, improved her conditions in prison]. If you give us cases, then I promise that you'll get a meeting with your son." Despite the fact that I had already confessed [to my own crimes], they put me in solitary confinement again.[103]

By the end of 1951, the Supreme Court leadership complained angrily by letter to the Department of Administrative Organs about the methods that procuracy investigators used in several of these cases. Among other specific incidents, the letter complained that one lawyer was kept in solitary confinement for twenty-eight months before he was tried, a clear violation of Soviet law. Investigators once came to his cell and handed him a list of all the members of the Supreme Court. They said, "Slavkin, help us. Tell us, who among them takes bribes?"[104]

For his part, Prosecutor General Safonov steadfastly refused to acknowledge that his investigators ever undertook illegal or improper methods of investigation. He labeled any such statements "slander." Safonov denied numerous specific claims that his investigators used coercion to extract information, despite a great deal of evidence to the contrary.[105]

Planning the Trials and the Decision on Secrecy

By the spring of 1949, party leaders had begun to plan trials for those charged in the cases of the RSFSR and USSR Supreme Courts and the Moscow City Court, even as procuracy investigators continued to gather evidence and interrogate people held in Butyrsk prison. The Politburo resolved that there must be absolutely no publicity about the arrests or the trials. This was a significant decision, made for reasons that are quite telling. An April 30, 1949 letter, composed jointly by the minister of justice, the procurator general, and the chair of the Supreme Court, was sent to Malenkov at the Central Committee. The three legal chiefs urged that the high court cases never be mentioned in the press.[106] They argued that complete silence was critical "to avoid spreading information about these crimes." If the cases were tried with "regular" (*obychnyi*) procedures (that is, in a public trial) involving the "unavoidable" participation of multiple procuracy and defense lawyers who would spread information about the trials, the resulting publicity would "affect the authority of the court organs in a negative way." The concern was that the lawyers would talk about the trials to friends, family, and colleagues, spreading news of the scandal and thus weakening the Soviet courts' ability to enforce "socialist legality." During this period of mass arrests for economic and property crime, party leaders did not wish to undermine the notion that, although the courts (and judges) were extremely strict in the execution of justice for criminals, they were still honest, fair to all, and above reproach.

In addition, the chiefs of the legal agencies wrote that they feared that foreign enemies would use any public bribery trials to defame the Soviet Union. As the jointly authored letter notes, "Leaks of information about these crimes could be used in the interests of hostile propaganda." This reasoning is revealing: party leaders were concerned that trials of judges would discredit the agencies of Soviet justice, undermine public confidence in the courts, and be used by foreign anti-Soviet propagandists.

The Politburo endorsed a plan to try the cases in special, closed sessions of the Military Collegium of the USSR Supreme Court in Moscow, presided over by a panel of three Supreme Court justices. Full secrecy about the scandal in the high courts was imposed. Surely, this Politburo decision about secrecy was also Stalin's own.[107] No mention of the cases was ever made in the press.[108]

These secret trials of the late Stalin period stand in marked contrast to the major public NEP-era bribery trials, in which bureaucrats were alleged to have accepted bribes and the Nepmen were said to have bought them off. In the 1920s, the dominant view in the party was that media *silence* about corruption among officials would discredit Soviet power in the eyes of the population. The 1920s legal and popular press discussed the problem of graft and the party's struggles against it. In contrast, between 1945 and 1953 only a very few references to bribery ever appeared in the press.

The cases at the center of the Affair of the High Courts were heard in multiple trials, in three general groups, between May and August 1949: cases pertaining to the Moscow City Court (in May–June 1949); the RSFSR Supreme Court (between May and December 1949); and the USSR Supreme Court (July–August 1949). A few related cases were tried later in 1949.[109] The trial of the defendants in the case of the Georgian Supreme Court was held in late 1949; the trial of the Ukrainian Supreme Court employees occurred in early 1952.

Most of the trials were organized in such a way that the current Supreme Court judges were forced to preside (and pass judgment) at the trials of accused judges and other employees dismissed from their own courts. One can speculate that, for Stalin, having these trials of former Supreme Court judges overseen by current justices of the same courts was intended as a combination of bullying intimidation and a test of loyalty. The new chairman of the Soviet Supreme Court, Volin, was ordered to preside over the trials of USSR Supreme Court employees. (Volin fell ill before the trial began, and he was replaced by one of his deputy chairmen.)[110] For his part, Bitiukov, the newly appointed chairman of the RSFSR Supreme Court, chaired the trial of the former judges and employees of that court. Stalin was constantly assessing the trustworthiness of leading cadres.[111] The new court leaders might have been afraid—understandably—that they would be the next to sit on the defendants' bench.

The main trials featured between twenty-five and forty defendants each, and each trial lasted approximately two weeks. Guards brought the defendants from Butyrsk prison to the courtroom each day. Because the Politburo resolution had banned lawyers from the courtroom, it was the judges who asked questions of the defendants; the defendants were also allowed to ask each other questions. Most proclaimed their innocence, although several judges and staff pled guilty. With very rare exceptions, defendants were found guilty. Nearly all the accused judges were found guilty, including three from the USSR Supreme Court, five from the RSFSR Supreme Court, and five from the Moscow City Court. In later trials, six judges on the Supreme Court of the Georgian SSR were convicted, as were two from the Supreme Court of the Ukrainian SSR.

The judges convicted of accepting bribes were uniformly given sentences of ten years in prison (regardless of whether they had pled guilty or cooperated with the prosecution), while bribe givers and intermediaries received between two and five years in prison, as stipulated by the criminal code. In addition, perhaps 275 bribe givers and intermediaries were convicted and given two- to five-year terms. (Acquittals among bribe givers were quite rare, and generally occurred only if the defendant was elderly, disabled, or pregnant.) The Department of Administrative Organs continued closely to follow the outcome of the cases, as evidenced by the fact that Supreme Court Chair Volin sent copies of the verdicts to the department immediately upon the conclusion of the trials.[112]

The proceedings in these cases mainly followed the procedures of regular trials: the presentation of evidence and multiple witnesses; attempts by the prosecution to prove quid pro quo; allowing people to deny their guilt, explain their actions, and ask other defendants questions; and the fact that they stretched over weeks. In some ways, however, they bore the hallmarks of overtly political trials: especially notable are the secrecy, the absence of defense lawyers, the nearly guaranteed convictions (sometimes only on the basis of denunciations), the use of some coerced testimony, and the emphasis on certain defendants' moral failings together with their crimes. Still, these trials were not nearly as politicized as the brief, sham trials of "enemies of the people" in the 1930s. Each charge received a full hearing, including complete testimony of the accused and witnesses. Even the indictments against high court judges did not allege that they *intended* to sabotage the party or Soviet power. No one in these trials was charged with "counterrevolutionary" acts or other Article 58 crimes.

PART II. MAKING DEALS IN THE HIGH COURTS

The procuracy claimed to have exposed a nest of bribery in a number of important courts in 1948 and 1949. In the prosecution of the high court bribery cases, accusations pinpointed both the judges' criminal activities and their personal corruption, stressing (often intersecting) patterns of sexual deviance, participation in underground capitalism and infection with a "capitalist mentality," and dangerous ethnic clannishness.[113] Significantly, none of the official accusations focused on structural explanations such as poor pay, red tape, or inadequate working conditions. Court employees were said to be participating in criminal conspiracies, but not political or counterrevolutionary conspiracies. In these postwar allegations, bribe-taking judges were not said to be foreign spies, traitors, or disguised "enemies of the people." Judging by the transcripts of the trials and prosecutors' interviews with defendants, it appears that the cases were intended to demonstrate, first, the professional and moral corruption of certain judges; and second, that the judges' alleged degradation created a dangerous environment that encouraged further improper behavior among their subordinates. Party and procuracy officials typically explained bribery as a natural by-product of various types of moral dissolution that could contaminate both individuals and institutions.[114]

Yet these official explanations for the existence of bribery in the high courts answer very few questions. Indeed, they obscure the real situation. Only by looking more closely at the unusual conditions in the high courts, which encouraged face-to-face contacts and negotiations, can we understand court employees' willingness—at times—to make deals. An earlier chapter explored the factors that encouraged the making of informal deals between petitioners and judicial employees in the lower courts of the USSR. We will now consider motivating factors in the country's highest appeals courts as we piece together a key puzzle: what caused some employees of prominent high courts to enter into illicit, if profitable, deals with citizens, an activity that clearly carried very substantial risks?

It is important to emphasize again that we are by no means arguing that all, or most, judges took bribes. There is no evidence that this was the case, of course. Rather, we are exploring the reasons why those who did enter into such deals chose to do so.

Appeals as Opportunity

Between 1946 and 1952, the highest Soviet courts were deluged with appeals brought by ordinary citizens. In the wake of a crucial 1938 change in the appeals process, and particularly after the war, hundreds of thousands of people were inspired to pursue appeals of—or to file formal appeals about—criminal convictions all the way to the RSFSR and USSR Supreme Courts. Moreover, the harsh June 4 decrees on theft—and laws targeting other nonpolitical crimes—had unanticipated effects on Soviet society and the legal system. The discussion here focuses on their effects on the late Stalin-era appeals courts in particular.

When a person wished to appeal what they considered to be an unjust conviction, the process was as follows: as of 1930, "people's courts" occupied the lowest rung on the judicial ladder; each region of a province had at least one people's court. A person convicted by a judge in a people's court could immediately ask for an automatic review in cassation (*kassatsiia*) at the next highest level: the provincial (oblast') court. This cassational review verified that the lower court had followed proper procedure (and they often had not) and handed down the correct sentence. Cassation typically did not revisit the evidence in the case or otherwise review the case on its merits. This review was done quickly, normally within ten days. The cassational courts rarely overturned lower court decisions.[115] Once an appeal was rejected by the court in cassation, the conviction went into effect.

Any citizen who was still dissatisfied with the court's ruling had the right to appeal further, to the republic-level Supreme Court, in a process known as *nadzor* (or supervisory review). There were two types of appeals under nadzor. Procurators could bring an appeal in the form of a protest (*protest*). Procurators typically appealed sentences on the grounds that they were too light, not too harsh. For our purposes, a second type of appeal is much more relevant: a "complaint" (*zhaloba*) brought by an ordinary citizen. Such appeals could be formally submitted by any citizen (or his or her family or lawyer) whose convictions had been confirmed in cassation in the provincial court.[116] Court staff members called "legal consultants" (konsultanty) in the courts were normally the first to review complaints, deciding whether to reject the complaint immediately or pass it on to a judge for further examination. According to standard Soviet legal procedure, a citizen's appeal in nadzor could result in a case being "pulled for review" by a judge. The judge could then reverse the decision of the lower court, acquitting the person who had been convicted, reducing the sentence, or recommending that the case be reviewed further.

In the fall of 1938, there had been an unusual and extremely important development in this process of filing appeals. Beginning with the August 16, 1938 Law on Court Organization, the all-Union Supreme Court suddenly was given the right to review and revise sentences emanating from nearly any court of first instance in the country.[117] Before August 1938, the USSR Supreme Court could only hear appeals that had been ruled on by the republican supreme courts, and then only if the USSR Procuracy had referred the case.[118] The law of August 16, however, created a major change in the way the appeals courts functioned. Beginning in the fall of 1938 (to quote Peter Solomon), the Supreme Court "acquired almost unrestricted power to hear in its supervisory capacity appeals from trial directly after the obligatory cassation review. Thus, the court could examine any case tried in a people's court and reviewed in cassation at a provincial court, bypassing entirely the republican supreme courts that were also empowered to review court decisions."[119]

To put it another way, Soviet people who had been convicted in lower courts now had the right to bring appeals of sentences all the way to the USSR Supreme Court, skipping the republic level completely.[120] The purpose of this post-purge law was to restore a sense of legitimacy and legality to the courts by raising the prominence of the USSR Supreme Court and allowing it to reverse lower courts' all-too-frequent improper convictions.[121] As of August 1938, judges in the RSFSR and USSR Supreme Courts evidently believed that they could correct glaring errors that had been made by the lower courts, often made under the influence of meddling local political officials. Supreme Court judges (normally working in three-judge panels), for example, had the ability to reverse any politically tainted convictions made by lower-level people's courts during the years 1936–1938.[122] But there were other, unexpected consequences as well.

Once this law was published in 1938, tens of thousands of people took their appeals directly to Moscow, clearly believing that they would have a better chance at a satisfactory (and expedited) outcome.[123] Lawyers and lower-level judges apparently often recommended that their clients file an appeal so that a Supreme Court judge would fairly review their convictions. In the postwar Stalin years, however, this high degree of centralization of the appeals process caused unanticipated problems, leaving the USSR Supreme Court (and, to a lesser degree, the republican supreme courts) overburdened with an enormous—and growing—deluge of cases and appeals.[124]

The new right to bring one's appeal all the way to the USSR Supreme Court epitomized the Soviet ideal of citizens' universal right to petition authorities at all levels. (A 1936 statute had made this right explicit, and it was widely publicized as a key prerogative of the citizen under newly constructed socialism.)[125] As one defendant put it at her trial, contrasting petitioning (which she believed she was doing in the case of her husband) with bribery (which she denied undertaking): "Under Soviet power, it is possible to petition everywhere, but I did not give money to anyone. . . . Whether [my husband] was convicted correctly or incorrectly, I had to petition for him."[126]

Yet in practice, in a period of mass arrests for petty crimes the right to petition had serious effects on the appellate courts. It encouraged the population to seek out direct contact with officials regarding their individual grievances. In principle, anyone could personally consult with a Supreme Court justice about his or her case. Such official consultations (during judges' office hours) with justices of the USSR Supreme Court in fact occurred at least several hundred times a month by 1947.

At the same time, growing numbers of convictions for nonpolitical crimes precipitated a sharp upsurge in the number of formal appeals that citizens filed. Statistics on appeals were never published in the Stalin period, but justice archives show that the number of appeals grew quickly after 1938. In 1936, the Supreme Court reviewed fewer than 11,000 appeals in supervision. Nearly as soon as the new law on appeals went into effect in August 1938, however, that figure jumped sixfold. In the period between 1938 and 1940, an average of about 70,000 appeals from citizens per year were reviewed in supervision by the USSR Supreme Court.[127] The war naturally saw a significant drop in the quantity (to about 49,000 in 1944, and 55,000 for 1945). But in 1946, the number of appeals received by the Soviet Supreme Court jumped to 97,000.[128]

The June 4, 1947 decree on theft of state property, with its seven-year minimum sentences, created another very large increase in the number of appeals that landed in the USSR Supreme Court. Shortly after the issuance of the June 4 edicts, the family members of those convicted under them began to swamp the courts with appeals of sentences they regarded as incorrect, unfair, or even "illegal." By 1950, nearly 40 percent of the cases that were reviewed in the Collegium for Criminal Cases of the USSR Supreme Court concerned just one law—the June 4, 1947 law on theft of state property.[129]

In 1948 alone, nearly 135,000 appeals of convictions, for all varieties of crime, came into the USSR Supreme Court as the full impact of the wave of appeals of theft convictions reached Moscow.[130] There were times when appeals came into the Supreme Court at the rate of 1,000 *per day*.[131] An enormous backlog of files built up.[132] Supreme Court Chairman Goliakov wrote that in the first half of 1948 he had personally reviewed 500 citizen appeals about convictions for theft alone.[133] A severe shortage of staff made it very difficult "to register, examine, [and] consider" the appeals. Goliakov pointed to the August 1938 law that made the Supreme Court the destination for appeals from all over the country as one of the main factors exacerbating the court's space problems. He noted sardonically that the law "required that the Supreme Court become closer to the population." Goliakov's use of the expression "closer to the population" seems to have been delivered with a generous dose of irony, considering the great shortage of space to meet with and process the petitioners. "The Supreme Court has become a destination where significant numbers of petitioners, complainants, and defense lawyers from all corners of the Union congregate."

Once they reached the high courts, these appeals were often given a brief and cursory review. Over 80 percent of the appeals about criminal cases that reached the Supreme Court were rejected immediately (mainly because there were "no grounds" for review), with about 10 percent typically referred to a more appropriate institution.[134] By 1952, 87 percent were rejected, and only 4 percent resulted in the pulling of a case for review.[135] In light of this huge volume, one can imagine the quick glance the appeals received, and the mounting dissatisfaction of petitioners. A senior legal consultant for the RSFSR Supreme Court responsible for screening appeals, Kuz'ma T. Popov, testified that because of staffing shortages, he had to review seventy to eighty appeals a day, which led to "the superficial review of cases." Delays in handling appeals undoubtedly led to frustration among prisoners' families, and increased demand for back-door approaches to resolve this bureaucratic intransigence.[136] At trial, Popov described the opportunities that this mass of appeals gave him for making deals with frustrated, and often desperate, petitioners.[137] (He was convicted of accepting at least eight bribes.)

Similar testimony was provided by F. P. Umanskaia, who was arrested in June 1948. As chief of the Department of the Judicial Supervision (*Otdel sudebnogo nadzora*), Umanskaia's job had been to supervise the handling of the "mountains of appeals" that poured into the Supreme Court. So Umanskaia was very well positioned to make side deals with disgruntled petitioners. Indeed, the legal consultants who first reviewed the appeals were a prime target for bribe givers. Umanskaia confessed to accepting at least fifteen bribes. Solodilov's secretary, N. G. Ivanovskaia, was likewise in an excellent position to negotiate, build informal relationships, and, for an extra "fee," locate and pull files for review. She also admitted to having received numerous bribes.[138]

The effects of the June 4 decree had tremendous staying power inside the court system that has been overlooked by historians. Even as the number of convictions fell after their peak in late 1947, the number of appeals to the all-union and republican supreme courts continued to grow steadily. Indeed, the number of appeals increased annually by tens of thousands between 1946 and 1952. As late as June 1952, USSR Supreme Court Chairman Volin wrote to the Council of Ministers lamenting that his staff was still buried in appeals. Volin wrote that while 192,000 appeals had been submitted to the USSR Supreme Court in 1949, by 1951 that figure had jumped to a remarkable 251,000 appeals in a single year. Thus, the number of appeals filed by citizens had nearly doubled in the three years since 1948 (when the total was 135,000).[139] Ultimately, this increased volume of appeals in nonpolitical cases resulted in more opportunity for judges and court staff to make illegal deals with complainants in exchange for pulling a case for review.

The very process of filing an appeal seems to have invited the pursuit of extralegal methods to achieve satisfaction. In principle, this method of redress highlighted a laudable aspect of the Soviet administrative system: at any time, any citizen could formally complain in writing about the wrongful decision of any agency and expect a timely response. One did not need to follow a certain formula in writing the appeal, although often the defendant or their family hired a lawyer to draft an appeal. There was also no time limit on filing an appeal. In the courts, petitioners (or their lawyers) sometimes dropped the appeals in a box in the court's reception area; such "complaint boxes" were present even in the lobby of the Soviet Supreme Court. Frequently, though, complainants lined up from early in the morning, hoping to meet personally with a legal consultant or even a judge. (Entrepreneurial lawyers sometimes recruited clients from among the mass of desperate petitioners waiting in line to file appeals.) Such meetings were held for a few hours per day; those who did not succeed in arranging a personal meeting could leave their appeals in the box or with a staff member.[140]

This process, on the one hand, symbolized the pretext of egalitarianism in the appeals process—in principle any Soviet person could submit a complaint to any agency and anticipate a quick reply. On the other hand, the process was fraught with extreme impersonality and potential futility for the family members of the accused.[141] The frustrating procedures and uncertain results inclined many people to seek help any way they could, including through under-the-table arrangements.[142]

Working and Living Conditions in Moscow's High Courts

Financial hardship helps to explain why high court employees, just like other officials in Soviet administrations, were sometimes willing to accept illegal payments and gifts. The economic position of many judges became even more dire during the war. In a letter to Molotov received on August 7, 1944, the chairman of the USSR Supreme Court, Ivan Goliakov, complained that "in wartime conditions the material situation of members of the Supreme Court has worsened sharply."[143] Surprisingly, perhaps, the financial situation of high court judges was not substantially different from that of lower court judges, described earlier in this book. Most judges who worked in the country's supreme courts were not particularly well paid or adequately housed, especially before living standards began to improve slightly in 1948–1949.[144] In February 1948, a Ministry of Justice official complained that the average police officer earned more than some members of the Soviet Supreme Court (who earned 1,350 rubles per month).[145] A. G. Gusev, a Supreme Court justice and the chair of the court's party cell, wrote, "It is impossible for members of the Supreme Court to dress more or less decently; they often wear threadbare suits." Some judges said they could not afford food at times.[146]

If the opportunity arose, various Supreme Court employees sometimes succumbed to accepting a bribe out of need, the desire to improve poor living conditions, or a wish for extra income.[147] The RSFSR Supreme Court judge Shevchenko admitted that he had traded cash for favors over the course of several years precisely because his financial situation was precarious.[148] He was in such desperate need for money that he had to look for part-time work as a porter at the city's railroad stations. Shevchenko testified that when he returned to Moscow from evacuation in 1943, he found that a German incendiary bomb had seriously damaged his apartment. Bribes provided him with the income he needed to make the repairs to his apartment and make ends meet.[149] Two other members of the USSR Supreme Court staff solicited cash bribes to buy medicine on the black market for their seriously ill husbands. Safronova needed what she called "Canadian penicillin" for her husband, who suffered from a lung abscess. The RSFSR Supreme Court judge Kumekhov told the court that eleven of his nephews and six of his cousins had been killed in the war, and he had committed himself to supporting their widows. "My difficult material situation enabled every kind of go-between, persuader, and pusher to play on my need and, taking advantage of my exhaustion, put me on the criminal path, where I committed many crimes."[150]

Living conditions for Supreme Court judges and employees could also be quite poor, as Georgian judge Levan K. Chichua's stint in Moscow's Evropa Hotel illustrates (in chapter 4). In fact, about half of the judges appointed to the USSR Supreme Court during 1946 did not show up because they had nowhere to live and no space in which to work. The situation was so challenging that the Department of Administrative Organs ordered Goliakov to find a way to force the new judges to come to Moscow to take up their new positions.[151]

Moreover, the working conditions in both the RSFSR and USSR Supreme Courts encouraged dubious contact between court employees and petitioners. The postwar space shortage in Soviet cities did not spare the agencies of the judiciary. Conditions in the USSR Supreme Court offices were atrocious. The Supreme Court did not even have its own building. It shared space with the USSR Procuracy at 25 Pushkin Street (now Bol'shaia Dmitrovka Street), in a building that had been a merchant's mansion.[152] When the government returned to Moscow from evacuation in 1942, according to Goliakov, the USSR Procuracy, on its own volition, simply took over six rooms that had belonged to the Supreme Court, infuriating court staff.[153] As Goliakov wrote with exasperation to Molotov at the Council of Ministers in July 1945, the Supreme Court's offices were a noisy, overcrowded, helter-skelter assembly of judges, staff, lawyers, and petitioners, affording space and professional distance to no one.[154] Such conditions were conducive to illicit contact between court employees and the petitioners who had come to file appeals at the Supreme Court building. For its part, the RSFSR Supreme Court shared its cramped building with the Russian Republican Ministry of Justice, which occupied two middle floors. After the return from evacuation, the RSFSR Supreme Court lost the fifth floor of the building when it too was taken over by the Ministry of Justice.[155] The court had only two small courtrooms; many hearings were carried out in small offices.

For years, the chairman of the Supreme Court requested an appropriate building. During the evacuation of Moscow, the Supreme Court's space problems were put on the back burner, but after the war the problem again became a priority. As Goliakov put it, "The absence of space is creating an unequivocally catastrophic situation. Conditions for work are absolutely inconceivable." Several justices of the court are crammed together in tiny rooms "as if in a barn," one person complained, making it impossible to concentrate.[156] Moreover, court hearings were held in these small rooms—incredibly enough, the USSR Supreme Court building contained no courtrooms. The court had to limit the number of petitioners in the building "since there is literally nowhere to receive them. It is obvious that this is completely intolerable for the highest court, which should be open for any person who has reason to be dissatisfied with the decision of a lower court." Of the hundreds of complainants who came to the court building each day, only a small fraction could be seen.[157]

As soon as A. A. Volin took over as head of the USSR Supreme Court in the fall of 1948, he assigned new urgency to these grievances. On September 14, 1948, his first day as Supreme Court chairman, Volin wrote to Stalin that teetering piles of tens of thousands of unreviewed appeals and files crowded the court offices. More than 11,000 case files and 14,000 files containing appeals languished in the already-cramped offices of the Supreme Court. "Case files and appeals are unregistered, spilling out on the floor under tables or in sacks, where they have sat for a long time without any progress." He went on: "As a result, the USSR Supreme Court, as the highest court organ, often sets a bad example for lower courts." In a letter to Stalin a month later, Volin insisted that the USSR Supreme Court must have its own building: "From the perspective of the law, the discharging of justice in the USSR Supreme Court occurs in extremely difficult, or more truthfully, in totally impossible and unacceptable conditions." His conclusion was concise, damning, and highly plausible: "That the USSR Supreme Court is in such a condition discredits it as the highest institution of justice, and to a substantial degree demeans the authority of Soviet justice itself."[158]

A consideration of the everyday working conditions in the high courts of Moscow—and the new deluge of appeals after mid-1947—greatly complicates the official story produced by the top levels of the party and USSR Procuracy, which depicted "organized" conspiracies of morally deficient judges and "criminal" petitioners and intermediaries. A confluence of factors led to the development of illicit relationships in the high courts. Petty bribery and related gift-giving traditions and practices thrived on fertile ground in the courts and perhaps especially in the appeals courts. Opportunities were legion for bribe givers, bribe takers, and intermediaries, especially in the context of social disruption, chaos, shortages, and other effects of war and reconstruction. People were highly motivated to make deals as they struggled to navigate the legal system. Overworked and underpaid officials also had many reasons to consider accepting bribes.

Why Here? Why Now?

The present study argues that the postwar Affair of the High Courts (including the assault on the Military Collegium discussed in the previous chapter) was an attack on the Soviet courts, certainly approved of by Stalin, if not wholly initiated by him, and guided by the Department of Administrative Organs of the Central Committee Secretariat (under the leadership of A. A. Kuznetsov).

Why were the Soviet high courts the venue for such an incendiary scandal, and why did party leaders attack the courts with such vehemence? We cannot answer these intriguing questions definitively. We do not have perfect information, and many archival documents are still unavailable. Further research may shed new light on this question, which focuses our attention on the mechanisms of political power in late Stalinism. Nevertheless, it seems that a combination of factors peculiar to the postwar Stalinist moment propelled the scandal forward between 1947 and 1949. Party leaders' attack on the staff of the high appeals courts was mainly a function of the courts' intersection with several of Stalin's goals in the first postwar years.

Stalin's aspirations on the "legal front" in 1947–1949 provide an important clue to the origins of the scandal. After the war, the party leadership wished to restore discipline in the courts, which were an important part of the command-administrative system. Stalin certainly saw the courts primarily as the punitive arm of the socialist state, a tool in the revolutionary struggle. In the words of Supreme Court Chairman Goliakov and Minister of Justice Rychkov, "All these tasks insistently require that our courts be a sufficiently flexible and responsive weapon in the hands of the party and the government, which every day, every hour, can use the courts to carry out their policy."[159] According to Stalin, however, the judicial system in the wake of the war was not answering the party's call to defend state property vigorously. (Stalin had a similar understanding of the military courts' failure to punish collaborators, "counterrevolutionaries," and other political criminals.) Unofficial relationships and patronage in the courts would have particularly corrosive effects, leading officials argued. Justice or procuracy officials who altered decisions or mitigated sentences on the basis of hidden material incentives would weaken the party's control over the legal agencies. In party leaders' view, the full implementation of the June 4 decree on theft of state property and other repressive laws depended on the willingness of prosecutors to ask for, and judges to apply, the most severe penalties. Arrests and investigations sent a message to the country's major appeals courts that any hint of weakness would be severely punished. Thus, for Stalin the scandal most likely served as a way to discipline leaders of the major appeals courts for their insufficient efforts to prosecute and harshly sentence accused counterrevolutionaries, collaborators with the Nazis, thieves of state property, speculators, and others whose actions would have undermined the state and the foundations of the economy. The exposure of numerous cases of actual bribery, using evidence obtained from aggressive investigations and a steady stream of denunciations, gave Stalin and other party agencies the opportunity to dismiss and disgrace—and in some cases, to arrest and imprison—judges and other employees of the courts.

Stalin also remained concerned about the loyalty of individuals and institutions; for the courts, this loyalty meant an unswerving enforcement of the party's draconian penal policies. The crackdown on corruption reinforced a crucial goal of the regime after the Nazis' defeat, namely the fortification of trustworthy state institutions as part of the postwar recentralization of power.[160] Stalin aspired to rein in any hints of autonomy in Soviet institutions, which he understood as insubordination. At the same time, Stalin had to guarantee the repressive power of the courts in order to maintain political authority and social order.[161]

Not surprisingly, the way this affair evolved seems also to be intertwined with bureaucratic politics.[162] In February 1948, as the investigation into bribery in the high courts was spreading, a changing of the guard took place in the legal agencies. As the new USSR procurator general, Safonov might have been trying to make a name for himself by pursuing the investigation with special zeal. It was certainly in the interests of the USSR Procuracy to portray the scandal as being as large and far-reaching as possible, and for Safonov to declare that his investigators had uprooted and broken apart a widespread criminal conspiracy led by senior judges. Likewise, investigators undoubtedly believed that they could build their careers by netting big fish, attacking key judges as corrupt and rotten. Indeed, in late 1949 an article lauding two of the main investigators in the scandal, K. V. Bulaev and D. L. Golinkov, appeared in the national journal of the procuracy, *Sotsialisticheskaia zakonnost'* (*Socialist Legality*).[163] Of course, the article did not mention the bribery cases, which were entirely secret, but it praised the investigators' dedicated efforts to smoke out major bribe takers and thieves of state property and to crush their subversive activities. The Central Committee's Department of Administrative Organs encouraged Safonov and his staff in their enthusiastic, if not obsessive, approach to the investigations, even though it occasionally pulled back on the reins to slow investigations.

Perhaps more important politically was the role of Central Committee Secretary Aleksei A. Kuznetsov. If any top party leader, apart from Stalin, was the driving force in moving the scandal forward, it may have been Kuznetsov, whose power and influence were peaking at around this time. In his capacity as head of the Cadres Directorate, he was in charge of reestablishing strict party control over the employees of the state apparatus (including the courts) in this period. Kuznetsov made it his mission to use the party to root out moral corruption from the state agencies he targeted, claiming that with weak leadership came the types of "deviance" and moral abuses that were exposed among the accused in the Affair of the High Courts.[164] Without direct evidence, one can only speculate.

For his part, Stalin, suffering from exhaustion and ill health, increasingly withdrew from domestic issues after 1946–1947, as he focused primarily on Cold War foreign policy struggles.[165] He became less involved in matters of state than he had been before and during the war. He likely left the details of the prosecutions to Kuznetsov at the Department of Administrative Organs and Safonov at the procuracy. To be sure, matters involving the courts probably rarely caught Stalin's attention after the war. Among the major exceptions, however, would have been the courts' role in prosecuting "counterrevolutionaries" and "political criminals" (including collaborators) and thieves of state property, two of his major criminal justice priorities. It seems that the attack on corruption in the courts had as much to do with guaranteeing the harsh punishment of "betrayers of the homeland" and thieves of state property as it did with actual concerns about bribery. The postwar attack on these courts, the far-reaching, "united, massive," and "campaign-style blow (udar)" against the courts, as one defendant called it, occurred in part because the courts were not living up to their responsibilities.[166] The party intervened with a sledgehammer, sometimes wielded indiscriminately.

Once Solodilov fell under a cloud of suspicion and investigators began looking into his relationships, it must have become clear that deal-making between petitioners and judges was occurring in many Moscow courts to an unexpected extent. Judging by the reaction of party leaders, and by the fact that investigations were launched in several courts almost simultaneously, the party almost surely had not anticipated the extent of bribery in the high courts. Cases of bribery in these courts were a manifestation of the types of informal relationships, patronage, and negotiation going on in courts (and many other bureaucracies) around the country; it was only the setting—and the degree of risk—that was more elevated than usual.

The scandal further demonstrates Stalin's continuing commitment to resolving political and social problems through rather haphazardly aimed, ad hoc bursts of arrests and explosive campaigns rather than by structural reform or substantial changes in the criminal code. Between 1948 and 1950—precisely during the period of arrests, interrogations, and trials that comprised the scandal—the procuracy and Ministry of Justice sent several proposals to Stalin that recommended toughening the laws on bribery. He rejected, or simply ignored, all of them.[167] Proposals modestly to increase sentences for bribery, as described in chapter 5, seem almost quaint in the retrospective light of the storm of arrests in the courts of Moscow and other regions.

In the context of the party's sharp criticism of the courts for their insufficiently rigorous sentencing of "dangerous" criminals, the Bakanov case in the Moscow military courts and the Solodilov case in the USSR Supreme Court seem to have served as pretexts for major assaults on any hint of corruption among high court judges and their staffs, whether real or invented. Ultimately, the Solodilov case seems to have been a pretext for attacking the USSR Supreme Court and its chairman Goliakov. The procuracy encouraged the assault on supposedly serious deficiencies in the courts by providing the Department of Administrative Organs with a steady stream of new information about judges' alleged bribe taking—much of it stemming from denunciations that were unverified and ultimately shown to be false—obtained during investigations and interrogations in 1947–1949.[168] The logic of Stalinist law enforcement convinced investigators that bribery in the courts must be widespread and conspiratorial.

It is striking that the careers of so many prominent Stalin-era judges unraveled amid corruption scandals after World War II. In the immediate postwar years, the chair of the Soviet Supreme Court Goliakov and both of his deputies, Ul'rikh and Nikitchenko, were accused not of *treason* (as they would have been in 1936–1938), but of *bribery*. The RSFSR Supreme Court justice Shevchenko and at least four other judges serving on that court were accused of bribery, not counterrevolution. Vasnev and four other judges on the Moscow City Court were convicted of bribery and abuse of office. The same goes for many other judges between 1948 and 1952. Accused of bribery or other types of official corruption, they either were sentenced to prison or were forced into retirement under a cloud of disgrace. They nevertheless avoided the death sentences handed down to "enemies of the people" during the purges, often by these same judges.

In the wake of Stalin's apparent decision to purge the courts bloodlessly, party and procuracy investigators recast hundreds of instances of petty bribery, spread across many years and courts, as a major, interlocked criminal conspiracy, undergirded by moral decay and capitalist degeneration that threatened the foundations of socialist legality. As discussed in the previous chapter, in the post–mass terror state such accusations of bribery became a tool to defame individuals whose alleged crimes would have called for violent repression in earlier times. Investigators compiled a long list of allegations—especially conspiracy, but also moral depredation, clannishness, and an insatiable appetite for profiteering—from which they could draw. After the war, bribe takers were not charged with invented political conspiracies inspired by Trotskyism, Bukharinism, or treason, but rather with regular *criminal* activities, even if in a highly politicized context. Some people were never charged with a crime at all, despite the procuracy's best efforts to build corruption cases against them (Ul'rikh, Goliakov, and Nikitchenko, for example). This strategy represents a major political change in the regime's handling of accusations of corruption, and one that remained a hallmark of the Khrushchev and Brezhnev periods.

Stalin changed tactics after the war. Believing that fascism and Trotskyism had been vanquished, he moved away from claims that poorly performing officials were "enemies of the people," and turned instead to allegations of corruption. Moreover, since violence was no longer being used to punish whole categories of criminals after the war, it seems clear that these accusations of bribery served a critical purpose—such allegations would not simply discredit the accused parties' credibility as trustworthy representatives of Soviet power, but would also embarrass them personally, undermine them morally, and destroy them as carriers of revolutionary truth and defenders of socialist legality. Several of the cases in the high courts scandal highlight not only a desire to remove leading figures in important Moscow courts, but also its additional aim to disgrace them. For a party member after the war, an accusation of bribery was debilitating. A Soviet official convicted of taking a bribe was thought to be no better than an American or German bureaucrat or a tsarist chinovnik. Bribery was such an effectively destructive accusation because it implied the moral and political decay of the whole person (at the heart of the concept of corruption), not just a one-time mistake.

CONCLUSION

One sees in this scandal the solidification of a new, post-Terror mosaic of explanations for the existence of corruption. The scandals in the courts exemplify how postwar narratives about corruption differed from those relied upon during the purges. It was during the late Stalin period that charges of moral corruption and professional malfeasance against officials were permanently de-coupled from allegations of treasonous activity. Judges who would have been purged in the 1930s as enemies under Article 58 were now accused of regular white-collar crimes. In the immediate postwar years, one sees a transition from the 1930s, when the NKVD labeled entire categories of people as dangerous enemies of the people or "criminal elements" and then arrested them en masse, often as part of a large counterrevolutionary conspiracy. After the war, on the other hand, law enforcement mostly operated on the principle that individuals committed crimes alone or in small groups, each with their own motives and methods.[169] Even in cases where the authorities alleged that criminal groupings were at work, postwar law enforcement agencies aimed primarily to show that instances of corruption were isolated occurrences of individuals falling from grace.

What, in fact, explains the wave of bribery in the Soviet high courts in the years just after World War II? Although they are by no means unbiased documents, the trial transcripts and investigative materials themselves bring out in vibrant detail many of the political and structural causes of the scandal, while recording the types of informal relationships that pervaded Soviet life. By detailing the tribulations of ordinary Soviet people, both officials and non-officials, the trials greatly complicate any narrative that lays full blame on the moral or political failings of court employees, lawyers, and bribe givers. Indeed, while many indictments contained allegations of "coordinated criminal conspiracies," prosecutors presented no evidence at trial that such machinations actually existed, beyond sketching normal friendships and collegial relations among co-workers (albeit portrayed in the most ominous light), compounded by the usual attempts of people engaged in a crime to avoid discovery. To determine the roots of unofficial deals in postwar Soviet society, one need look no further than conditions that the trials unintentionally lay bare: low pay, shortages of apartments and other essential goods, family illnesses and other problems, and people's aspirations not only to survive but to improve their living standards, which were at a low point in the wake of the catastrophes of the collectivization of the peasantry, breakneck industrialization, and war. If one adds to the mix other structural factors highlighted throughout this book, including the arbitrary and poorly trained bureaucracy, an economy of scarcity, and chaotic and unprofessional working conditions (not to mention normal human avarice), it becomes much clearer what in fact propelled court employees and petitioners alike along the "bribe trail" in the Soviet courts.

Ironically, perhaps, party watchdogs were right on one score: bribery in the courts was indeed a threat to the legitimacy of the Soviet legal system, though not, as the official narrative would have it, because of a series of plots by deeply corrupted people who were consciously aspiring to tear apart socialism. Rather, as the trials and appeals make clear, bribes in many cases were a result of the party-state's disrespect for the rule of law, extraordinarily overburdened courts, and the unexpected consequences of mass arrests and outrageously severe sentences for petty crimes against state property and the national economy. All of these conditions taken together, along with the thickets of red tape that hindered the execution of justice, encouraged the development of vibrant informal relationships in the shadows of Soviet life.

Many elements of the schemes—and the accusations that accompanied them—continued to echo well into the post-1953 period. The "art of the bribe" did not die with Stalin. This makes perfect sense: the USSR was still a state that both suppressed and unintentionally promoted entrepreneurial activity, still a multicultural world of people who negotiated among themselves to get by and find solutions to intractable problems, to find an education and work and justice, and who aspired to acquire goods and services and improve their standards of living. Although Stalin passed from the scene, the conditions that sowed the seeds for informal deal-making between officials and ordinary Soviet people still remained.

Conclusion
The Bribe and Its Meaning

CONSIDERING THE NEARLY OMNIPRESENT DISCUSSIONS of corruption in contemporary Russia and the late Soviet era, the subject of bribery may seem familiar. The phenomenon is worthy of a new approach, however, one that examines bribery as a crucial, yet mostly hidden, social practice with implications for legal, political, ideological, ethical, and institutional spheres in the Stalin years (and beyond). Corrupt relationships based on bribes flourished in some situations not because of the persistence of "capitalist outlooks" among a small slice of the population (as Soviet regimes insisted). Rather, both the givers and receivers of bribes learned to use the bribe as a flexible tool for maneuvering inside a disorganized economy and rigid bureaucratic system. This study illuminates the texture and culture of Stalinist society through the lens of shadow economy activity. Traditional practices of giving gifts to officials to express gratitude, common to many groups inside the Soviet Union, shaped the art of offering (and accepting) bribes. Much of the public did not consider the paying of bribes to be deviant. In an extraordinarily difficult postwar environment, Soviet people, including mid- and lower-level government officials, faced very trying and often bizarre circumstances, from housing and food shortages to nearly indiscriminate arrests, convictions, and imprisonment for petty nonpolitical crimes. Much of the evidence presented here has aimed to humanize—but not to romanticize—the logic and dynamics of these transactions as Soviet people developed schemes to get things done in chaotic times.

Amid the massive disruptions caused by the war, the population became even more dependent on arbitrary government agencies for official paperwork regarding housing, trade, migration, and work. Often, disputes over these documents were handled by local government administrations and the courts, offering officials excellent leverage to resolve these disputes—in exchange for illicit "fees." In law enforcement agencies, the mass prosecution of petty crimes after the war, reflecting the state's growing obsession with protecting state resources from theft and embezzlement, inadvertently created conditions that accelerated the spread of bribe giving. Some people risked paying off judges, police, or procurators in order to shield themselves or their loved ones from harsh mandatory sentences. Criminal justice and other law enforcement officials sometimes risked accepting illegal payments to supplement their meager incomes.

For the authorities, the persistence of bribery over time became a particularly keen reminder of the resilience of corrupt practices. Although it was incompatible with Soviet values of public culture and official propriety, bribery proved immensely difficult for the party and law enforcement to recognize and fully understand, never mind to eradicate, from a system that seemed to nourish it. It crossed the revolutionary divide from the tsarist civil service to the new Soviet state, albeit in somewhat modified forms, adapted to Soviet conditions. Both the pre-revolutionary intelligentsia and Bolshevik idealists saw bribery as endemic to a stifling bureaucracy. No act better symbolized the parasitical official than the simple informal demand for cash or other valuables in exchange for a favor. In Imperial times, the intelligentsia and middle classes saw bribery as the defining characteristic of a corrupt administration that employed many of the country's least enlightened and civic-minded people. Bribery symbolized the chasm between the officials of the decrepit state—who served only their own private interests—and the disenfranchised, victimized ordinary people. For Soviet leaders, bribe taking further served as a metaphor for the grossly exploitative, and surely doomed, system of capitalism.

In both the Soviet and late Imperial periods, bribery represented much more than its simple legal definition—a payment or other gift of value in exchange for an illegal benefit, obtained through an official's abuse of his position. Bribery symbolized an entire social, economic, and political infrastructure, a set of unjust, rigged arrangements that served to repress ordinary people. Revolutionaries idealized an alternative vision: rule by well-educated and honest people who would never demand money or gifts simply to do the right thing. They overlooked the fact that bribery emerged from a set of practices and attitudes that, in many cases, could serve certain practical functions, from distributing scarce goods and services, to establishing personalized relationships among state functionaries and citizens, to cutting through red tape. Both intelligentsia critics of the tsarist administration and Soviet critics of enduring "capitalist mentalities" unintentionally reinforced the stereotype of the eternally corrupt Russian bureaucrat.

Soviet ideology lent a peculiar coloration to discussions of bribery. In Soviet times, as is the case in many societies, gift giving was widely employed as a method of cementing relationships, establishing reciprocity, and ensuring the smooth functioning of local administration. Yet, in contrast to capitalist societies, where crime was considered a regrettable but largely inevitable part of life, Soviet ideology held that bribery was completely foreign to socialism. Indeed, until the late 1980s the word "*korruptsiia*" (corruption) was used in Soviet parlance to describe a phenomenon that existed *exclusively* in the bourgeois-capitalist world. Socialism in theory should eliminate the objective reasons for all crime, and especially crime among officials, who were supposed to be the cream of the Soviet crop. Bribery was akin to a disease that would be eradicated once the cruelties and injustices inherent to capitalism— poverty, exploitation, unemployment, and class hatred—disappeared in the process of perfecting this revolutionary society.

To party leaders, the bribe was a shameful reminder of the "backwardness" of parts of society, a primitive by-product of a dying way of life. If steel, factories, locomotives, rockets, modern collective farms, booming cities, and, perhaps most of all, the military victory over fascism symbolized the glories of Soviet progress and achievement, the bribe was an ugly remnant of a "dark" and "archaic" past. To some, the corrupt actions by Soviet officials represented conspiratorial and disloyal activity of all kinds, epitomizing underground deals and trickery. Public discussion of bribery was something that party leaders wanted to sweep under the rug, a symbol of postwar social and moral breakdown.

Amid the patriotic pride in winning the war and building a powerful country, the persistence of bribery was embarrassing. The regime hid bribery scandals and trials from the public. They refused to allow the phenomenon to be widely discussed, as the secret "campaign" of 1946 and the closed trials of high court judges in 1948–1952 demonstrate.

The years of recovery from the war led to new priorities for the regime, such as the capture and prosecution of collaborators and the restoration of control over the entire state administration. These goals merged with ongoing concerns that became even more urgent at war's end: securing state-controlled property and resources, fortifying the socialized economy, and vigilantly defending against the laxity of party cadres—all while creating a morally upright Soviet officialdom. Each of these concerns was reflected in the regime's attempts to rein in corruption. In this context, the Soviet regime saw bribery among its civil servants as a highly virulent form of malfeasance.[1] The acceptance of bribes by officials combined several particularly worrisome features that could damage and embarrass the country abroad, including a blatant disregard for professional duty, a perversion of revolutionary goals and party ethics, and a duplicitous disloyalty to the party-state.

Most of all, bribery in the agencies of law enforcement (or even the *rumors* of bribery) alarmed those concerned with preserving the legitimacy of the regime among the population. Officials were supposed to be the gatekeepers of law and order—when they could be "bought," chaos and anarchy might ensue. At the same time, the inherent unfairness of bribery could undercut popular support for the Soviet government. Corruption could undercut the party's use of the legal system as a weapon to punish criminals severely and otherwise to further the regime's goals. The law and the courts were adapted to serve the needs of the regime. In the words of Kathryn Hendley, "Both the czars and the Communist Party leadership routinely used law as a blunt instrument to advance their interests, enforcing it strictly against the powerless, but stretching it beyond recognition to accommodate themselves and their favorites. Laws were often written in the broadest terms possible so as to give officials maximum flexibility."[2]

The approach taken in this book results in a focus on areas of life in the Stalin-era USSR that have rarely been explored. It further challenges the view that in the postwar Stalin years there were only two major actors: an all-powerful and repressive state machine that hovered above, and a powerless, victimized society below. Intermediaries in bribery transactions, for example, employed an impressive degree of "entrepreneurial" initiative. They pursued opportunities, sometimes by "translating" local demands to central authorities, and other times by negotiating with those authorities directly. Intermediaries established connections, creating lines of communication between social and state actors. Resilient networks of contacts, friends, and relatives thrived as people tried to work through or around the bureaucracy. Some people could use such networks to find a partner with whom to make a deal— sometimes this could involve blat, if one were fortunate enough to have the necessary connections. (Most people were not so lucky.) Although there was a degree of risk in either strategy—working through intermediaries or approaching officials directly—many people calculated that the potential outcomes were worth the chance.

Both bribery and blat were informal relationships that served related functions in the Stalinist USSR. Blat could be more effective than money in certain situations, if one were lucky enough to have acquaintances in a position to help. Blat and bribery often intersected: a blat relationship could serve as a stepping-stone on the path to a bribe. At times, then, "blat relations mediate bribery."[3] But for most Soviet people, their connections were not adequate to solve all their problems. In cases where blat was not sufficient, or if a high degree of risk was involved, they might have to move beyond the realm of "the mutual exchange of favors" and into the realm of the outright *purchase* of favors from officials. For the well-connected, to quote a common saying, blat could be "more influential than the Council of Ministers" and even "higher than Stalin." (*Blat vyshe Sovmina! Blat vyshe Stalina!*) But for the person who lacked the right contacts, *Vziatka vyshe blata!* (Bribery is higher than blat!)

Ultimately, Soviet ruling elites were trapped in a contradiction of their own creation—they attempted to control corruption while simultaneously maintaining a system that created the conditions in which it thrived. In every society, power relations help to determine who will be prosecuted for corruption and who will avoid penalties. Many activities among the elites that could fairly be described as "abuse of office for personal profit" were never prosecuted. After all, the system was built on certain legal privileges for those at the top of the hierarchy. The party certainly did not consider the high salaries, dachas, fancy automobiles, exclusive medical care, opportunities for travel and relaxation, access to scarce supplies, and other perquisites for the elite and their families (with these privileges carefully calibrated according to one's rank in the hierarchy) to be a product of "corruption." Expulsions from the party for corruption dropped sharply after 1953, and party members at all levels of the hierarchy were only rarely charged with crimes.[4] Even as newspapers contained more coverage of crimes by officials after Stalin's death, corruption among elites was almost never mentioned in the press. Self-enriching bureaucrats at all levels of the state and economic administrations came to personify an increasingly inflexible and self-serving system. And with the collapse of the regime in 1991, officials who had locked in their positions and their access to state-owned resources found themselves perfectly placed to profit to an extent that was inconceivable in Soviet times.[5]

Notes

1. Crime among party officials in the 1930s has received more attention, notably in Peter H. Solomon's excellent study of the Stalinist legal system. Peter Solomon, *Soviet Criminal Justice under Stalin* (Cambridge, 1996). On police measures against speculation in the 1930s, see Paul Hagenloh, *Stalin's Police.*

2. An exception is an article by Cynthia V. Hooper, who argues that the party covered up crimes by elites in exchange for their support of the regime's policies. The state, Hooper argues, would allow functionaries to profit criminally from their offices in exchange for carrying out the regime's commands without question, partly by discouraging or ignoring reports about wrongdoing from ordinary people that had kept elites off balance, and their grip on power tenuous, in the 1930s. "A Darker 'Big Deal': Concealing Party Crimes in the Post–Second World War Era," in Juliane Fürst, ed., *Late Stalinist Russia: Society between Reconstruction and Reinvention* (London, 2006), 142–163. Julie Hessler has contributed important research on the "informal" but legal private sector in this period. This study of the development of bazaars and private production and trade during and after the war, both official and unofficial, highlights growing government accommodation with certain varieties of unsponsored economic activity that the regime came to believe it could never fully control. Moreover, Hessler's work shows that mechanisms outside the state's complete control, such as bazaars, were essential for enabling people to acquire things and get things done after the war. Hessler coins the phrase "the survivalist consensus"—a sense that, in this time of dire poverty, the repression of certain unsanctioned solutions to desperate problems would be relaxed. Julie Hessler, *A Social History of Soviet Trade: Trade Policy, Retail Practices, and Consumption, 1917–1953* (Princeton, NJ, 2004).

3. Most scholarly studies of Soviet corruption written in the 1970s–1990s devote space to a survey of prerevolutionary Russia and the years immediately after the 1917 Revolution, but skip over the 1930s, 1940s, and 1950s with little or no

comment, on their way to a discussion of the ripening of corruption in the period of "stagnation" under the leadership of Leonid Brezhnev and his successors (1964–1985). (Mikhail S. Gorbachev used the term "stagnation" to smear his predecessors and his political opponents.) One person to challenge this interpretation was the émigré lawyer Konstantin Simis, in his 1982 memoir, *USSR: The Corrupt Society* (New York, 1982). Considering a later period than this study, he describes an utterly corrupt legal system, which, in his telling, took root in the late 1950s. Though he sometimes seems to exaggerate (he describes what he calls "an orgy of corruption"), Simis points out important phenomena in the courts, including widespread bribery, political pressures on the court system, and party interference in prosecutions. His discussion of the late Stalin period is largely based on rumors and personal anecdote (he began practicing law in the early 1960s and left the Soviet Union in the late 1970s).

4. Among the most important examples of scholarly work that reference such activities are Stephen Kotkin, *Magnetic Mountain: Stalinism as Civilization* (Berkeley, CA, 1995); Elena Osokina, *Ierarkhiia potreblieniia. O zhizni liudei v usloviiakh Stalinskogo snabzheniia: 1928–1935 gg.* (Moscow, 1993); David Shearer, *Policing Stalin's Socialism: Repression and Social Order in the Soviet Union, 1924–1953* (New Haven, CT, 2009); Paul Hagenloh, *Stalin's Police: Public Order and Mass Repression in the USSR, 1924–1941* (Baltimore, 2009); and Sheila Fitzpatrick, *Everyday Stalinism: Ordinary Life in Extraordinary Times: Soviet Russia in the 1930s* (New York, 1999). See also the memoirs of Gennady Andreev-Khomiakov for insight into informal relationships in the 1930s, *Bitter Waters: Life and Work in Stalin's Russia.* Trans. by Ann E. Healy (Boulder, CO, 1997). On theft and profiteering among soldiers during the war, see Catherine Merridale, *Ivan's War: Life and Death in the Red Army, 1939–1945* (New York, 2006). O. L. Leibovich provides several interesting case studies of economic crimes by party elites in the Molotov region in his *V gorode M. Ocherki sotsial'noi povsednevnosti sovetskoi provintsii* (Moscow, 2008).

5. Max Weber, for example, believed that some "Orientals" were more prone to corruption than Europeans; Samuel Huntingdon argued the same for "mulatto states." Robert Klitgaard, "Gifts and Bribes," in *Strategy and Choice,* ed. Richard Zeckhauser (Cambridge, MA, 1991), 223. For a recent example of an author who finds something eternally criminal—and "slavish"—in "Russian national character" and "the Russian mentality" see the Russian journalist Vladimir Soloviev, *Empire of Corruption: The Territory of the Russian National Pastime* (London, 2014). Discussing contemporary Russia, he writes, "The system characterized by a corrupt elite and bribery, for which our own period appears to be so famed, has actually existed since the dawn of time. It is, I stress, a national tradition" (63). A few pages later he argues, "The Russian people cannot see that corruption is unacceptable, because a strong clan instinct has lived in the collective conscience from ancient times"; and finally, "Russian corruption is linked to our slave mentality" (78).

6. James C. Scott, *Comparative Political Corruption* (Englewood Cliffs, NJ, 1972), 10.

7. Only a small part of the vast literature can be mentioned here (more is discussed below). See, for example, Susan Rose-Ackerman, *Corruption and Govern-*

ment: Causes, Consequences, Reform (Cambridge, 1999); Arnold Heidenheimer, et al., eds., *Political Corruption: A Handbook* (Edison, NJ, 2001). For very useful discussions of definitional aspects of corruption, see Leslie Holmes, *The End of Communist Power: Anti-Corruption Campaigns and Legitimation Crisis* (Cambridge, 1993); and his *Rotten States? Corruption, Post-Communism, and Neo-Liberalism* (Durham, NC, 2006), 17–43. On corruption in the USSR and Russia during and since the collapse of the Soviet Union, see, for example, Stephen Solnick, *Stealing the State: Control and Collapse in Soviet Institutions* (Cambridge MA, 1998); Stephen Kotkin, *Armageddon Averted* (Oxford, 2008). On informal mechanisms of all kinds, Alena Ledeneva, *How Russia Really Works: The Informal Practices That Shaped Post-Soviet Politics and Business* (Ithaca NY, 2006); on the machinations surrounding the rise to power of Putin and his circle, see Karen Dawisha, *Putin's Kleptocracy: Who Owns Russia?* (New York, 2014). On organized crime, see Mark Galeotti, ed., *Russian and Post-Soviet Organized Crime* (London and Ashgate, 2002). See also Leonid Kosals and Anastasia Maksimova, "Informality, Crime and Corruption in Russia: A Review of Recent Literature," *Theoretical Criminology* 19 (May 2015): 278–288.

8. Susan Rose-Ackerman points out that Weberian definitions of corruption can be poorly suited to polities where distinctions between notions of public and private are blurred. Rose-Ackerman, *Corruption and Government* (Cambridge, 1998).

9. Very fine empirical research on Brezhnev-era corruption, based mainly on reports in the Soviet press, was undertaken by scholars including William Clark, F. J. M. Feldbrugge, Nick Lampert, and Charles Schwartz, who mainly published their studies in the 1970s and 1980s. F. J. M. Feldbrugge, "Government and Shadow Economy in the Soviet Union," *Soviet Studies*, 36, no. 4 (October 1984): 528–543; William Clark, *Crime and Punishment in Soviet Officialdom: Combating Corruption in the Political Elite, 1965–1990* (Armonk, NY, 1993); Nick Lampert, "Law and Order in the USSR: The Case of Economic and Official Crime," *Soviet Studies* 36, no. 3 (July 1984): 366–385; Charles A. Schwartz, "Economic Crime in the USSR: A Comparison of Khrushchev and Brezhnev Eras," *The International and Comparative Law Quarterly* 30, no. 2 (April 1981): 281–296. In his highly perceptive book *Crime and Punishment in Soviet Officialdom*, William Clark uses the periodical press and other published sources to discuss the 1970s and 1980s; the study focuses on scandals at the highest levels of the Communist Party. The émigré lawyer Konstantin Simis labels the wake of the 1956 Secret Speech "the turning point in the spread of corruption," as party members lost both their scruples and their faith in the system. See his article "The Machinery of Corruption in the Soviet Union," *Survey* (1977): 35. See also Yoram Gorlizki, "De-Stalinization and the Politics of Russian Criminal Justice, 1953–64," unpublished D. Phil Thesis, University of Oxford, 1992. Katsenelinboigen's classic study of "coloured markets" provides one example of corruption from the "late fifties"; all others are from later periods. Aron Katsenelinboigen, "Coloured Markets in the Soviet Union," *Soviet Studies* 29 (January 1977). Nick Lampert's study begins with the 1960s. On other types of crime in the late Stalin and Khrushchev eras see, for example, Brian La-Pierre, *Hooligans in Khrushchev's Russia* (Madison, WI, 2012); and Miriam Dobson, *Khrushchev's Cold Summer: Gulag Returnees, Crime, and the Fate of Reform*

after Stalin (Ithaca, NY, 2009). The various forms of illicit "horse trading" among managers in industry lie outside the parameters of this study. On informal bartering in industry in the 1930s, see David Shearer, "Wheeling and Dealing in Soviet Industry: Syndicates, Trade, and Political Economy at the End of the 1920s," *Cahiers du monde russe* 36, no. 1/2 (1995): 139–160; and Paul Gregory, *The Political Economy of Stalinism: Evidence from the Soviet Secret Archives* (Cambridge, 2004). For more recent work on the 1970s–1980s, see the study of corruption in two important Moscow trade administrations in the 1980s, based on materials located in part in the KGB archive: Luc Duhamel, *The KGB Campaign against Corruption in Moscow, 1982–1987* (Pittsburgh, 2010). See also the recent study of police attempts to rein in economic crime in the late Soviet and post-Soviet years, even as law enforcement often became the partners of criminals: Gilles Favarel-Garrigues, *Policing Economic Crime in Russia: From Soviet Planned Economy to Privatization* (London, 2011).

10. This is not to argue that bribery is a moral evil—such judgment is best left to ethicists and philosophers. Many political thinkers, it is true, traditionally defined an official's susceptibility to wrongdoing as a symptom of moral degeneration, a personal failing of virtue, or a sign of sinfulness. Glib condemnations of bribery as a simple moral or spiritual failure, both inside and outside Russia, are perhaps more common—and less revealing—than ever. Contemporary social scientists and historians have largely rejected this moralistic approach. For a discussion of such categories of analysis, see John M. Kramer, "Political Corruption in the USSR," *The Western Political Quarterly* 30, no. 2 (June 1977): 213–224. In Soviet authorities' discussions of corruption, moralistic explanations of its causes were common.

11. Mass casualties during the war meant that two-thirds of party members had joined since 1941. On the development of Russian national identity, see Brandenberger, *National Bolshevism: Stalinist Mass Culture and the Formation of Modern Russian National Identity, 1931–1956* (Cambridge, MA, 2002).

12. On this process, see Moshe Lewin, "Rebuilding the Soviet Nomenklatura"; Jean Levesque, "Into the Grey Zone: Sham Peasants and the Limits of the Kolkhoz Order in the Post-War Russian Village, 1945–1953," in Juliane Fürst, *Late Stalinist Russia: Society between Reconstruction and Reinvention* (London, 2006), 163–189; Donald Filtzer, *Soviet Workers and Late Stalinism: Labour and the Restoration of the Stalinist System after WWII* (Cambridge, 2002). John Barber and Mark Harrison, *The Soviet Home Front 1941–1945: A Social and Economic History of the USSR in World War II* (London, 1991). In the words of Yoram Gorlizki, "Postwar reconstruction in the Soviet Union entailed a concerted effort to recreate, often from a most uncompromising base, a system of centralized Stalinist relations in almost all walks of life." Gorlizki, "Ordinary Stalinism: The Council of Ministers and the Soviet Neopatriomonial State, 1946–1953," *Journal of Modern History* 74 (December 2002): 699.

13. Vera Dunham, *In Stalin's Time: Middleclass Values in Soviet Fiction* (Cambridge, 1976). Katerina Clark has also emphasized that postwar Soviet citizens wished to demonstrate an air of greater sophistication; upright people wanted to

exhibit their style and status with luxury goods and travel. Katerina Clark, *The Soviet Novel: History as Ritual* (Chicago, 1981), 197–198. Anne E. Gorsuch, "There's No Place like Home": Soviet Tourism in Late Stalinism," in *Slavic Review,* Vol. 62, No. 4 (Winter 2003): 760–785.

14. Accepting bribes has drawn opprobrium throughout history. Bribery by a judge has been a cause of special condemnation in many societies, as John Noonan has shown throughout his book, *Bribery* (Berkeley, CA, 1988). For the case of France, see Natalie Z. Davis, *The Gift in Sixteenth Century France* (Madison, WI, 2000), 85–99.

15. Catriona Kelly, "Self-Interested Giving: Bribery and Etiquette in Late Imperial Russia," in *Bribery and Blat in Russia: Negotiating Reciprocity from the Middle Ages to the 1990s,* ed. Stephen Lovell, Alena V. Ledeneva, and Andrei Rogachevskii (New York, 2000), 65–94.

16. See, for example, Josiah Heyman and Alan Smart, "States and Illegal Practices: An Overview," in *States and Illegal Practices,* ed. Josiah Heyman (Oxford, 1999), 1–24; Italo Pardo, *Between Morality and the Law: Corruption, Anthropology and Comparative Society* (Aldershot, UK, 2004); Caroline Humphrey, *The Unmaking of Soviet Life: Everyday Economies after Socialism* (Ithaca, NY, 2002).

17. The "informal institutions" and the culture of reciprocity that supported them were by no means unique to the USSR, of course. For a classic study, see Gretchen Helmke and Steven Levitsky, "Informal Institutions and Comparative Politics: A Research Agenda," *Perspectives on Politics* 2, no. 4 (December 2004): 725–740.

18. Ledeneva, *Russia's Economy of Favours: Blat, Networking and Informal Exchange* (Cambridge, 1998). Ledeneva was inspired by the pioneering work of Raymond Bauer, Alex Inkeles, and Joseph Berliner, each of whom worked on the interviews with émigrés during the "Project on the Soviet Social System" (informally known as the Harvard Interview Project) in the early 1950s, and which noted that corrupt practices seemed to be both necessary and largely tolerated by the state as long as they served the goal of plan fulfillment. These scholars were mainly interested in industry, but their observations also apply to certain aspects of civilian administration and daily life. R. A. Bauer, A. Inkeles, and Clyde Kluckhohn, *How the Soviet System Works: Cultural, Psychological, and Social Themes* (Cambridge, MA, 1956), 89–93. Sheila Fitzpatrick has examined this practice (and many others) in the 1930s, using interviews with Soviet émigrés who left during World War II made by Harvard scholars in the early 1950s. Sheila Fitzpatrick, "Blat in Stalin's Time," in *Bribery and Blat in Russia,* ed. Stephen Lovell, et al., 166–182. This article briefly notes respondents' observation that blat and bribery could be related, yet were usually regarded as quite distinct from each other. Fitzpatrick did not study bribery. For some thoughts on blat in the 1930s, see also Vladimir Andrle, *A Social History of Twentieth Century Russia* (London, 1994), 200–202. See also the observations of the journalist Edward Crankshaw, in *Khrushchev's Russia* (Harmondsworth, 1959). In the words of Moshe Lewin, "The unwieldy party-state machinery could continue to function on condition of accepting informal arrangements by all involved, and adapting to widespread behavior that made many formal

procedures irrelevant." Lewin, "Rebuilding the Soviet Nomenklatura 1945–1948," *Cahiers du monde russe* 44 (2003/2–3): 243. Sheila Fitzpatrick, "Blat in Stalin's Time," in *Bribery and Blat in Russia,* ed. Lovell et al, 166–182.

19. For the expression "rules of the game," see James Scott, *Comparative Political Corruption.*

20. Cicero and Seneca, for example, each wrote guides to gift giving.

21. Like all important Soviet legal records and nearly all Communist Party documentation, these files were inaccessible before the collapse of the USSR in 1991; most of the records cited in this text became available to researchers only in 2001 or later.

22. The interesting work of L. V. Borisova on the 1920s contains little from the point of view of those *giving* bribes. "Tret'ii vrag revoliutsii: Bor'ba so vziatochnichestvom i khoziaistvennymi prestupleniiami v nachale NEPa," *Soviet and Post-Soviet Review* 30, no. 3: 245–277.

23. Heidenheimer's "Introduction" (pp. 3–14), for example, discusses existing moral codes in various societies, but focuses mainly on the codes concerning the *taking* of bribes. These are the codes of the official, and do not touch on the behavior of the people offering gifts to people in positions of authority.

24. Arnold J. Heidenheimer, Michael Johnston, and Victor Levine, *Political Corruption: A Handbook* (Edison, NJ, 2001).

25. Charles Schwartz adopted this color-coded scheme for the Soviet case. See Charles Schwartz, "Corruption and Political Development in the USSR," *Comparative Politics* 11, no. 4 (July 1979): 425–443. Of course, it must be taken into account that not all citizens agree on what constitutes a corrupt act.

26. Two social historians, Moshe Lewin and Sheila Fitzpatrick, are credited with pioneering the nuanced study of Soviet society in the Stalin years. Among other topics, Lewin focused on the unanticipated consequences of state actions and Stalinist repression. His enduring studies of the Stalinist state system, with its contradictions and often self-defeating and even self-destructive elements, inspired scholars to dig more deeply into how the system worked. Fitzpatrick has long focused on Soviet people as "survivors" in chaotic times, as they struggled to cope. Both have concentrated much more on the 1930s than on the postwar period. Much of her *Everyday Stalinism* focuses on urban consumption and the fight to obtain goods in the 1930s. On the dearth of published sources on the postwar Stalinist legal system, see Peter Solomon, "Understanding the History of Soviet Criminal Justice: The Contribution of Archives and Other Sources," *Russian Review* 74, no. 3 (July 2015): 401–418. Conducting oral interviews proved to be impractical a full fifty to sixty years after the conclusion of the period examined.

27. Stephen Lovell has called the years of postwar Stalinism an "unloved" period among scholars. See *The Shadow of War: Russia and the USSR, 1941 to the Present* (Chichester, UK, 2010), 14.

28. See, for example, Amir Weiner, *Making Sense of War: The Second World War and the Fate of the Bolshevik Revolution* (Princeton, NJ, 2002).

29. Yoram Gorlizki and Oleg Khlevniuk's study is a collaboration that exhaustively examines high politics, and especially the political actions and role of Stalin. Gorlizki and Khlevniuk, *Cold Peace: Stalin and the Soviet Ruling Circle, 1945–1953*

(Oxford, 2004). Informed by previously inaccessible archival documents, the authors shed new light on the postwar relationships between Stalin and his closest associates that earlier could only tentatively be gleaned from a few memoirs and limited newspaper coverage.

30. Lovell has noted this in *The Shadow of War*. Chris Ward has made the point that until relatively recently the narrative of late Stalinism largely excluded social history. Chris Ward, "What is History? The Case of Late Stalinism," *Rethinking History*, no. 8 (2004): 439–458. The first major study of late Stalinist society was a collection of articles edited by Susan Linz, *The Impact of World War II on the Soviet Union* (Totowa, NJ, 1985). A recent valuable collection of articles that focuses on social and cultural approaches is Juliane Fürst, *Late Stalinist Russia: Society between Reconstruction and Reinvention* (London, 2006).

31. Amir Weiner, *Making Sense of War*; Mark Edele, *Soviet Veterans of World War II: A Popular Movement in an Authoritarian State* (Oxford, 2008). Karl Qualls has written about the creation of the myth of Sevastopol' as a "hero-city" and the contested challenge of rebuilding Soviet cities after the war. Karl Qualls, *From Ruins to Reconstruction: Urban Identity in Soviet Sevastopol after World War II* (Ithaca, NY, 2009). See also Lisa Kirschenbaum's penetrating *The Legacy of the Siege of Leningrad, 1941–1995* (Cambridge, 2004). In his fine study of Rostov-na-Donu between 1943 and 1948, Jeffrey Jones devotes one chapter to a discussion of corruption in party ranks in one major Soviet city. Using research in archives and the local press, Jones describes the contradictory ways that party elites discussed corruption in closed party forums and in the press. Jones suggests a high degree of tolerance for corruption inside the party. Jones, *Everyday Life and the "Reconstruction" of Soviet Russia during and after the Great Patriotic War, 1943–1948* (Bloomington, IN, 2008). Donald Filtzer's studies of industrial workers and urban life in late Stalinism are major contributions. See Donald Filtzer, *Soviet Workers and Late Stalinism: Labour and the Restoration of the Stalinist System after WWII* (Cambridge, 2002); and the remarkable *The Hazards of Urban Life in the Late Stalinist USSR, 1943–1953* (Cambridge, 2010). On provincial life, see also Jean Levesque, "Into the Grey Zone: Sham Peasants and the Limits of the Kolkhoz Order in the Post-War Russian Village, 1945–1953," in Fürst, *Late Stalinist Russia: Society between Reconstruction and Reinvention* (London, 2006), 163–189. See also Kees Boterbloem, *Life and Death under Stalin: Kalinin Province, 1945–1953* (Montreal and Kingston, 1999). On regional power networks in the 1930s see James Harris, *The Great Urals: Regionalism and the Evolution of the Soviet System* (Ithaca, NY, 1999).

32. In the final chapter of his book on repression and social order in Stalinism, for example, David Shearer notes a key "shift in the mechanics of repression" after the war. He notes that the postwar discourse of repression "was cast in the language of social discipline and not the rhetoric of the danger of political insurgency" (423). David Shearer, *Policing Stalin's Socialism*. For another example, see Mark Edele, *Soviet Veterans of World War II*. On the demographic and social effects of the postwar famine, see Nicholas Ganson, *The Soviet Famine of 1946–47 in Global and Historical Perspective* (New York, 2009). The Russian scholar Elena Iu. Zubkova's influential research was among the first to take the war's impact on Soviet

society into full account. Zubkova concentrates especially on public attitudes toward the state and social life. She discusses public perceptions of a wave of crimes against persons, arguing that the population exaggerated the growth in criminal activity after the war. She does not delve deeply into the question of white-collar crime or corruption, though she argues that many people were angered by abuse of office by some local officials. Elena Iu. Zubkova, *Poslevoennoe sovetskoe obshchestvo: Politika i povsednevnost'*, *1945–53* (Moscow, 2000), 89–90; an earlier edition was translated into English as *Russia after the War: Hopes, Illusions, and Disappointments, 1945–1957*, trans. and ed. Hugh Ragsdale (Armonk, NY, 1998), 38–39. A fascinating 2003 collection, *Sovetskaia zhizn'*, which compiles a wide variety of documents from Soviet archives about daily life in the period, contains a section on "The Postwar Criminal" (189–210). This collection, however, does not include documents that mention bribery or white-collar crime, focusing rather on theft, hooliganism, murder, and assault. E. Iu. Zubkova, et al., eds., *Sovetskaia zhizn'* (Moscow, 2003).

33. Peter H. Solomon, Jr., *Soviet Criminal Justice under Stalin* (Cambridge, 1996), chapters 11 and 12; Yoram Gorlizki, "Rules, Incentives and Soviet Campaign Justice after World War II," *Europe-Asia Studies* 51, no. 7 (November 1999): 1245–1265; Juliette Cadiot, "Equal before the Law? Soviet Justice, Criminal Proceedings against Communist Party Members, and the Legal Landscape in the USSR from 1945 to 1953," *Jahrbücher für Geschichte Osteuropas* 61, no. 2 (2013): 249–269; Juliette Cadiot, "Avocat sous Staline. Profession accessoire, profession témoin (1945–1953)," *Les Annales HSS* 71, no. 1 (January–February 2016), 139–170. See also, for example, John Hazard, *Law and Social Change in the USSR* (London, 1953); Harold Berman, *Justice in the USSR: An Interpretation of Soviet Law* (Cambridge, MA, 1963); Charles Hachten, "Property Relations and the Economic Organization of Soviet Russia, 1941–1948," unpublished PhD dissertation (University of Chicago, 2005).

34. Some notable recent examples include Oleg Khlevniuk, *Master of the House: Stalin and His Inner Circle* (New Haven, CT, 2008); David Shearer, *Policing Stalin's Socialism: Repression and Social Order in the Soviet Union, 1924–1953* (New Haven, CT, 2009); Paul Hagenloh, *Stalin's Police;* J. Arch Getty, *Yezhov: The Rise of Stalin's "Iron Fist"* (New Haven, CT, 2008); Stephen Barnes, *Death and Redemption: The Gulag and the Shaping of Soviet Society* (Cambridge, MA, 2011); Marc Jansen and Nikita Petrov, *Stalin's Loyal Executioner: People's Commissar Nikolai Ezhov* (Palo Alto, CA, 2002). Peter Solomon's work on the application of justice in Stalin's time examines issues mainly from the point of view of the legal agencies and their personnel. His studies are highly valuable because (among other things) they illustrate the education of legal specialists, the tensions among certain party and state agencies, the process of drawing up and carrying out draconian wartime and postwar decrees, and a degree of push-back by some judges against the regime's most repressive laws. Solomon notes that the party tried to fight corruption when certain prominent cases came to its attention. (Peter Solomon, *Soviet Criminal Justice*, chapters 11 and 12.) Solomon also states that bribery was widespread in the Moscow courts in the 1920s. Cynthia V. Hooper's work has focused on popular participation in rooting out crimes among party members, and the corre-

sponding resistance at high levels to exposing elite wrongdoing. Hooper, "Terror from Within: Participation and Coercion in Soviet Power, 1924–1964," unpublished PhD dissertation (Princeton University, 2003). In a separate article, Hooper highlights how party leaders were increasingly tolerant of crimes by party officials after the war, and argues that, in marked contrast to the more effective control "from below" (mainly via denunciations) of the 1930s, party leaders after the war were able to smother public and intra-party discussion—and stifle prosecution—of high-level abuses by the *nomenklatura*. Cynthia Hooper, "A Darker 'Big Deal,'" 142–163. Edward Cohn examines the party's highly uneven punishment of corrupt party members in "Disciplining the Party: The Expulsion and Censure of Communists in the Post-War Soviet Union, 1945–1961," unpublished PhD dissertation (University of Chicago, 2007). See also Eric Duskin, *Stalinist Reconstruction and the Confirmation of a New Elite, 1945–1953* (Basingstoke, UK, 2001).

35. Joseph Berliner, *Factory and Manager in the USSR,* 160–230; and his "Blat is Higher than Stalin!" *Problems of Communism* 3, no. 1 (Jan.–Feb. 1954): 22–31. In the 1970s, Gregory Grossman and Vladimir Treml issued several crucial studies of the relationship between the Soviet "second economy" and state corruption in the Brezhnev period. They described the active second economy that provided the consumer goods and essential services that the planned economy could not produce in sufficient amounts. For example, Gregory Grossman, "The 'Second Economy' of the USSR"; Gregory Grossman, "Notes on the Illegal Private Economy and Corruption," in *The Soviet Economy in a Time of Change,* Joint Economic Committee (Washington, 1979). Émigrés and a few journalists described, mostly anecdotally, a thriving black market, widespread blat, and official malfeasance in the 1940s and 1950s. See, for example, David Dallin, "The Black Market in Russia," *American Mercury* 69 (1949): 676–689; Kirill Alexeiev, "Russia's Underground Capitalism," in *Plain Talk,* December 1949, 19–24; Boris A. Konstinovsky, *Soviet Law in Action: The Recollected Cases of a Soviet Lawyer,* edited by Harold J. Berman (Cambridge, MA, 1953). For examples of black market dealings and theft by employees in the 1930s, see Elena Osokina, *Ierarkhiia potrebleniia. O zhizni liudei v usloviiakh Stalinskogo snabzheniia: 1928–1935 gg.* (Moscow, 1993). In his classic study of the planned economy, Janos Kornai showed that in a system with what he called "soft budget constraints," managers' practice of hoarding resources typically was not punished by central planners. Janos Kornai, *Economics of Shortage and the Socialist System* (Amsterdam, 1980).

36. Gregory Grossman, "The 'Second Economy' of the USSR," *Problems of Communism,* Sept.–Oct. 1977, 25–40 (quote at 32–33). As Stephen Kotkin has noted about the city of Magnitogorsk in the 1930s, it is nearly impossible to separate the official economy from the unofficial economy; the second economy was "a corollary to the official economy; it was the shadow economy that permitted the official economy to function, and vice versa." Stephen Kotkin, *Magnetic Mountain,* 274. Eugenia Belova, "Economic Crime and Punishment," in *Behind the Façade of Stalin's Command Economy: Evidence from the Soviet State and Party Archives,* ed. Paul Gregory (Stanford, 2001).

37. To be sure, certain aspects of the legal system, including judges' and prosecutors' political dependency on the party and the nomenklatura that created this

dependency, have been discussed by scholars. See, for example, Peter Solomon, *Soviet Criminal Justice under Stalin* (Cambridge, 1996).

38. Katherine Verdery's study of Eastern European (including Soviet) socialist societies provides a productive framework for examining corruption in the late Stalin period. Katherine Verdery, *What was Socialism, and What Comes Next?* (Princeton, NJ, 1996), especially 20–28. Verdery has argued that socialist states and economies had special features that helped to shape the parameters of corruption. In the absence of free markets, Verdery argues, socialist states maintained legitimacy to the extent that they could fulfill their promises of "social distribution and social welfare." Verdery argues that these states tried to gain allegiance through "socialist paternalism," which meant meeting the population's basic needs by collecting and redistributing the fruits of society's production, including apartments, education, transportation, work, and social welfare for the needy. I would add to this list the promise of equal and complete justice—that the system would punish wrongdoers and, equally importantly, protect the innocent. People in socialist societies came to expect that the state would meet these basic needs, which was their "right." Yet the poorly planned, over-centralized, and inefficient production and distribution systems failed to provide for those needs. Verdery has noted that people in a position to profit from illegal deals in Soviet-style economies were often those at key points in the distribution networks, who had the power to divert resources in exchange for illicit payments. Bribery threatened the regime's monopoly on distribution, adding new (paid) links to the chain. Managers would "game the system" because they did not have the resources necessary to fulfill plan targets; further shortages resulted. Monopolies in the allocation of scarce goods, concentrated in the hands of planning officials, also compelled mid- and low-level managers and ordinary people to bargain to obtain what they needed. At the same time, the state's abolition of markets, neglect of personal consumption, and centralized planning system gave rise to an enormous underground economy in scarce products and in services.

39. Vera Dunham used a reading of Soviet "lowbrow" fiction of the late Stalinist era to observe that the regime was granting people's desire for consumer goods to accommodate the growing professional elites (or upper middle class). Dunham, *In Stalin's Time.*

40. As many scholars have shown, officially outlawed forms of corruption continued to co-exist both with the official procedures for obtaining goods and services (whether the permitted markets or the "normal" bureaucratic channels) and with informal but not strictly illegal methods such as blat. Gregory Grossman, "The 'Second Economy' of the USSR"; Julie Hessler, *A Social History of Soviet Trade*; Stephen Kotkin, *Magnetic Mountain: Stalinism as a Civilization*, 238–279; Alena V. Ledeneva, *Russia's Economy of Favours*; Sheila Fitzpatrick, "Blat in Stalin's Time," in *Bribery and Blat in Russia*, ed. Stephen Lovell, et al.

41. Although the "Affair of the High Courts" has not been closely examined in studies by scholars using archival sources since the collapse of the Soviet Union, other high-level political affairs have. Yoram Gorlizki and Oleg Khlevniuk, *Cold Peace*. David Brandenberger and Benjamin Tromly have used archives to examine the Leningrad Affair: Benjamin Tromly, "The Leningrad Affair and Soviet Patron-

age Politics," *Europe-Asia Studies* 56, no. 5 (July 2004): 707–729; David Brandenberger, "Stalin, the Leningrad Affair, and the Limits of Postwar Soviet Ethnocentrism," *Russian Review* 63: 3 (2004), 241–255; Richard Bidlack, "Ideological or Political Origins of the Leningrad Affair? A Response to David Brandenberger," *The Russian Review* 64 (January 2005): 90–95;" Lovell, *The Shadow of War*; N. L. Krementsov, *The Cure: A Story of Cancer and Politics from the Annals of the Cold War* (Chicago, 2004); Joshua Rubenstein and Vladimir Naumov, eds., *Stalin's Secret Pogrom: The Postwar Inquisition of the Jewish Anti-Fascist Committee* (New Haven, CT, 2001); Arno Lustiger, *Stalin and the Jews* (New York, 2002). One of the first studies of late Stalinist high politics is Robert Conquest, *Power and Policy in the USSR: The Study of Soviet Dynastics* (New York, 1951).

CHAPTER ONE. THE LANDSCAPE OF BRIBERY AND CORRUPTION IN THE SHADOWS OF STALINISM

1. On the famine and provisions shortages that accompanied the end of the war, see Nicholas Ganson, *The Soviet Famine of 1946–47 in Global and Historical Perspective* (New York, 2009); Michael Ellman, "The 1947 Soviet Famine and the Entitlement Approach to Famines," *Cambridge Journal of Economics* 24 (2000): 603–630; V. F. Zima, *Golod v SSSR, 1946–47 godov: Proiskhozhdenie i posledstvie* (Moscow, 1996); Zubkova, *Poslevoennoe Sovetskoe obshchestvo*, 61–77 (Moscow, 2000); and Zubkova, *Russia after the War* (Armonk, NY, 1998), 40–50. Donald Filtzer, *Soviet Workers and Late Stalinism* (Cambridge, 2002), 41–76.

2. Stanislaw Pomorski, among others, makes this point in his "Perversions of Soviet Administrative Law," in *Soviet Administrative Law: Theory and Policy*, ed. George Ginsburgs, et al. (Dordrecht, 1989), 114.

3. Historians believe that the practice dates back to the seventeenth century or earlier. Cathy J. Potter, "Payment, Gift or Bribe? Exploring the Boundaries in Pre-Petrine Russia," in *Bribery and Blat in Russia*, ed. Stephen Lovell, et al., 20; Janet Hartley, "Bribery and Justice in the Provinces in the Reign of Catherine II," in *Bribery and Blat in Russia*, ed. Stephen Lovell, et al., 52–54. See also Valerie Kivelson, *Autocracy in the Provinces: The Muscovite Gentry and Political Culture in the Seventeenth Century* (Palo Alto, CA, 1996), chapter 7; Nancy S. Kollmann, *Crime and Punishment in Early Modern Russia* (Cambridge, 2012). For the entry on bribery in the *Entsiklopedicheskii slovar'* of F. A. Brokgaus and I. A. Efron, see "Vziatochnichestvo." *Entsiklopedicheskii slovar'* (Saint Petersburg, 1890–1907), tom VI (1894), 213–216.

4. Stephen Hoch, *Serfdom and Social Control in Russia: Petrovskoe, A Village in Tambov* (Chicago, 1989). Neil Weissman, "Regular Police in Tsarist Russia, 1900–1914," *Russian Review* 44 (1985): 52–59.

5. Nancy Kollmann, *Crime and Punishment*, 98.

6. Cathy J. Potter and L. F. Pisar'kova have explored varied cultural and legal understandings of notions of the gifts or fees accepted by officials in the seventeenth century. Cathy J. Potter, "Payment, Gift or Bribe? Exploring the Boundaries in Pre-Petrine Russia," in *Bribery and Blat in Russia*, ed. Stephen Lovell, et al., 20–34;

Liubov' F. Pisar'kova, "K istorii vziatok v Rossii (po materialam sekretnoi kantse-liarii Kn. Golitsynykh pervoi poloviny XIX v.)," *Otechestvennaia istoriia* 5 (2002): 33–49.

7. L. F. Pisar'kova, "K istorii vziatok," 46–47. Fundukel' was governor from 1839 to 1852.

8. Pisar'kova and Golosenko emphasize this point. I. A. Golosenko, "Na-chal'stvo. Ocherki po istorii Rossiiskoi sotsiologii chinovnichestva kontsa XIX–nachala XX vv," *Zhurnal sotsiologii i sotsial'noi antropologii* (2005), tom 8, no. 1: 54–85.

9. For the period of Catherine the Great, Hartley notes, "Within this broader context the existence, and prevalence, of bribery within the judicial system were only symptomatic of general arbitrariness, poor public standards, and weak proce-dures in Russia." The same could be said about large sections of the legal system during the late Imperial period. Hartley, "Bribery and Justice in the Provinces," 62.

10. Richard Wortman, *The Development of a Russian Legal Consciousness* (Chicago, 1976).

11. Kelly, "Bribery and Etiquette," 74–75.

12. Pisar'kova, "K istorii vziatok v Rossii," 47.

13. Herzen, "The Year 1860," in *A Herzen Reader,* Aleksandr Herzen (trans. and ed. Kathleen Parthé) (Evanston, IL, 2012), 107. See also pp. 268, 323. On the prereform judiciary's reputation for corruption, see Sergei Kazantsev, "The Judicial Reform of 1864 and the Procuracy in Russia," in *Reforming Justice in Russia, 1864–1996: Power, Culture, and the Limits of Legal Order,* ed. Peter Solomon (New York, 1997). See also Laura Engelstein, "Combined Underdevelopment: Dis-cipline and the Law in Imperial and Soviet Russia," *American Historical Review* (April 1993): 338–53.

14. Cited by Pomorski, in "Perversions of Administrative Law," 114. As Susanne Shattenberg has noted, in the nineteenth century nearly all of Russian society was united in its belief that bureaucrats were corrupt. "Kul'tura korruptsii, ili K istorii rossiiskikh chinovnikov," *Neprikosnovennyi zapas* 42: 4 (2005).

15. Irina Davydova, "Bureaucracy on Trial: A Malaise in Official Life as Repre-sented in Nineteenth-Century Russian Thought," in *Bribery and Blat in Russia,* ed. Stephen Lovell, et al., 94–113. As Davydova observes, "Our contemporary picture of the tsarist administration as extremely corrupt and open to bribery is in part a stereotype derived from the radical discourse which was itself a product of, and a weapon in, this struggle" (108).

16. Lenin himself wanted even stricter punishments. As he wrote to Minister of Justice Kurskii (no later than May 8, 1918), "It is necessary immediately, with de-monstrative speed, to introduce into the law [on bribery] that the punishment for bribery . . . should be no less than ten years in prison, on top of which should be ten years of forced labor." On the regime's general antipathy for law in the 1920s, see Robert Sharlet, "Pashukanis and the Withering Away of the Law in the USSR," in *Cultural Revolution in Russia, 1928–1931,* ed. Sheila Fitzpatrick (Bloomington, IN, 1978), 176–180.

17. *Ezhenedel'nik sovetskoi iustitsii,* 1922, no. 35, appendix, p. 11. Upon the launch of the campaign against bribery on October 9, 1922, Article 114 of the Law

Code was strengthened further, in particular by setting minimum sentences. Postanovlenie VTsIK i SNK, October 9, 1922. Cited in Epikhin and Mozokhin, *VChK-OGPU v bor'be*, doc. 31: 369–370. Those who accepted bribes would get no less than one year in prison. Accepting a bribe with aggravating circumstances would land an official a three-year minimum with strict isolation. The death penalty could be assigned in especially aggravating circumstances. A new article, number 114a, was added, which grouped together the giving of bribes and acting as an intermediary.

18. Borisova, "*Tret'ii vrag*," 250–251.

19. "*Vypiska iz protokola VChK no. 21: O bor'be s vziatochnichestvom,*" in Epikhin and Mozokhin, *VChK-OGPU v bor'be*, 315. On July 15, 1922, Dzerzhinskii ordered the creation of a special commission inside the GPU to fight bribery on the railroads. *Prikaz* no. 1310, "On Bribery on the Railways," in Epikhin and Mozokhin, *VChK-OGPU v bor'be*, 334.

20. See, for example, Tracy McDonald, *Face to the Village: The Riazan Countryside under Soviet Rule, 1921–1930* (Toronto, 2009), 72, 92–98. For her discussion of forest guards, see 173–175.

21. V. Makashvili, "Strogo vypolnyiat' trebovaniia zakona ob otvetstvennosti za vziatochnichestvo (Sudebnaia praktika Verkhovnogo Suda SSSR)," *Sotsialisticheskaia zakonnost'*, no. 2 (1953): 40.

22. See, for example, Catriona Kelly, "Bribery and Etiquette," 65–90.

23. For one case of an alleged kulak bribing the chairman of a local soviet to obtain identity documents, see Sheila Fitzpatrick, *Everyday Stalinism*, 133. This phenomenon of giving gifts to local officials was denounced using the traditional name *magarych* (sometimes spelled *mogarych*) which implied the giving of a gift to wrap up a deal. (Of course, it was not only the "wealthy" peasants who had reason to try to curry favor with local officials, and magarych was not always offered voluntarily by rural dwellers.) Officials placed the blame on peasants who supposedly offered the gifts of food and drink rather than the officials who quite often demanded them. Still, the Plenum of the USSR Supreme Court issued an instruction in April 1929 stating that the acceptance of magarych by any official would be considered equivalent to taking a bribe. "Postanovlenie Plenuma Verkhovnogo Suda SSSR ot 15 April 1929," in *Sbornik raz'iasnenii Verkhovnogo Suda SSSR za 1929 god* (Moscow, 1930), 62–63.

24. The Harvard Interview Project contains many examples, some of which are discussed in chapter 3 of this book. For the Magnitogorsk trial of a supply official who stole materials to build a dacha, then covered up his actions with bribes to his underlings, see Stephen Kotkin, *Magnetic Mountain*, 261.

25. Safonov made similar charges in a circular letter to procuracy employees around the Soviet Union. (GARF, f. 8131, op. 32, d. 1023, l. 17–22. Undated, but likely composed May–July 1952 based on surrounding documents in file and internal evidence.) See, for example, a July 1952 report by Sverdlov, the head of the USSR Procuracy department responsible for supervision of police agencies, to Deputy Procurator-General Khokhlov. (GARF, f. 8131, op. 32, d. 941, l. 305.) As Peter Solomon shows, it had long been common practice that officials would be charged with Article 109 rather than something more serious, and courts would assign them punishments up to one year in prison, as a way of minimizing the effect of the

conviction. Peter H. Solomon, Jr., *Soviet Criminal Justice under Stalin* (Cambridge, 1996), 437–438.

26. GARF, f. 9492, op. 2, d. 49, l. 275 (Report entitled "Obzor osnovnykh dannykh o sudimosti v SSSR za 1947 god," signed by K. Gorshenin). On secrecy and plan fraud, see Mark Harrison, "Forging Success: Soviet Managers and Accounting Fraud, 1943–1962," *Journal of Comparative Economics* 39, no. 1 (2011): 43–64; and Harrison, "Secrecy, Fear and Transaction Costs: The Business of Soviet Forced Labour in the Early Cold War," *Europe-Asia Studies* 65, no. 6: 1112–1135.

27. For a more detailed discussion of the June 4, 1947 decree on theft of socialist property, see James Heinzen, "Corruption among Officials and Anticorruption Drives in the USSR, 1945–1964," in *Russian Bureaucracy and the State: Officialdom from Alexander III to Putin*, ed. Don K. Rowney and Eugene Huskey (Basingstoke, UK, 2009), 169–188. On pilfering and profiteering by soldiers during World War II, see Catherine Merridale, *Ivan's War: Life and Death in the Red Army, 1939–1945* (New York, 2006), 270–274.

28. On the 1947–1948 campaign against theft of socialist property, see especially Peter Solomon, *Soviet Criminal Justice under Stalin,* 410–412; and Yoram Gorlizki, "Rules, Incentives and Soviet Campaign Justice after World War II," *Europe-Asia Studies* 51, no. 7 (November 1999): 1245–1265.

29. GARF, f. 9492, op. 2, d. 63, ll. 32–33. In Gorshenin's words, "This information reflects only that material damage which was uncovered by the courts in the course of investigations, but the investigations make clear what enormous losses the theft of state and socialist property have inflicted on the economy." For some examples of theft by officials during and after the war, see Cynthia Hooper, "A Darker 'Big Deal,' " 145–146.

30. Statistics from the Department of Court Statistics of the Supreme Court of the USSR. Reprinted in *Istoriia Stalinskogo Gulaga: Massovye repressii v SSSR*, tom 1 (Moscow, 2004), 613. Military tribunals convicted 24,372 people for theft of state property in 1947. Ibid., 618.

31. RGANI, f. 6, op. 6, d. 25, ll. 2–3.

32. As Donald Filtzer points out, only in the year 1947 were more collective farmers than workers arrested under the June 4 ukaz. Filtzer, *Soviet Workers and Late Stalinism,* 28–29.

33. Stalin's *osobaia papka* (the "special portfolio" of especially secret materials) is full of reports sent to him in 1944–1947 documenting large schemes involving theft of state property. *Osobaia papka I. V. Stalina*, ed. V. A. Kozlov and S. V. Mironenko (Moscow, 1994), from materials of the Secretariat of the NKVD-MVD, 1944–53. The regime sounded the call about corruption in the trade and distribution systems partly to scapegoat them because the economy was not producing enough.

34. GARF, f. 9492, op. 2, d. 37, ll. 65–66 (Letter from Dvinskii to Mikoian, deputy chairman of the USSR Sovmin, September 30, 1946). Many examples of tips reported by informers pertain to functionaries profiting illegally during the course of their official duties (see chapter 6).

35. GARF, f. 5446 (Council of Ministers USSR), op. 48a, d. 1614, ll. 102–198. Reprinted in *Istoriia Stalinskogo Gulaga: Massovye repressii v SSSR*, tom 1: 557–559. The number of collective farm chairpersons convicted of theft of state prop-

erty, for example, increased from 935 in 1948 to 1,483 in 1949. GARF, f. 9492, op. 2, d. 63, l. 37 (Report by Gorshenin, sent to Stalin).

36. Peter Solomon, *Soviet Criminal Justice,* 408–414.

37. Peter Solomon, *Soviet Criminal Justice,* 124–125. Scholars have tended to focus on the punishment of collective farmers for petty theft of food during the famine under the decree. "Iz prigorov raionnykh narsudov o privlechenii k ugolovnoi otvetstvennosti kolkhoznikov po Ukazu 1947 g.," *Sovetskie arkhivy* 3 (1990): 55–60. On the development of the black market and the theft of government property in the industrial city of Magnitogorsk in the 1930s, especially within and from the highly stressed and stratified supply network, see Stephen Kotkin, *Magnetic Mountain,* 242–260. See also David Shearer, "Wheeling and Dealing: Syndicates, Trade, and Political Economy at the End of the 1920s," *Cahiers du Monde Russe* 36: no. 1/2 (1995)"; and Hessler, *A Social History of Soviet Trade: Trade Policy, Retail Practices, and Consumption, 1917–1953* (Princeton, NJ, 2004). For instances of speculation schemes, embezzlement, and petty theft in the context of the failures of the food supply system in the 1930s, see Elena Osokina, *Za fasadom "Stalinskogo izobiliia": raspredelenie i rynok v snabzhenii naseleniia v gody industrializatsii, 1927–1941* (Moscow, 1998). The book is translated into English as *Our Daily Bread: Socialist Distribution and the Art of Survival in Stalin's Russia, 1927–1941* (Armonk, NY, 2001).

38. A secret 1952 draft instruction, written by USSR Procurator-General Safonov for the Supreme Court, sheds light on the prosecution of crimes committed by officials under Article 109. (GARF, f. 8131, op. 32, d. 1023, ll. 2–6.) The report chastises judges for several reasons. Too often, it notes, judges hand out harsh prison sentences when corrective labor on the job would serve the purpose. Officials are groundlessly convicted of serious crimes. This is "a politically harmful practice" that "does serious harm to the task of strengthening the state apparatus." Yet, in other cases (the report continues), when "serious harm is done to state interests"—in certain cases of negligence (Article 111) that result in major material losses, for example—the Justice Ministry complained that officials were not punished harshly enough. In April 1953, the Ministry of Justice noted that many people convicted of negligence were guilty only of inexperience. Fifty-seven thousand people were convicted under Article 111 in 1952. GARF, f. 9492, op. 2, d. 93, l. 62 (Gorshenin comments on draft law code).

39. An indication of the seriousness with which the regime took theft of state property is that the postwar amnesty of Gulag prisoners excluded those convicted under the August 7, 1932 law. "Ob amnistii v sviazi s pobedoi nad gitlerovskoi Germaniei" of July 7, 1945. *Amnistiia i pomilovanie v SSSR* (Moscow 1959), 71–72.

40. The law recognized as "officials" all individuals who were employed in a permanent or temporary position of responsibility in all political, social, and economic organizations of state, including managers of factories or social organizations, collective and state farm chairmen, and union officials. Soviet law criminalized many infractions by officials that will not be considered "corruption" in this book. Negligence and other crimes of inaction, the malicious non-fulfillment of contracts, report padding, and the production of shoddy goods, for example, were "crimes by

officials" or "economic crimes" under the very broad provisions of the criminal code. Since in most cases they would not have resulted in self-enrichment, I am not treating them as the type of corruption this book is investigating.

41. GARF f. 8131, op. 38, d. 299, l. 11 ("Materials on combating bribery, 1946–47"). After the December 1947 monetary reform and the abolition of rationing, the role of money in the economy increased. Before the reform, one encounters more cases of bribes offered in the form of food or goods. In September 1946, prices on some rationed food items were increased by two to three hundred percent. These price increases made goods more desirable as inducements for bribes. A September 27, 1946 decree took ration cards away from 23 million people in rural areas. In these circumstances, food made for a potent bribe. See Zubkova, *Russia after the War: Hopes, Illusions, and Disappointments, 1945–1957*, 70–75. For crimes among party elites in Molotov region associated with the monetary reform, see Oleg Leibovich, *V Gorode M: Ocherki sotsial'noi povsednevnosti sovetskoi provintsii* (Moscow, 2008), 72–113.

42. GARF, f. 9492, op. 6, d. 14 (Statistics on convictions, 1937–1956). Individuals who paid a bribe because it was extorted from them could escape punishment if they immediately and voluntarily informed the authorities.

43. A May 30, 1946 report on the state of bribery in 1944–1945, written by a consultant to the Ministry of Justice's general courts administration, states that "the quantity of people convicted for bribery (the accepting of bribes and the giving of bribes) in certain republics and in the USSR is extremely insignificant on the whole." GARF, f. 9492, op. 1a, d. 478, l. 33.

44. Susan Rose-Ackerman, *Corruption and Government: Causes, Consequences, and Reform* (Cambridge, 1998), 98.

45. *Sotsialisticheskaia zakonnost'*, no. 9 (September 1946), 1.

46. John Barber and Mark Harrison have written a comprehensive history of the war's economic aspects, including industrial and agricultural production, distribution, and trade, in *The Soviet Home Front, 1941–45: A Social And Economic History of the USSR in World War II* (London, 1991).

47. Donald Filtzer describes the economic crisis that paralleled the political and social crises of the postwar years described by Elena Zubkova and Vera Dunham. Filtzer, *Soviet Workers and Late Stalinism*.

48. GARF, f. 9492, op. 2, d. 49, l. 245 ("Summary data on Convictions in the USSR for 1947," signed by Gorshenin, dated 1948).

49. GARF, f. 9492, op. 2, d. 49, ll. 35–40 (Gorshenin's survey of crime data for 1947).

50. GARF, f. 8131, op. 38, d. 282, l. 62 (Documents on 1946 antibribery campaign).

51. GARF, f. 9474, op. 16, d. 355, l. 90 (1950 report on bribery in Ukraine by Stepko of Ukrainian Supreme Court).

52. According to the study, "On the basis of a study of cases and materials sent to us from the localities, the administration of living space is the system where bribery is most widespread and where the most crimes have been uncovered." (GARF, f. 8131, op. 38, d. 299, l. 57.) The study reported that the most common types of bribery cases brought during the two years after the end of the war involved law

enforcement and judicial personnel, housing officials, and food procurement agents, in that order. For a case involving the Moscow housing administration, see GARF, f. 8131, op. 32, d. 66, l. 4 (Report on struggle against bribery in 1950). For a study of conflicts between returning evacuees and housing officials, see Rebecca Manley, "'Where Should We Resettle the Comrades Next?' The Adjudication of Housing Claims and the Construction of the Postwar Order," in *Late Stalinist Russia,* ed. Juliane Fürst, 233–246. On the abysmal condition of much Soviet housing stock after the war, see Donald Filtzer, "Standard of Living versus Quality of Life: Struggling with the Urban Environment in Russia during the Early Years of Post-War Construction," in *Late Stalinist Russia,* ed. Juliane Fürst, 84–89.

53. On the hierarchies of supply and distribution of scarce products in the 1930s, see Elena Osokina, *Za fasadom "Stalinskogo izobiliia": Raspredelenie i rynok v snabzhenii naseleniia v gody industrializatsii, 1927–1941* (Moscow, 1998). For brief reports about several cases of bribery in Leningrad drawn from newspaper accounts and local archives, see I. V. Govorov, *Prestupnost' i bor'ba s nei v poslevoennom Leningrade (1945–1953): Opyt istoricheskogo analiza* (St. Petersburg, 2004).

54. On Sevastopol', see Karl Qualls, *From Ruins to Reconstruction,* 18. See also Eric Duskin, *Stalinist Reconstruction and the Confirmation of a New Elite,* 12. On the Belorussian SSR, see GARF, f. 9474, op. 16, d. 283, l. 29 (Letter to Rychkov, Gorshenin, and Goliakov, July 17, 1945).

55. GARF, f. 8131, op. 37, d. 4216, l. 191 (Letter to K. P. Gorshenin from Procuracy Commission investigating bribery among procuracy and court employees). For an October 1946 letter written by the chair of the Supreme Court, Goliakov, to the deputy chief of the Cadres Administration of the Central Committee, noting competition for living space between returning evacuees and government offices, see GARF, f. 9474, op. 16, d. 294, ll. 27–28. For examples of bribes paid to recover apartments, see GARF, f. 8131, op. 37, d. 4216, l. 191; and GARF, f. 9474, op. 16, d. 294, ll. 27–28 (Correspondence between USSR Supreme Court and the Central Committee on legal and judicial questions). GARF, f. 8131, op. 38, d. 299, ll. 3–3 ob. For cases of corruption in the housing administration in the city of Rostov, see Jeffrey Jones, *Everyday Life and the "Reconstruction" of Soviet Russia during and after the Great Patriotic War, 1943–1948* (Bloomington, IN, 2008), 252–253, 264. For a 1946 case of bribery in the housing department of Dauvgavpils, Latvia, see Geoffrey Swain, *Between Stalin and Hitler: Class War and Race War on the Dvina* (London and New York, 2004), 193.

56. See Zubkova, *Poslevoennoe sovetskoe obshchestvo,* 28–29. On demobilization, see Eric Duskin, *Stalinist Reconstruction,* 17. On the plight of postwar veterans, see Mark Edele, *Soviet Veterans of World War II: A Popular Movement in an Authoritarian State* (Oxford, 2008); and Robert Dale, "Rats and Resentment: The Demobilization of the Red Army in Postwar Leningrad, 1945–50," *Journal of Contemporary History* 45, no. 1 (January 2010): 113–133.

57. GARF, f. 8131, op. 38, d. 299, l. 12.

58. GARF, f. 8131, op. 23, d. 11, l. 138, for a newspaper article on a 1946 case in Odessa. For a case of a man who falsely claimed to be a demobilized officer to gain advantage in a housing dispute, see RGANI, f. 6, op. 6, d. 1609, ll. 114–115.

59. Eric Duskin, *Stalinist Reconstruction*, 12.

60. GARF, f. 9492, op. 1a, d. 376, ll. 1–4 (Letter from K. P. Gorshenin to V. M. Molotov, November 2, 1944; "Obvinitel'noe zakliuchenie po obiveniiu grazhdan.")

61. GARF, f. 9474, op. 16, d. 294, ll. 27–28 (October 22, 1946 letter to deputy chief of the Cadres Directorate, V. D. Nikitin).

62. Evidence at later trials indicated that at least one Supreme Court employee had a close—and highly dubious—relationship with legal consultants at the housing department of the Moscow City Soviet. According to Umanskaia's testimony, Kudriavtsev, an employee of the Military Collegium of the Supreme Court, was in close contact with two legal consultants of the Moscow housing department, Ishchenko and Savel'ev. They may have been exchanging bribes. Umanskaia had heard that Ishchenko was a "blatant bribe taker." GARF, f. 9474, op. 7, d. 824, l. 22 (Testimony of Umanskaia).

63. GARF, f. 9401, op. 2, d. 171 (Osobaia papka Stalina), ll. 19–28 (A report on bribery and measures to fight it in January–July 1947, by the organs of the MVD).

64. GARF, f. 9401, op. 2, d. 171, l. 26. *Pravda* reported on August 1, 1946, that a certain N. Ignat'ova was sentenced to ten years' imprisonment, and an inspector received eight years, for taking bribes up to 3,000 rubles for illegally assigning rooms.

65. GARF, f. 8131, op. 29, d. 4, ll. 86–90 ob.

66. GARF, f. 8131, op. 32, d. 3, ll. 121–123 (Letter of G. Safonov on bribery in Moscow city soviet housing administration, dated January 29, 1951). See also GARF, f. 8131, op. 32, d. 3, ll. 124–129 (Report by the procuror of the city of Moscow, Vasil'ev, to the General Procuror USSR, G. N. Safonov).

67. In the Moscow city procuracy's summary report on bribery cases in 1950, the case is mentioned, but none of the elites involved are named or referred to. The report mentions only the employees of the Moscow Soviet housing administration who were implicated. "Sixteen people are being held, including former employees of the *Biuro obmen* in the Moscow housing department: Iakovleva, Eremina, Abramenko, Shul'gina, and several others without specific jobs." "Despite the complexity of the case," the report went on, "the Moscow Procuracy must take measures to complete the investigation quickly." (GARF, f. 8131, op. 32, d. 66, l. 7.) Geoffrey Roberts, *Stalin's General*, 251.

68. On the cults of Vasilii Chapaev and the Civil War, see David Brandenberger, *National Bolshevism: Stalinist Mass Culture and the Formation of Modern Russian Identity, 1931–1956* (Cambridge, 2002); Nina Tumarkin, *Lenin Lives! The Lenin Cult in Soviet Russia* (Cambridge, 1983); and Justus Hartzok, "Children of Chapaev: The Russian Civil War Cult and the Creation of Soviet Identity," unpublished doctoral dissertation (University of Iowa, 2009). Vasilii Chapaev adopted the two daughters of his friend and fellow soldier in 1917. At the time of the scandal, Vera Chapaeva lived with her husband, Dupak, "an artist in the Stanislavskii Theater." (This is possibly Nikolai Dupak, a film actor and the director of the Taganka Theater for many years.)

69. See the transcript of Zheleznikov's interrogation in GARF, f. 8131, op. 37, d. 4043, ll. 10–15.

70. Eric Duskin, *Stalinist Reconstruction*, 12–16.

71. Rebecca Manley, *To the Tashkent Station*, 139–140, 158, 241–244.

72. Sometimes soldiers refused to pay anything, and they just grabbed seats without tickets. RGASPI, f. 17, op. 121, d. 464 ll. 27–28 (KPK report to Malenkov). For a conductor demanding bribes for tickets on the Kirov railroad, see GARF, f. 9492, op. 1, d. 514, l. 35. This incident was reported in the newspaper *Leninskoe znamia* on October 18, 1946.

73. *Pravda*, August 1, 1946. The scholar Stanislaw Pomorski writes that in 1942 he witnessed "how a desperate family at a small God-forsaken railroad station at Kazakhstan had to surrender one of its last pillows to a cashier in order to purchase tickets." See Pomorski, "Perversions of Soviet Administrative Law," in *Soviet Administrative Law: Theory and Policy*, ed. George Ginsburgs et al. (Dordrecht, the Netherlands, 1989), 116.

74. GARF, f. 9492, op. 2, d. 38, ll. 119–22. For cases of bribery on the railroads, see *Sudebnaia praktika Verkhovnogo suda SSSR* (1947), vyp. 1 (XXXV): 3–5. See also GARF, f. 8131, op. 37, d. 2817, l. 6 (Documents on drafting 1946 prikaz).

75. GARF, f. 9492, op. 4, d. 716, l. 117. For the 1948 Supreme Court review, see GARF, f. 9492, op. 2, d. 51, l. 187. A 1952 report by the Ministry of Justice stated that bribery was but one variety of crime on the railways. Railway employees were able to earn extra cash by falsifying receipts. (GARF, f. 9492, op. 2, d. 88, ll. 130–31.) Ineffective auditing procedures rarely caught discrepancies.

76. On internal migration after the war, see Ganson, *The Soviet Famine of 1946–47*, ch. 4.

77. GARF, f. 8131, op. 38, d. 299, l. 34.

78. Donald Filtzer, *Soviet Workers and Late Stalinism*, 179.

79. GARF, f. 9474, op. 16, d. 355, l. 106.

80. RGANI, f. 6, op. 6, d. 1590, ll. 51–56 (KPK investigative report). In addition, the 1947 currency reform created numerous opportunities for officials to profit illegally. Where supervision was lax, or where auditors had been paid off, bank employees took bribes from citizens in exchange for backdating deposits so they did not suffer when the currency was devalued. RGANI, f. 6, op. 2, d. 135, ll. 39–50.

81. Medical personnel rarely seem to have been prosecuted for bribery unless they used their *official* powers for issuing documents illegally, not simply for taking a gift or payment for seeing a patient or doing a certain procedure. See, for example, HIP, Schedule A, case 191, p. 12. Conniving doctors had been the targets of satire in late Imperial Russia. The writer Anton Chekhov, who himself had medical training, made a teasing allusion to the venality of physicians in his play *The Cherry Orchard*: "The doctor keeps talking, talking, but his eyes keep darting, darting to my fist—wondering if I'll give him a crisp blue-colored bill." Anton Chekhov, *The Cherry Orchard*, 1904 (cited by Gradirovski and Esipova, 2006).

82. GARF, f. 9492, op. 1, d. 514, l. 14 (Ministry of Justice report on fighting bribery). Whether they were convicted is not noted in the file. See also GARF f. 8131, op. 38, d. 299, ll. 66–67.

83. On the Stalingrad dentist, see GARF, f. 8131, op. 38, d. 299, l. 67. On Rovno, see GARF, f. 9474, op. 16, d. 355, l. 95. Such activity was especially pronounced in the militarized sectors of the economy, including heavy industry and the railroads. In 1946, for example, a man was charged with offering a bribe of fourteen pounds

of meat to exempt his father from mandatory forestry work. (GARF, f. 8131, op. 38, d. 299, l. 65.) Such cases underscore Donald Filtzer's point that people negotiated through informal channels to avoid unpleasant work assignments, often with the complicity of local authorities. Donald Filtzer, *Soviet Workers and Late Stalinism*, 236–247. On postwar medical administration, see Chris Burton, "Medical Welfare during Late Stalinism," unpublished PhD dissertation (Chicago, 2000).

84. On veterinarians, see GARF, f. 9492, op. 1, d. 514, l. 33. On the legal markets and bazaars, see Julie Hessler, *A Social History of Soviet Trade*. Another veterinarian in Ternopol' oblast' illegally charged fifty to seventy rubles to castrate animals in the local veterinary hospital. (GARF, f. 9474, op. 16, d. 355, l. 95.) He was sentenced to three years in prison in September 1949.

85. GARF, f. 8131, op. 32, d. 58, l. 133. The investigation pointed out that, once accepted into the institute, Khitrova "behaved herself completely inappropriately and did not take her studies seriously." She performed badly in several courses her first year, and got in trouble with the Komsomol organization, which tried to direct her to study properly. The charges seem to have been confirmed in the main, and the case was passed on to the next level. (RGANI, f. 6, op. 6, d. 1594, ll. 65–67.) In a case, described in an article in *Pravda*, a provincial director for the arts in Penza took bribes from artists to produce their concerts and dramas inside Penza theaters. Boris Lavrenev, "Korolev and Others," *Pravda*, November 12, 1949, p. 3.

86. See, for example, GARF, f. 8131, op. 38, d. 449, ll. 8–14 (Report by D. Salin, Procurator of the Lithuanian SSR, to Mokichev, of April 14, 1947). Of the postwar countryside as reflected in the popular literature of late Stalinism, Vera Dunham has observed: "Despite the rococo veneer, rural unrest became evident even in these tales. Wartime bribery, speculation, the black market had flourished. Yet, these liberties, granted by default, had worked for the system's advantage. But now the 'law' clamped down on all sorts of irregularities as well as on peasant tribalism. The institutional mutations that had helped the peasant to survive were now fiercely investigated." Dunham, *In Stalin's Time: Middleclass Values in Soviet Fiction*, 226.

87. GARF, f. 9492, op. 1, d. 514, l. 31. For cases in Ukraine, see GARF f. 9474, op. 16, d. 355, ll. 93–94. V. F. Zima has written about crime during the famine. Zima focuses on wide-scale "theft" (out of desperation) of food and other kolkhoz property by collective farmers rather than stepped up white-collar crime. See especially *Golod v SSSR*, 96–128. See also Ganson, *The Soviet Famine of 1946–47*, 86–89. Jean Levesque has shown how rural areas were devastated during the war. Jean Levesque, "Into the Grey Zone: Sham Peasants and the Limits of the Kolkhoz Order in the Post-War Russian Village, 1945–1953," in *Late Stalinist Russia*, ed. Juliane Fürst, 103–119. On rural poverty, see also Stephen Lovell, *In the Shadows of War*, 72. On Krasnodar krai, see GARF, f. 8131, op. 32, d. 58, l. 133. For more examples of bribery in the requisitioning system, including bribes to obtain phony receipts for cotton requisitions, see GARF, f. 8131, op. 29, d. 299, l. 11.

88. For a comparison, note the case of the New York City crane inspector who accepted bribes to clear for service cranes that had not been inspected. "N.Y. Crane Inspector Goes to Prison for Accepting Bribes," *New York Times*, June 16, 2010. Accessed on-line on August 3, 2010.

89. GARF, f. 9401, op. 2, d. 171 (*Osobaia papka Stalina*). For the case of two

inspectors in the RSFSR Ministry of State Control accused of taking bribes to cover up theft in wood cooperatives in Moscow oblast' that came to the attention of the Department of Administrative Organs, see RGASPI, f. 17, op. 136, d. 190, ll. 26–30. On the 1949 Odessa case, see GARF, f. 9474, op. 16, d. 355, l. 94.

90. GARF f. 9492, op. 1, d. 514, l. 16. Some inspectors demanded hush money when they uncovered cases of theft by bookkeepers and other officials. See the OBKhSS report in GARF, f. 9415, op. 5, d. 98, str. 43. For the case of a bookkeeper who demanded bribes to cover up shortages, see GARF, f. 8131, op. 32, d. 58, l. 133. See also a 1946 Procuracy report in GARF, f. 8131, op. 32, d. 299, l. 68.

91. For theft and bribery schemes in artisanal cooperation, see GARF, f. 8131, op. 29, d. 7, ll. 152–181; f. 8131, op. 29, d. 8, ll. 10–31, 196–203.

92. Such deals could be negotiated on collective farms as well. The Party Control Commission investigated a district agronomist, I. Ia. Vostrikov, who worked on a Machine-Tractor Station in Voronezh. Two shepherds accused the agronomist of "disgracing the name of communism" by attempting to extort bribes from them to silence his claim that they allowed sheep to overgraze and damage the winter wheat. Fearing arrest, the shepherds each paid the agronomist 200 rubles to keep him from filing a complaint against them, then immediately went to the authorities to report the blackmail. After a hearing, the agronomist was excluded from the ranks of the Communist Party. (The file does not mention whether the case was ever turned over to prosecutors.) GARF, f. 9492, op. 1, d. 514, l. 32. Paying bribes to evade taxes is hardly unusual worldwide, of course. See the 2010 report by the Brookings Institution that notes that about a quarter of Greek taxes went unpaid, as an estimated one in seven taxpayers pay bribes to tax inspectors (as reported in the *New York Times*, May 1, 2010). Another vulnerable segment of the economy that often tried to shield their activities with blankets of illicit payments, authorities said, were private traders who sold their wares in city marketplaces. In 1946, for example, tax inspectors and other employees of a regional financial department were accused of taking bribes from private traders who sold their goods at the central market in Kishinev, Moldavian SSR. Inspectors accepted bribes of money, food, wine, and other valuables and, in exchange, lowered the taxes on the traders' dealings. A group of seven inspectors garnered a total of 800,000 rubles. GARF, f. 8131, op. 38, d. 299, l. 11–13.

93. GARF, f. 9415, op. 5, d. 87, ll. 241–242 (Letter to chiefs of OBKhSS administrations of republics, krais, oblast's and cities). Gregory Grossman referred to this giving of valuable gifts to one's superiors and others "in proximate authority" as a continuous factor in the history of the Russian bureaucracy. Grossman, "The 'Second Economy' of the USSR," *Problems of Communism* 26 (September—October 1977): 25–40.

94. GARF, f. 8131, op. 37, d. 2817, l. 10.

95. Stephen Kotkin, *Magnetic Mountain: Stalinism as Civilization,* 254.

96. The police agency responsible for combating crimes against socialist property and the socialist economy (OBKhSS) reported that bribery was common in supply and trade organizations. Employees took bribes in exchange for scarce goods. As a February 1947 report put it, "practical experience confirms that in these systems [trade and supply] bribery is very widespread, but also most difficult to expose."

GARF, f. 8131, op. 38, d. 299, l. 67. In his memoir, Gennady Andreev-Khomiakov writes that a bribe of 2,000–3,000 rubles to a restaurant manager would buy a position as a waiter in a crowded restaurant. *Bitter Waters: Life and Work in Stalin's Russia* (Boulder, CO, 1997), 103.

97. On Moscow, see GARF, f. 9492, op. 2, d. 81, ll. 335–338 (Protest directed to the Plenum of the USSR Supreme Court from Volin, undated but likely from 1951). On Krasnovodsk, see GARF, f. 8131, op. 32, d. 58, ll. 13 (Report of Aleksandrov to Safonov, June 1952).

98. For a treatment of a campaign against corruption in Moscow food distribution and retail trade administrations in the 1970s and 1980s, see Luc Duhamel, *The KGB Campaign against Corruption in Moscow, 1982–1987* (Pittsburgh, PA, 2010). For a feuilleton about the head of a personnel department who takes bribes from employees to guarantee promotion or secure jobs, see Sem. Narinyani, "Feuilleton—The Simpletons," *Komsomolskaya Pravda*, September 19, 1952, p. 3.

99. RGANI, f. 6, op. 2, d. 100, ll. 72–79 (KPK investigation of anonymous denunciation, 1946).

100. RGANI, f. 6, op. 6, d. 1590, l. 50. Moscow's TsUM was also a popular location for speculators to congregate. Julie Hessler, "A Postwar Perestroika? Toward a History of Private Enterprise in the USSR," *Slavic Review* 57, no. 3 (Autumn 1998): 516–542.

101. As a report to Stalin from Kruglov, head of the Ministry of Internal Affairs, summarized things in late 1947: "Investigations in these cases have established that bribery is widespread in trade-supply organizations, in financial and insurance organs, and in housing agencies." (GARF, f. 9401, op. 2, d. 171, ll. 19–28). On prewar retail trade, see Amy Randall, *The Soviet Dream World of Retail Trade and Consumption in the 1930s* (Basingstoke, UK, 2008).

102. RGANI, f. 6, op. 6, d. 1595, ll. 46–47 (KPK investigation, 1952).

103. RGANI, f. 6, op. 2, d. 158, ll. 114–124 (Protocol no 142: session of the Biuro of the KPK, April 15, 20, and 21, 1950).

104. Moshe Lewin, "Rebuilding the Soviet Nomenklatura," 229–230, 237. Lewin describes documents produced by the Cadres Directorate of the Central Committee Secretariat in 1946–1948 expressing frustration with the "bribing" with gifts or favors (in Kuznetsov's words) of party officials by economic administrators or managers subordinate to them. The party hierarchy sometimes used this language to describe the close relationships of party supervisors and administrators such as factory directors in the economic apparatus, who "paid off" the people who were supposed to be guiding them politically. Often this "bribery" entailed factory directors providing banquets, prizes, or other material rewards to their party supervisors.

105. RGANI, f. 6, op. 2, d. 126, ll. 22–36.

106. On April 18, 1949, the head of the main alcohol committee was excluded from the ranks of the Communist Party, the first step towards criminal prosecution. As usual, there is no mention in his file about his fate after exclusion from the party.

107. RGANI, f. 6, op. 2, d. 194, ll. 1–7 (Letter to Malenkov from Shkiriatov, February 19, 1951).

108. The minister later claimed that he offered to pay for the gifts, but that the Georgian refused payment.

109. Managerial bartering (sometimes referred to as blat) was first described in detail by Joseph Berliner, based on interviews made during the Harvard Project on the Soviet Social System (better known as the Harvard Interview Project), mostly concerning managers' experiences in the 1930s. Managers would pad reports, barter with managers of other enterprises, and hoard supplies. Joseph Berliner, *Factory and Manager in the USSR* (Cambridge: Harvard University Press, 1957), 160–230. See also David Shearer, "Wheeling and Dealing in Soviet Industry." For a lively first-hand account of bartering in the lumber industry, see Andreev-Khomiakov, *Bitter Waters*, 69–79. As he notes, "It was often impossible to sort out the swindlers and scoundrels from the good people who were obliged by vicious necessity to resort to scheming" (79).

110. See, for example, GARF, f. 8131, op. 38, d. 299, ll. 60–61, for a procuracy report stating that bribe givers often defended themselves by saying that they did so "in the interests of production."

111. GARF, f. 9492, op. 1, d. 514, l. 15.

112. RGANI, f. 6, op. 6, d. 220, ll. 62–66. For the 1944 case of a director of a machine-tractor station in Saratov oblast' who traded the use of the MTS automobile for forty-five liters of vodka, which his wife then sold on the black market, see RGANI, f. 6, op. 6, d. 1587, ll. 48–49.

113. His request to have the reprimand removed, however, was turned down in November 1951 (GARF, f. 9474, op. 16, d. 355, l. 92.) An employee of an industrial artel' in Odessa oblast' was sentenced to ten years in prison for taking bribes to distribute barrels to collective farms. Knowing that barrels were in high demand, he took a bonus of 2,000 rubles for every twenty barrels delivered. In other cases, managers paid bribes to obtain better quality materials or the best assortment of products for their factories or stores. For examples, see RGANI, f. 6, op. 2, d. 1887, ll. 60–60 ob.; GARF, f. 8131, op. 32, d. 299, l. 68; GARF, f. 8131, op. 32, d. 299, l. 68.

114. Vera Dunham has argued that an insecure postwar Stalinist leadership, aware of a great deal of discontent within wide swaths of the population and concerned about possible opposition, made concessions to an emerging middle class as a way of cementing a social base. In the second half of the late Stalin era, one sees growing consolidation of the elites. Dunham, *In Stalin's Time*. Juliane Fürst has highlighted that some young people in the late Stalin years began to define themselves as much by consumption as by ideology. Fürst, *Stalin's Last Generation: Soviet Post-War Youth and the Emergence of Late Stalinism* (Oxford, 2010). See also Moshe Lewin, "Rebuilding the Soviet Nomenklatura 1945–1948," *Cahiers du monde russe* 44, no. 2/3 (2003): 219–252; Monica Ruthers, "The Late Stalinism on Moscow Gorkii Street: Space, History, and *Lebenswelten*," in *Late Stalinist Russia*, ed. Juliane Fürst. Just as the regime denied orphans, veterans, and victims of war traumas the luxury of attributing their sufferings to the war itself (Fürst, "Introduction," in *Late Stalinist Russia*, ed. Juliane Fürst, 5–6; Jeffrey Brooks, *Thank You Comrade Stalin*, 195–232) official postwar narratives never acknowledged that the war forced many people to engage in crime to survive. Those implicated in giving bribes were given no slack, just as, according to the official narrative, those who stole food from the collective farms to survive were in no way "victims" of catastrophic food shortages, but simply thieves.

115. Katherine Verdery, *What Was Socialism, and What Comes Next?* (Princeton, NJ, 1996).

CHAPTER TWO. "PICK THE FLOWERS WHILE THEY'RE IN BLOOM"

1. GARF f. 9474, op. 7, d. 855, l. 320 (Trial of Vasnev et al., May 24–June 11, 1949, testimony of Praushkina).

2. The definitive study of the procuracy and courts during the entire Stalin period is Peter H. Solomon, Jr., *Soviet Criminal Justice under Stalin* (Cambridge, 1996).

3. GARF, f. 9415, op. 5, d. 95, str. 16 (OBKhSS Annual Report for 1946, dated April 2, 1947). On the "informal" but legal private sector in this period, see Julie Hessler's *A Social History of Soviet Trade: Trade Policy, Retail Practices, and Consumption, 1917–1953* (Princeton, NJ, 2004). Hessler's work is somewhat less concerned with how various products found their way to the markets (often a result of theft from workplaces and illegal transport, aided by widely distributed bribes) and the officials involved in this activity.

4. Authorities targeted those who had exploited their insider knowledge of the monetary reform. For the case of a man who purchased large quantities of cigarettes and vodka to resell after the issuance of the reform, see GARF, f. 9474, op. 7, d. 958, l. 124 (Trial of Murzakhanov, et al., Nov–Dec 1949).

5. While 15.5 percent of speculators received sentences of six years or more between 1937 and 1940, that figure nearly doubled to 30.1 percent between 1946 and 1952. The number of people convicted for speculation nearly tripled between 1939 (12,547) and 1948 (36,396), when it peaked. GARF, f. 9492, op. 6s, d. 14, ll. 14–15, 30 (Ministry of Justice statistics on convictions). On speculation in the bazaars and other offenses regarding ration cards, see Julie Hessler, *A Social History of Soviet Trade,* 271–273.

6. See Amir Weiner, *Making Sense of War.* Eric Duskin notes that the technical intelligentsia was also largely free from fear of arrest after the war. Duskin, *Stalinist Reconstruction,* 130.

7. Donald Filtzer, *Soviet Workers and Late Stalinism,* 28–29. This is still a large number of people, of course. The prosecution of "counterrevolutionary" and political criminals—and their appeals—will have important implications later in this book in chapter 7.

8. GARF, f. 9492, op. 6, d. 14, ll. 14–15. Also reprinted in Afanas'ev et al., eds., *Istoriia Stalinskogo Gulaga,* 1: 632, 635. This figure includes convictions under Article 162 of the RSFSR Criminal Code. See also Peter Solomon, *Soviet Criminal Justice,* 435–438, esp. n70. On the drafting of the June 4, 1947 laws, see especially Solomon, *Soviet Criminal Justice,* chapter 12.

9. For the year 1940, see J. Arch Getty, Gabor T. Rittersporn, and Viktor N. Zemskov, "Victims of the Soviet Penal System in the Pre-War Years," *American Historical Review* 98, no. 4 (October 1993): 1031. For the year 1953, see GARF, f. 9414, op. 1, d. 118, l. 96 ("Materialy perepiski s TsK KPSS"). Data from January 1 of each year.

10. The penalties for theft of state property soared beginning in 1946, going

from an average of 2.3 years for a prison term between 1937 and 1940, to 3.2 years between January 1946 and June 1947, to 8.7 years between June 1947 and December 1952.

11. GARF, f. 9492, op. 6, d. 14, l. 30. As Supreme Court chair Volin noted in 1949, it was incongruous that, once the death penalty was abolished in May 1947, a person could receive twenty years deprivation of freedom for stealing state property but only ten years for murder. GARF, f. 9474, op. 16, d. 337, ll. 84–85.

12. Peter Solomon, *Soviet Criminal Justice,* 443.

13. Donald Filtzer, *Soviet Workers and Late Stalinism,* 28.

14. GARF, f. 9474, op. 16, d. 330, l. 209. (Survey of cases of police employees accused of bribery, reviewed by Military Collegium of USSR Supreme Court, May 3, 1948.)

15. RGANI, f. 6, op. 6, d. 1590, l. 94 (KPK investigative materials).

16. GARF, f. 9474, op. 16, d. 355, l. 106 (Ukrainian Supreme Court report on bribery in Ukraine).

17. Several of the Harvard Interview Project respondents noted an upsurge in bribery during the war. One alleged that in the city of Moscow, police took bribes to pay no mind to illegal activity. HIP, Schedule B, case no. 144, p. 3. "By February or March 1942, there were thousands of buyers on the kolkhoz market in town. Often there would be only one or two collective farm salespersons with a sack of carrots or beets. The militiamen stood aside, with money bribes to let people buy what they could." Similarly, in occupied territories, German police and soldiers also took bribes for not interfering in spontaneous market activity on the streets: "At times the Germans endeavored to control the markets etc., but they were bribed, and left people alone." HIP, Schedule B, case no. 59, p. 5. One man said that bribery was widespread in the German-occupied town of Polotok in the Belorussian Republic, where he lived. HIP, Schedule B, case no. 488, pp. 5–6. Police accepted many illegal payments for access to apartments; the Germans had seized a lot of it for themselves. "The [German] police took bribes all the time: for lodgings, land, permits, railway tickets, and [work] positions."

18. GARF, f. 8131, op. 32, d. 814, ll. 2–40 (Report sent to Safonov on police bribery in Ivanova oblast', May 1952).

19. GARF, f. 9474, op. 16, d. 330, l. 209.

20. RGASPI, f. 17, op. 135, d. 88, ll. 24–26 (Report by Mekhlis of Goskontrol', "On the results of the review of the trade-financial activities of Tsentrosoiuz," July 12, 1949). Kees Boterbloem notes that a MVD report decried numerous cases of bribery among MVD employees in Kalinin Province in 1946. *Life and Death under Stalin: Kalinin Province, 1945–1953* (Montreal, 1999), 162.

21. RGANI, f. 6, op. 6, d. 1595, ll. 33–34. For an example of the OBKhSS chief in the city of Baku and two of the department heads taking bribes, see GARF, f. 9415, op. 3, d. 820, ll. 203–206 (Spravka on bribery case in OBKhSS, May 9, 1951).

22. Interestingly, the procuracy's investigation did not find any links to their superiors. P. V. Subbotin, who worked in the Novo-Kubansk raion MGB in Krasnodar, was accused of accepting a bribe from a certain Trutnia, a person who had committed a crime during the war. Because he was afraid of being exposed, Trutnia

offered Subbotin a bribe of 4,300 rubles and one *pood* of flour. Subbotin said that he had accepted the bribe to delay Trutnia from leaving the area, and that he intended to return the money, but that his material situation was so bad that he could not. Instead, Subbotin recruited Trutnia as an informant for the MGB. Subbotin was removed from the party for these transgressions. His appeal for restoration to the ranks of the party was heard in January 1957, but it was denied. RGANI, f. 6, op. 4, d. 580, l. 30–30 ob.

23. GARF, f. 8131, op. 29, d. 27, l. 143 (Report to Safonov on the struggle with bribery in Moscow, August 18, 1950).

24. GARF, f. 8131, op. 38, d. 299, ll. 33–34. The Russian GAI has recently been renamed DPS.

25. RGANI, f. 6, op. 6, d. 1587, ll. 106–112 (Letter to Shkiriatov from Alekseeva, undated, but reviewed at a 1947 session of KPK).

26. RGANI, f. 6, op. 6, d. 1587, l. 110. For a case of a police inspector taking bribes of food and shoes from chauffeurs in exchange for giving them back their right to drive, see RGANI, f. 6, op. 2, d. 1398, ll. 128–129.

27. Three secretaries for the judges were also charged with acting as intermediaries. In 1944, a certain Golubeva gave a judge in the Moscow City Court a bribe in exchange for assisting her son, who had received a sentence of three years in prison the year before. (The trial transcript does not include the crime for which the son had been convicted.) The bribe included cash, two pairs of trousers, a dress, and a dressing gown. (GARF, f. 9474, op. 7, d. 855, ll. 86–89, 300: Trial of Vasnev et al.). The sizable proportion of the cases described in this chapter that involve female judges reflects the position of authority that many women occupied in the courts after the deaths of so many male judges during the war.

28. GARF, f. 9474, op. 16, d. 271, ll. 47–50; RGASPI, f. 82 (Molotov fund), op. 2, d. 418, l. 382.

29. For the case of Sprimon, see GARF, f. 9492, op. 1, d. 15, ll. 289 ob.-290; and GARF, f. 8131, op. 37, d. 3024, l. 2. For an example of a boss who bribed judges to keep his employees from jail, see RGANI, f. 6, op. 4, d. 585, ll. 21–22.

30. GARF, f. 9492, op. 1, d. 515, l. 288 ob.

31. RGANI, f. 6, op. 3, d. 1, l. 28 (KPK Protocols of meetings and additional materials, 1952–1956; meeting of October 15, 1952).

32. Peter Solomon has shown that some judges sought various legal ways of mitigating these harsh mandatory sentences for theft. See *Soviet Criminal Justice under Stalin,* chapter 12.

33. GARF, f. 9492, op. 1a, d. 553, ll. 132–133, 135.

34. Similarly, the Party Control Commission (KPK) put pressure on the Georgian Supreme Court in early 1947 because it was assigning sentences that were too moderate in theft cases. RGANI, f. 6, op. 6, d. 1587, ll. 21–24.

35. See the case of N. Ia. Anisimova, whose husband was sentenced to ten years in 1945 for violating the law of August 7, 1932, and a number of the cases discussed below. GARF, f. 9474, op. 7, d. 984 (Trial of Anisimova, et al.).

36. Peter Solomon focuses on the drafting of the law and a degree of discontent among some judges to its most outrageous elements. Donald Filtzer focuses on the effect on workers in his *Soviet Workers and Late Stalinism* (Cambridge, 2002),

28–29. For another discussion of the June 4 laws see Nicolas Werth, *La terreur et le desarroi: Staline et son système* (Paris, 2007).

37. People convicted of speculation and theft of state property (or their relatives) comprised the majority of the eighteen people arrested for offering bribes in a 1948 Moscow City Court scandal. RGASPI, f. 17, op. 118, d. 133.

38. For an example of an alternative to bribery, see the case of E. V. Kochetovyi and E. I. Chistilina, who set a fire in the local courthouse in Putilovskii raion, Sumsk oblast', in order to destroy evidence in the case of their relative. GARF, f. 9492, op. 1a, d. 535, l. 14.

39. The author of an anonymous letter received by the Party Control Committee in 1952 alleged that he had overheard someone in a bar say that he had offered a bribe to the chairman of the USSR Supreme Court's Judicial Collegium to get his 18-year-old daughter out of prison. The accused, a bank cashier, had been sentenced to ten years under the June 4, 1947 decree for illegally backdating bank deposits at the time of the December 1947 monetary reform. Her father was the former director of the Solikamsk Combine (*kombinat*). The KPK investigation of the allegations contained in the letter did not confirm the accusation. The letter does show, however, that rumors about bribery in the courts spread in society. Such rumors would have fed the widespread perception that regular channels would not work; that back-door deals were a necessity. RGANI, f. 6, op. 6, d. 1594, ll. 61–62.

40. GARF, f. 9474, op 7, d. 912, l. 340 (Trial of Shevchenko, et al. Protocol of closed session of USSR Supreme Court, July 1949). See also l. 281.

41. GARF, f. 8131, op. 37, d. 4041, ll. 372–375.

42. GARF, f. 9474, op. 7, d. 1045, l. 13. He claimed that he did not even know for what crime his sister had been convicted. She had received ten years for violating the June 4 decree on theft of state property. GARF, f. 9474, op. 7, d. 1045, l. 15 (Trial of Chichua et al.).

43. GARF, f. 9492, op. 1, d. 542, ll. 201–202. Italics added.

44. GARF, f. 8131, op. 37, d. 4666, ll. 81–88 (Letter of T. Z. Saraev to Deputy Chair of the Council of Ministers L. P. Beria, November 18, 1948).

45. He writes that, in the wake of victory in the war, the Soviet Union is stronger, as the "forces of democracy and communism are stronger." Yet, he notes, "the war also had its dark sides." A very small part of the Soviet population—those who spent time abroad—"absorbed capitalist influences." Many of these unreliable "elements" sold out to foreign intelligence. The state located, arrested, and severely punished these counterrevolutionaries for their crimes. The author separates out this minority of true counterrevolutionary types who deserve to be treated ruthlessly for their betrayal.

46. Saraev also writes angrily about the actions of procuracy investigators. Their mistakes border on crimes against the state. During investigations, they treat the accused rudely and coerce them, so that they confess to nonexistent crimes. Investigators threatened Saraev that he would be shot if he did not sign the phony statements. If he did sign, he would get ten years for violating the August 7, 1932 law on theft of state property. He recommends that Procurator-General Safonov educate himself by spending one or two years in a camp. "Then he would have a real understanding, not an abstract conception, of what ten–twenty-five years of

prison means. He would look at things differently, correctly. Behind the documents of investigators and the sentences of the courts, he would see real people. Then Safonov would lead a decisive battle against those who handle a man's fate in this formal bureaucratic way."

47. One Georgian judge refused to take a 10,000-ruble bribe because the "crime" (tried under Article 58, paragraph "b") resulted in the deaths of many people and he was afraid to mitigate the maximum sentence. GARF, f. 9474, op. 16, d. 355, l. 14 ob (Sentences in trials of members of Georgian Supreme Court, December 1949).

48. GARF, f. 9474, op. 7, d. 912, ll. 193–194. There is also evidence for this tendency in the 1930s. For an example from the late 1930s, see the fifty-year-old former army officer respondent in the Harvard Interview Project who claimed knowledge of NKVD techniques and noted, "If it is a political prisoner, no bribery will help. Then the person who has freed you may be arrested himself." Harvard Interview Project, schedule A, no. 175, p. 28. In the late 1940s, David Dallin speculated that blat would not help people accused of crimes under Article 58, because law enforcement officials feared the consequences of improper activity in a political case. Dallin, "The Black Market in Russia," *American Mercury* (December 1949): 678–682.

49. The Armenian Supreme Court USSR judge Arutiunian was accused of accepting a bribe in 1947 from an acquaintance whose son was accused of rape. (GARF, f. 8131, op. 29, d. 4, ll. 208–211.) The father was a dentist who testified that, when he noticed that Arutiunian was missing two teeth, he offered to have an acquaintance replace them. Procurator-General Safonov wrote to the Central Committee in March 1950 declaring that Arutiunian "has grossly violated his official responsibilities." (Letter from Safonov to Panomarkenko, March 28, 1950.)

50. The August 7, 1932 law was classified as an Article 58 crime; for all its severity, the June 4 decree on theft of state property was not categorized as Article 58. It was therefore not as risky for judges to take bribes in cases under the June 4 decrees or thefts prosecuted under other articles of the criminal code.

51. In 1939, the Ministry of Justice eliminated the possibility of lawyers practicing privately (with a few exceptions). The legal consultation bureaus of the courts absorbed defense lawyers. Fee schedules were set that determined how much lawyers could charge for every service. Eugene Huskey, *Russian Lawyers and the Soviet State* (Princeton, NJ, 1986), 216–217. One can reasonably infer that this official limitation on lawyers' fees was a major impetus for the charging of mikst.

52. Eugene Huskey's excellent study of lawyers in the first two decades of Soviet power, *Russian Lawyers and the Soviet State,* discusses the fees that lawyers took, and mentions the phenomenon of mikst as a likely by-product of the stricter regulation of fees that lawyers could charge. I have found dozens of instances of mikst accepted during the war, but in general, it seems that the practice became much more common after the war. The first person to direct the attention of Western scholars to the phenomenon of mikst seems to have been Dina Kaminskaya, an émigré defense lawyer who participated in a numbers of famous cases, including that of the writers Siniavskii and Daniel. Referring to the 1960s and 1970s in her 1982 memoir, she wrote, "In all my years as an *advokat,* I knew very few colleagues

who took no mikst at all." She expresses some embarrassment about its prevalence: "This system hardly redounds to the credit of Soviet advocacy." Kaminskaya, *Final Judgment: My Life as a Soviet Defense Lawyer* (New York, 1983), 29–31. See also Yuri Luryi, "The Right to Counsel in Ordinary Criminal Cases in the USSR," in *Soviet Law after Stalin, Part I: The Citizen and the State in Contemporary Soviet Law,* ed. D. Barry, G. Ginsburgs, and P. Maggs, no. 20(1) (Alphen aan den Rijn, the Netherlands, 1977), 105–115. The first references to mikst that I can find in published sources date from a few Soviet newspaper articles in 1961–1963, and a few Western journalistic and scholarly accounts from the period, which rely on the same articles in the Soviet press. See, for example, the article by Yuri Klasov in *Izvestiia,* February 24, 1961 (page 4), which mentions a lawyer who charged 5,000 rubles for every year's reduction of a sentence he could obtain for his clients. According to the article, the higher the amount of mikst, the harder the lawyer would work on behalf of the client. I have found no references to mikst in the Stalin-era press.

53. GARF, f. 9474, op. 7, d. 1025, l. 108 (Trial of Pashutina, et al., May–June 1951).

54. GARF, f. 9474, op. 7, d. 1025, l. 89.

55. RGASPI, f. 17, op. 136, d. 168, l. 143.

56. RGANI, f. 6, op. 6, d. 1587, ll. 85–86 (KPK investigation of mikst in the Moscow defense bar. Letter from I. Kuz'min to Zhdanov, August–September 1946).

57. GARF, f. 9492, op. 1a, d. 858, ll. 13–15. As punishment for taking mikst from his clients, Lugovskoi lost his party membership, but he was not prosecuted criminally. (Letter to Rubichev, June 4, 1956.)

58. For an example, see f. 9474, op. 7, d. 936, l. 82 ob. (File of Suslo.)

59. For the case of a lawyer who demanded extra fees from an MVD officer whose wife had been arrested, see GARF, f. 9492, op. 1, d. 169, ll. 35–40. Sometimes, a mikst payment was given personally to the lawyer, rather than through the office of the legal consultancy, as was mandated. GARF, f. 9492, op. 2, d. 50, ll. 113–117. (Letter from Gorshenin to Secretary of the Moscow City Party Committee Popov, May 23, 1948.)

60. GARF, f. 9474, op. 7, d. 1025, l. 219.

61. GARF, f. 9492, op. 2, d. 88, ll. 7–9.

62. GARF, f. 9474, op. 7, d. 912, l. 274.

63. For these three statements, see GARF, f. 9474, op. 7, d. 912, l. 279; GARF, f. 9474, op. 7, d. 961, l. 232; GARF, f. 9474, op. 7, d. 824, ll. 279–80.

64. GARF, f. 9474, op. 7, d. 912, l. 229.

65. GARF, f. 8131, op. 29, d. 7, ll. 302–03. (Letter from Safonov to Deputy Chair of the Council of Ministers Beria, September 29, 1950.) As a prikaz of the USSR Ministry of Justice put it in September 1948: "Several judges are captive to cunning lawyers who, by fair means or foul, push forward the cases of their clients, often misleading the court; they get the cases pulled [for review] and get penalties reduced even in those instances when there are no grounds for this; they artificially delay cases, even when average citizens often do not have the opportunity to enjoy the timely and fair review of their cases."

66. GARF, f. 9474, op. 7, d. 958, ll. 82–83.

67. GARF, f. 9474, op. 7, d. 824, ll. 105–107. The lawyer Tavgazov testified at trial that after he was demobilized from the army, "I had to serve in the [Moscow] bar, and every respectable person becomes a bribe taker from the very first days on the job there, including the young advocates." GARF, f. 9474, op. 7, d. 958, l. 133.

68. One lawyer, N. V. Paramonov, a war invalid who had been kicked out of the bar, wrote a bitter letter to Stalin claiming that "wreckers" in the persons of the USSR Minister of Justice, Gorshenin, and his deputy, Kudriavtsev, had slandered him. GARF, f. 9492, op. 2, d. 58, ll. 441–46 (From N. V. Paramonov to Stalin, dated June 7, 1949; and written statement of October 17, 1949).

69. GARF, f. 9474, op. 7, d. 982, l. 158. For a wartime case of mikst in Georgia, see GARF, f. 9492, op. 1a, d. 415, ll. 6–12.

70. The chair of the Soviet Supreme Court, A. Volin, had a much harsher take on the phenomenon of mikst, regarding it not as a friendly gesture by willing clients, or as a reasonable fee for extra work, but as a form of bribery. He laid the blame squarely on dishonest lawyers. In July 1949, Volin argued that the soliciting of mikst by crooked lawyers corrupted otherwise innocent Soviet petitioners. He wrote with venom that there are many "underground defense lawyers and various adventurists" who are "deceiving convicts and their relatives, distorting the contents of court cases in phony appeals." GARF, f. 9474, op. 16, d. 337, ll. 79–80 (Volin reply to KPK review, July 1949).

71. GARF, f. 9492, op. 1, d. 542, ll. 565–66. At the same meeting, a certain Lukov noted, "There are lawyers in the Moscow defense bar who are so corrupted that for them it is nothing to take 20,000 or 30,000 rubles. I will not mention their names. Everyone knows who they are." (GARF, f. 9492, op. 1a, d. 542, l. 576.) Lukov went on to say that "if we had announced a battle against bribe takers, then we wouldn't have any more, but no battle has been waged against them" (l. 576). For further cases of mikst, see GARF, f. 9492, op. 2, d. 542, l. 576 ff. For Safonov's scathing report sent to the Central Committee denouncing widespread mikst and passing of bribes in the Moscow College of Advocates, see GARF, f. 8131, op. 37, d. 3410, ll. 137–142.

72. For a 1953 letter comparing the "bandits" who had been released from the Gulag to Germans, see Miriam Dobson, *Khrushchev's Cold Summer: Gulag Returnees, Crime, and the Fate of Reform after Stalin* (Ithaca, NY, 2009), 41.

73. Central Committee Secretary Kuznetsov, whose purview included the ideological preparedness of party members, expressed concern in 1949 to Goliakov about the declining morality of Soviet lawyers. (GARF f. 9492, op. 2, d. 50, ll. 239–241.) It is possible that judges might have harbored a class-based resentment of "bourgeois" lawyers' acceptance of extra fees. Judges considered themselves poorly paid, and this could have played a role in the increased attacks on mikst. In the words of Eugene Huskey commenting on the 1930s, "For most judges, the advocates represented the decaying bourgeois world that the Soviet state was dedicated to eliminating." Huskey, *Russian Lawyers*, 177–178. Moreover, a degree of anti-Semitism might have had a part in the party's stepped up assault on mikst, since throughout the Stalin period a large proportion of the bar was comprised of Jewish lawyers. (There were very few Jewish judges.) The pointedly anti-Semitic

1931 tract (translated as *Pack of Wolves: Notes of a Member of the Collegium of Defense Lawyers*), published by the RSFSR Ministry of Justice's press, is an attack on Jewish lawyers. V. Valerin, *Vol'chia staia: Zapiski chlena kollegii zashchitnikov* (Moscow, 1931).

74. V. I. Lenin, "O dvoinom podchinenii zakonnosti," in *Sovetskaia prokuratura: sbornik vazneishikh dokumentov* (Moscow, 1972), 100–102.

75. Alec Nove, "Some Aspects of Soviet Constitutional Theory," *Modern Law Review* 12, no. 1 (January 1949): 32.

76. GARF, f. 8131, op. 38, d. 282, l. 62. In 1946, 210 people's judges in the RSFSR were removed for bribery or abuse of office; 120 were charged with a crime. Eighty-seven employees of procuracy agencies were arrested for bribery that year. GARF, f. 9492, op. 2, d. 44, l. 116 (Letter from Bakakin to Kuznetsov, February 20, 1947).

77. GARF, f. 8131, op. 38, d. 282, l. 63.

78. GARF, f. 8131, op. 38, d. 449, l. 94. For cases of bribery in courts and among procuracy employees in the Tatar ASSR, see RGANI, f. 6, op. 2, d. 160, ll. 1–35.

79. In another case, the chief bookkeeper of a grain collection point in Barnaul offered a bribe to a prosecutor to have him soften his sentence when the case was brought to the oblast' court. RGANI, f. 6, op. 2, d. 1888, ll. 140–140 ob.

80. GARF, f. 8131, op. 38, d. 449, l. 96 (Procuracy report on the struggle against bribery, 1946–47). One man paid a bribe to have his wife transferred to a prison camp closer to their home city. She was serving a ten-year term. GARF, f. 9474, op. 7, d. 912, l. 246.

81. RGANI, f. 6, op. 3, d. 573, ll. 36-ob (KPK summary report).

82. Another type of self-enrichment by legal officials was the "shameful" stealing of property confiscated from arrested people, or the theft of evidence to be used in cases. For examples, see GARF, f. 9492, op. 2, d. 88, l. 55.

83. RGANI, f. 6, op. 2, d. 129, l. 55.

84. RGANI, f. 6, op. 2, d. 158, ll. 93–109.

85. The former chief of the MGB for Krasnoiarsk krai, Bovshuk-Bekman, was given a reprimand. (RGANI, f. 6, op. 2, d. 158, l. 93.) Babenko's request to have the reprimand lifted was rejected by the KPK in February 1952. RGANI, f. 6, op. 2, d. 227, l. 62.

86. For more examples of large-scale bribery cases during wartime, see GARF, f. 8131, op. 37, d. 3024, ll. 1–3.

87. GARF, f. 9474, op. 16, d. 355, ll. 105–106. According to law enforcement sources, the offering of bribes in kind was a more common practice in the rural parts of the USSR. In 1948, for example, a judge in Cheliabinsk oblast' was accused of accepting a bribe of a goose and ten kilograms of flour. GARF, f. 9492, op. 2, d. 58, l. 144.

88. In the time of Catherine the Great, the legal system was an especially fruitful venue for deals. Extra fees were paid to judges to decide a case in one's favor. Multiple fees, both legitimate and under-the-table, pervaded the system. Hartley points out, "Although there was nothing improper about this practice in itself it meant

that 'paying' for justice was an established part of the judicial procedure." Janet Hartley, "Bribery and Justice in the Provinces in the Reign of Catherine II," in *Bribery and Blat*, ed. Stephen Lovell, et al., 48–64.

89. RGANI, f. 6, op. 3, d. 1, l. 28 (KPK Protocols of meetings and additional materials, 1952–1956; meeting of October 15, 1952).

90. Yoram Gorlizki, "Campaign Justice," 1252; Peter Solomon, *Soviet Criminal Justice*, 428–445.

91. Natalie Z. Davis, *The Gift in Sixteenth Century France* (Madison, WI, 2000), 86–87.

92. William Clark has argued that corruption was a perfectly reasonable response to the structural incentives present within the Soviet bureaucracy. Clark, *Crime and Punishment in Soviet Officialdom: Combating Corruption in the Political Elite, 1965–1990* (Armonk, NY, 1993), 64–65.

93. For an argument emphasizing very strong continuity between cultures of governing and acquiring food from the Muscovite to the Soviet periods, see Tamara Kondrat'eva, *Kormit' i pravit': o vlasti v Rossii XVI-XX vv* (Moscow, 2006). For a study of party interference in the prosecution of party members for theft of state property in the late Stalin period, see Juliette Cadiot, "Equal before the Law? Soviet Justice, Criminal Proceedings against Communist Party Members, and the Legal Landscape in the USSR from 1945 to 1953," *Jahrbücher für Geschichte Osteuropas* 61, no. 2 (2013): 249–269.

94. For references to metaphors of the shadow economy serving as a "lubricant," see Gregory Grossman, "The Second Economy of the USSR," *Problems of Communism* 26, no. 5 (September–October 1977): 40; Charles Schwartz, "Corruption and Political Development in the U.S.S.R.," *Comparative Politics* 11 (July 1979): 425–443.

CHAPTER THREE. "THE WORD 'BRIBE' WAS NEVER MENTIONED"

1. Alena V. Ledeneva, *Russia's Economy of Favours: Blat, Networking and Informal Exchange* (Cambridge, 1998). Ledeneva briefly refers to "economic crime" and blat relations in the 1940s and 1950s as background for the later period. Ledeneva's work demonstrated the importance of blat as a continuing feature of Soviet life, and she is very careful to distinguish blat from bribery.

2. On such traditions in the late imperial and early Soviet periods, see Catriona Kelly, "Self-Interested Giving: Bribery and Etiquette in Late Imperial Russia," in *Bribery and Blat in Russia*, ed. Stephen Lovell, et al., 79–80, 86.

3. Zubkova, *Poslevoennoe Sovetskoe obshchestvo*, 118–124; Zubkova, *Russia after the War*, 76–82.

4. See, for example, Amir Weiner, *Making Sense of War: The Second World War and the Fate of the Bolshevik Revolution* (Princeton, NJ, 2002); Mark Edele, "Soviet Veterans as an Entitlement Group, 1945–1955," *Slavic Review* 65, no. 1 (Spring 2006): 111–137.

5. One can see something of a parallel in wartime attitudes toward crime. Julie Hessler has written about the wartime "survivalist" ethic. Her work addresses speculation in scarce goods and the violation of travel restrictions by people accused of

speculation. "It is impossible to ascertain the prevalence of this attitude, but it must have resonated with many people who were left out of, or left behind by, the system, especially in the villages and smaller towns. The impact of the war was to bring it back to the cities. . . . From 1942 on (1941 in the occupied territory), however, they, too, adopted survivalism as their moral standard . . ." See also Richard Bidlack and Nikita Lomagin, *The Leningrad Blockade, 1941–1944* (New Haven, CT, 2012), 262–328.

6. The bribe-taking judge Shevchenko was called a "leech" by the wounded veteran Solov'ev at a hearing in 1949. GARF, f. 9474, op. 7, d. 912, l. 245.

7. Caroline Humphrey, "Rethinking Bribery in Contemporary Russia," in *Bribery and Blat in Russia,* ed. Stephen Lovell, et al., 218.

8. Similar attitudes seem to have existed in late imperial Russia. As Catriona Kelly puts it, "A refusal to give on the part of the individual would be an act of socio-economic suicide." Kelly also points out that "many Russians, both before and after the Revolution, accepted that bribery was a fact of life, and that there was nothing so particularly immoral about it, and especially not in *giving* bribes. . . . All in all, the central question for many Russians in the late imperial era was not whether to give bribes, but how to give them." Catriona Kelly, "Self-Interested Giving," 79–81, 86. Using a color-coded scheme of corruption, Arnold Heidenheimer observes that authorities and populations do not always define "corrupt" behavior the same way. Heidenheimer, *Political Corruption: Readings in Comparative Analysis* (New York, 1970), 26–28.

9. GARF, f. 9474, op. 7, d. 1006, l. 175 (Findings of the Procuracy in the case of A. V. Vol'skii, July 15, 1950). For his sentence, see l. 222 ob. Sheila Fitzpatrick and Golfo Alexopolous note that petitioners in the 1930s often cast themselves in the role of "victims" of one or another agency or official. Fitzpatrick, "Supplicants and Citizens: Public Letter-Writing in Soviet Russia in the 1930s," *Slavic Review* 55, no. 1 (Spring 1996): 78–105; Alexopolous, "Victim Talk: Defense Testimony and Denunciation under Stalin," *Law and Social Inquiry* 24, no. 3 (Summer, 1999): 637–654.

10. For example, GARF, f. 8131, op. 26, d. 10, ll. 36–38. For a parallel, Peter Solomon has discussed party allegations that some judges were overly sympathetic to those convicted of theft of state property, and that judges sought ways to reduce the excessive sentences of those convicted of petty theft under the June 1947 law. Peter Solomon, *Soviet Criminal Justice,* 428–444.

11. GARF f. 9492, op. 1a, d. 491, l. 153.

12. GARF, f. 9474, op. 7, d. 958, l. 45.

13. GARF, f. 9474, op. 7, d. 824, l. 288.

14. *Sotsialisticheskaia zakonnost',* 1953, no. 2: 40–41.

15. "Nepravil'nyi glagol," *Krokodil,* no. 31 (November 10, 1945): 7; "Zhestokii romans," *Krokodil,* no. 33 (November 30, 1945); "Dali, vziali. Vziali, dali," *Krokodil,* no. 23 (August 20, 1946).

16. For a summary of a Supreme Court ruling declaring that a gift "after the fact" was also a bribe, see V. Makashvili, "Strogo vypolnyiat' trebovaniia zakona ob otvetstvennosti za vziatochnichestvo (Sudebnaia praktika Verkhovnogo Suda SSSR)," *Sotsialisticheskaia zakonnost'* (1953) no. 2: 40–49.

17. "On Forgotten 'Details' in Supplying Services to the Kiev Population," *Pravda Ukrainy,* July 26, 1950, p. 3.

18. The first two sayings are mentioned in M. P. Karpushin and P. S. Dmitriev, *Vziatochnichestvo—pozornyi perezhitok proshlogo* (Moscow, 1964), 4. A respondent in the Harvard Interview Project recalled an official citing the third saying. HIP, schedule A, no. 5, p. 16. The fourth and fifth expressions are found an appendix of commonly used phrases in the Harvard Interview Project. See also HIP, schedule A, no. 108, p. 110.

19. One can speculate that this strong reluctance to label one's own activities as bribery (or to confess to criminal activity of any kind) may help explain why respondents in the Harvard Interview Project rarely referred to bribery but often openly discussed blat relations at length. Such a situation, in my view, contributed to the project's sophisticated discussion of blat, even as it undervalued the role of bribery in Soviet society. For a contemporary comparison, see the work of Jakob Rigi, who, during eighteen months of fieldwork studying corruption in Kazakhstan in 1995–96, could not find a single person who admitted to taking a bribe. Rigi, "Corruption in Post-Soviet Kazakhstan," in *Between Morality and the Law: Corruption, Anthropology and Comparative Society,* ed. Italo Pardo (Aldershot, UK, 2004), 109–110. Humphrey, "Rethinking Bribery," 221–222.

20. GARF, f. 9474, op. 7, d. 912, l. 239.

21. See, for example, GARF, f. 9474, op. 7, d. 1006, l. 175. Testimony of Vol'skii, stating that a payment to a lawyer in the *iuridkonsul'tatsiia* was a "gift" of gratitude. Prosecutors tried to establish that not only had the parties in bribery cases exchanged money or goods but that they had no prior personal relationship, in order to demonstrate that favors were "purchased" improperly. The accused were then forced to explain how they had innocently given a substantial quantity of money to a complete stranger. As a certain Ninidze described his situation: "I cannot explain this contradiction: that is, it turns out that I am sending money to an unknown person and, moreover, that a stranger is living in my house." GARF, f. 9474, op. 7, d. 912, l. 241.

22. GARF, f. 9474, op. 7, d. 935, l. 35 (Testimony of Silaev).

23. GARF, f. 9474, op. 7, d. 855, l. 301.

24. See also, for example, GARF, f. 9474, op. 7, d. 855, l. 32.

25. Anonymous letter to editor of *Daria Vostoka* newspaper, entitled "Gobsek v iubke." GARF, f. 8131, op. 26, d. 82, ll. 2–5, 1949.

26. GARF, f. 8131, op. 37, d. 4666, l. 179 (Testimony of Obukhov).

27. GARF, f. 9474, op. 7, d. 801, ll. 33–34. For an anonymous denunciation of trade workers taking bribes, see RGANI, f. 6, op. 2, d. 100, ll. 72–79.

28. GARF, f. 9474, op. 7, d. 960, l. 232.

29. GARF, f. 9474, op. 7, d. 802, l. 105.

30. GARF, f. 9474, op. 7, d. 912, l. 319.

31. GARF, f. 8131, op. 37, d. 4667, l. 255 ("Spravka" from Golinkov, Investigator in Most Important Cases, April 1949).

32. GARF, F. 9474, op. 7, d. 958, ll. 72, 74. Entertaining with alcohol as a form of bribe was discussed in the collegium on criminal cases of the USSR Supreme

Court on July 17, 1950, in the case of Radzivichus. *Sudebnaia praktika verkhovnogo suda,* no. 8 (1950): 11.

33. See V. Makashvili, "Strogo vypolnyiat' trebovaniia zakona ob otvetstvennosti za vziatochnichestvo," 42–43.

34. For testimony highlighting how a judge and an intermediary explained to one petitioner how to present a bribe disguised as a gift after the fact, see GARF, f. 9474, op. 7, d. 855, ll. 86–89.

35. GARF, f. 9474, op. 7, d. 958, l. 76. See also the testimony of Gadzhieva, who defended herself from a charge of bribe giving by saying that she told the accused intermediary–defense lawyer that she would give him a gift after her son was released from prison: "In the event of a favorable resolution of the case of my son, I would arrange some good company for him, that is, I would treat [the lawyer] to a meal [*usgostit'*]."

36. Janet Hartley, "Bribery and Justice in the Provinces," in *Bribery and Blat,* ed. Stephen Lovell, et al., 48–49.

37. N. S. Timasheff, "The Impact of the Penal Law of Imperial Russia on Soviet Penal Law," *American Slavic and East European Review* 12, no. 4 (December 1953): 460–461, citing a provisional law of January 31, 1916.

38. The article was entitled "O mzdoimstve i likhoimstve," in the section concerning crimes and violations in government and civil service. F. A. Brokgauz and I. A. Efron, "Vziatochnichestvo," *Entsiklopedicheskii slovar'* (Saint Petersburg, 1890–1907), tom VI (1894), 213–216.

39. Note in *Sotsialisticheskaia zakonnost',* 1948, no. 9.

40. In NEP conditions, a "hidden" bribe had been a payment or reward for a state official that was disguised as a "commission" in an exchange either between the private and public sectors, or within the public sector itself. On hidden bribes, see Feliks Dzerzhinskii's circular in *Izvestiia VTsiK,* October 6, 1922. As Borisova notes, bribes became "an essential part of the economic mechanism" of NEP ("Tret'ii vrag," 253). As Julie Hessler has noted with regard to Soviet trade networks during NEP, "There can be no doubt that bribery was more than a figment of the Bolsheviks' imagination; it played a pivotal role in the commercial representatives' milieu." Julie Hessler, *A Social History of Soviet Trade,* 85.

41. GARF, f. 8131, op. 38, d. 449, l. 91.

42. GARF, f. 9474, op. 7, d. 1025, l. 90 (Testimony of Kudroshova).

43. GARF, f. 9474, op. 7, d. 912, l. 277.

44. Leonid Lench, "Tochnoe dokazatel'stvo," *Krokodil,* no. 15 (May 30, 1946): 4.

45. HIP, Schedule B, case no. 441, p. 22.

46. GARF, f. 9474, op. 7, d. 802, l. 111.

47. Testimony of Morozov, February 9, 1949. (GARF, f. 9474, op. 7, d. 879, l. 38.) A certain Gomzina told the court that "I went on the criminal path because I had a difficult situation, that is, my child was one and a half years old, I was eight months pregnant, and my husband was in prison at that time." GARF, f. 9474, op. 7, d. 882, l. 220.

48. On the September 27, 1946 law, see Donald Filtzer, "The Standard of Living

of Soviet Industrial Workers in the Immediate Postwar Period, 1945–48," *Europe-Asia Studies* 51, no. 6 (September 1999): 1020–1026.

49. GARF, f. 8131, op. 38, d. 449, l. 96.

50. A Moscow judge hinted to a complainant that he was in poor financial shape; the complainant then offered him money. Testimony of Digilov, GARF, f. 9474, op. 7, d. 958, l. 80.

51. GARF, f. 8131, op. 38, d. 449, ll. 99–103.

52. GARF, f. 8131, op. 38, d. 449, l. 97.

53. Of course, this process always had to be done without witnesses. As one confessed bribe giver stated, "It's not a secret to anyone that you can't give a bribe in the presence of a third person." GARF, f. 9474, op. 7, d. 958, l. 71.

54. One judge said that he found it impossible to refuse a petitioner's request for an illegal intervention in a case once he had accepted *zakuski* and alcohol at the petitioner's apartment. As he put it, "This was a masked bribe—*zakuski* and drinks—after which I couldn't refuse his request." GARF, f. 9474, op. 7, d. 912, l. 311.

55. GARF, f. 8131, op. 38, d. 449, l. 99.

56. GARF, f. 9474, op. 7, d. 882, ll. 109–121 (Closed session of Supreme Court, May 1949). The transcripts of hearings are such a rich source in part because Soviet judges and prosecutors were allowed to ask defendants very direct questions, such as "Where did you go wrong?" and "What led you down the criminal path?"

57. GARF, f. 8131, op. 38, d. 449, ll. 99–100. The document does not state the crime with which Solov'ev had been charged.

58. The investigator was sentenced to five years and the bribe giver to two years in prison. GARF, f. 8131, op. 38, d. 449, ll. 94, 99 (Testimony of Shevchenko).

59. The most useful answers are from refugees who had reached adulthood before the war, had enjoyed some formal education, drew on first-hand experience, and did not make simple, generalized statements pertaining to things about which they had little or no personal knowledge.

60. HIP, Schedule A, case 124, p. 8.

61. HIP, Schedule B, case no. 1758, p. 38.

62. HIP, Schedule B, case no. 1758, pp. 31–32, 36–37.

63. HIP, Schedule B, case no. 1758, pp. 36–37.

64. HIP, Schedule B, case no. 1800, p. 17. "In a big city polyclinic it is impossible to accept a gift and if you do it is a big scandal."

65. HIP, Schedule B, case no. 1158, p. 38.

66. HIP, Schedule B, case no. 26, pp. 56–57.

67. For a discussion of court practice in treating intermediaries, see Makashvili, "Strogo vypolniat'," 45–48. One person accused of being an intermediary noted that investigators had not charged a "giver" or "acceptor" of the alleged bribe, just a middleman. Charges against him, he argued, should therefore be dropped. (GARF, f. 9474, op. 7, d. 855, l. 324. Testimony of Zheleznikov.) At least one procuracy investigation emphasized that bribe givers typically sought an intermediary from inside their circle of acquaintances. GARF, f. 8131, op. 38, d. 449, l. 97.

68. GARF, f. 9474, op. 7, d. 984, ll. 55 and 162 (Deposition of P. I. Kisliakova in Butyrsk prison, September 9, 1949). Kisliakova was a witness who overheard

Anisimova's conversations with Mushailov in her apartment. It is unknown what happened to Anisimova's husband.

69. For the return of an advance, see GARF, f. 9474, op. 7, d. 1006, ll. 5 and 8. For the case of an intermediary asking for a 25,000-ruble advance on a 50,000-ruble bribe, see GARF, f. 9474, op. 7, d. 984, ll. 162–163. For interesting observations about the institution of "brokerage" in corrupt exchanges in contemporary Hungary, see David Jancsics, "A Friend Gave Me a Phone Number—Brokerage in Low-Level Corruption," *International Journal of Law, Crime, and Justice* 43 (2015): 68–87.

70. GARF, f. 9474, op. 7, d. 1006, ll. 5–9, 169–170.

71. GARF, f. 9474, op. 7, d. 984, l. 163.

72. Golfo Alexopoulos, "Portrait of a Con Artist as a Soviet Man," *Slavic Review* 57, no. 4 (Winter 1998): 774–790; Sheila Fitzpatrick, "The World of Ostap Bender: Soviet Confidence Men in the Stalin Period," *Slavic Review* 61, no. 3 (Fall 2002): 535–557.

73. Fitzpatrick, "The World of Ostap Bender," 550.

CHAPTER FOUR. "GREETINGS FROM SUNNY GEORGIA!"

1. For a stimulating study of Stalin's path from Georgian to Russian identity, see Alfred J. Rieber, "Stalin, Man of the Borderlands, in *American Historical Review* 106 (December 2001): 1651–1691.

2. Natalie Zemon Davis, *The Gift in Sixteenth Century France* (Madison, WI, 2000).

3. GARF, f. 9474, op. 7, d. 1045, l. 34 (Stenogram of Trial of L. K. Chichua, et al., February 22–March 5, 1952).

4. To handle this enormous task, the Supreme Court was quite large, with seventy justices by 1946. Chapter 8 will examine in detail a series of bribery cases that swept through the USSR Supreme Court.

5. See the December 17, 1949 request from Chair of the USSR Supreme Court Volin to the Secretary of the Communist Party of Georgia, asking him to recommend a Georgian jurist who speaks Russian well to review cases from Georgian Republican courts "in consideration of local conditions and all particularities of a case." GARF, f. 9474, op. 16, d. 337, ll. 63 (Letter to Secretary of Georgian SSR Central Committee). On the appointment of Chichua to the Supreme Court, see RGASPI, f. 17, op. 121, d. 612, l. 60.

6. For Volin's recommendation to dismiss Chichua from the Supreme Court, see RGASPI, f. 17, op. 136, d. 22, ll. 58–59 (Letter of Bakakin to Molotov, November 22, 1949). Because Chichua was removed from the Supreme Court on December 14, 1948, he had no opportunity to act in the case of Bukiia's sister, even if he had wished to do so. Note that this case is not related to the Mingrelian Affair, Stalin's attack on Lavrenty Beria's alleged patronage network, which resulted in the arrest of hundreds of people of Mingrelian descent from Western Georgia. The events leading to that scandal had their genesis in September 1951, and peaked a year later. On the Mingrelian Affair, see Oleg Khlevniuk, "Kreml'—Tbilisi. Chistki, kontrol' i problemy gruzinskogo natsionalizma v pervoi polovine 1950-x godov,"

paper presented at workshop on "Georgian Nationalism and Soviet Power," Joensuu, Finland, August 27, 2012.

7. On speculation, see Julie Hessler, *A Social History of Soviet Trade,* 271–273.

8. GARF, f. 9474, op. 7, d. 1045, l. 28. When he was first appointed to the USSR Supreme Court in March 1946, Chichua protested to the Central Committee department responsible for overseeing the courts that he was not ready for such an important position, having graduated from a juridical institute just five years earlier in 1941. GARF, f. 9474, op. 7, d. 1045, l. 26.

9. GARF, f. 9474, op. 7, d. 1045, l. 35.

10. GARF, f. 9474, op. 7, d. 1045, l. 97.

11. GARF, f. 9474, op. 7, d. 1045, l. 12. For allegations of bribery among lawyers in the Georgian Supreme Court, see GARF, f. 9492, op. 2, d. 58, ll. 412–414 (Letter of Kudriavtsev to Bakakin at Central Committee, December 15, 1949).

12. As an example, the North Ossetian lawyer Tavgazov was accused of illegally working with the RSFSR Supreme Court judges Kumekhov and Murzakhanov, both of whom were also from the North Caucasus, to modify the sentences of his many North Ossetian clients. North Ossetia was a small region in the North Caucasus, just north of the Georgian Republic (GSSR). See GARF, f. 9474, op. 7, d. 958, especially ll. 128–153 (Trial of Murzakhanov et al.). A good deal of evidence was introduced into the trial that Tavgazov had aggressively recruited North Ossetian clients by claiming close relationships with the judges Kumekhov and Murzakhanov on the basis of shared ethnic ties. Similarly, ethnic Russians seem to have typically sought out ethnic Russian intermediaries. See the major bribery trial of court employees in Krasnodar. GARF, f. 9492, op. 2, d. 60, ll. 42–57.

13. Erik R. Scott, "Familiar Strangers: The Georgian Diaspora in the Soviet Union," unpublished PhD dissertation, University of California, Berkeley (2011), 124.

14. GARF, f. 9474, op. 7, d. 824, l. 25 (Trial of Safronova et al., July 1949). Melik-Nubarov had gotten in trouble for offering a bribe in Georgia in 1944. This may be why he traveled to Moscow to earn his living there as a semi-legal *advokat.* See GARF, f. 9492, op. 1a, d. 415, ll. 6–12.

15. GARF, f. 9474, op. 7, d. 984, l. 8 (Interrogation of A. S. Mazur by Investigator Gol'st, July 1, 1949. Mazur was the deputy chief of the Chancellery for the Military Collegium).

16. Erik R. Scott, "Familiar Strangers," 125.

17. GARF, f. 9474, op. 7, d. 982, ll. 147–148. Mersakov was born in Georgia, though he had a Russian-sounding last name. Mushailov introduced himself as Murdashvili to court employees and to clients. GARF, f. 9474, op. 7, d. 958, l. 96.

18. GARF, f. 9474, op. 7, d. 982, l. 8.

19. GARF, f. 9474, op. 7, d. 984, l. 15.

20. GARF, f. 9474, op. 7, d. 958, l. 97. For an exploration of many dimensions of "imposture" in Soviet history, see the essays in Sheila Fitzpatrick, *Tear off the Masks! Identity and Imposture in Twentieth-Century Russia* (Princeton, NJ, 2005).

21. GARF, f. 9474, op. 7, d. 1045, l. 18.

22. GARF, f. 9474, op. 7, d. 1045, l. 34. A procuracy or court official who later

read this trial transcript underlined the phrases, "As a Georgian, I could not re-fuse" and "This was my weakness and this is also our Georgian tradition."

23. Marcel Mauss, *The Gift: The Form and Reason for Exchange in Archaic Societies,* trans. W. D. Halls (New York, 1990), 13.

24. In fact, the judge's way of handling this very difficult situation was quite reasonable. Chichua said that he accepted gifts of alcohol, but he never drank them himself, serving it, rather, to others who came to see him (GARF, f. 9474, op. 7, d. 1045, l. 26).

25. Indeed, apples were so rare that in the fall of 1945 some members of the Supreme Court were implicated in an illicit deal involving the fruit. According to an investigation by the Party Control Commission, court employees, including the chair of the Supreme Court of the Russian Republic, Nesterov, paid Georgian contacts to bring fruit from the Caucasus to Moscow, where they sold it for profit on the very grounds of the building that housed the Supreme Court. (This incident will be discussed in more detail in chapter 8.) RGANI, f. 6, op. 2, d. 132, ll. 37–48; d. 199, ll. 18–23.

26. James Scott, *Comparative Political Corruption,* 11.

27. GARF, f. 9474, op. 16, d. 355, ll. 102–03. The file does not explain what became of the case or the defendant.

28. RGASPI, f. 17, op. 121, d. 612, ll. 59–61. Similarly, in December 1944 Go-liakov sent a letter to Molotov begging for money for clothing and shoes for Su-preme Court judges. He even asked for underwear. The letter notes that fifteen members of the Supreme Court, having arrived from the Soviet republics, "for many years have lived in hotels with their families, and several of them have raised the possibility of quitting their work and leaving Moscow." Members of the Su-preme Court, unlike most government elites (the so-called nomenklatura), could not use the dining room at the Kremlin. GARF, f. 9474, op. 16, d. 271.

29. RGASPI, f. 17, op, 121, d. 612, ll. 59–61. The first session of the Supreme Soviet chose new members of the Supreme Court USSR in March 1946. Several of the new judges were from other union republics.

30. GARF, f. 9474, op. 7, d. 1045, l. 29. Chichua testified in his final statement to the court: "I received them courteously. I went to the chair of the Supreme Court, Goliakov, and asked him to create normal living conditions for me, but they did not meet me half way (l. 72)." Other judges also had many visiting petitioners.

31. GARF, f. 9474, op. 7, d. 1045, l. 73.

32. GARF, f. 9474, op. 7, d. 1045, l. 72. On a Georgian search for a "strong sense of localness" outside the home community, see Rieber, "Stalin, Man of the Border-lands," 1661.

33. GARF, f. 9474, op. 7, d. 1045, l. 23. The court found both Chichua and the doctor, Efrem G. Mikhelashvili, not guilty of a crime in this incident.

34. For the phrase "cult of hospitality" with reference to Georgian traditions, see, for example, Peter Nasmyth, *Walking in the Caucasus* (New York, 2006).

35. GARF, f. 9474, op. 7, d. 1045, l. 72.

36. GARF, f. 9474, op. 7, d. 1045, l. 26.

37. GARF, f. 9474, op. 7, d. 912, l. 279 (Trial of Shevchenko, et al., July 1949).

38. GARF, f. 9474, op. 7, d. 1045, l. 21. In another case, Mirelashvili said that he treated people according to "our Georgian *obychai* [customs]." As Chichua said, "I knew Dzhavakhiia as a communist and a Georgian, and I could not drive him out of my room either [since] I knew him very well."

39. GARF, f. 9474, op. 7, d. 1045, ll. 32–33, 72.

40. GARF, f. 9474, op. 7, d. 1045, l. 72. The reason for the visit is not recorded in the files. Gelovani also showed up at a gathering to which an RSFSR Supreme Court judge, Shevchenko, was invited. GARF, f. 9474, op. 7, d. 912, l. 288.

41. GARF, f. 9474, op. 7, d. 1045, ll. 303–304. A North Ossetian lawyer, Tavgazov, who was himself a former member of the RSFSR Supreme Court, also faced charges of bribery in 1949. Tavgazov was accused of taking bribes at his apartment during meetings with clients. He offered a defense very similar to Chichua's—such was the tradition among his people, he told the court. "I understand that it was incorrect to receive clients at home . . . I also understood that not all Caucasian traditions are good outside the Caucasus but, nevertheless, I received my fellow natives at home. All of this has led me here to the defendants' bench." GARF, f. 9474, op. 7, d. 958, l. 44.

42. Vladimir Dal', *Tolkovyi slovar' zhivogo velikorusskogo iakyka,* 1880–82: vol. 2: 92. Quoted in Catriona Kelly, "Self-Interested Giving: Bribery and Etiquette in Late Imperial Russia," in *Bribery and Blat,* ed. Lovell, et al., 65. For a translation of the satirical but spot-on 1980s pamphlet "A Small Handbook for the Bribe Giver: Tokens of Gratitude," published independently in Poland, see *Survey* 29, no. 3 (Autumn 1986): 195–198.

43. GARF, f. 9474, op. 7, d. 1045, l. 44.

44. For more examples of gifts of fruit and meals raising red flags among prosecutors in Georgia, see the sentence of ten people from April 1951. GARF, f. 9492, op. 2, d. 81, ll. 265–277.

45. GARF, f. 9474, op. 7, d. 912, l. 217.

46. With regard to corruption and the second economy in the Brezhnev era, Gregory Grossman wrote, "Georgia has a reputation second to none. . . . In form this activity may not differ greatly from what takes place in other regions, but in Georgia it seems to have been carried out on an unparalleled scale and with unrivaled scope and daring." Grossman, "The Second Economy," 35.

47. Gerald Mars and Yochanan Altman, "How a Soviet Economy Really Works: Cases and Implications," in *Corruption: Causes, Consequences and Control,* ed. Michael Clarke (New York, 1983), 260–261.

48. GARF, f. 9474, op. 7, d. 912, l. 311. Summing up a common sentiment, one Georgian general ruefully said to the Supreme Court judge Shevchenko, "*Kak riumka vodki, tak novaia obiazannost*'" ("With each shot of vodka comes a new obligation"). The general wanted Shevchenko to do him a favor after they had had a drink together. Shevchenko understood what this implied—that if you accept someone's vodka (or other offering), you are in debt to that person.

49. GARF, f. 9474, op. 7, d. 1045, l. 73.

50. GARF, f. 9474, op. 7, d. 1045, l. 44.

51. Echoing this theme of the stigma associated with bribe taking, the Supreme Court judge Bukanov stated that, had he been aware that his good friend on the

RSFSR Supreme Court, the judge Shevchenko, was taking bribes, "I would have strangled him with my own hands." GARF, f. 9474, op. 7, d. 960, l. 317 (Trial of Bukanov, September 1951).

52. Still, he concluded, "I am ready to sacrifice myself for the Party." GARF, f. 9474, op. 7, d. 1045, ll. 72–74.

53. GARF, f. 9474, op. 7, d. 1046, ll. 222–251 (Materials for Procuracy review of Chichua conviction). After his release from prison, the intermediary Eremadze recanted his statement that he had passed Chichua a bribe. He said that he had been forced to denounce Chichua by Georgian investigators. On the basis of this recantation, Chichua appealed more than once to have his conviction overturned. His appeals were denied; the final perfunctory official rejection in his case file is dated 1966 (l. 251).

54. On the Stalinist ideal of the "New Soviet Person," see David L. Hoffman, *Stalinist Values: The Cultural Norms of Soviet Modernity* (Ithaca, NY, 2003).

CHAPTER FIVE. "A GRAVE EVIL AND DANGER"

1. Heyman and Smart, "States and Illegal Practices," 5.

2. Raymond Bauer, Alex Inkeles, and Clyde Kluckhohn noted in 1956 the persistence of certain types of "adjustive, informal mechanisms," including theft and bribery, and the state's apparent willingness to abide them. Raymond A. Bauer, Alex Inkeles, and Clyde Kluckhohn, *How the Soviet System Works* (Cambridge, MA, 1956), 89–93. Oleg Khlevniuk has argued that as long as official "malfeasance and ineffectiveness" did not pose a threat to the regime, Stalin did not believe he needed to take serious measures to combat it. *TsK VKP(b) i regional'nye partiinye komitety, 1945–1953*. Oleg Khlevniuk, et al., eds. (Moscow, 2004), 8. Julie Hessler's study of markets and bazaars points out the Stalin regime's willingness to embrace semi-formal pathways as a way of distributing scarce products. Bribery can be considered a similar mechanism or institution for distributing services and goods. Hessler, *A Social History of Soviet Trade*.

3. See, for example, I. A. Golosenko, "Nachal'stvo. Ocherki po istorii Rossiiskoi sotsiologii chinovnichestva kontsa XIX–nachala XX vv," *Zhurnal sotsiologii i sotsial'noi antropologii,* tom 8, no. 1 (2005): 54–85.

4. GARF, f. 9492, op. 2, d. 44, ll. 227–229 (Letter from Minin to Stalin, May 3, 1946).

5. For a letter from a citizen complaining that banditism was like an "epidemic," see Miriam Dobson, *Khrushchev's Cold Summer,* 41. For similar concerns that hooliganism was "infectious" during the NEP, see Tracy McDonald, *Face to the Countryside,* 208–209. Some argue that it is not merely the existence of bribery that erodes the legitimacy of government. Rather it is a government's perceived *toleration* of bribery that damages its legitimacy. See, for example, Gbenga Lawal, "Corruption and Development in Africa: Challenges for Political and Economic Change," *Humanity & Social Sciences Journal* 2, no. 1 (2007): 1–7. Indeed, one can speculate that a vigorous public campaign to crush bribery in the Soviet Union might have helped to buttress the legitimacy of the regime among some parts of the population.

6. See, for example, the May 20, 1946 report on bribery in 1944–1945, written by Beldiugin of the Ministry of Justice, which states that the "the quantity of people convicted for bribery (the accepting of bribes and the giving of bribes) in certain republics and in the USSR is extremely insignificant on the whole." GARF, f. 9492, op. 1a, d. 478, l. 33.

7. Statistics found in GARF, f. 9492, op. 6s, d. 14. These documents were recently reprinted in *Istoriia Stalinskogo Gulaga: Massovye repressii v SSSR,* tom 1, Iu. N. Afanas'ev et al., eds. (Moscow, 2004), 633, 636.

8. The outcome for Minin is unknown, but there is no evidence in the files that he faced negative consequences for writing the letter. The Ministry of Justice categorized bribe taking by judges as both a crime and a "moral transgression." See, for example, GARF, f. 9492, op. 1a, dd. 376, 465, 491, 525–527.

9. Zhdanov was the party's chief of ideology, and he expressed deep concern about the morality of party cadres. In an editorial in mid-July 1946, two months after the Minin letter, Zhdanov wrote that economic administrators (such as factory directors) gave bribes to party officials so that the latter would ignore corruption. Jonathan Harris, *The Split in Stalin's Secretariat* (Lanham, MD, 2010), 95, citing *Partiinoe stroitel'stvo,* no. 11 (1946): 1–4.

10. V. A. Kozlov, "Denunciation and its Functions in Soviet Governance: A Study of Denunciations and their Bureaucratic Handling from Soviet Police Archives, 1944–1953," *Journal of Modern History* 68, no. 4 (December, 1996): 867–898; Sheila Fitzpatrick, "Signals from Below: Soviet Letters of Denunciation of the 1930s," *Journal of Modern History* 68, no. 4 (December, 1996): 831–866.

11. As Yoram Gorlizki and Oleg Khlevniuk have argued, archives show that Zhdanov could do almost nothing, including launching campaigns, without Stalin's permission. In their words, "Rather than initiating these campaigns, as some earlier scholars have surmised, the archives show that Zhdanov was Stalin's compliant, hard-pressed, and ultimately rather bewildered agent." Gorlizki and Khlevniuk, *Cold Peace,* 31.

12. As Gordon B. Smith noted in reference to a later period, Soviet campaigns against crime were "the coordinated efforts of several law enforcement related agencies and institutions to reduce the incidence of certain types of crime.... Ideally, campaigns represent an integrated, total approach to combating crime, incorporating investigations, prosecution, follow-up supervision, and preventative measures.... Campaigns against crime assume a central position in the Soviet system of criminal justice." The campaign against bribery, flawed as it was, fulfilled this definition. Gordon B. Smith, "Procuratorial Campaigns against Crime in the USSR," in *Soviet Law Since Stalin,* ed. Donald Barry, George Ginsburgs, and Peter Maggs (Leiden, 1979), 146. Smith goes on: "In actuality, campaigns serve four separate functions; (1) to uncover, punish, and, by example, prevent violations; (2) to communicate new policies or laws to officials and the public; (3) to inform Party and state officials of the state of legality in a region; and (4) to provide an outlet for ritualistic participation in government."

13. Dated 1922, draft prikaz on the *Ugolovnyi rozysk* of the Republic. A. Iu. Epikhin and O. B. Mozokhin, *VChK-OGPU v bor'be s korruptsiei v gody novoi ekonomicheskoi politiki* (Moscow, 2007), document 58: 415. This volume of doc-

uments (apparently sponsored by the FSB) includes the authors' mostly laudatory commentary about the secret police campaign against corruption during NEP. Corruption, the authors say, was often engaged in by "terrorists."

14. Speech of October 17, 1921, by V. I. Lenin, *Polnoe sobranie sochinenii*, 5th ed. (Moscow, 1964), vol. 44: 173–174.

15. L. V. Borisova, "NEP v zerkale pokazatel'nykh protsessov po vziatochnichestvo i khoziaistvennym prestupleniiam," *Otechestvennaia istoriia*, no. 1 (January 2006): 84. For a nuanced analysis of the conflict between traditional norms and the new revolutionary values as reflected in allusions to bribery in NEP-era and early Stalinist literature, see Stephen Lovell, "Reciprocity and the Soviet Cultural Revolution: The Literary Perspective," in *Bribery and Blat in Russia,* ed. Stephen Lovell et al., 141–165.

16. Prikaz of GPU no. 255, October 12, 1922. Epikhin and Mozokhin, *VChK-OGPU v bor'be,* document no. 33: 374.

17. In their efforts to combat bribery, the Bolsheviks rejected all the experience of the tsarist government, which for decades had been working on ways to reform administration by strengthening internal audits and elevating professional ethics. The Bolsheviks instead took a "people's *kontrol'*" (supervision) approach, attempting to stimulate popular participation in exposing corrupt officials. "Protokol Kollegii GPU, August 31, 1922." In Epikhin and Mozokhin, *VChK-OGPU v bor'be,* doc. 1: 340. By secret decree of September 1, 1922, the STO, in close coordination with the GPU, created a new agency, the Central Commission on Bribery, which coordinated antibribery efforts. Dzerzhinskii was its chief.

18. Epikhin and Mozokhin, *VChK-OGPU v bor'be,* doc 10: 336. "Vypiski iz protokola no. 23 zasedaniia Politbiuro TsK RKP, August 24, 1922."

19. "Protokol kollegii GPU, August 31, 1922." In Epikhin and Mozokhin, *VChK-OGPU v bor'be,* doc. 14: 341. The Economic Administration (EKU) of the GPU played the major role in this process of cleansing agencies of bribe takers.

20. Undated NKVD instruction, probably October or November 1922. In Epikhin and Mozokhin, *VChK-OGPU v bor'be,* doc 45: 394.

21. As the antibribery commission in the Commissariat of Internal Affairs wrote in a letter to the Commissariat's employees: "No matter what position he occupies—anyone who takes bribes or commits fraud awaits severe punishment." Undated letter to NKVD employees from the Commission to combat bribery within NKVD, Epikhin and Mozokhin, *VChK-OGPU v bor'be,* doc no. 46: 396.

22. Borisova, "NEP v zerkale," 84–85. As early as February 1922, Lenin had urged the Commissariat of Justice to hold public show trials of bribe-taking officials. For a sample of articles in the legal press that mention the campaign, see *Ezhenedel'nik sovetskoi iustitsii,* no. 10, March 13, 1923: 219–220; no. 21, May 31, 1923: 492.

23. Tracy McDonald writes that local judges in Riazan' province were susceptible to gifts of "mutton and moonshine" and other in-kind presents during the NEP. McDonald, *Face to the Village,* 94.

24. Borisova, *Tret'ii vrag,* 264. The continued social toleration for various forms of reciprocity between officials and the population caused frustration among the leaders. In 1923, the head of the trade commission, A. M. Lezhava, wrote a petition

calling for a halt in trials of trade employees for petty bribery, and for an end to the application of the death penalty for convicted bribe takers. The petition illustrates both the consternation the trials were causing among honest trade officials, and the excessive harshness of the attack on bribery: "Our trials do not expose with blinding clarity the darkest forms of embezzlement and bribery, which alone would justify the application of the highest punitive sanction. The general impression that remains from the recent trials is that we instead are using the death penalty to wage a struggle against a centuries-old, mundane fixture of Russian life." Cited in Julie Hessler, *A Social History of Soviet Trade*, 85–86.

25. "Vsem, vsem, vsem. Vozzvanie," [No author] GARF, f. 9550, op. 4, d. 5988, l. 1.

26. Epikhin and Mozokhin, *VChK-OGPU v bor'be*, 114, citing contemporary sources, 137. At the conclusion of the campaign in March, over 3,300 people had been convicted, according to official statistics. Nearly half of all those convicted received sentences of two years in prison or less. Published statistics for the 1920s, on the other hand, provide a picture of declining numbers of convictions as the decade progressed. According to incomplete data, 9,258 people were convicted for bribery in 1923; only 4,623 were convicted in 1927. From *Statistika osuzhdennykh v SSR, 1923–24* (Moscow, 1927), p. 15, 94; and *Statistika osuzhdennykh v SSSR, 1925, 1926 i 1927* (Moscow, 1930): 10–11.

27. See, for example, *Ezhenedel'nik sovetskoi iustitsii*, 1927, no. 16: 475, which notes that "by the end of 1926, bribery occupies an insignificant place among other crimes."

28. Epikhin and Mozokhin, *VChK-OGPU v bor'be*, 114.

29. Convictions for bribery, 1943–1945:

	1943	1944	1945
Bribe taking:	528	685	981
Bribe giving:	992	1404	1858

Sources: GARF, f. 9492, op. 2, d. 38, ll. 119–122; GARF, f. 9492, op. 2, d. 49, l. 277; GARF, f. 8131, op. 37, d. 2817, l. 3.

30. This turn of phrase is quoted in N. P. Kucheriavyi, *Otvetstvennost' za vziatochnichestvo po sovetskomu ugolovnomu pravu* (Moscow, 1957), 3.

31. In June 1949, the Supreme Court declared that bribery was intrinsic to capitalism. For the published 1949 *postanovlenie* of the Supreme Court, "On Court Practice in Cases of Bribery," which emphasized that bribery resulted from "a remnant of capitalism in the consciousness of the people" and reiterated its "social danger," see GARF, f. 8131, op. 26, d. 10, ll. 36–39 (USSR Procuracy correspondence with USSR Supreme Court). For textbooks on Soviet law that took this line, concentrating on crimes by officials and crimes against state property, see T. L. Sergeeva, *Ugolovno-pravovaia okhrana sotsialisticheskoi sobstvennosti v SSSR* (Moscow, 1954); B. A. Kurinov, *Ugolovnaia otvetstvennost' za khishchenie gosudarstvennogo i obshchestvennogo imushchestva* (Moscow, 1954), 12–13; G. R. Smolitskii, *Dolzhnostnye prestupleniia* (Moscow, 1947). See also K. P. Gorshenin, *Sotsialisticheskaia zakonnost' na sovremennom etape: Stenogramma publichnoi lektsii*

prochitannoi 17 avgusta 1948 goda v Tsentral'nom lektorii obshchestva v Moskve (Moscow, 1948).

32. The chairman of the Soviet Supreme Court expressed the general approach to the problem of crime, stating that it would eventually disappear under Soviet socialism, even as a small percentage of the population lagged. "In the Soviet state, crime is declining quite noticeably, in contrast to capitalist countries, because it is alien to the nature of socialist society. In our state, all the socio-economic conditions for the complete liquidation of crime have been created. At the same time, one should not minimize the still-existing threat of crime. If the socio-economic roots of crime have been liquidated here, then the remnants of capitalism in the consciousness of a certain part [*neskol'ko chast'*] of the people have not been liquidated." A. Volin, "Strogo sobliudat' zakonnost' v rabote sudov," *Sotsialisticheskaia zakonnost'*, no. 1 (1950): 5. Letter to Malenkov of August 3, 1953, signed by Voroshilov, Shvernik, Gorshenin et al. GARF, f. 7523 (USSR Supreme Soviet), op. 85, d. 34, l. 19.

33. Aleksandr Nekrich, *Forsake Fear: Memoirs of a Historian* (Boston, 1991), 9.

34. John Hazard made this point in "Socialism, Abuse of Power, and Soviet Law," *Columbia Law Review* 50, no. 4 (April 1950): 452–453.

35. For the case of the concerns about maintaining the appearance of a "paternal state" in provisioning postwar Sevastopol', see Karl Qualls, *From Ruins to Reconstruction*, chapter 3.

36. See, for example, John Barber and Mark Harrison, *The Soviet Home Front, 1941–1945: A Social and Economic History of the USSR in World War II* (London and New York, 1991), 49.

37. Yoram Gorlizki and Oleg Khlevniuk, *Cold Peace.*

38. GARF, f. 8131, op. 38, d. 282, l. 76.

39. GARF, f. 8131, op. 38, d. 449, l. 31. It is notable that Minin complained that some party members had begun attending church during the war. He lamented that the rank and file of the party had succumbed to two ideologicial vices under the pressure of war: religion and bribery.

40. See, for example, GARF, f. 8131, op. 38, d. 282, l. 33.

41. GARF, f. 8131, op. 37, d. 4041, ll. 27–28 (Letter from Safonov, March 8, 1948).

42. See, for example, "Meeting of the Tbilisi (Tiflis) City Party Organization 'Aktiv,'" *Zarya Vostoka,* January 27, 1952, p. 2.

43. Expressing a fundamental principle of Soviet legal theory, the Procurator-General A. Ia. Vyshinskii wrote in a 1939 pamphlet that mass illegality in capitalist societies stems from several factors: the greed of capitalist elites, their exploitation of the working masses, and the poverty that ensues. The October Revolution obliterated the foundations for these evils by crushing the doddering state structures of the old regime, socializing the economy, and creating a society imbued with a new morality. "The very reason for the success of the struggle against crime in the USSR is to be found in the very organization of the new, socialist society, a society that rests upon a new economic basis and is protected from the ulcers and corruptions of the old world by a new, socialist culture, by socialist democracy and socialist law." A. Ia. Vyshinskii, *Crime Recedes in the USSR* (Moscow, 1939).

44. GARF, f. 9492, op. 2, d. 31, ll. 27–28 (May 1944 letter from Butov, Deputy Chief of the Cadres Directorate of the Central Committee, to Malenkov).

45. GARF, f. 9492, op. 2, d. 49, l. 17. The party leadership also expressed similar concerns about raw, untrained party cadres. See Rittersporn, *Simplifications stali-niennes et complications sovietiques: Tensions socials et conflits politiques en U.R.S.S* (Paris, 1988). Cynthia S. Kaplan, *The Party and Agricultural Crisis Management in the USSR* (Ithaca, NY, 1987).

46. GARF, f. 9492, op. 2, d. 49, ll. 206, 234–235.

47. RGASPI, f. 17, op. 136, d. 71, ll. 1–3 (Letter from Safonov to Andreev in Central Committee, Janaury 29, 1949).

48. GARF, f. 9492, op. 2, d. 50, ll. 144–46.

49. In 1946, Rychkov wrote to Molotov at the Council of Ministers asking for 100,000 rubles to be dedicated to improving the material conditions of court employees. (RGASPI, f. 82, op. 2, d. 420, l. 102.) See also GARF, f. 9492, op. 2, d. 58, ll. 3–38.

50. RGASPI, f. 17, op. 136, d. 29, l. 144 (Report of Dukel'skii).

51. GARF, f. 9492, op. 2, d. 49, l. 234 (Letter from Gorshenin to Stalin, no date, but likely from December 1948 based on other documents in file).

52. See GARF, f. 9492, op. 2, d. 41, ll. 92–110, for 1945 correspondence on ranks and uniforms for prosecutors and judicial employees.

53. RGASPI, f. 17, op. 121, d. 612, ll. 72–73. Shvernik supported the proposal in a letter of May 13, 1947. As of January 1, 1947, there were 3,097 employees with ten years or more of uninterrupted service in procuracy agencies. Safonov noted that such medals were commonly awarded to employees of the police force, engineers on railroad transport, and others.

54. GARF, f. 9492, op. 2, d. 41, ll. 92–94 ("Descriptions of uniforms for staff of the courts and the organs of the Ministry of Justice"). Goliakov and Gorshenin both supported the Ministry of Justice's proposal. GARF, f. 9492, op. 2, d. 41, ll. 102–103 and 109–110. See also GARF, f. 9492, op. 2, d. 49, l. 206, for Gorshenin's 1948 request for rewards for long-term service. Several years later (in 1952), the minister of justice lobbied the Presidium of the USSR Council of Ministers for the status of court bailiffs to be elevated. The minister of justice noted that "bailiffs do not have uniforms; they are dressed in ill-fitted clothing, sometimes poorly. This does not provide them with the necessary authority as officials, performing functions such as assigning and carrying out the sentences and decisions of the court regarding the confiscation of property, recovering monetary sums, removing citizens from housing, etc. It is necessary to introduce uniforms for bailiffs." GARF, f. 9492, op. 2, d. 88, l. 56 (Letter from Gorshenin to the Council of Ministers, March 28, 1952).

55. The report of a procuracy commission established to study the causes of bribery also cited these causes as crucial for its spread. GARF, f. 8131, op. 37, d. 4216, ll. 188–91.

56. GARF, f. 8131, op. 37, d. 4216, ll. 188–191 (Sent to Gorshenin). Given the special complexity of bribery cases, only prosecutors with proper qualifications and experience should be assigned to investigate them. For a case of prosecutors failing to turn in one of their own, see the letter from Mokichev to the prosecutor

general of Lithuanian SSR, regarding the case of Kondrat'eva, of November 10, 1947. GARF, f. 8131, op. 38, d. 449, l. 15. (Gorshenin replaced Rychkov as Minister of Justice USSR in January 1948.) For a complaint about party officials' interference in a case of the military tribunal on the railroads, see GARF, f. 9492, op. 2, d. 44, ll. 51–52 (Letter from Rychkov to Zhdanov, August 13, 1947).

57. RGASPI, f. 17, op. 136, d. 167, l. 3. The Commission's report noted that in prerevolutionary Russia, legal and judicial officials were very well compensated. Moreover, in Great Britain, France, and the United States, prosecutors were paid at a level higher than other professionals.

58. GARF, f. 8131, op. 37, d. 4216, ll. 188–191.

59. For such an assertion by the procuracy, see GARF, f. 8131, op. 38, d. 299, l. 42.

60. GARF, f. 8131, op. 38, d. 449, l. 91. A 1949 report from the MVD's economic crime police, OBKhSS, similarly described how difficult it was to uncover major bribery cases. GARF, f. 9415, op. 3, d. 820, l. 21.

61. GARF, f. 9492, op. 2, d. 44, l. 227.

62. Zhdanov was thinking quite a bit about corruption among party members at this time; just three days later, on May 18, the Central Committee Secretariat issued an instruction prohibiting party members from taking "gifts" or other bonuses from factory directors or enterprise employees, or from any government representative. Kees Boterbloem, *The Life and Times of Andrei Zhdanov, 1896–1948* (Montreal, 2004), 478, n. 170.

63. GARF, f. 9492, op. 2, d. 38, ll. 119–22.

64. GARF, f. 8131, op. 37, d. 2817, l. 2.

65. GARF, f. 8131, op. 37, d. 2817, l. 6.

66. Party agencies sometimes aggressively pressured procurators and judges to acquit or go easy on party members accused of abuse of office, especially those who were high-ranking or well connected. On the late Stalin period, see Hooper, "A Darker 'Big Deal.'" For a study of regional party intervention to apply pressure on prosecutors and judges to dismiss or lighten sentences of party members convicted of theft, see Juliette Cadiot, "Equal before the Law? Soviet Justice, Criminal Proceedings against Communist Party Members, and the Legal Landscape in the USSR from 1945 to 1953," *Jahrbücher für Geschichte Osteuropas* 61, no. 2 (2013) 2: 249–269. On friction between the procuracy and party control officials, see Edward Cohn, "Disciplining the Party: The Expulsion and Censure of Communists in the Post-War Soviet Union, 1945–1961," unpublished PhD dissertation (University of Chicago, 2007), esp. 190–199. Legal authorities complained that party organizations interfered in prosecutions of party members. Procuracy archives document cases of interference by local party leaders in the prosecution of criminal cases, including cases of officials arrested for theft of state property or other types of corruption. Procuracy officials complained that *obkom* or *gorkom* secretaries pressured procurators to refrain from bringing cases to court, to dismiss the charges, or to recommend lenient sentences. One 1949 procuracy report, for example, describes party officials' attempts to influence prosecutions. The report, which runs to ninety-seven pages, lists dozens of instances of interference in the year 1948 alone. (GARF, f. 8131, op. 29, d. 11, ll. 133–219.) These are solely cases involving the

railroads. In some cases, local party bosses may have intervened in the prosecution of friends or colleagues. In other cases, however, they may have been arguing that managers guilty of a minor infraction should not be given sentences that would remove them from the workplace for an extended period. Peter Solomon points out that "few local politicians were willing to have key managers removed from their posts." Solomon, *Soviet Criminal Justice,* 429. Officials often protected each other from prosecution, and it follows that many party members seem to have had a sense of impunity that effectively encouraged more extravagant self-enrichment. On the Communist Party's ability to protect its members from criminal prosecution in the 1960s–1970s, see Robert Sharlet, "The Communist Party and the Administration of Justice in the USSR," in *Soviet Law after Stalin,* Part 3 of No. 20, Law in Eastern Europe Series, ed. Donald Barry et al. (Alphen aan den Rijn, Netherlands, 1979).

67. In 1944–1945, the Ministry of Justice Rychkov had accused local judges of "liberalism" for their soft sentencing for this "especially dangerous crime." Rychkov implied that some corrupt jurists were accepting bribes in exchange for light sentences. The Ministry of Justice, Rychkov notes, had responded to this laxity by instructing the courts to intensify the struggle, and emphasizing that lenient sentences could not be assigned in bribery cases. An internal directive letter issued by the People's Commissariat of Justice in December 1944 noted that many judges had "weakened the struggle against bribery" by assigning overly lenient sentences. GARF, f. 9492, op. 1a, d. 314, l. 32 (Directive letter of December 26, 1944). See also the postanovlenie mentioned in GARF, f. 9492, op. 1a, d. 542, l. 14, and Rychkov's telegram of June 7, 1946, demanding that local justice officials implement the conditions of the directive and report back to Moscow with the results. GARF, f. 9492, op. 1, d. 148, l. 1.

68. In 1941, 71.7 per cent of persons convicted of giving bribes were sentenced to prison time. By 1945, that figure had dropped to just under half (48.6 percent). Of those convicted of accepting bribes or acting as an intermediary in 1945, about two-thirds (64.8 percent) were given jail time by judges. GARF, f. 9492, op. 1, d. 478, ll. 30–33. See also GARF, f. 9492, op. 1, d. 514, l. 7.

69. This tendency to punish the givers of bribes less severely is reflected in many documents, including the Ministry of Justice survey of bribery for the year 1945, dated May 20, 1946. GARF, f. 9492, op. 1a, d. 478, ll. 30–33.

70. The procuracy made this point itself. See, for example, GARF, f. 8131, op. 37, d. 4216, ll. 188–91.

71. In December 1946, Rychkov was privately writing that the number of people charged by the police and procuracy was still "extremely insignificant." (GARF, f. 9492, op. 2, d. 38, l. 117.) Rychkov blamed the poor work of police and procuracy employees. He wrote that "I have informed the Procurator-General, comrade Gorshenin, about the unsatisfactory work of the organs of the police and procuracy in exposing bribe takers." Gorshenin was appointed procurator-general of the USSR on November 13, 1943. He left the procuracy in February 1948, and was confirmed as the new minister of justice on May 29, 1948. He served in that capacity until May 31, 1956, and died in Moscow on May 27, 1978.

72. Historians have noted institutional conflict in late Stalinism. Donald Filtzer,

for example, highlights tensions between local procuracy, militia, economic, and party officials in his *Soviet Workers and Late Stalinism*, 177. On institutional conflict among economic agencies in the 1920s, see James Heinzen, *Inventing a Soviet Countryside: State Power and the Transformation of Rural Russia, 1917–1929* (Pittsburgh, PA, 2004).

73. GARF, f. 8131, op. 37, d. 2817, l. 10.

74. GARF, f. 8131, op. 37, d. 2817, ll. 2, 10–11.

75. While the evidence is inconclusive, it is possible that it was the Ministry of Internal Affairs under S. N. Kruglov that pressed most strongly for a special public decree on bribery.

76. The decree would have been issued by the Presidium of the Supreme Soviet of the USSR. The Ministry of Justice drafted at least two versions of an ukaz. The first is dated June 25, 1946, and the second is dated July 4. GARF, f. 9492, op. 1, d. 148, l. 2; f. 8131, op. 37, d. 2817, 1. 17. The first draft called for a three-year minimum sentence for any official (*dolzhnostnoe litso*) guilty of accepting a bribe. If the guilty party occupied a "responsible position," was taking bribes "systematically," or was extorting bribes, a five-year minimum punishment with the confiscation of property was prescribed. Under particularly aggravating circumstances, the draft called for the death penalty and confiscation of property. The giving of bribes, or acting as an intermediary in giving bribes, should be punished by a three-year minimum term. The minimum penalties were raised in the subsequent draft. The draft decree also forbade a person convicted of bribery from ever again occupying an administrative or economic job in any state, cooperative, or social organization or enterprise. GARF, f. 8131, op. 37, d. 2817, l. 17.

77. GARF, f. 9492, op. 2, d. 38, l. 122 (Letter from Rychkov to Zhdanov, May 23, 1946).

78. Although no direct consultation on this question has been found in the archives, the procuracy also apparently opposed creating a special decree, as evidenced by the fact that its editors crossed out a paragraph in the draft Central Committee postanovlenie that called for issuing one. GARF, f. 8131, op. 37, d. 2817, l. 14.

79. GARF, f. 9474, op. 16, d. 294, l. 30. May 17, 1946.

80. Cynthia Hooper also makes the point that the regime did not want to reveal the full extent of the problem of corruption to the public. Cynthia V. Hooper, "A Darker 'Big Deal': Concealing Party Crimes in the Post-Second World War Era," in *Late Stalinist Russia*, ed. Juliane Fürst (London, 2006), 142–163.

81. GARF, f. 9474, op. 16, d. 284, l. 19.

82. Golfo Alexopoulos, "Amnesty 1945: The Revolving Door of Stalin's Gulag," *Slavic Review* 64, no. 2 (2005): 274–306. Peter Solomon, *Soviet Criminal Justice*, 406.

83. For the final version of the secret prikaz "Ob usilienii bor'by so vziatochnichestvom," no. 036/0210/126s, of July 15, 1946, see GARF, f. 8131, op. 38, d. 299, ll. 1–2. For more on internal discussions surrounding the postwar drive against bribery, see James Heinzen, "A Campaign Spasm: Graft and the Limits of the 'Campaign' against Bribery after the Great Patriotic War," in *Late Stalinist Russia*, ed. Juliane Fürst, 123–141. For a discussion of the growing use of regulations

and laws classified as secret to express legal norms, see Peter Solomon, *Soviet Criminal Justice,* 418–426.

84. Rychkov urged placing articles describing bribery trials in the national newspapers *Pravda* and *Izvestiia,* and in local newspapers. GARF, f. 9492, op. 2, d. 38, ll. 119–22. Western newspapers on rare occasions made mention of stories about bribery that appeared in the Soviet press in the second half of 1946. See "Six Moscow Officials Jailed in Campaign to End Bribery and Corruption in Nation," *New York Times,* July 8, 1946.

85. In 1957, N. P. Kucheriavyi noted that no articles in Soviet legal journals had been dedicated to the question of bribery between 1937 and 1957, apart from one article that came out in 1953. Kucheriavyi, *Otvetstvennost' za vziatochnichestvo po sovetskomu ugolovnomu pravu* (Moscow, 1957), 6. He missed several articles published in the year 1946 and one in 1947, but his point that legal journals essentially ignored the topic of bribery is correct.

86. Cynthia V. Hooper has written that police newspapers were not allowed to publish satirical cartoons or feuilletons targeting police officials in the post-war years. "A Darker 'Big Deal,'" 148–150.

87. GARF, f. 5446, op. 51a, d. 5339, ll. 4–5. (Letter from Safonov to Stalin, May 14, 1948.) Several other crimes, such as rape and making homebrew, did see their penalties increased at this time. Peter Solomon, *Soviet Criminal Justice,* 427–428.

88. GARF, f. 5446, op. 51a, d. 5339, ll. 43–44 (Letter from Gorshenin to Stalin, May 19, 1948).

89. For an early draft of a new criminal code sent to Stalin on July 1, 1948, see RGASPI, f. 17, op. 136, d. 19, ll. 50 (Letter to Stalin, signed by Gorshenin, Volin, Safonov, Abakumov, et al.) The draft criminal code was being reviewed by the Supreme Soviet as of October 19, 1949 (l. 65). A legal expert in the Council of Ministers wrote that one reason that bribery was so widespread was because it was "uncovered extremely rarely." GARF, f. 5446, op. 51a, d. 5339, l. 23.

90. In a note of September 8, 1951, the idea of raising penalties for bribery was again said to have been tabled in 1949. GARF, f. 5446, op. 51a, d. 5339, l. 60.

91. For some discussions, see, for example, GARF, f. 9492, op. 2, d. 77, ll. 7–27.

92. GARF, f. 8131, op. 37, d. 4668, ll. 2–3 ob. (Unsigned letter forwarded to Safonov by Bakakin on June 19, 1949). The author complained that this situation was especially aggravating since procuracy staff were mostly well educated, while "the bosses of the MVD and the MGB in rural regions are illiterate, with [only] four to seven years of education." The author claims that he has some higher education and ten years of experience, yet he receives one-third the pay of the regional MVD chief, who earns 2,990 rubles per month. He complains that even the technical secretary of the regional MGB office, a "young girl" with five years of education who only works three or four hours a day, earns more than he does.

93. GARF, f. 5446, op. 80a, d. 9701, ll. 131–34.

94. Safonov complained that a procurator of a raion earns 900 to 1,100 rubles per month, while an inspector earns 600 to 800 rubles.

95. GARF, f. 5446, op. 80a, d. 9701, l. 124. (Safonov sent the same note to Malenkov.) GARF, f. 8131, op. 37, d. 4669, l. 193.

96. GARF, f. 9492, op. 1, d. 269, ll. 96–97.

97. An October 23, 1951 letter from Safonov to Gosplan chair M. Z. Saburov noted that local procuracy offices were under-resourced. (GARF, f. 8131, op. 32, d. 6, ll. 87–88.) Of 5,670 offices, only 966 had their own buildings. Some offices were located in basements, in school buildings, in collective farm buildings, or in hotels. More than 3,000 procuracy offices had no safes for important documents. 2,430 offices had no typewriters, and 2,125 regional procuracy offices had no transportation. Safonov asked for money to supply these things. Judges and procurators essentially argued that they were compelled "by objective conditions" to break the law. Moreover, Safonov complained that the USSR Procuracy's office did not have a single dacha or sanatorium at its disposal. Judges also remained relatively inexperienced. By early 1952, 40 percent of people's judges in the country had less than three years experience, and this was considered a major improvement from earlier years. In the previous two years, the proportion of judges with higher legal education went from 13.5 percent in 1949 to 21 percent in 1951; the proportion with only middle education went from 48.5 percent to 60.8 percent, and with no legal education whatsoever dropped from 17.9 percent to 8.3 percent. (RGASPI, f. 17, op. 136, d. 167, ll. 23–24.) For a discussion of some of the organizational implications of poor, though gradually improving, training of judges between 1945 and 1956, see Yoram Gorlizki, "Anti-Ministerialism and the USSR Ministry of Justice, 1953–56: A Study in Organisational Decline," *Europe-Asia Studies* 48, no. 8 (December 1996): 1279–1318.

98. The campaign also hints at how accusations of corruption began to emerge as a potent tool in the postwar period when allegations of counterrevolutionary crime against officials were on the decline, a topic taken up in more detail in chapters 7 and 8.

99. The Procuracy General pointed out that prosecution of bribery cases was highly uneven in different parts of the Soviet Union; prosecutors worked most "vigilantly" in the RSFSR and the Ukrainian SSR but did very little in most other republics. (GARF, f. 9492, op. 1, d. 514, l. 36.) During the first three quarters of 1946, the courts of the Armenian SSR prosecuted a grand total of four people for bribery; the Kazakh SSR convicted only five; and during those nine months the Turkmen SSR could find only thirteen people who took bribes.

100. GARF, f. 9492, op. 2, d. 49, l. 277.

101. Thus, in the first three quarters of 1946, 322 employees had been fired from the organs of justice and the procuracy for various "amoral infractions, among which bribery enjoys a prominent position." During the same period, 210 judges in the RSFSR had been removed for bribery and abuse of position. Yet only 120 of them (57 per cent) were charged with a crime. In the procuracy agencies, 249 employees were charged with various crimes, with eighty-seven being accused of bribery. GARF, f. 9492, op. 2, d. 44, l. 116.

102. According to procuracy figures, the number of people charged union-wide with accepting bribes dropped each year, from 3,291 people in 1948, to 2,499 in 1949, to 1,903 in 1950, to 1,298 in 1951. The 1951 total amounted to less than half the 1948 number. The quantity of people charged with *offering* a bribe declined in similar fashion: from 3,080 in 1948, to 2,716 in 1949, to 2,003 in 1950,

to 1,863 in 1951. GARF, f. 8131, op. 32, d. 58, l. 115 ("Dokladnaia zapiska o rabote organov prokuratury po delam o vziatochnichestvo za 1951 g." Dated April 7, 1952).

103. GARF, f. 8131, op. 29, d. 27, l. 2.

104. GARF, f. 8131, op. 32, d. 66, l. 2 (Dokladnaia zapiska, addressed to G. N. Aleksandrov, from Khivtsov, procurator of the investigations section, April 17, 1951).

105. GARF, f. 8131, op. 32, d. 58, l. 19. ("Doklad o rabote prokuratury Moskovskoi oblasti po bor'be so vziatochnichestvom vo vtorom polugodii 1951 goda." Sent to Procurator-General Safonov, February 1952.) According to Timothy Colton, *Moscow: Governing the Soviet Metropolis* (Cambridge, MA, 1995), the population of the city of Moscow was approximately four million in 1947 (p. 758).

106. The majority of these cases involved housing problems, typically centering on falsely obtaining permission to live in subsidized housing.

107. GARF, f. 8131, op. 32, d. 58, l. 116 ("Dokladnaia zapiska o rabote organov prokuratury po delam o vziatochnichestve za 1951 g." Dated April 7, 1952).

108. GARF, f. 8131, op. 32, d. 58, l. 116.

109. GARF, f. 8131, op. 32, d. 58, ll. 132–34. "Dokladnaia zapiska," Dated June 1952.

110. GARF, f. 8131, op. 32, d. 58, l. 134.

CHAPTER SIX. INFORMERS AND THE STATE

1. GARF, f. 9415 (OBKhSS), op. 5, d. 87, ll. 241–242. (Letter from D. Lebin to chiefs of OBKhSS administrations of republics, krais, oblast's and cities.)

2. According to respondents in the Harvard Interview Project, one could offer a bottle of vodka or another significant gift to one's supervisor or a worksite engineer to be named a "Stakhanovite," or shock worker. HIP, Schedule A, case no. 119, p. 5. Stakhanovites were eligible for higher rations and valuable bonuses. Vyshinskii warned about bribes disguised as "loans" to officials. See A. Ia. Vyshinskii, *Sudebnye rechi* (Moscow, 1948), 27.

3. Robert Gellately, "Denunciations in Twentieth-Century Germany: Aspects of Self-Policing in the Third Reich and the German Democratic Republic," *Journal of Modern History* 68 (December 1996): 966. This chapter defines an informer as a person who reports violations of the law or misconduct to an agent or official of the government. The terms "informer" and "informant" are used interchangeably. For more detail, see a longer version of this chapter: James Heinzen, "Informers and the State under Late Stalinism: Informant Networks and Crimes against 'Socialist Property,' 1940–1953," *Kritika: Explorations in Russian History* 8, no. 4 (Fall 2007): 789–815.

4. On the 1930s, see David Shearer, *Policing Stalin's Socialism: Repression and Social Order in the Soviet Union, 1924–1953* (New Haven, CT, 2009); Paul Hagenloh, *Stalin's Police: Public Order and Mass Repression in the USSR, 1924–1941* (Baltimore, 2009). For an overview of the administrative history of political policing in the 1920s, see Stuart Finkel, "An Intensification of Vigilance: Recent Perspectives on the Institutional History of the Soviet Security Apparatus in the

1920s," *Kritika* 5, no. 2 (Spring 2004): 299–320. For the example of secret police surveillance of one prominent Ukrainian academic in the 1920s, see Iurii Shapoval, "The Mechanisms of the Informational Activity of the GPU-NKVD: The Surveillance File of Mykhailo Hrushevsky," *Cahiers du monde russe,* 42, no. 2/4 (April–December 2001): 207–230. On state practices of surveillance and information gathering in the early years of Soviet power, seen in a comparative framework, see Peter Holquist, "'Information is the Alpha and Omega of Our Work': Bolshevik Surveillance in its Pan-European Perspective," *Journal of Modern History* 69, no. 3 (September 1997): 415–450.

5. An in-depth treatment of the question of the degree to which the theft of state property was regarded by some people as a "political" or counterrevolutionary crime lies outside the parameters of this chapter. To be sure, certain party officials placed extraordinary pressure on the Ministry of Justice, the procuracy, and the Supreme Court in 1947–1948 to punish defendants with great severity. Rhetoric trumpeting the need to defend state property, and thereby to prevent harm to the interests of the socialist state, overlay the campaign. In late 1952 and early 1953, renewed attention focused especially on politicizing "organized" and "large-scale" theft of state property. As Peter Solomon and others have pointed out, the language treating "political crime" in the 1926 RSFSR Criminal Code was so vague that nearly all crimes could be considered "counterrevolutionary." Article 58 defined a "counterrevolutionary" crime as "any action directed toward the overthrow, subversion, or weakening of the power of worker-peasant soviets . . . or toward the subversion or weakening of the external security of the USSR and the fundamental economic, political, and national achievements of the proletarian revolution." At any time, and for any reason, authorities could temporarily politicize nearly any crime (Solomon, *Soviet Criminal Justice under Stalin,* 28). This "temporary politicization" of the theft of state property occurred with the promulgation of the August 1932 law (the prosecution of which had all but died out by 1933) and in the June 4, 1947 decree, which was highly politicized for approximately one year. Nevertheless, there were a number of distinctions between the June 4, 1947 decree and political crimes. In the postwar Stalin period, theft of state property was handled by the regular police force, and prosecuted by regular procurators in regular courts. The prosecution of property crimes did not bear the hallmarks of "political" cases or trials. Public perceptions of state property and its theft in the Stalin era is an important topic that awaits further research.

6. Statistics compiled by the Supreme Soviet for the years 1940–1955, reprinted in *Istoriia stalinskogo Gulaga: Massovye repressii v SSSR,* vol. 1 (Moscow, 2004), 611–612.

7. Sheila Fitzpatrick, "Signals from Below: Soviet Letters of Denunciation of the 1930s," *Journal of Modern History* 68, no. 4 (December 1996): 831–866; V. A. Kozlov, "Denunciation and its Functions in Soviet Governance: A Study of Denunciations and their Bureaucratic Handling from Soviet Police Archives, 1944–1953," *Journal of Modern History* 68, no. 4 (December, 1996): 867–898. These articles are part of a special issue of the *Journal of Modern History* devoted to practices of denunciation. The introduction to this issue, by Fitzpatrick and Robert Gellately, defines denunciations as "spontaneous communications from individual citizens

to the state (or to another authority, such as the church) containing accusations of wrongdoing by other citizens or officials and implicitly or explicitly calling for punishment" (747).

8. In two significant articles, David Shearer has argued that in the Soviet case individual denunciations and informant networks were less important in 1930s policing than scholars have believed. David R. Shearer, "Social Disorder, Mass Repression, and the NKVD during the 1930s," *Cahiers du monde russe* 42, no. 3 (April–December 2001): 505–534; and "Elements Near and Alien: Passportization, Policing, and Identity in the Stalinist State, 1932–1952," *Journal of Modern History* 76, no. 4 (December 2004): 835–881. With the end of the Great Purges and mass operations in 1938, and continuing during the war, there was a renewed emphasis on direct surveillance, as police and party policy moved away from hauling in certain categories of people during mass police sweeps, and focused instead on regularizing police procedures and operations. Policing again regained its classic reliance on investigation and informant networks. Economic and property crime again became a major target of police investigation. OBKhSS informants and the investigative apparatus emerged as critical elements in strategies for combating property crimes, speculation, and crimes by officials.

9. This is unlike the denunciations analyzed by Sheila Fitzpatrick, V. A. Kozlov, or Cynthia V. Hooper. Cynthia Hooper, "Terror from Within: Participation and Coercion in Soviet Power, 1924–1961," unpublished PhD dissertation (Princeton, NJ, 2003).

10. This informant network usually required an ongoing, personal relationship between the police supervisor and the informant. No letters of denunciation from informants are contained in the accessible archives. Only surviving materials produced by the police, such as reports, instructions, and correspondence, are available.

11. The instruction, signed by Stalin and Molotov, is reprinted in *Istoriia Stalinskogo Gulaga: Massovye repressii v SSSR,* tom 1 (Moscow, 2004), 305–308.

12. GARF, f. 9492, op. 2, d. 49, l. 245. The law recognized as "officials" all persons who were employed in permanent or temporary office in all political, social, and economic organizations of state, including managers of factories or social organizations, collective and state farm chairmen, and union officials.

13. GARF, f. 9415, op. 5, d. 95, ll. 1–2.

14. On the 1947 campaign against theft of socialist property, see especially Peter Solomon, *Soviet Criminal Justice under Stalin,* 410–412; and Yoram Gorlizki, "Rules, Incentives and Soviet Campaign Justice after World War II," *Europe-Asia Studies,* 51, no. 7 (November 1999): 1245–1265, and his "De-Stalinization and the Politics of Russian Criminal Justice, 1953–64," unpublished D. Phil thesis (University of Oxford, 1992).

15. See G. Aleksandrov, "Otvetstvennost' nedonositelei po ukazam Prezidiuma verkhnogo soveta SSSR ot 4 Iunia 1947 g." *Sotsialisticheskaia zakonnost',* 1950, no. 7: 26–33. On December 15, 1952, *Pravda* reported about family members who failed to inform authorities about the thieving and embezzling activities of their relatives, and argued that the family members who failed to inform should themselves be punished.

16. B. A. Kurinov, *Ugolovnaia otvetstvennost' za khishchenie gosudarstvennogo i obshchestvennogo imushchestva* (Moscow, 1954), 111–112.

17. K. P. Gorshenin, *Sotsialisticheskaia zakonnost' na sovremennom etape*, 16–18. This echoed a 1926 speech by Stalin. In his study of East Germany and the Third Reich, Gellately highlights a "denunciatory atmosphere" that existed "in the cultural and social context of an interventionist system that fostered instrumentalist relations between citizens and regime." Robert Gellately, "Denunciations in Twentieth-Century Germany," 949.

18. According to the Ministry of Justice, 3,688 people were convicted in 1948 for nedonesenie (failure to inform) under Article 5 of the June 4, 1947 decree on theft of socialist property. In 1949, that number declined slightly, to 3,483. It fell to 708 in the first quarter of 1950 (GARF, f. 9492, op. 2, d. 63, l. 34). This concept of "failure to inform" is best understood in the context of Soviet legal theory, which held that passive behaviour or inaction, if in the form of a conscious failure to inform the proper authorities (whether the police or one's direct supervisor), is itself a criminal act. A criminal's relatives were not exempt from the obligation to inform. Before the publication of the June 4, 1947 law, failure to inform about theft of state property did not take a specific legal shape. See also G. Aleksandrov, "Otvetstvennost' nedonositelei po ukazam Prezidiuma Verkhovnogo Soveta SSSR ot 4 Iunia 1947 g.," *Sotsialisticheskaia zakonnost'*, 1950, no. 7, 26–33.

19. Political crime was left to the OGPU/GUGB, which in turn dissolved its Economic Department and no longer pursued economic crime. For a discussion of the creation of OBKhSS, see Shearer, "Social Disorder, Mass Repression, and the NKVD," 527–528; and Paul Hagenloh, "Policing Speculation after the Great Terror," unpublished paper presented at the Southern Conference for Slavic Studies, March 2004. Amir Weiner and Aigi Rahi-Tamm have done research on MGB surveillance networks in the Western borderlands. "Getting to Know You: The Soviet Surveillance System, 1939–57," *Kritika* 13, no. 1 (Winter 2012): 5–45. Local NKVD administrations contained OBKhSS branches in cities and rural areas all over the country.

20. This description of the informant network is taken from several OBKhSS documents, cited below, and from a 1935 letter from Ezhov to Stalin describing the network of informants in the political police. RGASPI, f. 671, op. 1, d. 118, ll. 3–10.

21. GARF, f. 9415, op. 5, d. 98, str. 7; d. 95, str. 5; d. 100, str. 4.

22. GARF, f. 9415, op. 5, d. 87, ll. 223–226 ("Orientirovka.").

23. See, for example, the letter from the chief of GURKM NKVD USSR, Police Inspector Galkin, of October 1940. GARF, f. 9415, op. 5, d. 87, l. 65.

24. GARF, f. 9415, op. 5, d. 91, ll. 6–8.

25. GARF, f. 9415, op. 5, d. 91, l. 2 ff. For an overview of the wartime economy, including industrial and agricultural output, supply, and distribution, see John Barber and Mark Harrison, *The Soviet Home Front* (London, 1991).

26. GARF, f. 9415, op. 5, d. 93, l. 7. (MVD *prikazy* of February 13, 1943 (No. 00316) and July 22, 1943 (No. 001020).

27. GARF, f. 9415, op. 3, d. 820, l. 23.

28. GARF, f. 9415, op. 5, d. 91, l. 12. One OBKhSS report noted that even as the informant network grew in 1942/43, the amount of crime remained about the

same. The report attributed this to the fact that much of the "criminal element" already had been drafted or imprisoned. Moreover, the report went on, the women left at the home front were less likely than men to participate in large-scale or organized criminal activity. GARF, f. 9415, op. 5, d. 91, l. 23.

29. James Heinzen, "Korruptsiia v Gulage: Dilemmy chinovnikov i uznikov," in *Gulag: Ekonomika prinuditel'nogo truda,* ed. L. I. Borodkin, P. Gregory, O. V. Khlevniuk (Moscow: Rosspen, 2005); also published as "Corruption in the Gulag: Dilemmas of Officials and Prisoners," *Comparative Economic Studies* 47, no. 2 (June 2005), 456–475.

30. GARF, f. 9415, op. 5, d. 93, l. 8, 10.

31. GARF, f. 9415, op. 3, d. 820, l. 24. A 1950 report argued that, in those enterprises where the potential for economic crime was especially high, the number of informants should increase by two or three times.

32. GARF, f. 9415, op. 3, d. 820, l. 21.

33. GARF, f. 9415, op. 5, d. 95, str. 10. This proportion ranged from 0.4 percent of cases in the Lithuanian SSR and 8 percent in Orel oblast', to 56.3 percent in the Azerbaizhan SSR and 41.7 percent in Gorkii oblast'.

34. Data taken from annual reports of OBKhSS; for 1945–46: GARF, f. 9415, op. 5, d. 95, l. 10; for 1947: GARF, f. 9415, op. 5, d. 98, l. 13; for 1948: GARF, f. 9415, op. 5, d. 100, l. 13. A brief comparison with the two major German informant networks of the twentieth century, those run by the Gestapo and the Stasi, is apt here. Unlike the Gestapo, OBKhSS did not have trouble finding criminals on its own, even without informants. In an evaluation of the relative effectiveness of the OBKhSS informant network, this ability stands as one sign of its success. OBKhSS was not as dependent on informers as the Nazis seem to have been. About two-thirds of OBKhSS cases came from sources other than informers, as opposed to only 25–40 percent of the Gestapo's cases. Information that the Gestapo gathered was typically offered voluntarily by the population. Indeed, the Gestapo complained of being swamped by voluntary denunciations, many of which were false. Robert Gellately, "Denunciations in Twentieth-Century Germany," 951. The cases that Gellately analyzes, however, were all overtly political, whether they concerned race or listening to foreign radio broadcasts. In contrast, the cases discussed in this study are not political crimes, and OBKhSS would not have handled them if they had been. OBKhSS itself actively sought out information about property and official crime, in a manner more similar to that of the Stasi, which was actually rather suspicious of unsolicited information. Like the Stasi networks, OBKhSS channels for gathering information were institutionalized and highly regulated, even bureaucratized. One is struck by how the OBKhSS description of its own informant network resembles typical Soviet discourse about bureaucracy, including language emphasizing the need for efficiency, timeliness, and rationality, while deploring turnover and communication breakdowns.

35. For a 1948 comment that the quality of the informant network "has been extremely unsatisfactory for several years," see GARF, f. 9415, op. 5, d. 98, str. 5–6.

36. GARF, f. 9415, op. 5, d. 87, ll. 65–66.

37. GARF, f. 9415, op. 5, d. 98, str. 9.

38. GARF, f. 9415, op. 5, d. 100, str. 7.

39. This figure can be compared to a figure of approximately 10 percent of Stasi informants who were dropped from the rolls each year. Robert Gellately, "Denunciations in Twentieth-Century Germany," 955. A December 30, 1945 NKVD prikaz ordered the replacement of incompetent agents and informants with new recruits. GARF, f. 9415, op. 5, d. 95, str. 5. Prikaz of NKVD SSSR No. 001558.

40. GARF, f. 9415, op. 5, d. 88, l. 4.

41. GARF, f. 9415, op. 5, d. 100, str. 7. According to David Shearer, several of these criticisms—including the high rates of turnover and the low quality of informants—echo criticisms of NKVD networks made by Ezhov and Iagoda between 1935 and 1939. Shearer, *Policing Stalin's Socialism.*

42. GARF, f. 9415, op. 5, d. 100, str. 7.

43. GARF, f. 9415, op. 5, d. 100, str. 6.

44. Research on the Stasi has drawn the same conclusion. Catherine Epstein, "The Stasi: New Research on the East German Ministry of State Security," in *Kritika* 5, no. 2 (Spring 2004): 321–348.

45. See complaints in GARF, f. 9415, op. 5, d. 95, str. 11–12; GARF, f. 9415, op. 3, d. 820, l. 21.

46. GARF, f. 9415, op. 3, d. 820, ll. 22, 110.

47. GARF, f. 9415, op. 3, d. 820, l. 22.

48. GARF, f. 9415, op. 5, d. 100, l. 2. Officials repeated this sentiment in 1951, lamenting that thieves, bribe takers and speculators had become more cautious and clever. GARF, f. 9415, op. 3, d. 820, l. 22.

49. GARF, f. 9415, op. 3, d. 820, l. 144. The civilian police force (*militsiia*) was transferred from the MVD to the MGB in October 1949. In April 1943, the NKVD had been divided into two independent commissariats: a smaller NKVD, responsible for nonpolitical policing, prison administration and management, the passport system, and so on; and the new Commissariat of State Security (NKGB), responsible for investigating "political crime." Each was renamed "ministry" in 1946, earning the new names MVD and MGB. The two ministries were recombined on March 10, 1953.

50. The literature on popular participation in communist regimes, including informing and denunciations, includes Jan T. Gross, "A Note on the Nature of Soviet Totalitarianism," *Soviet Studies* 34, no. 3 (July 1982): 367–376; and his *Revolution from Abroad* (Princeton, NJ, 1988); Stephen Kotkin, *Magnetic Mountain: Stalinism as Civilization* (Berkeley, CA, 1995), and "The State—Is it Us? Memoirs, Archives, and Kremlinologists," *Russian Review* 61 (January 2002): 35–51; and Cynthia Hooper, "Terror from Within." Sheila Fitzpatrick, "Soviet Letters of Denunciation," and V. Kozlov, "Denunciation and its Functions in Soviet Governance," discuss motivations on the basis of numerous letters of denunciations. It is not clear whether some people informed because they regarded theft of state property as a "political" crime that undermined the foundations of Soviet society and that had "political" consequences. This question deserves further research.

51. Similar to the Gestapo (as Gellately recounts it), OBKhSS does not seem to have cared much about what motivated people to denounce others, as long as they were providing accurate information. For OBKhSS, the key was obtaining information that would lead to arrest and conviction; how and why it reached them seems

to have been of little interest. Gellately's samples indicate that only about a quarter to 30 percent of individual denouncers in the Third Reich evinced any political or ideological ("systemic-loyal") motivation. Robert Gellately, "Denunciations in Twentieth-Century Germany," 944.

52. See, for example, GARF, f. 9415, op. 5, d. 127, l. 50. This was also a leading method for recruiting informants by the political police in this period. See, for example, KGB Lithuanian archives, op. 3, d. 1433, l. 61. Report by Chief of uezd MGB department, Kobelev, sent to General Major Efimov about activities for February 1948, Minister of State Security for Lithuanian SSR. Cynthia Hooper has argued that the MVD developed a "virtual science of blackmail" in the post-war years. "A Darker 'Big Deal,'" 153.

53. GARF, f. 9415, op. 5, d. 93, l. 10–11.

54. GARF, f. 9415, op. 5, d. 87, l. 67.

55. GARF, f. 9415, op. 5, d. 95, str. 8.

56. OBKhSS employees could "converge" with criminals, as was the case in Riazan' oblast' in 1952. GARF, f. 9415, op. 5, d. 124, ll. 11–13.

57. For example, GARF, f. 9415, op. 5, d. 100, str. 6.

58. GARF, f. 9415, op. 5, d. 127, l. 217. ("Obzor nedostatkov i oshibok, dopuskaemykh nekotorymi organami militsiia v rabote s agenturoi.")

59. GARF, f. 9415, op. 4, d. 127, l. 219.

60. GARF, f. 9415, op. 5, d. 127, l. 52. This document cites several similar examples.

61. See, for example, GARF, f. 9415, op. 5. d. 127, ll. 219–220.

62. For an example of these significant risks on a unique stage, see James Heinzen, "Corruption in the Gulag."

63. J. M. Montias and Susan Rose-Ackerman, "Corruption in a Soviet-Type Economy: Theoretical Considerations," in *Economic Welfare and The Economics of Soviet Socialism. Essays in Honor of Abram Bergson,* ed. Steven Rosefielde (Cambridge, UK, 1981), 62.

64. Joseph Berliner, *Factory and Manager in the USSR,* 182–206.

65. GARF, f. 9415, op. 3, d. 820, l. 123. "List of Criminal Cases," by Lebin, September 1951.

66. In one example, OBKhSS complained that managers in the trade administrations conspired with inspectors and lower-level employees to cover up thefts. GARF, f. 9415, op. 5, d. 100, str. 26–27.

67. "Otchet o rabote partkollegii KPK pri TsK VKP (b) za period posle XVIII S"ezda VKP(b)." RGANI, f. 6, op. 6, d. 6, l. 8.

68. GARF, f. 8131, op. 38, d. 299, l. 65. For another case in the Kirov regional housing administration, see GARF, f. 8131, op. 29, d. 27, l. 144.

69. See, for example, Rose-Ackerman, *Corruption and Government,* 92–102; Alena V. Ledeneva, *Russia's Economy of Favours: Blat, Networking and Informal Exchange* (Cambridge, 1998). See also Sheila Fitzpatrick's discussion of blat practices in the 1930s in her "Blat in Stalin's Time."

70. Bauer, Inkeles, and Kluckhohn noted in 1956 the persistence of certain types of "adjustive, informal mechanisms," including theft and bribery, and the state's

apparent willingness to abide them. Raymond A. Bauer, Alex Inkeles, and Clyde Kluckhohn, *How the Soviet System Works* (New York, 1956), 91–93.

71. R. W. Davies, *Soviet History in the Yeltsin Era* (London, 1997), 185.

72. A tolerant attitude among workers toward the theft of state property was noted by the émigré lawyer Boris A. Konstinovsky in 1953 in his *Soviet Law in Action*, 19. It is revealing that the regime issued two decrees the same day: one punishing theft of *socialist* property, and another punishing theft of *personal* property. The two decrees may have served to reinforce this distinction between the two types of property in people's minds.

73. Sheila Fitzpatrick and Robert Gellately, "Introduction," *Journal of Modern History* 68, no. 4 (December 1996): 751.

74. Kozlov, "Denunciation and its Functions in Soviet Governance."

75. The most developed historical literature addressing informant networks in European dictatorships examines the cases of the Gestapo and, even more often, the East German Ministry of State Security, commonly known as the Stasi. Robert Gellately's work on denunciations in the Third Reich and in East Germany forms a useful comparative framework. Gellately does not distinguish, however, between denunciations to the authorities about political crimes and informing on nonpolitical acts. In fact, the Nazi-era racial and foreign-radio cases that Gellately examines all concerned explicitly "political" violations. Thanks to laws providing extraordinary access to the records of both the informants and the informed-upon, the case of the Stasi offers the best view to date of an informant network in a communist state. The Soviet and East German networks were not identical: The Stasi was mainly concerned with setting its informants against the intelligentsia, potential émigrés, and others whom the police perceived as a *political* (rather than economic) danger to the regime. The present study focuses on informants who were to expose those profiting *materially,* irrespective of their real or alleged political orientation. Parallels did exist, nevertheless. In the words of Catherine Epstein, despite the East German Ministry's reputation for omniscience and omnipotence, "The Stasi, it turns out, was often surprisingly inefficient, ineffective, and even counterproductive. As scholars have learned, it performed numerous state functions, but its power remained circumscribed. It dispatched hordes of snoopers, but it often had great difficulty controlling its informants." Catherine Epstein, "The Stasi: New Research," 322.

CHAPTER SEVEN. MILITARY JUSTICE AT THE INTERSECTION OF
COUNTERREVOLUTION AND CORRUPTION

1. Eugene Lyons, *Assignment in Utopia* (New York, 1937), 568. In the 1930s, Ul'rikh kept a special file containing NKVD reports about judges serving on military tribunals who acquitted or modified sentences of people condemned by the NKVD. Peter Solomon, *Soviet Criminal Justice under Stalin*, 248. For documents pertaining to Ul'rikh's role in disciplining judges in military tribunals in the 1930s and 1940s, see A. I. Muranov and R. E. Zviagintsev, *Sud nad sud'iami: Osobaia papka Ul'rikha* (Kazan, 1993).

2. Marc Jansen and Nikita Petrov, "Mass Terror and the Court: The Military Collegium of the USSR," *Europe-Asia Studies* 58, no. 4 (June 2006): 589–602; Michael Parrish, *The Lesser Terror: Soviet State Security, 1939–1953* (Westport, CT, 1996), 207. Ul'rikh also apparently chaired the hearing that judged General Andrei A. Vlasov, a former Soviet officer whom the Germans captured, and who then led an army of Soviet defectors against the Red Army in 1944.

3. Jansen and Petrov, "Mass Terror," 591–592.

4. Jansen and Petrov, "Mass Terror," 600–601.

5. According to a 1934 instruction of the USSR Central Executive Committee. (GARF, f. 9474, op. 16, d. 326, ll. 179–180.) In the wake of the purges, Stalin appointed many of the judges of the Military Collegium to the country's leading legal posts. In 1938, Ivan T. Goliakov was appointed chairman of the USSR Supreme Court, having served on the Military Collegium during the war. Of the Military Collegium judges who served during the purges, only Matulevich, Orlov, and Ul'rikh remained as of 1939. O. F. Suvenirov, "Voennaia kollegiia,"143. After a stint as a member of the Military Collegium, Andrei P. Solodilov became chairman of the RSFSR Supreme Court in October 1937, and a deputy chairman of the USSR Supreme Court in September 1938. Ioan Nikitchenko was appointed a second deputy chair of the USSR Supreme Court, and N. M. Rychkov became the USSR Minister of Justice. Ia. P. Dmitriev was appointed RSFSR Minister of Justice. N. Rychkov served on the three-judge panel of the Military Collegium of the USSR Supreme Court, together with Ul'rikh and I. O. Matulevich (deputy chairman of the Military Collegium), that sat in judgment of the old Bolsheviks Piatakov, Radek, Sokolnikov, and others in the second major show trial, which took place January 23–30, 1937. Matulevich and Ul'rikh presided over the third show trial, sitting in judgment of Bukharin, Rykov, Yagoda, and others. Whether Stalin regarded these judges as especially loyal because they had passed swift and lethal judgment on condemned party leaders, prominent Old Bolsheviks, and the officer corps is unknown. To be sure, Stalin was fond of testing people by making them accessories in the purging of their comrades; these men seem to have passed that test with flying colors.

6. The definitive archive-based study of postwar Stalinist high politics, including Stalin's relationships with his top lieutenants, is Yoram Gorlizki and Oleg Khlevniuk, *Cold Peace: Stalin and the Soviet Ruling Circle, 1945–1953* (Oxford, 2004).

7. For some notable examples, see Ivan Krastev, *Shifting Obsessions* (Budapest, 2004); William A. Clark, *Crime and Punishment in Soviet Officialdom: Combating Corruption in the Political Elite, 1965–1990* (Armonk, NY, 1993); Virginie Coulloudon, "Russia's Distorted Anticorruption Campaigns," in *Political Corruption in Transition: A Sceptic's Handbook,* ed. Stephen Kotkin and András Sajó (Budapest, 2002), and the "Introduction" to Kotkin and Sajó, *Political Corruption in Transition.*

8. On the punishment of collaborators in Ukraine, see Amir Weiner, *Making Sense of War: The Second World War and the Fate of the Bolshevik Revolution* (Princeton, NJ, 2002). On Soviet military justice, see Harold Berman and Miroslav Kerner, *Soviet Military Law and Administration* (Cambridge, MA, 1955); Berman and Kerner, eds., *Documents on Soviet Military Law and Administration* (Cambridge, MA, 1955); Aleksandr E. Epifanov, *Otvetstvennost' gitlerovskikh voennykh*

prestupnikov i ikh posobnikov v SSSR (istoriko-pravovoi aspekt) (Volgograd, 1997); Vanessa Voisin, "Law and the Soviet Purge: Domestic Renewal and International Convergences," in *Dealing with Wars and Dictatorships: Legal Concepts and Categories in Action,* ed. Liora Israël and Guillaume Mouralis (The Hague, 2014).

9. GARF, f. 9492, op. 2, d. 44, ll. 113–118. (Letter from Nikitin, Bakakin, and Lopukhov of Cadres Directorate to Kuznetsov, dated February 14, 1947, located in the archives of the Ministry of Justice.) Kuznetsov had been given leadership of the Cadres Directorate on April 13, 1946 (Khlevniuk et al., eds., *Politbiuro TsK VKP (b),* 32). This summary letter probably was written in response to a report about the case sent to the Central Committee by the USSR Procuracy or by the Chief Military Procuracy (though I have not located such a report in the archives). The records of the Central Military Procuracy and the military courts are located in the Defense Ministry of the Russian Federation, and are off limits to researchers as of the time of this writing.

10. Oleg Khlevniuk et al., eds., *Politbiuro TsK VKP(b) i Sovet Ministrov SSSR, 1945–53* (Moscow, 2002), 36.

11. GARF, f. 9492, op. 16, d. 319, l. 113. The case was originally handled by the Military Procuracy of the Moscow Military Garrison.

12. GARF, f. 9492, op. 2, d. 44, ll. 113–116.

13. GARF, f. 9492, op. 16, d. 319, l. 116.

14. In January 1946, Bakanov was transferred to that higher court (the military tribunal of the Moscow Military District), making it even easier for him to make promises of help with appeals.

15. GARF, f. 9474, op. 16, d. 319, ll. 119–125. Muranov and Zviagintsev state that between 1943 and 1993 only two military judges were convicted of accepting bribes (*Sud nad sud'iami,* 82). While this fact would be difficult to confirm, it reinforces the notion that the military courts had a reputation for the highest probity.

16. The dissident Lev Kopelev was acquitted by a military tribunal of the Moscow Military District in November 1946, but was re-arrested and convicted in March 1947, at which time he was sentenced to three years of hard labor. He eventually served ten years. He wrote in his memoir that he was arrested in April 1945 and charged with "bourgeois humanitarianism" for attempting to stop soldiers from looting homes and raping civilians in East Prussia.

17. GARF, f. 9492, op. 1a, d. 304, l. 44. (Letter from Rychkov to Shcherbakov, January 6, 1944.) The right to appeal was suspended during the war. Harold Berman and Miroslav Kerner, *Soviet Military Law and Administration,* 113; V. P. Maslov and N. F. Chistiakov, *Vopreki zakonu i spravedlivosti.* By late 1943, the Moscow Military Tribunal was hearing very few cases. Several cities formed military tribunals, including Leningrad, Gorkii, Voronezh, and others. Tribunals typically allowed defendants only one day to prepare their defense.

18. The forces of the NKVD also had tribunals, which handled most cases of collaboration. In 1943, tribunals gained the right to try foreigners. During the war, there was a huge increase in the number of sentences. On the treatment of Soviet collaborators and traitors, see Jeffrey Jones, "Every Family Has Its Freak: Perceptions of Collaboration in Occupied Soviet Russia, 1943–1948," *Slavic Review* 64, no. 4 (Winter 2005): 747–770.

19. Ilya Bourtman, "'Blood for Blood, Death for Death': The Soviet Military Tribunal in Krasnodar, 1943," *Holocaust and Genocide Studies* 22 (Fall 2008): 248. The Krasnodar military tribunal that Bourtman describes in detail was established under the auspices of the NKVD. The eleven defendants were Soviet citizens accused of collaborating with the Nazis. Another famous case was the December 1943 trial of German war criminals held in Khar'kov, which resulted in the public hanging of four defendants in the center of the city. Three of the four were German.

20. Tanja Penter, "Collaboration on Trial: New Source Material on Soviet Postwar Trials against Collaborators," *Slavic Review* 64, no. 4 (Winter 2005): 783, citing an FSB publication.

21. A. E. Epifanov, *Otvetstennost' za voennye prestupleniia, sovershenye na territorii SSSR v period Velikoi Otechestvennoi Voiny: 1941–1956* (Vologda, 2005). For statistics on convictions by military tribunals, 1940–1955, see *Istoriia Stalinskogo Gulaga*, vol 1: 618. The death penalty was reinstated on January 13, 1950, in cases of serious political crimes.

22. Peter Solomon, "The USSR Supreme Court," 129. This structure was similar to the Russian Imperial Senate (*Senat*), a prerevolutionary body that also acted as the country's highest court of appeals.

23. There was a substantial degree of imprecision and overlap between various paragraphs of Article 58. See Sergey Kudryashov and Vanessa Voisin, "The Early Stages of 'Legal Purges' in Soviet Russia (1941–1945)," *Cahiers du monde russe* 43, no. 2/3 (2008): 263–296. It is likely that about half a million civilian collaborators were punished. During the war, some were summarily executed by soldiers. Kudryashov and Voisin, "The Early Stages," 267.

24. Tanja Penter, "Collaboration on Trial," 784; Jeffrey Jones, "Every Family Has Its Freak."

25. Weiner, *Making Sense of War*, 108–111, 160–162, 183–187.

26. GARF, f. 9492, op. 2, d. 44, ll. 117–118.

27. No one from the Military Procuracy was convicted in the case.

28. GARF, f. 9492, op. 2, d. 44, ll. 113–116; GARF, f. 9474, op, 16, d. 319, l. 112.

29. GARF, f. 9474, op. 16, d. 319, l. 100.

30. GARF, f. 9474, op. 16, d. 319, l. 101.

31. GARF, f. 9474, op. 16, d. 319, ll. 100–113. Dokladnaia zapiska from Karavaikov addressed to Ul'rikh, August 2, 1947.

32. GARF, f. 9474, op. 16, d. 319, ll. 98–99.

33. GARF, f. 9474, op. 16, d. 319, ll. 98–99.

34. GARF, f. 9474, op. 16, d. 319, l. 116.

35. GARF, f. 9474, op. 16, d. 319, ll. 101–102. Karavaikov had begun work in the Military Collegium only on April 15, 1946 (GARF, f. 9474, op. 16, d. 307, l. 48). In his capacity as a member of the military tribunal of the Moscow Military District, Karavaikov had similarly complained about gross improprieties by prosecutors in cases of counterrevolution as early as October–November 1939. Karavaikov noted the "contrived artificiality of the charges, the bias and non-objectivity of the investigation and a whole array of information that points to the illegal

methods of the investigators, [including] the application of physical coercion [*vozde-istvie*]." Karavaikov had written about the "excesses" of the military procuracy in cases of counterrevolutionary crimes, including coerced confessions, as early as 1940. GARF, f. 9474, op. 16, d. 162, ll. 36–37 ob. (Letter from Goliakov to Malen-kov, January 21, 1940). By 1940, the Central Committee department on courts and procuracy organs requested regular updates from the Supreme Court about its re-views of counterrevolutionary cases. GARF, f. 9474, op. 16, d. 326, l. 61.

36. GARF, f. 9474, op. 16, d. 319, ll. 103–104.

37. GARF, f. 9474, op. 16, d. 319, ll. 104–105.

38. The Secretariat also placed blame for these shortcomings on the Ministry of Justice, which had responsibility for general supervision of all the country's courts, and on the USSR Supreme Court. RGASPI, f. 17, op. 118, d. 131, ll. 162–163. ("On the condition of matters in the Supreme Court." Dated August 20, 1948. Resolu-tion from Central Committee Secretariat sent to Malenkov.)

39. An undercurrent in discussions of leniency in sentencing was the suspicion that some judges accepted bribes in exchange for assigning relatively weak sen-tences, or for overturning sentences on appeal. Solomon argues that crackdowns on bribery were a way of putting pressure on judges not to show leniency. Peter Solomon, *Soviet Criminal Justice*, 381–383. Judges who gave sentences below the maximum level could be accused of having "material interest" in the case.

40. For Ul'rikh's comments on this in 1946, see GARF, f. 9474, op. 16, d. 307, l. 79.

41. Kudryashov and Voisin, "The Early Stages," 283–286, 292. See also Muranov and Zviagintsev, *Sud nad sud'iami*, 77–81. Beginning in 1946, however, the Central Committee attacked the Military Collegium for this practice of reducing sentences, giving it the damning label of "liberalism."

42. As Amir Weiner has also noted, higher military tribunals often overturned the verdicts of lower courts. *Making Sense of War*, 186.

43. Amir Weiner, *Making Sense of War*, 187.

44. RGASPI, f. 17, op. 118, d. 96, ll. 135. (Report of Kuznetsov, sent to Malen-kov, July 8, 1948.) The "Akt" of September 24, 1948 which accompanied the change of leadership in the Supreme Court also made this point. See *Istoriia Sta-linskogo gulaga: Massovye repressii v SSSR*, vol. 1: 608, for data on the length of sentences assigned by military tribunals, 1939–1953. Sentences that were "obvi-ously too light" probably meant sentences of fewer than six years. (GARF, f. 9474, op. 16, d. 322, ll. 32–76.) On the military tribunals, see Tanja Penter, "Collabora-tion on Trial," 782–790. The article is based on material contained in the collec-tions of the U.S. Holocaust Memorial Museum. The Ministry of Justice also issued numerous instructions scolding military tribunals for the "soft" sentences they gave to betrayers of the homeland. Muranov and Zviagintsev, *Sud nad sud'iami*, 83–84.

45. Before August 1948, judges on the Military Collegium had had "a liberal attitude toward enemies," as the new chairman of the Military Collegium, A. A. Cheptsov, claimed in February 1950 (transcript of meeting of Military Collegium party cell). RGASPI, f. 17, op. 136, d. 171, l. 84. On the second and third quarters of 1947, see GARF, f. 9474, op. 16, d. 319, ll. 145–172.

46. The report noted, "In 1947 the Military Collegium reduced punishments

after sentences were assigned by the military tribunals of the army, including those for 1,328 people convicted for betrayal of the homeland [and] 1,066 people convicted for anti-Soviet agitation. This totals 44.4 percent of cases reviewed by the Military Collegium for anti-Soviet agitation." (GARF, f. 9474, op. 16, d. 322, l. 88. Letter from Volin to Stalin, November 1948.) The RSFSR Supreme Court was similarly attacked in an instruction of the Ministry of Justice collegium for failing to supervise the lower courts' handling of cases involving counterrevolutionary crimes. The September 9, 1948 instruction noted that many lower courts assigned light sentences to active collaborators with the German-fascist aggressors, and the RSFSR Supreme Court usually did not challenge those sentences. This also went for crimes against the state (*gosudarstvennye prestupleniia.*) (GARF, f. 9492, op. 1a, d. 516, l. 177.) Located in the files of the Department of Administrative Organs is a handwritten note written by Kuznetsov calling Gorshenin to the Central Committee offices for a conversation. The note is located just before the September 9 prikaz of the USSR Ministry of Justice. RGASPI, f. 17, op. 136, d. 19, l. 81.

47. According to Goliakov, tribunals were applying Article 51 of the RSFSR Criminal Code too liberally. Article 51 allowed for lower penalties for those serving in the military in cases of betrayal of the homeland (Articles 58–1-a and -b and Article 58–3). Goliakov warned Ul'rikh that Article 51 should only be used in extraordinary cases where there were especially mitigating circumstances. (GARF, f. 9474, op. 16, d. 355, ll. 134–134 ob. Letter from Goliakov to V. V. Ul'rikh of November 27, 1947.) According to Volin, in the year 1947 the Military Collegium reduced upon review the sentences of 554 people convicted by local military tribunals for betrayal of the homeland under Articles 58–1-a and 58–1-b. This figure constituted 8.7 percent of appeals reviewed by the Military Collegium (not including death penalty cases). Nikitchenko sent a table to the Central Committee showing that in 1946, 1947, and the first six months of 1948 the Military Collegium had annulled the sentences of 2,742 people. RGASPI, f. 17, op. 136, d. 22, l. 9.

48. GARF, f. 9474, op. 16, d. 322, ll. 53–56. There were also complaints that military tribunals failed adequately to punish the theft of state property. (See GARF, f. 9474, op. 16, d. 319, l. 146, for example.) Interestingly, charges of weakness on the part of the military courts, including the Military Collegium, echoed accusations that Stalin made about the Soviet contingent's role at the Nuremberg trials—that they had disappointed the country by failing to secure the harshest possible sentences for all defendants.

49. In July 1948, Safonov forwarded to Central Committee Secretary Popov an excerpt from the testimony of a lawyer implicating an inspector in the Military Collegium for passing a bribe to an unnamed Military Collegium judge in 1947. (GARF, f. 8131, op. 37, d. 4042, ll. 187–188.) This lawyer told investigators that a colleague of his was representing a certain colonel who had been accused of stealing valuables in Germany and bringing them home to the Soviet Union. The colonel's wife offered 60,000 to 70,000 rubles for a favorable decision in the case. It is not possible to verify the accusation, nor to know whether the judge ever received the money if it is true. See also the case of Anisimova and her lawyer, who appealed to the Military Collegium. GARF, f. 9474, op. 7, d. 984, ll. 1–76.

50. GARF, f. 8131, op. 32, d. 3, ll. 54–55 (Report of Bulaev on Goliakov's alleged crimes, January 19, 1951, likely sent to Safonov).

51. GARF, f. 8131, op. 37, d. 4940, ll. 101–117 (Procuracy materials on the case of L. N. Kudriavtsev). Kudriavtsev admitted to "perhaps, an ethical violation." He said that he pulled two cases for review based on complaints given him by two lawyer friends. (GARF, f. 8131, op. 37, d. 4938, l. 153. Procuracy materials on case of L. N. Kudriavtsev.) For more on the Kudriavtsev case, see GARF, f. 8131, op. 37, d. 4924. A late-1949 trial of judges on the RSFSR Supreme Court also indicates that the procuracy was still looking to indict employees of the Military Collegium. Note the testimony of the intermediary/phony lawyer Mushailov, who was repeatedly asked by the presiding judges about his allegedly corrupt connections with Military Collegium staff, including Mazur, Serdiuk, and Khokhlov (GARF, f. 9474, op. 7, d. 984).

52. The best evidence indicates that Kudriavtsev was not guilty of the charges lodged against him. The only witnesses who testified against Kudriavtsev were accused of slander by several other defendants and witnesses. Kudriavtsev's appeals and other pertinent information can be found in GARF, f. 8131, op. 37, d. 4938. In an October 1953 complaint addressed to Procurator-General Rudenko, Kudriavtsev compared his leading accuser, a female lawyer, to a female doctor who accused the Kremlin doctors of conspiring to kill Stalin in the so-called "Doctor's Plot." GARF, f. 8131, op. 37, d. 4938, l. 173.

53. This "major political error" by Karavaikov was singled out by the Cadres Directorate in its scathing July 8, 1948 report concerning the political reliability of the cadres of the USSR Supreme Court. (The Supreme Court Plenum annulled the reduced sentence.) (RGASPI, f. 17, op. 118, d. 96, l. 136.) By July of 1948, the Cadres Directorate had added a new charge against Kopelev—The "American spy," a certain Suchkov, had spoken out in his defense. (RGASPI, f. 17, op. 118, d. 96, l. 136.) On the Kopelev case, see also the letter from Goliakov to the Party Control Commission of the Central Committee, January 5, 1948. GARF, f. 9474, op. 16, d. 322, l. 1. Judge Orlov also sat on the three-judge panel.

54. It is not clear whether the Politburo took up the question formally. (RGASPI, f. 17, op. 116, d. 348, pt. 79. Protocols of Orgbiuro/Secretariat of April 24, 1948.) Karavaikov appears to have avoided arrest, however, at least for the time being. On December 19, 1946, Karavaikov had received a strict reprimand from the KPK for his role in obtaining trophy goods when he was the chair of a military tribunal for a group of occupation forces in Germany. He had allegedly "made a deal with a German—he bought a piano, home furnishings, and two electric refrigerators, and he obtained a receipt for the goods he acquired" (GARF, f. 9474, op. 16, d. 294, l. 51). Of course, many officers acquired trophy goods in Germany; most were never prosecuted. Such accusations were a staple of postwar disciplinary proceedings against party members who had spent time working abroad.

55. Pt. 109 on that day's agenda. (Referred from S-t from April 30, 1948, pr. No. 348, p. 79-gs.)

56. In the case of the alleged Trotskyist Kopelev, the Cadres Directorate implicated General-Major of Justice Orlov in addition to Karavaikov. RGASPI, f. 17, op. 118, d. 96, l. 136.

57. RGASPI, f. 17, op. 118, d. 96, l. 136.

58. Francine Hirsch has considered the Soviet delegation's role in the formulation of the indictment at the Nuremberg tribunal. "The Soviets at Nuremberg:

International Law, Propaganda, and the Making of the Postwar Order," *American Historical Review* 113 (June 2008): 701–730. Born in 1895, Nikitchenko died in 1967.

59. GARF, f. 8131, op. 37, d. 4938, l. 168. The chief of the Department of Judicial Supervision of the USSR Supreme Court, Umanskaia, was asked at her July 1949 trial if she "knew anything bad" about Nikitchenko. The former USSR Supreme Court judge Chursina (a highly unreliable source) testified at her closed trial that Nikitchenko's assistant had informed her that Nikitchenko had illicitly "arranged" several cases. GARF, f. 9474, op. 7, d. 824, ll. 23, 183.

60. GARF, f. 8131, op. 37, d. 4938, ll. 152–153, 168. "Complaint" from L. N. Kudriavtsev to USSR Procurator General Rudenko, September 12, 1953.

61. RGASPI, f. 17, op. 118, d. 96, l. 135. Chursina alleged that Nikitchenko had an affair with the lawyer Orlova while they were both at Nuremberg, and that this made Nikitchenko susceptible to accepting bribes through Orlova. (GARF, f. 9474, op. 7, d. 824, l. 183.) That Chursina, who was exposed in telling multiple lies about high court judges, would make this claim is further evidence that prosecutors were pressuring witnesses to provide incriminating evidence against Nikitchenko, Ul'rikh, Dobrovol'skii and other members of the Military Collegium. Nikitchenko had been one of the presiding judges at one show trial (the August 19–24, 1936 trial of Zinov'ev and Kamenev et al.). Chursina also alleged at her trial that an employee of the Military Collegium had told her that Ul'rikh took bribes, along with many other unnamed employees of the Collegium. GARF, f. 9474, op. 7, d. 824, l. 183.

62. GARF, f. 9474, op. 16, d. 322, l. 94. (Letter from Volin to Stalin, October 26, 1948, "On measures to improve the work of the Supreme Court USSR.")

63. At the time of his removal, Nikitchenko was chairman of the Railways Collegium of the USSR Supreme Court. (GARF, f. 9474, op. 16, d. 337, l. 31.) The Politbiuro discussed Nikitchenko's fate on June 14, 1949 (Protocol of Secretariat meeting from June 10, 1949, pr. No. 437, p. 267-s).

64. The details of Bukanov's biography are based on his testimony at trial on September 19, 1951, the transcript of which can be found in GARF, f. 9474, op. 7, d. 960 (here at ll. 314–15). See also GARF, f. 9474, op. 16, d. 144, l. 29 (Letter from Goliakov to Andreev at the Central Committee, February 7, 1939).

65. This damning information came from Shevchenko, the former judge of the RSFSR Supreme Court, following his arrest for accepting bribes earlier that year. Shevchenko, an old friend and drinking buddy of Bukanov, was undergoing interrogation in prison. GARF, f. 9492, op. 2, d. 50, ll. 359–360 (Joint letter from Safonov and Gorshenin of November 4, 1948, to the chief of the Department of Administrative Organs); GARF, f. 8131, op. 37, d. 4044, ll. 145–146 (Letter to Kuznetsov, October 6, 1948).

66. GARF, f. 9474, op. 7, d. 960, ll. 195–200.

67. For a reference to Bukanov's first trial (the transcript of which has not been found), see GARF, f. 9474, op. 16, d. 960, l. 195.

68. GARF, f. 9474, op. 7, d. 960, l. 332.

69. GARF, f. 9474, op. 7, d. 912, ll. 181 ff. The chair of the Moscow City Court, Vasnev, also complained bitterly about physical coercion. GARF, f. 9474, op. 7, d. 800, ll. 94–99 (Letter from Vasnev to Chair of the USSR Supreme Court, A. F.

Gorkin, November 26, 1959). At trial, Karakhanov alleged that Dvorkin told him, "You have fallen into my hands and you won't tear yourself loose. I, Dvorkin, am alone in the USSR and whatever Dvorkin says will be done by the court." Karakhanov also testified, "Dvorkin threatened to arrest my family, my children." GARF, f. 9474, op. 7, d. 855, l. 165 (Trial of Vasnev et al.).

70. GARF, f. 9474, op. 7, d. 960, l. 336.

71. Judges in these high court cases understood that the procuracy could arrest members of their families. For a similar threat in the case of RSFSR Supreme Court justice Murzakhanov, see GARF, f. 9474, op. 7, d. 958, l. 90.

72. GARF, f. 9474, op. 7, d. 960, l. 337. The Military Collegium judge Bukanov made almost the same observation at his trial: "The investigator wanted to find a representative person who occupied a major post and place him at the head of a bribery [conspiracy]." Later, he said, "Investigators wanted to place a major figure at the head of a group of petty bribe takers and they 'set a trap' for me, using the accusations of other people." GARF, f. 9474, op. 7, d. 960, ll. 319 and 355.

73. GARF, f. 9474, op. 7, d. 912, l. 237.

74. GARF, f. 9474, op. 7, d. 960, l. 356.

75. This question is, of course, quite pertinent. As a member of the Military Collegium, one would imagine that Bukanov understood perfectly the role that some party leaders would have played in the trial of high-ranking judges.

76. Report of Kuznetsov, sent to Malenkov, July 8, 1948. RGASPI, f. 17, op. 118, d. 96, l. 134.

77. RGASPI, f. 17, op. 118, d. 96, l. 134. Kassel' said she had worked in Lenin's Secretariat.

78. RGASPI, f. 17, op. 118, d. 96, ll. 133–134.

79. As early as April 9, 1945, personal tensions among members of the Military Collegium of the Supreme Court had been reported by Bakakin, a deputy department head of the Cadres Directorate, who described to Central Committee Secretary Malenkov "the very unhealthy environment in the USSR Military Collegium of the Supreme Court." Ul'rikh allegedly had gotten drunk at a party at his dacha where many members of the Military Collegium and their wives were present. Ul'rikh cursed at Orlov, a fellow justice on the Military Collegium. As Orlov was leaving the room, Ul'rikh called him an idiot and referred to his "Yid face." He then turned to everyone in the room and said, "I am the the chief here; if I want I can throw everyone out." He again used the words "Yid face" to describe some of the victims of the purge trials he presided over in the 1930s, including Ezhov. Nikitchenko and several members of the Military Collegium, including Bukanov, Orlov, and Klimin, had earlier complained to the Cadres Directorate that there were poor relations among the Military Collegium's members, which Ul'rikh only made worse. They complained that Ul'rikh was a heavy drinker who was in relationships with two different women. Bakakin stated that this situation has taken on "an ugly, anti-party form." "All this undermines the authority of comrade Ul'rikh, as the leader of the Collegium, in the eyes of his subordinates." Malenkov forwarded Bakakin's report to Molotov, recommending that a commission be formed to address the problem. Molotov agreed, though in the documents there is no indication about what occurred. Ul'rikh remained in his position for more than three more

years. GARF, 9474, op. 16, d. 283, ll. 48–49 (Letter from Bakakin in Cadres Directorate to Kuznetsov).

80. Yoram Gorlizki and Oleg Khlevniuk, 114–116.

81. RGASPI, f. 17, op. 136, d. 22, l. 19. Ul'rikh pressed Dobrovol'skii for the
information for a long time and finally went to find the information himself. Ul'rikh
adds that Minister of Justice Rychkov hired Dobrovol'skii without clearing it with
him in May 1946, and asks that Dobrovol'skii be fired. Ul'rikh had had conflicts
with Dobrovol'skii in the past. RGASPI, f. 17, op. 136, d. 22, ll. 1–3.

82. RGASPI, f. 17, op. 136, d. 22, ll. 14–18. A November 5, 1948 memo accompanying this letter to the Central Committee archive states that Ul'rikh's pleading
letter had not gone far enough: "The former deputy chair of the Supreme Court
USSR, comrade Ul'rikh, presented to the Central Committee a note in which he
tries to show only isolated flaws in the work of the Supreme Court USSR, without
touching on the serious political mistakes tolerated in the work of the Military
Collegium of the Soviet Union under his direction."

83. GARF, f. 9474, op. 7, d. 824, l. 183. The Main Military Procurator of the
Soviet Army, Afanas'ev, was removed in 1950, charged with many of the same
transgressions—in particular, showing weakness in prosecuting traitors and counterrevolutionaries. RGASPI, f. 17, op. 136, d. 175, ll. 11.

84. GARF, f. 9474, op. 7, d. 960, ll. 202–203. Bukanov's trial was held in secret
in November 1950. Prosecutors also continued to try to find compromising evidence against the Military Collegium judge Dobrovol'skii. At the bribery trial of
USSR Supreme Court judge Solodilov's colleagues in July 1949, the presiding judges
asked one defendant whether Dobrovol'skii had taken bribes. GARF, f. 9474, op. 7,
d. 824, l. 27.

85. Yoram Gorlizki and Oleg Khlevniuk, *Cold Peace*, 110–111. See also Oleg
Khlevniuk, "Kreml'—Tbilisi: Chistki, kontrol' i problemy gruzinskogo natsionalizma v pervoi polovine 1950-x godov," paper presented at workshop on "Georgian
Nationalism and Soviet Power," Joensuu, Finland, August 27, 2012; and Khlevniuk,
ed, *Politbiuro TsK VKP (b) i Sovet Ministrov SSR,* 167–168, 354–355.

86. On Brezhov, see William A. Clark, *Crime and Punishment in Soviet Officialdom;* Virginie Coulloudon, "Russia's Distorted Anticorruption Campaigns."

87. David Shearer, "Crime and Social Disorder"; David Hoffman, *Stalinist Values,* 176–179. For mention of a Purge-era case in which party investigators linked
officials' wasteful spending on banquets with accepting bribes for "Trotskyist" activities, see Hoffman, 76.

88. During the party purges of the 1930s, the Military Collegium had sentenced
several of its own former members to death as traitors, including Valentin Trifonov,
Ul'rikh's predecessor as chairman. Jansen and Petrov, "The Military Collegium of
the USSR," 599.

CHAPTER EIGHT. THE DEATH OF A JUDGE

1. Coincidentally, the day of Solodilov's suicide was the one-year anniversary
of issuance of the extraordinary June 4, 1947 decree condemning the theft of state

property, the law that set the stage for the tremendous pressure on the legal system that played a major role in this scandal.

2. A. P. Solodilov and G. N. Amfiteatrov, *Pravo nasledovaniia v SSSR* [*The Right of Inheritance in the USSR*] (Moscow, 1946).

3. GARF, f. 9474, op. 16, d. 283, ll. 17–17 ob. (Letter from Goliakov to Malenkov, June 11, 1945.)

4. GARF, f. 9474, op. 7, d. 797, l. 97.

5. Figures calculated from physical finding aid of trials overseen by the Supreme Court's Military Collegium (GARF, f. 9474, seventh *opis'*).

6. In his 1982 memoir, Konstantin Simis notes in passing that, when he worked as a young lawyer in Moscow, he heard legends for years about bribe-taking judges in the Supreme Court of the Russian Republic (RSFSR) in the late 1940s and 1950s. (He was not more specific about the dates.) These rumors circulated in legal circles. He certainly could not have known whether or not all the accused were guilty. Nevertheless, he assumes with a very healthy dose of exaggeration, "The presumption was: every functionary of the legal system is infected by corruption." Simis, *USSR: The Corrupt Society* (New York, 1982), 117. It was Simis who first alluded to the cases in print. He knew none of the details, mentioned no names, and referred to the story only fleetingly. He writes about the rumors as a tidbit of anecdotal evidence that corruption in the Soviet courts stretched back to the time of postwar Stalinism, or so legal professionals in the late 1950s and 1960s whispered among themselves. In his magisterial study of the Stalinist legal system, Peter Solomon writes briefly that several high court judges were indeed charged with bribery and arrested in 1948. He notes that the scandal caused a shake-up in the leadership of the USSR Supreme Court and its Military Collegium. Peter Solomon, *Soviet Criminal Justice under Stalin,* 381–382. Solomon writes about these allegations in the context of his larger focus on the pressure brought upon the courts after the war by procuracy and party officials intent on ensuring that judges assigned the maximum sentences allowable. Solomon thus places the cases in the context of the party's campaign against acquittals and its counterproductive obsession with secrecy. See Peter Solomon, "The Case of the Vanishing Acquittal: Informal Norms and the Practice of Soviet Criminal Justice," *Soviet Studies* 39, no. 4 (October 1987): 531–555; and his *Soviet Criminal Justice under Stalin,* chapter 11. The third and final brief published reference to the high court scandals of which I am aware appeared in an article in the contemporary Russian press, published in 2008 in the business supplement of the newspaper *Kommersant.* (Evgenii Zhirnov, "Chleny Verkhovnogo suda brali vziatki" ["Members of the Supreme Court Took Bribes"] *Vlast',* August 11, 2008.) It summarizes several cases of bribery among judges over the course of the entire Soviet period. The article's purpose is sensationalism. The author drops Solomon's cautious approach to the documents and ignores any larger perspective. Much like Simis, the author uses the article as evidence that the Soviet court system and nearly everyone who ever worked in it were entirely corrupt. The author of this journalistic piece takes every document at face value, accepting every word of the indictments as fact. He quotes parts of two documents produced by procuracy investigators, though he says nothing about their provenance. On the

late Stalin period, the article cites RGASPI, f. 17, op. 118, d. 131, ll. 162–163 (a Central Committee resolution of August 1948), and one document on a case of alleged bribery in the Bashkir Supreme Court.

7. Important documents pertaining to these cases are spread out across several archives and collections, including the USSR Procuracy, the Ministry of Justice, and the USSR and RSFSR Supreme Courts. RGASPI also contains critical documentation sent to, and produced by, party agencies. The procuracy sent reports of its investigations to the Politburo, the Secretariat of the Central Committee, and the Orgbiuro, all of which composed their own reports on the scandal and sent them to Stalin and/or the Politburo, which put the situation on its agenda several times. Some of the most sensitive material is stored in the top-secret Osobaia papka (Special Portfolio) of the Politburo. Files of the Department of Administrative Organs of the Central Committee (RGASPI, f. 17, op. 136) were briefly open when the Soviet Union collapsed, then closed until 2009, when I was given limited but useful access. These cases represent the only time that the word "bribery" (*vziatochnichestvo*) appears in the published indices to the Politburo protocols for the period between 1930 and 1953. *Politbiuro Ts RKP(b)-VKP(b). Povestki dnia zasedanii. Tom III. 1940–1952. Katalog* (Moscow 2001).

8. *Politbiuro TsK VKP*, 59–60.

9. Central Committee departments were renamed and reorganized by a July 10, 1948 postanovlenie of the Central Committee. (*Politbiuro TsK VKP(b) i Sovet Ministrov SSSR, 1945–53*, 60–61.) "The fundamental task of the otdely is the selection of cadres for the corresponding branches [of government] and the verification of the implementation of Central Committee and government decisions" (61).

10. The Moscow City Court heard appeals both in *nadzor* (supervision) and cassation.

11. GARF, f. 9474, op. 7, d. 855, ll. 53–55 (Trial of Vasnev, Chursina, et al., May 24–June 11, 1949). During the war, Bakanov had known many employees of the Moscow City Court when it temporarily functioned as the military tribunal for the city of Moscow. Khalin had been a member of the Moscow Military Tribunal during the war.

12. RGASPI, f. 17, op. 118, d. 151, l. 133 (Letter from Safonov to Malenkov, August 31, 1948).

13. GARF, f. 9492, op. 2, d. 50, ll. 32–35 (Letter from Gorshenin to Central Committee Secretary A. A. Kuznetsov, May 8, 1948). By December 1948, eleven lower court judges in Moscow's city courts had been arrested for bribery. GARF, f. 8131, op. 37, d. 4045, ll. 380–382 (December 29, 1948 letter from Safonov to Popov at the Central Committee). Each of them eventually was convicted and sentenced to ten years in prison. RGASPI, f. 17, op. 118, d. 151, l. 133.

14. August 28, 1948 letter from Lopukhov to Kuznetsov. RGASPI, f. 17, op. 136, d. 29, l. 44. See also GARF, f. 9492, op. 1a, d. 527, l. 142; RGASPI, f. 17, op. 118, d. 151, l. 135.

15. V. V. Gutorkina was convicted of accepting bribes on June 11, 1949, and sentenced to ten years in prison. Gutorkina pled guilty at trial, saying that she took 10,000 rubles through the lawyer Senderov. Like many defendants at trial and in depositions, she testified that she made mistakes under the poisonous influence of

her colleague, Chursina. Her husband wrote to the Party Control Commission in 1952, asking that she be released early because she was ill. The request was denied. Her fate is unknown. RGANI, f. 6, op. 6, d. 1609, ll. 118–119 (Letter from Kalistratov, responsible controller for KPK, to Skiriiatov, March 1952).

16. GARF, f. 9474, op. 7, d. 855, l. 2.

17. Several defendants accused Chursina of being "sick" or "crazy." She described herself as "eccentric." GARF, f. 9474, op. 7, d. 855, l. 45. The transcript of the trial of Moscow City Court employees can be found in GARF, f. 9474, op. 7, d. 855.

18. Protocol of the interrogation of F. P. Umanskaia, June 7, 1947. GARF, f. 9474, op. 7, d. 803, l. 3, 8.

19. During interrogations and at her closed trial, Chursina implicated the leaders of several high courts, including the deputy chair of the USSR Supreme Court, Solodilov; another justice of the USSR Supreme Court, Tsvetkov; a deputy chair of the RSFSR Supreme Court, Davydova; a Military Collegium secretary, Kudriavtsev; the chairman of the Moscow City Court, Vasnev; and others. Chursina also provided evidence of bribery that was later shown to be false in cases of at least two high court judges: the chair of the USSR Supreme Court Goliakov (who was never charged); and V. V. Bukanov of the Military Collegium (who was eventually acquitted). RGASPI, f. 17, op. 118, d. 151, l. 134.

20. GARF, f. 9474, op. 7, d. 855, l. 2; Viktor Kravchenko, *I Chose Freedom: The Personal and Political Life of a Soviet Official*, 355–356.

21. GARF, f. 9474, op. 7, d. 855, especially ll. 45–54. While one cannot be sure in retrospect, of course, there is a large amount of evidence that Judge Vasnev was not guilty of the charges for which he was tried. Vasnev claimed that he had been falsely denounced by two judges who had confessed to taking bribes, Chursina and Gutorkina, and who had wanted to lighten their own sentences. Vasnev protested his innocence in a letter to Stalin after his conviction, arguing that Chursina had lied about him to investigators because she hoped to improve her conditions in confinement (RGANI, f. 6, op. 6, d. 1608, ll. 7–21. Letter from Vasnev to Stalin. Received December 6, 1949). See also Vasnev's 1960 appeal to the USSR Supreme Court in GARF, f. 9474, op. 7, d. 857, ll. 94–108. At trial, Vasnev said that Chursina was slandering him because he had refused to marry her. Bribery charges against him were eventually dropped for lack of evidence, though he was convicted of abuse of office. Vasnev wrote several angry letters protesting the way his case was handled and insisting that he was not guilty. He pointed out that literally dozens of the original charges against him were based almost exclusively on uncorroborated hearsay provided by his colleagues on the bench, Chursina and Gutorkina.

22. See Vasnev's letter of appeal: GARF, f. 9474, op. 7, d. 800, l. 100; and his trial: GARF, f. 9474, op. 7, d. 855, especially l. 312. Vasnev's appeals seem to have resonated within the Department of Administrative Organs after Kuznetsov's removal in 1949. A major investigation of the claims in Vasnev's appeal was undertaken, beginning in November 1949 and lasting until May 1950.

23. *Sotsialisticheskaia zakonnost'*, no. 4 (1945): 4.

24. Vasnev was accused of involvement in the case of a certain Chertov, who in 1943 had been accused of grand theft of manufactured goods. In exchange for a bribe, Vasnev supposedly re-qualified the charge to the much less serious crime of

"abuse of office." (RGASPI, f. 17, op. 118, d. 151, ll. 132–134.) Chertov was charged with violating the theft law of August 7, 1932.

25. RGASPI, f. 17, op. 136, d. 29, l. 44. August 28, 1948 letter from Lopukhov to A. A. Kuznetsov, citing L. R. Sheinin and Gorshenin. According to V. N. Safronova, Chursina told her that Vasnev had hit her in the face during a quarrel. GARF, f. 9474, op. 7, d. 801, l. 54 (Protocol of interrogation of Safronova, June 16, 1948, Butyrsk prison).

26. GARF, f. 8131, op. 37, d. 4666, ll. 175–185 (Letter from Safonov to Bakakin at Department of Administrative Organs, February 16, 1949).

27. GARF, f. 8131, op. 37, d. 4666, l. 176.

28. GARF, f. 8131, op. 37, d. 4666, l. 179. Vasnev later wrote to Stalin, "At first, [the procuracy investigator] Dvorkin slandered me as an organizer, heading a group of bribe takers in the Moscow City Court, and then simply as a bribe taker, and then, as these accusations were disproved and Dvorkin and the USSR Procuracy were put in a difficult position, he had to artificially create a case under Article 109 [abuse of office] and Article 114" (rendering an improper legal decision). "As a result," he went on, "I am a ruined man" (RGANI, f. 6, op. 6, d. 1608, l. 15). He wrote that once the USSR Procuracy could find no evidence that Vasnev took bribes, to avoid the embarrassment of releasing a person they had sought permission to be arrested, they found other accusations to pour on him, including that he was a drunk and a morally corrupt person. (GARF, f. 9474, op. 7, d. 855, l. 317.) Vasnev wrote to Stalin that Gutorkina and Chursina should be charged under Article 58 as anti-Soviet wreckers for their false accusations. He writes that Chursina's husband was German, and he may have been an "enemy." "My arrest and my conviction can serve as a shining example of the destruction of an honest and innocent man, devoted to his Motherland, party and government." (RGANI, f. 6, op. 6, d. 1608, l. 18.) At his trial, Vasnev told the court that the first time he met the procuracy investigator Dvorkin, before a party meeting about Vasnev, "he looked at me as at a person who must be destroyed, and quickly." (GARF, f. 9474, op. 7, d. 855, l. 316.) Dvorkin told the Department of Administrative Organs that Vasnev had to be kept in solitary confinement during the investigation because of the "poor quality reaction from the criminal element" in the prison's general population who would be in danger of violence if they found out that Vasnev was a judge. "This could end extremely sadly for Vasnev." (RGASPI, f. 17, op. 136, d. 70, l. 187. Letter from Dvorkin to Gromov, April 29, 1950.) Vasnev interrupted the trial with shouts that Chursina was lying. (See, e.g., f. 9474, op. 7, d. 855, l. 37.)

29. GARF, f. 8131, op. 37, d. 4666, l. 180–181.

30. GARF, f. 9474, op. 7, d. 855, l. 47; RGASPI, f. 17, op. 118, d. 151, ll. 133–135.

31. GARF, f. 8131, op. 37, d. 4666, ll. 179–180.

32. Another judge who appears to have been incorrectly accused (in 1950) was the chair of the Gulag court of Moscow oblast', Aleksei A. Kupriianov. As had been the case with the Bukanov, he was removed from his position after the initial wave of arrests in 1948. The USSR Procuracy accused Kupriianov of accepting a wardrobe in December 1946 from a certain E. M. Guseva. He was further alleged to

have accepted a meal in the summer of 1947 from Chursina and Migunova. GARF, f. 9492, op. 2, d. 67, l. 179; and d. 68, ll. 110–113 (Spravka from Skorokhodov, hand-dated July 24, 1950). For a summary of the pertinent testimony of Chursina implicating Kupriianov, dismissed by the Ministry of Justice as false, see GARF, f. 9492, op. 2, d. 67, ll. 180–183. After reviewing the material in the possession of the USSR Procuracy, Gorshenin argued in an April 5, 1950 letter to Gromov at the Department of Administrative Organs that the procuracy's request to charge Kupriianov with a crime was "groundless and premature" (GARF, f. 9492, op. 2, d. 67, l. 181). Kupriianov categorically denied the charges against him. Implying that witnesses were lying, Gorshenin called for "close scrutiny" of the testimony of Chursina, Guseva, Migunova, and the witness Pimenov.

33. GARF, f. 9492, op. 2, d. 50, ll. 32–35 (Letter from Gorshenin to Kuznetsov).

34. GARF, f. 8131, op. 37, d. 4669, ll. 2–10 (Letter from Safonov to Party Control Commission, followed by report, June 1949).

35. See RGASPI, f. 17, op. 118, d. 151, l. 132.

36. For a February 16, 1949 USSR Supreme Court determination on the situation in the RSFSR Supreme Court, see GARF, f. 8131, op. 37, d. 4669, l. 12–13 (Finding signed by Bitiukov). In addition to its ongoing investigations in several other courts, the procuracy immersed itself in the situation in the RSFSR Supreme Court. (RGASPI, f. 17, op. 136, d. 29, l. 55.) The RSFSR Supreme Court judge Pashutina testified that she told Bakakin, a deputy in the Central Committee apparatus, about the suspicious activities of Shevchenko and Murzakhanov. GARF, f. 9474, op. 7, d. 1025, l. 83.

37. For the transcript of Pashutina's 1951 trial, see GARF, f. 9474, op. 7, d. 1025. For the Politburo discussion of her case, see the materials for the Politbiuro protocols from August 22, 1950, pt. 113. RGASPI, f. 17, op. 163, d. 1558.

38. RGASPI, f. 17, op. 136, d. 29, l. 111 (Letter from Lopukhov to Tekhsekretariat, October 19, 1948). It is not clear whether the procuracy later charged Vasil'ev with bribery.

39. RGASPI, f. 17, op. 136, d. 29, l. 99. Aleksandr Mikhailovich Nesterov was born in 1905 in Tiumen' province, and studied law in Leningrad for two years from 1937 to 1939. He became head of the Altai krai court in 1940. Nesterov was appointed chairman of the RSFSR Supreme Court on May 4, 1945.

40. Politburo meeting of June 13, 1949, pt. 214.

41. RGANI, f. 6, op. 2, d. 132, ll. 37–48. The KPK heard Nesterov's appeal of his expulsion from the party in March 1951. The appeal was denied. RGANI, f. 6, op. 2, d. 199, ll. 18–23.

42. GARF, f. 8131, op. 37, d. 4669, ll. 2–11 (Spravka by Safonov, sent to Shvernik at KPK, June 9, 1949).

43. GARF, f. 8131, op. 37, d. 4669, l. 2.

44. GARF, f. 9474, op. 7, d. 881, l. 5 ("Obvinitel'noe zakliuchenie," March 25, 1949. Written by Safonov). GARF, f. 9474, op. 7, d. 882, l. 131. Kuz'ma T. Popov, a senior consultant in the RSFSR Supreme Court responsible for screening appeals who had been charged with (and confessed to) multiple counts of taking bribes (arrested July 26, 1948), described to prosecutors the overly comfortable, "nepotis-

tic" atmosphere that encouraged criminal activity in the offices of the Court. No one in a position of authority confronted (much less turned in) employees who inappropriately involved themselves in cases, he said.

45. GARF, f. 8131, op. 37, d. 4669, l. 15. All the names mentioned in this paragraph have been changed.

46. Just before her trial began, Ivanova wrote to Supreme Court Chair Volin, "I have committed no crimes, I did not take bribes, I am innocent!" GARF, f. 9474, op. 7, d. 882. l. 392. (Letter from Ivanova to Supreme Court of USSR, forwarded to Volin May 13, 1949.) For the transcript of her trial, see GARF, f. 9474, op. 7, d. 882, ll. 109–221.

47. At trial, Ivanova stated: "I confess, that since 1935 I have lived together with [and] was in close, intimate sexual relations with Rostova." At the same trial, Vasil'eva was called as a witness and forced to testify about their relationship. GARF, f. 9474, op. 7, d. 882, l. 211.

48. Ivanova told the court: "One can say that while I lived permanently with Rostova alone, Kiseleva changed women very often." GARF, f. 9474, op. 7, d. 882, l. 211.

49. GARF, f. 8131, op. 37, d. 4042, ll. 182–187 (Interrogation of Seifulina dated July 26, 1948, and sent by Safonov to Central Committee secretaries Popov and Kuznetsov on July 31, 1948).

50. GARF, f. 8131, op. 37, d. 4669, ll. 3–5 (Report from Safonov to Shkiriatov at KPK, June 9, 1949).

51. Luc Duhamel has written about the KGB's efforts in the 1980s to break apart Georgian criminal networks that had infiltrated the Moscow retail trade system. Duhamel, *The KGB Campaign against Corruption, 1982–1987* (Pittsburgh, PA, 2010).

52. See the transcript of Shevchenko's trial in GARF, f. 9474, op. 7, d. 912. Shevchenko used this very language when he testified in the trial of Bukanov, at which he was a witness: "I was acquainted with [the Georgian] Gogorishvili through his job in a snack bar in the Ramenskii region [of Moscow], where Bukanov and I met. As a result of falling into the company of his relatives and friends, I was bought by them and now, thanks to them, I am serving my punishment [in prison]." GARF, f. 9474, op. 7, d. 960, l. 331. See also Safonov's report to Shvernik about the RSFSR Supreme Court case. GARF, f. 8131, op. 37, d. 4669, ll. 6–7.

53. RGASPI, f. 17, op. 118, d. 151, ll. 138–139.

54. GARF, f. 9474, op. 7, d. 960, l. 347. At one point, Shevchenko and his wife were invited to the dacha of a Georgian food store manager to be the guests of honor. Forty people attended the party, including four generals and several colonels. The table, as he put it, was abundantly stocked with food and drinks, and it was clear that the Georgians were trying to ingratiate themselves with him, to "buy" his help permanently. Shevchenko testified that his wife, surveying the gathering, warned him that "I had fallen into the company of scoundrels ['*zhuliki*'] and by associating with them I, myself, could become a scoundrel." (GARF, f. 9474, op. 7, d. 912, l. 188.) In the procuracy's correspondence on the scandal, one can sense just beneath the surface a simmering suspicion of ethnic groups from the Caucasus. One sees this especially in the investigation of malfeasance in the RSFSR

Supreme Court, which heard appeals of cases from areas located in the North Caucasus, such as Dagestan, Chechnya, and North Ossetia. For example, a person linked to many bribery charges, the Chief of Administration of the RSFSR Supreme Court, Bekoev, was a North Ossetian. In a letter about the RSFSR Supreme Court scandal, a senior legal consultant, the Russian Popov, is quoted saying that "Bekoev was involved in some kind of dark affairs. He very often had visitors, especially from North Ossetia, which is his birthplace, and he was always arranging some kind of deal. Bekoev was completely trusted by Supreme Court Chairman Nesterov. He was in good relations with everyone and could help in any case. He dragged me into these affairs too." GARF, f. 8131, op. 37, d. 4669, l. 8. Letter from Safonov to KPK, June 9, 1949.

55. Judge Shevchenko was sentenced to ten years of forced labor. As of 1950, he was doing hard labor on an MVD construction project in Moscow.

56. Alec Nove, "Some Aspects of Soviet Constitutional Theory," *The Modern Law Review* vol. 12, no. 1 (January, 1949): 32. After 1932, the Supreme Court sometimes issued "guiding explanations," which had the force of "quasi-law." Peter Solomon, *Soviet Criminal Justice under Stalin*, 404. For detail on how the Supreme Court was structured, see Peter Solomon, "The USSR Supreme Court: History, Role, and Future Prospects," *The American Journal of Contemporary Law* 38, no. 1 (Winter 1990): 129–130. The RSFSR Constitution established that the RSFSR Supreme Court served as the republic's final appeals court and supervised all courts in the Russian Republic, as did each union-republic and autonomous-republic supreme court.

57. For a brief biography of Solodilov, see the official website of the Supreme Court of the Russian Federation: www.supcourt.ru/vscourt_detale.php?id=18 (accessed on January 25, 2015). In the court's official history, some arrests and executions of RSFSR judges during the 1930s are mentioned, but, oddly, the website says nothing about the devastating bribery scandals that swept through the USSR and RSFSR Supreme Courts in 1947–1952, costing the leadership of the courts their jobs, and in many cases their freedom and reputations.

58. Stephen Lovell examines the intricacies of Soviet dacha ownership in *Summerfolk: A History of the Dacha 1710–2000* (Ithaca, NY, 2003). Officials were often accused of illegally using state-owned vehicles for transportation of construction materials.

59. According to his colleague, the legal consultant V. N. Safronova, this interview worried Solodilov, and he was on guard henceforth. (GARF, f. 9474, op. 7, d. 824, l. 17. Testimony of V. N. Safronova, July 19, 1949.) At a meeting introducing the new minister at the USSR Ministry of Justice in February 1948, one of the participants stated that rumors that Solodilov had built himself a dacha illegally were flying around the Supreme Court offices. (GARF, f. 9492, op. 1a, d. 542, l. 136.) Around the same time, Minister of Justice Rychkov had been taken to task by the Party Control Commission and the Ministry of State Control in January 1948 because he allegedly had built himself a large dacha using some government money. Rychkov also was alleged to have illegally acquired trophy goods that originated in Germany, including "several rugs, dishes, a piano . . . and even refrigerators" worth 47 thousand rubles. Ministry of Justice leaders were also rebuked for

failing fully to prosecute theft of state property. Rychkov was removed in February 1948. GARF, f. 9492, op. 1a, d. 542, l. 157.

60. In several of these cases, one sees continuity with what Cynthia Hooper has described as a tremendous suspicion of family ties in the 1930s. Hooper, "Terror of Intimacy: Family Politics in the 1930s Soviet Union," in Christina Kiaer and Eric Naiman, *Everyday Life in Early Soviet Russia: Taking the Revolution Inside* (Bloomington, IN, 2005).

61. A letter was received by Minister of Justice Rychkov in 1944 relating a comment made by an NKVD officer who was aware of a lawyer who had worked closely with Solodilov in Chkalov on several cases in which the results were suspicious. This lawyer had allegedly been acting as a middleman and passing bribes to Solodilov, though Solodilov was never charged in those cases. The NKVD officer said that Solodilov "long ago should have been thrown out of the organs of justice." (GARF, f. 9492, op. 1a, d. 357, ll. 6–9 ob.) Just after the war's end, Solodilov was ordered to move to Germany to serve in a new position. Goliakov intervened to stop the transfer, insisting that Solodilov's work was too valuable to the Supreme Court. GARF, f. 9474, op. 16, d. 283, ll. 17–17 ob.

62. GARF, f 9474, op. 16, d. 294, ll. 45–50. Letter from Nikitin at the Cadres Directorate to Goliakov, September 5, 1946.

63. GARF, f. 9474, op. 7, d. 824, l. 31.

64. GARF, f. 9474, op. 7, d. 798, l. 158 (Protocol of interrogation of Radchik, April, 1948).

65. GARF, f. 8131, op. 37, d. 4041, ll. 55–61. Copies to Kuznetsov and Molotov.

66. Safonov's report was based largely on the testimony of the judge Chursina, the USSR Supreme Court employee Vladarchuk, and the defense lawyer Berta Radchik, all of whom were in custody in Butyrsk prison. The summary of allegations against Solodilov took as its starting point a 1947 investigation into bribery in the courts of Chkalov oblast', near the border of the Kazakh Republic, where the USSR Supreme Court had been evacuated during the Nazi occupation. In 1938, the city of Orenburg, located 1500 kilometers southeast of Moscow, was renamed Chkalov, after the famed Soviet test pilot. The city reverted to its original name in 1957.

67. Testimony of Vladarchuk. GARF, f. 8131, op. 37, d. 4041, l. 66.

68. GARF, f. 9474, op. 7, d. 824, ll. 38–41. In her testimony, she did not state the reason why she had to leave her apartment.

69. See the statement of R. in GARF, f. 9474, op. 7, d. 804, ll. 84–88. She called Solodilov "disgusting" and a man utterly lacking in morality.

70. RGASPI, f. 17, op. 118, d. 151, l. 141.

71. David L. Hoffman, *Stalinist Values: The Cultural Norms of Soviet Modernity* (Ithaca, NY, 2003), 72–78.

72. David L. Hoffman, *Stalinist Values*, 75.

73. GARF, f. 8131, op. 37, d. 4041, l. 61.

74. The term "Politburo" must be used with caveats in this period since it met rarely and in various configurations at this time, at Stalin's whim. It was by no means a consultative body. See, for example, Gorlizki and Khlevniuk, *Cold Peace*.

75. Politburo protocol, May 19, 1948 (RGASPI, f. 17, op. 163, d. 1511, l. 155).

Solodilov was not actually dismissed until May 27, according to Safronova's testimony at trial. GARF, f. 9474, op. 7, d. 824, l. 107.

76. RGASPI, f. 17, op. 118, d. 96, l. 133; GARF, f. 9474, op. 7, d. 824, l. 196 (Testimony of Safronova. July 29, 1949).

77. Having served as a judge on the Military Collegium during the Great Terror, Solodilov knew that more important and connected people than he had been sentenced to death for committing minor crimes, or for no crimes at all. Suicide may have seemed like a desirable option as he imagined a fate similar to those he saw arrested, humiliated in front of him, and executed. In some ways, Solodilov's fate is reminiscent of that of the Minister of Culture under Brezhnev, Ekaterina Furtseva, the country's first female Politburo member. In 1973, she was charged with taking bribes and using state resources illegally to build a dacha. She committed suicide the following year.

78. In several instances, including that of Sergo Ordzhonikidze, V. V. Lominadze, and M. P. Tomskii, Stalin was angered when party officials committed suicide. Oleg Khlevniuk, *In Stalin's Shadow* (Armonk, NY, 1995), 69–77, 150–162.

79. RGASPI, f. 17, op. 118, d. 96, ll. 132–141.

80. RGASPI, f. 17, op. 118, d. 96, l. 132.

81. Politbiuro protocols, August 24, 1948, pt. 91. "On the situation in the USSR Supreme Court" (S-t from August 20, 1948, point no. 369, p. 15-s). The state of affairs in the USSR Supreme Court was the only item on the agenda that day. RGASPI, f. 17, op. 163, d. 1510.

82. RGASPI, f. 17, op. 118, d. 131, ll. 162–163.

83. RGASPI, f. 17, op. 136, d. 171, l. 31. For a discussion by Volin in late 1949 on how the Supreme Court had been reorganized, and the changes he proposed in the wake of the scandal, see GARF, f. 9474, op. 16, d. 338, l. 304. Volin was dismissed from his post at the Supreme Court on February 21, 1957. In a personal interview, Volin told Yoram Gorlizki that Stalin called him into a meeting of the Politburo in July 1948. (Personal conversation with Yoram Gorlizki.) At that meeting, Stalin told Volin personally that the Central Committee wanted him to "clean up the muck" in the Supreme Court. This sounds to me like an order fully to cooperate with the procuracy's investigation of the USSR Supreme Court (ordered by the Department of Administrative Organs), including the arrest, interrogation, and trial of many court employees. Volin also mentioned this, his first and only meeting with Stalin, in A. Zviagintsev and Iurii G. Orlov, *Neizvestnaia Femida: Dokumenty, sobytiia, liudi* (Moscow, 2003), 339. Even after Stalin's death, Volin frequently recounted to his colleagues that the Central Committee (meaning Stalin) had brought him into the USSR Supreme Court to clean out the "mud and rottenness" in the court. Yoram Gorlizki, "De-Stalinization and the Politics of Russian Criminal Justice, 1953–1964," 167–168; Dina Moyal, "Did Law Matter?—Law, State and Individual in the USSR, 1953–1982," unpublished PhD dissertation (Stanford University, 2011), 125.

84. RGASPI, f. 17, op. 118, d. 151, ll. 132–143.

85. RGASPI, f. 17, op. 118, d. 151, ll. 132–133. With the investigation still far from complete, Safonov wrote that 111 people had been arrested in Moscow alone

by late August 1948—twenty-eight court employees (including judges), eight lawyers, five legal consultants, and seventy others (mostly bribe givers and intermediaries).

86. On the 1937–1938 purges of USSR Supreme Court judges accused of being "wreckers" and "enemies," see GARF, f. 9474, op. 16, dd. 103, 128, 136, 138, and 144. See also Peter Solomon, "The USSR Supreme Court," 130.

87. Peter Solomon has discussed the procuracy's campaign to reduce the number of acquittals that courts issued. Peter H. Solomon, Jr., "The Case of the Vanishing Acquittal: Informal Norms and the Practice of Soviet Criminal Justice," *Soviet Studies* 39, no. 4 (October 1987): 531–555.

88. GARF, f. 8131, op. 37, d. 4043, ll. 226–228. The precise date of the letter introducing the postanovlenie is not noted. In this atmosphere, it seems that it may have been nearly impossible for the procuracy to dismiss the charges against any employees who had been arrested during the spring or summer of 1948, even if the evidence against them was weak.

89. Yoram Gorlizki and Oleg Khlevniuk, *Cold Peace,* 61.

90. The letter goes on: "On August 8, 1932 he was fired from the organs of the OGPU for applying unacceptable methods in relation to arrested people in the course of investigation. This year he made mistakes in reviewing cases about bribery by several workers of the Supreme Court RSFSR, expressed in the public arrest of Judge Shevchenko and the typist Goleva while they were at work. In August 1948, Kuznetsov directed Safonov's attention to this." RGASPI, f. 17, op. 136, d. 22, ll. 92–93.

91. GARF, f. 8131, op. 32, d. 3, ll. 51–58 (Spravka sledovatel'ia po vazhneishim delam, Gosudarstvennyi sovetnik iustitsii, K. Bulaev. Dated January 19, 1951). Bulaev was one of the lead investigators in these cases. Vladarchuk, an employee in the USSR Supreme Court who confessed to helping Solodilov illegally obtain building materials to construct his dacha, told prosecutors that Goliakov knew nothing of the scheme. Goliakov's dacha was built legally, Vladarchuk implied. (GARF, f. 8131, op. 37, d. 4041, l. 64.) Goliakov apparently felt most at home with academic work, at least at this point in his life. Goliakov wrote at least two books after 1953. According to the memoirs of the legal scholar B. S. Utevskii, Goliakov suffered from insomnia for the last dozen years of his life, between 1949 and his death in 1961. It is not difficult to imagine why. Utevskii, *Vospominaniia iurista* (Moscow, 1989), 278. Goliakov's study, *Sud i zakonnonst' v khudozhestvennoi literature (Courts and Legality in Belle Lettres),* was published in 1959. He is buried in Moscow's Novodevichii cemetery.

92. GARF, f. 9474, op. 16, d. 396, ll. 42–44 ob. For excerpts of Velichko's testimony of August 4–6, 1951, see ll. 46–57 ob.

93. Velichko testified that she made Goliakov's acquaintance in the summer of 1946 at the "Barvikha" sanatorium. Velichko alleged that Goliakov took separate bribes of 25,000 rubles, 20,000 rubles, and 15,000 rubles. In each case, she said, Goliakov kicked back 5,000 rubles to Velichko as her "fee." There is no evidence that there is any truth to Velichko's claims.

94. RGASPI, f. 17, op. 118, d. 151, ll. 142–143.

95. GARF, f. 8131, op. 37, d. 4043, ll. 230a–230d (Letter and report sent from

Baranov to Safonov, January 21, 1949). The procuracy also charged twelve employees of the retail trade network, including directors of stores and warehouses.

96. GARF, f. 9492, op. 2, d. 58, l. 238 (Letter from Deputy Minister of Justice I. Skorokhodov to R. A. Lopukhov, August 24, 1949). Their trial was held between November 10 and December 17, 1949. The Georgian Supreme Court judges charged included Nikolai R. Margiev, Nestor O. Shengeliia, Iosif G. Mchedlidze, Rostom G. Machavariani, Varlam Z. Georgobiani, and Pavel P. Kuparadze. All the justices were found guilty of accepting bribes. Five of the judges were sentenced to ten years in prison and one received eight years. For their sentences and a description of their alleged crimes, see GARF, f. 9474, op. 16, d. 355, ll. 5–31; GARF f. 9492, op. 2, d. 81, ll. 264–277.

97. For a transcript of the trial, see GARF, f. 9474, op. 7, d. 935. Procuracy correspondence on the cases includes GARF, f. 8131, op. 37, d. 4043, l. 230z.

98. On April 22, 1948, a detailed letter from a certain Mamedov accused a member of the Supreme Court of the Azerbaizhan SSR, Gusein Alekperov, of systematically taking bribes. The letter was forwarded to Safonov and Gorshenin, but there is no indication of the results of the investigation in the file. GARF, f. 9492, op. 1a, d. 527, ll. 136–138.

99. By April 30, 1949, 247 people had been arrested: twenty-seven of those who accepted bribes were persons "in positions of authority in the courts" (meaning judges, in the main), twenty-seven were defense lawyers, and twenty-two were legal consultants, secretaries, or other personnel in the courts; the rest were people charged with paying bribes and "enablers." GARF, f. 9492, op. 2, d. 58, ll. 140–141. Letter from Safonov, Gorshenin, and Volin to Malenkov at the Central Committee.

100. For N. V. Vasil'ev, see Politburo agenda from Jan. 12, 1948, pt. 65. Shevchenko testified that investigators told him that they were also targeting "*Bochkov*," which is very likely a typographical error obscuring the real person, deputy chair of the RSFSR Supreme Court *Bocharov* (though it could conceivably mean V. M. Bochkov, former USSR Procurator General); GARF, f. 9474, op. 7, d. 960, l. 352. Pashutina was arrested for bribery, as Safonov informed the Department of Administrative Organs in July 1950. The Procuracy alleged, on the basis of flimsy evidence, that in four cases she had taken bribes of cash and shoe leather in her capacity as a judge. Her trial began on May 28, 1951, but she was found guilty only of Article 109 (abuse of office, rather than bribery), and sentenced to just one year in prison. (GARF, f. 8131, op. 29, d. 6, ll. 111–117.) For the trial transcript, see GARF, f. 9474, op. 7, d. 1025, ll. 77–230.

101. Indeed, in an incredibly risky move, Shevchenko blurted out to the presiding judges during a July 1949 hearing: "They are laying a trap for Bukanov!" ("*Bukanovu roiut iamu!*") Shevchenko said this to let the presiding judges know that procuracy investigators had concocted evidence and had pressured him into lying. In September 1951, Bukanov was tried for bribery a second time in a closed session of the Military Collegium of the USSR Supreme Court. The judges found him not guilty and ordered him released. GARF, f. 9474, op. 7, d. 960, ll. 314–357. GARF, f. 9474, op. 7, d. 960, l. 352.

102. GARF, f. 9474, op. 7, d. 961, l. 228.

103. GARF, f. 9474, op. 7, d. 824, l. 29.

104. GARF, f. 9474, op. 16, d. 368, l. 57. As Minister of Justice Gorshenin scathingly summarized the methods of some procuracy investigators in March 1950: "Many procurators of republics, territories, and regions do not ask pointed questions about the personal responsibility of their [subordinate] employees, who act according to the method long ago condemned by the Party and the Government—'Arrest first, investigate later.' . . ." (GARF, f. 9492, op. 2, d. 68, l. 229.) Solomon points out that concerns about unfounded prosecutions began before the war (*Soviet Criminal Justice*, 368). The percentage of "unfounded arrests" was about 10 percent in 1948 and a relatively low 6.3 percent in 1947.

105. GARF, f. 9474, op. 16, d. 368, l. 58 (Letter from Morozov, Chairman of the Judicial Collegium for Criminal Cases of the USSR Supreme Court, to Lopukhov at the Department for Administrative Organs, December 17, 1951). In one case, Safonov stated, disingenuously and in spite of multiple specific complaints: "No lack of objectivity [*neob'ektivnost'*] has been observed in the investigatory work of the investigators, comrades Bulaev, Dvorkin, and Golinkov." A fifteen-page list of types of documents that were to be kept "secret" or "top secret," distributed in 1948, includes "cases of illegal methods of investigation." GARF, f. 8131, op. 37, d. 4041, ll. 268–283.

106. GARF, f. 9492, op. 2, d. 58, ll. 140–141. The letter notes that the first hearings, concerning individual episodes involving small groups of bribe takers, had already been conducted. At present, the letter goes on, the USSR Procuracy has completed investigations for the three major groups of accused. The evidence gathered in these cases "exposes the full scope of the character and scale of the criminal activities of the arrested court employees and testifies to their moral and personal corruption, their association with criminal elements, and their distortion of Soviet law."

107. This decision is located in the "Osobaia papka" ("Special File") of the Politburo, protocol no. 68, from May 9, 1949, pt. 362: ("On the procedure for reviewing cases of several organized groups of bribe takers who have been exposed in the USSR Supreme Court, the RSFSR Supreme Court, the Moscow City Court, and several people's courts in the city of Moscow"). The decision states that the cases of the employees of the USSR Supreme Court were to be heard by three judges from the USSR Supreme Court—Cherkov, Iakovlev, and Volin presiding; the RSFSR cases were to be reviewed by Bitiukov, the new chair of the RSFSR Supreme Court, together with to the justices Zeidin and Borisenko; and the Moscow City Court cases by deputy chair of the USSR Supreme Court Cheptsov, plus justices Uspenskii and Boiarkin. (RGASPI, f. 17, op. 162, d. 40, ll. 147–148.)

108. This was one of the rare instances when the USSR Supreme Court heard certain especially important cases as the court of first instance ("*po pervoi instantsii*"). The USSR Supreme Court did this in cases involving: a) Accusations of high responsible officials of Sovnarkom; b) Cases of extraordinary importance; and c) Legal arguments between Union republics. Safonov suggested that, just as in the cases of employees of the USSR and RSFSR Supreme Courts, the trials of employees of the Ukrainian Supreme Court should be conducted in closed session without lawyers. "Reviewing the given case in the usual manner with the participation of

parties [defense and prosecution lawyers] would lead to the divulging of information about the trial, and in such a way, negatively impact the authority of court organs." From introduction to the seventh published opis' for f. 9474 (the USSR Supreme Court).

109. The trial of RSFSR Supreme Court judges Murzakhanov and Kumekhov, for example, occurred in November–December 1949 (GARF, f. 9474, op. 7, d. 958).

110. This is reminiscent of the Mingrelian Affair, when Stalin forced Beria to preside at the April 1952 Plenum of the Georgian Communist Party, which denounced Beria's allies. Yoram Gorlizki and Oleg Khlevniuk, *Cold Peace*, 111–112. Stalin tested some of his top lieutenants' loyalty by arresting members of their families (for example, Molotov, Poskrebyshev, Kaganovich, and others).

111. GARF, f. 9474, op. 16, d. 337, l. 18 (Letter from Gorshenin and Zeidin to Malenkov, June 20, 1949).

112. See, for example, GARF, f. 9474, op. 16, d. 337, ll. 33–34; and d. 368, ll. 25, 36.

113. For more on narratives of corruption in the postwar Stalin period, see James Heinzen, "Intoxicated with the Easy and Happy Life: Scenarios of Bribery in the Stalinist High Courts," unpublished paper presented at the Southern Conference of Slavic Studies, March 29, 2012 (Savannah, GA).

114. During the purge trials of the 1930s, many of those shot for treason or counterrevolution were also accused of moral transgressions and sexual peccadilloes.

115. Another type of cassational appeal were protests (*protesty*) about improperly mild sentences or otherwise incorrect prosecutions, which could be initiated by procurators or by the chair of the USSR or republican supreme courts and which were made in much smaller numbers than citizen complaints. There was some controversy over whether appeals heard in cassation should include a substantive review of a case "on its merits" in some instances. See Samuel Kucherov, *The Organs of Soviet Administration of Justice* (Leiden, 1970), 621–640. On protests, see ibid., 642–651.

116. The law stated, "The right of complaint in the Soviet state has this essential characteristic, that . . . it is the means of defending the legal rights of citizens." Cited in Alec Nove, "Some Aspects of Soviet Constitutional Theory," *The Modern Law Review* 12, no. 1 (Jan. 1949): 34.

117. E. A. Smolentsev, "Na strazhe sotsialisticheskoi zakonnosti," in *Verkhovnyi sud SSSR*, ed. L. N. Smirnov, et al. (Moscow, 1974), 95–97.

118. Peter Solomon, *Soviet Criminal Justice*, 258.

119. Peter Solomon, "The USSR Supreme Court," 130.

120. The Supreme Court lost this extraordinary power in 1957, after which time it could only review decisions from the republican supreme courts. Peter Solomon, "The USSR Supreme Court," 132.

121. According to Peter Solomon, who interviewed people who worked with Goliakov, "Ivan Goliakov was the right man for the task of restoring the prestige and public image of the pinnacle of the legal system and by implication of the legal system itself." Peter Solomon, *Soviet Criminal Justice*, 262.

122. The law did not cover convictions by the political police, which issued the great majority of convictions for "counterrevolutionary" crimes.

123. The Judicial Collegiums (*Sudbenye kollegii*) of the Supreme Court reviewed complaints (especially the Judicial Collegium for Criminal Cases). Interesting studies of petitioning in the Soviet period include Golfo Alexopolous, *Stalin's Outcasts* (on the 1930s), and Christine Varga-Harris, "Forging Citizenship on the Home Front: Revising the Socialist Contract and Constructing Socialist Identity during the Thaw," in *The Dilemmas of De-Stalinization* (London, 2006), 101–116.

124. Goliakov made this point in a letter to Molotov at Sovnarkom in 1945 (GARF, f. 9474, op. 16, d. 284, l. 18.) In 1957, as Peter Solomon notes, Khrushchev-era reforms decentralized the courts. The Supreme Court could only accept protests from republican supreme courts, and then only if there was a possible conflict with USSR legislation. The size of the USSR Supreme Court quickly dropped to twelve justices. Most of the appellate work then fell upon the republican supreme courts. Peter Solomon, "The USSR Supreme Court," 131. One of Volin's first official acts (in November 1948) was to write to Stalin and ask for the load of appeals sent to the USSR Supreme Court to be reduced. (GARF, f. 9474, op. 16, d. 322, ll. 87–98.) In certain "important categories of cases, like theft of state and socialist property, about which up to two-thirds are appealed to higher courts with a complaint, 20 percent are annulled year to year, that is, every fifth sentence." (RGASPI, f. 17, op. 136, d. 167, l. 80. Letter from Dukel'skii to Malenkov. March 22, 1951.) Even if this is a somewhat exaggerated number, it is further evidence of the impact of the mass quantity of appeals for convictions for theft of state property.

125. Osborn, "Citizen vs. Administration in the USSR," *Soviet Studies* 17, no. 2 (October 1965): 228.

126. GARF, f. 9474, op. 7, d. 984, l. 187. (Testimony of Anisimova.)

127. E. A. Smolentsev, "Na strazhe sotsialisticheskoi zakonnosti," 97. Moreover, complaints could be forwarded to the Supreme Court by other agencies that received them, including the Central Committee, the Supreme Soviet, the Council of Ministers, and central newspapers.

128. GARF, f. 9474, op. 16, d. 310, l. 10 (Letter from Goliakov to the Central Committee, Comrade Kornev, March 6, 1947).

129. This collegium handled a bit more than half (54 percent) of the complaints that came into the USSR Supreme Court in 1950. (GARF, f. 9474, op. 17, d. 368, l. 72.) Thirty-nine percent of cases reviewed by the Collegium concern the June 4 decree on theft of state property (data for 1950). Data for 1949 indicates that 32 percent of cases reviewed by all collegiums (excluding the Military Collegium) were about the June 4 decree on theft of state property. These cases concerned 38 percent of the convictions reviewed. GARF, f. 9474, op. 16, d. 338, l. 320.

130. Letter from Volin to Malenkov, April 1, 1954. Document reproduced in A. Zviagintsev and Iu. Orlov, *Neizvestnaia Femida*, 341–343, citing GARF, f. 9474, op. 16, d. 434, ll. 173–178. The letter lists an average of 11,234 complaints per month coming into the USSR Supreme Court in 1948, for a total of 134,808. Another 96,910 poured into the Supreme Court just during the first six months of 1949. GARF, f. 9474, op. 16, d. 337, l. 79. ("Otchet o rabote Verkhovnogo suda SSSR po rassmotreniiu zhalob," signed by Volin, July 1949.) The RSFSR Supreme Court faced a similar flood of cases. In 1946, 66,990 cases and 97,081 complaints

were brought to the RSFSR Supreme Court. In 1948, 46,116 complaints came into the RSFSR Supreme Court; 15,645 came into the Ukrainian Supreme Court (GARF, f. 9492, op. 3, d. 76, l. 1. (Report on work of supreme courts for 1948.) In the first three quarters of 1950, 82,170 cases and 133,954 complaints were received by the court. Gorshenin requested that the RSFSR Supreme Court be expanded by twelve members to handle this increased volume. GARF, f. 9492, op. 2, d. 64, l. 39 (Letter from Gorshenin to the Council of Ministers, October 31, 1950).

131. RGASPI, f. 17, op. 136, d. 22, ll. 148–149. Appeals in languages other than Russian sat untouched for the longest time before they were reviewed, according to Volin. GARF, f. 9474, op. 16, d. 322, l. 72.

132. GARF, f. 9474, op. 16, d. 294, ll. 32–35 (Letter of November 15, 1946).

133. GARF f. 9492, op. 2, d. 51, ll. 206–208.

134. GARF, f. 9474, op. 7, d. 338, l. 316. In part because of the bribery scandal in the Supreme Court, an important reform was made. All cases that were pulled for review on the basis of a successful complaint now had to be cleared by the chairman of the Supreme Court or one of his deputies; all rejected complaints were to go to chairman of the relevant judicial collegium. GARF, f. 9474, op. 16, d. 379, l. 7.

135. GARF, f. 9474, op. 16, d. 405, l. 7. Judging by data from 1949–1951, only about five to eight percent of the complaints that were submitted to the Supreme Court resulted in a case being pulled for review. Ten percent were "sent to other institutions" (and one cannot feel optimistic about the chances for these transferred complaints caught in the bureaucratic shuffle). Between 81 and 85 percent were rejected outright.

136. A 1950 Party Control Commission review of appeals by the USSR Procuracy condemned the Supreme Court's review procedures as bogged down in "disgraceful red tape." RGANI, f. 6, op. 2, d. 166, l. 123. (Postanovlenie of KPK Biuro, dated June 13, 1950.) On September 20, 1949, the deputy chief of the Department of Administrative Organs discussed the slow review of complaints. RGASPI, f. 17, op. 136, d. 71, ll. 93–95. (Letter from Bakakin to Malenkov, September 20, 1949.) He noted that there was a great deal of delay when it came to reviewing protests of sentences for petty theft of state property.

137. GARF, f. 9474, op. 7, d. 882, l. 213.

138. GARF, f. 9474, op. 7, d. 824, ll. 30–31.

139. Each relevant employee of the USSR Supreme Court reviewed 650–700 complaints per month on average. (GARF, f. 9474, op. 16, d. 399, ll. 1–2.) Volin asked for twenty-five new staff to help review complaints. It is unclear whether the Council of Ministers fulfilled the request. In the year 1951, only about 5.7 percent of complaints resulted in a case being pulled for review. GARF, f. 9474, op. 16, d. 399, ll. 1–5 (Letter from Volin to USSR Council of Minister, June 9, 1952).

140. For the process, see GARF, f. 9474, op. 16, d. 310, ll. 10–12.

141. As a KPK report noted in 1949, petitioners began lining up outside the USSR Supreme Court offices at 3:00 or 4:00 in the morning. They often hoped in vain that they could consult with a judge who could make an immediate decision on their petition. GARF, f. 9474, op. 16, d. 337, l. 77.

142. As Peter Solomon has stated, "This situation was bound to make members of the public sense the arbitrary quality in the administration of criminal justice and distrust the law." Solomon, *Soviet Criminal Justice,* 444.

143. RGASPI, f. 82, op. 2, d. 418, l. 275 (Letter from Goliakov to Molotov, received on August 7, 1944).

144. "Despite the fact that all the members of the Supreme Court have the same rights and fulfill in essence the same work, all have varying material conditions. Thus, members of the Supreme Court working in the Military, Military Railroad, and Military Water transport collegiums earn salaries from 2,500 to 5,900 rubles, while members of the USSR Supreme Court working in other collegiums earn [only] 1,350 rubles." RGASPI, f. 17, op. 121, d. 612, ll. 59–61 (Letter from Gusev to Stalin, June 27, 1947).

145. He reported that those Supreme Court justices who came to Moscow from the national republics dreamed of returning to their families in their home republics, where they could earn more. GARF, f. 9492, op. 1a, d. 542, l. 135. ("Transcript of session of State Commission together with members of the Collegium, chiefs of administrations and sections of the USSR Ministry of Justice, February 5, 1948.")

146. RGASPI, f. 17, op. 121, d. 612, ll. 59–61.

147. In order to show the court that he had no reason to take bribes, the falsely accused judge Bukanov at his trial emphasized how much food he had access to during and after the war. GARF, f. 9474, op. 7, d. 960, l. 320.

148. Nesterov apparently planted potatoes during and after the war to feed the employees of the RSFSR Supreme Court. GARF, f. 9474, op. 7, d. 960, l. 322. In an apparently unrelated charge, prosecutors accused him of profiteering in vegetables on the grounds of the court.

149. GARF, f. 9474, op. 7, d. 912, ll. 178, 216, 288 (Transcript of trial, July 12–29, 1949).

150. GARF, f. 9474, op 7, d. 958, ll. 153–154.

151. RGASPI, f. 17, op, 121, d. 612, l. 60.

152. Peter Solomon, *Soviet Criminal Justice,* 397.

153. "The leadership organs [the Central Committee and the Council of Ministers] did not require the procuracy to return the space to us," despite Goliakov's bitter complaints. (RGASPI, f. 17, op. 136, d. 22, ll. 148–149.) See the report to L. Z. Mekhlis by Chebyshiv of the Ministry of Justice. No date, but judging by dates on surrounding documents, written in February–March 1948. (GARF, 9492, op. 1a, d. 544, ll. 338–339.) On October 8, 1946, Goliakov and Minister of Justice Rychkov had written to Beria asking for more space for the USSR Supreme Court offices, noting that thirteen people were sharing one small room of ten square meters. GARF, f. 9492, op. 2, d. 37, ll. 70–71.

154. GARF, f. 9474, op. 16, d. 284, ll. 18–19. Letter from Goliakov to Molotov, July 3, 1945.

155. GARF, f. 9492, op. 1a, d. 542, l. 189.

156. GARF, f. 9492, op. 1a, d. 542, l. 135.

157. GARF, f. 9474, op. 16, d. 322, l. 37. Another problem, Goliakov wrote to Molotov, is that it is not acceptable from a political standpoint for different categories of petitioners to mix in general reception areas. Those who have come to

complain about judgments regarding "counterrevolutionary crimes" (visiting the Military Collegium and the Collegium for the Gulag camps) must be kept separate from the others who were there about "regular" criminal cases. "It is completely undesirable to mix the petitioners of these *kollegiia* with other petitioners." (GARF, f. 9474, op. 16, d. 284, ll. 18–19.) Documents in state and party archives show that Goliakov continued to write repeatedly to the top levels of the government and party about these issues over the course of 1946, 1947, and 1948. Indeed, Goliakov asserted that he complained in writing about the court's building to party and state authorities *each of the ten years* that he was chair of the Supreme Court. RGASPI, f. 17, op. 136, d. 22, l. 150 (Letter from Goliakov, September 14, 1948). See also GARF, f. 9492, op. 1a, d. 542, l. 135.

158. GARF, f. 9474, op. 16, d. 322, ll. 95–96 (Letter to Stalin "On measures for improving the work of the USSR Supreme Court." October 26, 1948). For a description of the inefficient ways that complaints were reviewed in the Supreme Court, see GARF, f. 9474, op. 16, d. 322, ll. 69–75. In November 1948, Volin petitioned to have a new building constructed for the USSR Supreme Court. He asked that the Ministry of Internal Affairs be required to put the project on the list of forthcoming MVD construction projects. The new USSR Supreme Court building, therefore, should be built by forced labor. Volin later successfully requested that the court's offices be moved to 13 Vorovskaia Street, the home of the Moscow regional court. Finally the court got its new space.

159. GARF, f. 9474, op. 16, d. 162, l. 116 (Letter from Goliakov to Malenkov at the Central Committee. July 26, 1940).

160. A similar point was made by Peter Solomon about the 1930s. "The mid-1930s represented a turning point in the history of Soviet criminal justice. The criminal law remained an instrument serving Stalin, but the tasks served by the law changed. With collectivization nearly completed, Stalin sought to consolidate the new social order and create a strong centralized state. Such a state required respect for the laws that it issued, and it was not surprising that Stalin should decide to restore the authority of law and to create reliable, centralized agencies for its administration," *Soviet Criminal Justice*, 194. See also Yoram Gorlizki and Oleg Khlevniuk, *Cold Peace*.

161. As Peter Solomon has noted, "Underlying Soviet law, like Tsarist law before, was the cardinal assumption that the law was an instrument of rule, not an end in itself. The key difference was that Soviet socialist law would serve a new master, the 'ruling' proletariat represented by leaders of the Communist Party." Peter H. Solomon, Jr., "The USSR Supreme Court: History, Role, and Future Prospects," *The American Journal of Comparative Law* 38, no. 1 (Winter 1990): 127–142.

162. On high politics in this period, see Yoram Gorlizki and Oleg Khlevniuk, *Cold Peace*; R. G. Pikhoia, *Sovetskii soiuz: Istoriia vlasti, 1945–1991* (Moscow, 1998); Iu. N. Zhukov, "Bor'ba za vlast' v rukovodstve SSSR v 1945–1952 godakh," *Voprosy istorii*, no. 1 (1995): 23–39; Elena Zubkova, "Kadrovaia politika i chistki v KPSS (1945–1956)," *Svobodnaia mysl'*, nos. 3, 4, 6 (1999); A. Pyzhikov, "Leningradskaia gruppa: Put' vo vlasti (1946–1949)," *Svobodnaia mysl'*, no. 2 (2001): 89–104; and Kees Boterbloem, *The Life and Times of Andrei Zhdanov, 1896–1948* (Montreal, 2004).

163. F. Kamenskii, "Sledovateli po vazhneishim delam," *Sotsialisticheskaia zakonnost'*, November 1949 (11): 34–39.

164. Although the evidence is far from complete, one can speculate that Kuznetsov may have hoped to use the investigation into corruption in the high courts to strengthen his position against his rivals, Beria and Malenkov, in his struggle for control of the military and government spheres. Kuznetsov might also have been trying to reimpose central party control over the Military Collegium, the high courts, and the security organs, which he oversaw as Central Committee secretary. The paper trail left by the Affair of the High Courts reveals that Kuznetsov was involved in all of the key reports, either receiving them from the procuracy or summarizing them and sending them to Stalin. Clearly, Kuznetsov (with the assistance of his deputies) was the party's point person for the move against the high courts. He in turn might have fed Stalin this information, attempting to use the Affair of the High Courts to improve his standing in the Central Committee Secretariat. Kuznetsov may have pressured Safonov to provide him with evidence of corruption among court cadres, which he could then supply to Stalin. If so, Stalin tolerated Kuznetsov's actions—and the destabilizations and panic mongering they caused—which disrupted the high courts during the second half of 1948. He then, perhaps, pulled the rug out from under Kuznetsov near the beginning of 1949. In any case, we know that thousands of denunciations crossed Stalin's desk in these years, as they had for decades. Stalin encouraged people to denounce each other as a method of keeping control over party leaders, and had been doing so since the 1920s. Beria and Malenkov may have provided Stalin with inflammatory information about Kuznetsov, and vice versa. For the most part we simply do not know exactly how or why Stalin reacted to the intrigues going on in his inner circle. Ultimately, Kuznetsov lost his struggle with Beria and Malenkov. He was removed from the Central Committee in January 1949, and was executed as a central figure in the Leningrad Affair on October 1, 1950.

165. Eric Duskin, *Stalinist Reconstruction and the Confirmation of a New Elite*, 131. Yoram Gorlizki and Oleg Khlevniuk, *Cold Peace*.

166. GARF, f. 9474, op. 7, d. 826, l. 137. (Words of Pavel Takhtadzhiev in his 1957 appeal to the procuracy.)

167. GARF, f. 5446, op. 51a, d. 5339, ll. 1–60.

168. In Stalin's time, there had been a (post-purge) precedent for party leaders scapegoating judges to make them compliant with major initiatives from above. As Peter Solomon shows, judges were scapegoated in a 1940 "witch-hunt" (though not for bribery) in connection with alleged leniency in punishing the harsh new laws on labor discipline. Many were fired and typically accused of negligence. Peter Solomon, *Soviet Criminal Justice*, 309–318.

169. David Shearer has made this point in *Policing Stalin's Socialism* (Ithaca, NY, 2009).

CONCLUSION

1. The US Constitution names only two crimes for which a democratically elected president could be removed from office by Congress: treason and bribery.

2. Kathryn Hendley, "Rule of Law, Russian-Style," *Current History* (October 2009), 339–340.

3. Stephen Lovell, Alena Ledeneva, and Andrei Rogachevskii, "Introduction," in *Bribery and Blat in Russia,* ed. Stephen Lovell, et al., 7.

4. Edward Cohn, "Disciplining the Party: The Expulsion and Censure of Communists in the Post-War Soviet Union, 1945–1961," unpublished PhD dissertation (University of Chicago, 2007), 150.

5. Examples include Stephen Kotkin, *Armageddon Averted* (Oxford, 2008); Leslie Holmes, *Rotten States? Corruption, Post-Communism, and Neo-Liberalism* (Durham, 2006); and Stephen Solnick, *Stealing the State* (Cambridge, MA, 1998).

Bibliography

PRIMARY SOURCES

Russian Archives:

The State Archive of the Russian Federation (GARF):
f. 5446. Sovmin USSR (The USSR Council of Ministers)
f. 7523. Verkhovnyi Sovet SSSR (USSR Supreme Soviet)
f. 8131. Prokuratura SSSR (USSR Office of the Procuracy)
f. 9401. Osobaia papka Stalina (The Special Folder of Stalin)
f. 9414. Glavnoe upravlenie lagerei MVD (Gulag)
f. 9415. Otdel bor'by s khishcheniem sotsialisticheskoi sobstvennosti i spe-
    kuliatsiei MVD (OBKhSS)
f.9474. Verkhovnyi Sud SSSR (Supreme Court of the USSR)
f. 9492. Ministerstvo Iustitsii SSSR (USSR Ministry of Justice)
f. 9550. Kollektsiia listovok sovetskogo perioda (Leaflets of the Soviet
    period)

The Russian State Archive of Contemporary History (RGANI)
f. 6. Komitet Partiinogo Kontrolia TsK VKP(b) (Party Control Committee
    of the Central Committee).

The Russian State Archive of Social and Political History (RGASPI)
f. 17. The Central Committee of the Communist Party of the Soviet Union
    -op. 3. Protocols and materials to sessions of Politbiuro
    -op. 116–118 Secretariat and Organization Bureau of the Central Commit-
        tee of the Soviet Communist Party (Materials and Correspondence)
    -op. 121. Technical Secretariat of the Organization Bureau of the Cen-
        tral Committee of the Soviet Communist Party

-op. 122. The General Department
-op. 135. Planning-Financial Department
-op. 136. Department of Administrative Organs
-op. 162–163. The Special Folder (Osobaia papka) of the Politbiuro.
f. 82. Molotov
f. 671. Yezhov

Newspapers and Journals:
Christian Science Monitor
Current Digest of the Soviet Press
Daria Vostoka
Ekonomicheskaia gazeta
Ezhenedel'nik sovetskoi iustitsii
Izvestiia
Kommunist
Komsomolskaia Pravda
Krokodil
Leninskoe znamia
Moscow News
New York Times
Partiinoe stroitel'stvo
Plain Talk
Pravda
Pravda Ukrainy
Sotsialisticheskaia zakonnost'
Sovetskaia iustitsiia
Sudebnaia praktika Verkhovnogo suda SSSR
Trud
Vedomosti Verkhovnogo Soveta
Zarya Vostoka

Other Primary Sources:
Aleksandrov, G. "Otvetstvennost' nedonositelei po ukazam Prezidiuma verkhovnogo soveta SSSR ot 4 Iunia 1947 g." *Sotsialisticheskaia zakonnost'*, no. 7 (1950): 26–33.
Alexeiev, Kirill. "Russia's Underground Capitalism." *Plain Talk* (December 1949), 19–24.
Amnistiia i pomilovanie v SSSR. Moscow, 1959.
Andreev-Khomiakov, Gennady. *Bitter Waters: Life and Work in Stalin's Russia.* Boulder, 1997.
Cobbett, William. *Twelve Sermons.* London, 1823.
Dallin, David. "The Black Market in Russia." *American Mercury* (December 1949): 678–682.

Epikhin, A. Iu., and O. B. Mozokhin. *VChK-OGPU v bor'be s korruptsiei v gody novoi ekonomicheskoi politiki.* Moscow, 2007.

Gorshenin, K. P. *Sotsialisticheskaia zakonnost' na sovremennom etape: Stenogramma publichnoi lektsii prochitannoi 17 avgusta 1948 goda v Tsentral'nom lektorii obshchestva v Moskve.* Moscow, 1948.

The Harvard Project on the Soviet Social System (Harvard Interview Project or HIP)

"Iz prigorov raionnykh narsudov o privlechenii k ugolovnoi otvetstvennosti kolkhoznikov po Ukazu 1947 g." *Sovetskie arkhivy* 3 (1990): 55–60.

Konstinovsky, Boris A. *Soviet Law in Action: The Recollected Cases of a Soviet Lawyer,* ed. Harold J. Berman. Cambridge, MA, 1953.

Kravchenko, Viktor. *I Chose Freedom: The Personal and Political Life of a Soviet Official.* New York, 1946.

Kucheriavyi, N. L. *Otvetstvennost' za vziatochnichestvo po sovetskomu ugolovnomu pravu.* Moscow, 1957.

Kurinov, B. A. *Ugolovnaia otvetstvennost' za khishchenie gosudarstvennogo i obshchestvennogo imushchestva.* Moscow, 1954.

Lench, Leonid. "Tochnoe dokazatel'stvo." *Krokodil,* May 30, 1946.

Lenin, V. I. *Polnoe sobranie sochinenii,* 5th ed. Moscow, 1964.

Lyons, Eugene. *Assignment in Utopia.* New York, 1937.

Makashvili, V. "Strogo vypolniat' trebovaniia zakona ob otvetstvennosti za vziatochnichestvo (Sudebnaia praktika Verkhovnogo Suda SSSR)." *Sotsialisticheskaia zakonnost'* no. 2 (1953): 40–49.

Mironov, N. "Nasushchnye voprosy dal'neishego upkrepleniia sotsialisticheskoi zakonnosti." *Kommunist,* no. 1 (January 1963).

Muranov, A. I., and V. Zviagintsev. *Sud nad sud'iami: Osobaia papka Ul'rikha.* Kazan, 1993.

Politbiuro TsK VKP(b) i Sovet Ministrov SSSR, 1945–53. Ed. Oleg Khlevniuk and Nora S. Favorov. Moscow, 2002.

Reabilitatsiia—Politicheskie protsessy 1930–1950 godov. Moscow, 1991.

Sbornik raz"iasnenii Verkhovnogo Suda SSSR za 1929 god. Moscow, 1930.

Sbornik zakonov SSSR i ukazov Prezidiuma Verkhovnogo Soveta SSSR za 1938-noiabr' 1958 (Moscow, 1959), 418–420.

Sergeeva, T. L. *Ugolovno-pravovaia okhrana sotsialisticheskoi sobstvennosti v SSSR.* Moscow, 1954.

Smolitskii, G. R. *Dolzhnostnye prestupleniia.* Moscow, 1947.

Solodilov, A. P., and G. N. Amfiteatrov. *Pravo nasledovaniia v SSSR.* Moscow, 1946.

Sovetskaia zhizn'. 1945–53. Compiled by Elena Iu. Zubkova, L. P. Kosheleva, F. A. Kuznetsova, A. I. Miniuk, et al.

Valerin, V. *Vol'chia staia: Zapiski chlena kollegii zashchitnikov.* Moscow, 1931.

Volin, A. "Strogo sobliudat' zakonnost' v rabote sudov." *Sotsialisticheskaia zakonnost',* no. 1 (1950).

Vyshinskii, A. Ia. *Crime Recedes in the USSR.* Moscow, 1939.

———. *Sudebnye rechi.* Moscow, 1948.

Zviagintsev, A., and Iurii Orlov. *Neizvestnaia Femida: Dokumenty. Sobytiia. Liudi.* Moscow, 2003.

SECONDARY SOURCES

Adler, Nanci. *The Gulag Survivor: Beyond the Soviet System.* New Brunswick, NJ: 2002.

Alexopolous, Golfo. "Amnesty 1945: The Revolving Door of Stalin's Gulag." *Slavic Review* 64 (2005), 274–306.

———. "Portrait of a Con Artist as a Soviet Man." *Slavic Review* 57 (1998): 774–790.

———. "Victim Talk: Defense Testimony and Denunciation under Stalin." *Law and Social Inquiry* 24 (1999): 637–654.

Barber, John, and Mark Harrison. *The Soviet Home Front, 1941–45: A Social and Economic History of The USSR in World War II.* London, 1991.

Barnes, Stephen. *Death and Redemption.* Cambridge, MA, 2011.

Bauer, R. A., A. Inkeles, and Clyde Kluckhohn. *How the Soviet System Works: Cultural, Psychological and Social Themes.* Cambridge, MA, 1956.

Belova, Eugenia. "Economic Crime and Punishment." In *Behind the Façade of Stalin's Command Economy: Evidence from the Soviet State and Party Archives,* ed. Paul Gregory. Palo Alto, 2001.

Berlin, Isaiah, "Herzen and His Memoirs." In *The Proper Study of Mankind: An Anthology of Essays,* ed. H. Hardy and R. Hausheer. London, 1997.

Berliner, Joseph. "Blat Is Higher Than Stalin!" *Problems of Communism,* 3 (Jan-Feb. 1954): 22–31.

———. *Factory and Manager in the USSR.* Cambridge, MA, 1957.

Berman, Harold. *Justice in the USSR: An Interpretation of Soviet Law.* Cambridge, MA, 1963.

Berman, Harold, and Miroslav Kerner. *Soviet Military Law and Administration.* Cambridge, MA, 1955.

Bidlack, Richard. "Ideological or Political Origins of the Leningrad Affair? A Response to David Brandenberger." *Russian Review* 64 (January 2005), 90–95.

Bidlack, Richard, and Nikita Lomagin. *The Leningrad Blockade, 1941–1944*. New Haven, CT, 2012.

Borisova, L. V. "NEP v zerkale pokazatel'nykh protsessov po vziatochnichestvu i khoziaistvennym prestupleniiam." *Otechestvennaia istoriia* 1 (2006), 84–97.

———. "Tret'ii vrag revoliutsii: Bor'ba so vziatochnichestvom i khoziaistvennymi prestupleniiami v nachale NEPa." *The Soviet and Post-Soviet Review* 30 (2003), 245–277.

Boterbloem, Kees. *Life and Death under Stalin: Kalinin Province, 1945–1953*. Montreal, 1999.

———. *The Life and Times of Andrei Zhdanov, 1896–1948*. Montreal, 2004.

Bourtman, Ilya. "'Blood for Blood, Death for Death': The Soviet Military Tribunal in Krasnodar, 1943." *Holocaust and Genocide Studies*, vol. 22 (2008), 246–265.

Brandenberger, David. *National Bolshevism: Stalinist Mass Culture and the Formation of Modern Russian Identity, 1931–1956*. Cambridge, MA, 2002.

———. *Propaganda State in Crisis: Soviet Ideology, Indoctrination, and Terror under Stalin, 1927–1941*. New Haven, CT, 2012.

———. "Stalin, the Leningrad Affair, and the Limits of Postwar Soviet Russocentrism." *Russian Review* 63 (2004): 241–255.

Brooks, Jeffrey. *Thank You, Comrade Stalin: Soviet Public Culture from Revolution to Civil War*. Princeton, NJ, 2000.

Burbank, Jane. *Russian Peasants Go to Court: Legal Culture in the Countryside, 1905–1917*. Bloomington, IN, 2004.

Burton, Chris. "Medical Welfare during Late Stalinism." Unpublished PhD dissertation, University of Chicago, 2000.

Bushnell, John. "The 'New Soviet Man' Turns Pessimist." In *The Soviet Union since Stalin*, ed. Stephen Cohen, Alexander Rabinowitch, and Robert Sharlet. Bloomington, 1980.

Cadiot, Juliette. "Equal Before the Law? Soviet Justice, Criminal Proceedings against Communist Party Members, and the Legal Landscape in the USSR from 1945 to 1953." *Jahrbücher für Geschichte Osteuropas* 61 (2013): 249–269.

Cadiot, Juliette, and Tanja Penter. Introduction to special issue of *Jahrbücher für Geschichte Osteuropas* 61, "Law and Justice in Wartime and Postwar Stalinism" (2013).

Clark, Katerina. *The Soviet Novel: History as Ritual*. Bloomington, IN, 2000.

Clark, William. *Crime and Punishment in Soviet Officialdom: Combating Corruption in the Political Elite, 1965–1990*. Armonk, NY, 1993.

Cohn, Edward. "Disciplining the Party: The Expulsion and Censure of Communists in the Post-War Soviet Union, 1945–1961." Unpublished PhD dissertation, University of Chicago, 2007.

Colton, Timothy. *Moscow: Governing the Socialist Metropolis.* Cambridge, MA, 1995.

Conquest, Robert. *Power and Policy in the USSR: The Study of Soviet Dynastics.* New York, 1951.

Coulloudon, Virginie. "Russia's Distorted Anticorruption Campaigns." In *Political Corruption in Transition: A Sceptic's Handbook,* ed. Stephen Kotkin and Andras Sajo. Budapest, 2002.

David-Fox, Michael. *Showcasing the Great Experiment: Cultural Diplomacy and Western Visitors to the Soviet Union, 1921–1941.* Oxford, 2014.

Davies, R. W. *Soviet History in the Yeltsin Era.* London, 1997.

Davis, Natalie. *The Gift in Sixteenth Century France.* Madison, WI, 2000.

Davydova, Irina. "Bureaucracy on Trial: A Malaise in Official Life as Represented in Nineteenth-Century Russian Thought." In *Bribery and Blat in Russia,* ed. Stephen Lovell et al.

Djilas, Milovan. *The New Class: An Analysis of the Communist System.* New York, 1957.

Dobson, Miriam. *Khrushchev's Cold Summer: Gulag Returnees, Crime, and the Fate of Reform after Stalin.* Ithaca, NY, 2009.

Duhamel, Luc. *The KGB Campaign against Corruption in Moscow, 1982–1987.* Pittsburgh, 2010.

Dunham, Vera. *In Stalin's Time: Middleclass Values in Soviet Fiction.* Cambridge, 1976.

Duskin, Eric. *Stalinist Reconstruction and the Confirmation of a New Elite, 1945–1953.* Basingstoke, UK, 2001.

Edele, Mark. *Soviet Veterans of World War II: A Popular Movement in an Authoritarian State.* Oxford, 2008.

Ellman, Michael. "The 1947 Soviet Famine and the Entitlement Approach to Famines." *Cambridge Journal of Economics* 24 (2000): 603–630.

Epifanov, A. E. *Otvetstvennost' za voennye prestupleniia, sovershennye na territorii SSSR v period Velikoi Otechestvennoi Voiny: 1941–1956.* Vologda, 2005.

Epstein, Catherine. "The Stasi: New Research on the East German Ministry of State Security." *Kritika* 5 (2004): 321–348.

Evel'son, Evgeniia. *Sudebnye protsessy po ekonomicheskim delam v SSSR: shestidesiatye gody.* London, 1986.

Favarel-Garrigues, Gilles. *Policing Economic Crime in Russia: From Soviet Planned Economy to Privatization.* London, 2011.

Feifer, George. *Justice in Moscow.* New York, 1964.

Feldbrugge, F. J. M. "Government and Shadow Economy in the Soviet Union." *Soviet Studies,* 36, no. 4 (October 1984): 528–543.

Feofanov, Iurii. "The Trial of Ian Rokotov." In *Politics and Justice in Russia: Major Trials of the Post-Stalin Era,* ed. Iurii Feofanov and Donald Barry. Armonk, NY, 1996.

Filtzer, Donald A. *The Hazards of Urban Life in the Late Stalinist USSR, 1943–1953.* Cambridge, 2010.

———. *Soviet Workers and Late Stalinism: Labour and the Restoration of the Stalinist System after WWII.* Cambridge, UK, 2002.

———. "Standard of Living versus Quality of Life: Struggling with the Urban Environment in Russia during the Early Years of Post-War Construction." In *Late Stalinist Russia,* ed. Juliane Fürst. London and New York, 2006.

———. "The Standard of Living of Soviet Industrial Workers in the Immediate Postwar Period, 1945–48." *Europe-Asia Studies* 51 (September 1999): 1020–1026.

Finkel, Stuart. "An Intensification of Vigilance: Recent Perspectives on the Institutional History of the Soviet Security Apparatus in the 1920s." *Kritika* 5 (2004): 299–320.

Fitzpatrick, Sheila. "Blat in Stalin's Time." In *Bribery and Blat in Russia,* ed. Stephen Lovell et al. New York, 2000.

———. *Everyday Stalinism: Ordinary Life in Extraordinary Times: Soviet Russia in the 1930s.* New York, 2000.

———. "Signals from Below: Soviet Letters of Denunciation of the 1930s." *Journal of Modern History* 68 (1996): 831–866.

———. "Supplicants and Citizens: Public Letter-Writing in Soviet Russia in the 1930s." *Slavic Review* 55 (1996): 78–105.

———. *Tear off the Masks! Identity and Imposture in Twentieth-Century Russia.* Princeton, NJ, 2005.

———. "The World of Ostap Bender: Soviet Confidence Men in the Stalin Period." *Slavic Review* 61 (2002): 535–557.

Fürst, Juliane. "Introduction." In Juliane Fürst, ed., *Late Stalinist Russia: Society between Reconstruction and Reinvention.* London and New York, 2006: 1–19.

———, ed. *Late Stalinist Russia: Society between Reconstruction and Reinvention.* London and New York, 2006.

———. *Stalin's Last Generation: Soviet Post-war Youth and the Emergence of Mature Socialism.* Oxford, 2010.

Galeotti, Mark, ed. *Russian and Post-Soviet Organized Crime* (London, 2002).

Ganson, Nicholas. *The Soviet Famine of 1946–47 in Global and Historical Perspective.* New York, 2009.

Gellately, Robert. "Denunciations in Twentieth-Century Germany: Aspects of Self-Policing in the Third Reich and the German Democratic Republic." *Journal of Modern History* 68 (1996): 931–967.

Getty, J. Arch. *Yezhov: The Rise of Stalin's "Iron Fist."* New Haven, CT, 2008.

Getty, J. Arch, Gabor T. Rittersporn, Viktor N. Zemskov. "Victims of the Soviet Penal System in the Pre-War Years." *American Historical Review* 98, vol. 4 (October 1993): 1017–1049.

Ginsburgs, George. "The Soviet Procuracy and Forty Years of Socialist Legality." *American Slavic and East European Review,* vol. 18 (1959): 34–62.

Golosenko, I. A. "Nachal'stvo. Ocherki po istorii Rossiiskoi sotsiologii chinovnichestva kontsa XIX–nachala XX vv." *Zhurnal sotsiologii i sotsial'noi antropologii* 8, no. 1 (2005): 54–85.

Gorlizki, Yoram. "Anti-Ministerialism and the USSR Ministry of Justice, 1953–56: A Study in Organisational Decline." *Europe-Asia Studies* 48 (1996): 1279–1318.

———. "De-Stalinization and the Politics of Russian Criminal Justice, 1953–64." Unpublished D. Phil Thesis, University of Oxford, 1992.

———. "Rules, Incentives and Soviet Campaign Justice after World War II." *Europe-Asia Studies,* vol. 51 (1999): 1245–1265.

Gorlizki, Yoram, and Oleg Khlevniuk. *Cold Peace: Stalin and the Soviet Ruling Circle, 1945–1953.* Oxford, 2004.

Gorsuch, Anne E. "'There's No Place like Home': Soviet Tourism in Late Stalinism," *Slavic Review* 62, no. 4 (Winter 2003): 760–785.

Govorov, I. V. "Korruptsiia v usloviiakh poslevoennogo stalinizma (na materialakh Leningrada i Leningradskoi oblasti)." *Noveishaia istoriia Rossii* 1 (2011): 66–82.

———. *Prestupnost' i bor'ba s nei v poslevoennom Leningrade (1945–1953): opyt istoricheskogo analiza.* St. Petersburg, 2004.

Granick, David. *The Red Executive.* New York, 1961.

Gregory, Paul. *The Political Economy of Stalinism.* Cambridge, MA, 2004.

Gregory, Paul, and Mark Harrison. "Allocation under Dictatorship: Research in Stalin's Archives." *Journal of Economic Literature* 43, no. 3 (2005): 721–761.

Gross, Jan T. "A Note on the Nature of Soviet Totalitarianism." *Soviet Studies* 34 (1982): 367–376.

———. *Revolution from Abroad: The Soviet Conquest of Poland's Western Ukraine and Western Belorussia.* Princeton, NJ, 1988.

Grossman, Gregory. "Notes on the Illegal Private Economy and Corruption." In *The Soviet Economy in a Time of Change,* Joint Economic Committee. Washington, 1977.

———. "The 'Second Economy' of the USSR." *Problems of Communism* (1977): 25–40.

Hachten, Charles. "Property Relations and the Economic Organization of Soviet Russia, 1941–1948." Unpublished PhD dissertation, University of Chicago, 2005.

Hagenloh, Paul. *Stalin's Police: Public Order and Mass Repression in the USSR, 1924–1941.* Baltimore, MD, 2009.

Harris, James. *The Great Urals: Regionalism and the Evolution of the Soviet System.* Ithaca, NY, 1999.

Harris, Jonathan. *The Split in Stalin's Secretariat.* Lanham, MD, 2010.

Harrison, Mark. "Forging Success: Soviet Managers and Accounting Fraud, 1943–1962." *Journal of Comparative Economics* 39, no. 1 (2011): 43–64.

———. "Secrecy, Fear and Transaction Costs: The Business of Soviet Forced Labour in the Early Cold War." *Europe-Asia Studies* 65, no. 6 (2013): 1112–1135.

Hartley, Janet. "Bribery and Justice in the Provinces in the Reign of Catherine II." In *Bribery and Blat in Russia,* ed. Stephen Lovell et al. New York, 2000.

Hartzok, Justus. "Children of Chapaev: The Russian Civil War Cult and the Creation of Soviet Identity." Unpublished PhD dissertation, University of Iowa, 2009.

Hazard, John. "Socialism, Abuse of Power, and Soviet Law." *Columbia Law Review,* vol. 50 (1950): 448–474.

Heidenheimer, Arnold, Michael Johnston, and Victor T. Le Vine, eds. *Political Corruption: A Handbook.* Edison, NJ, 2001.

Heinzen, James. "The Art of the Bribe: Corruption and Everyday Practice in the Late Stalinist USSR." *Slavic Review* 66, no. 3 (Fall 2007): 389–412.

———. "Corruption among Officials and Anticorruption Drives in the USSR, 1945–1964." In *Russian Bureaucracy and the State: Officialdom from Alexander III to Putin,* ed. Don K. Rowney and Eugene Huskey. Basingstoke, UK, 2009.

———. "Informers and the State under Late Stalinism: Informant Networks and Crimes against 'Socialist Property,' 1940–1953." *Kritika: Explorations in Russian History* 8 (2007): 789–815.

———. "Korruptsiia v Gulage: Dilemmy chinovnikov i uznikov." In *Gulag: Ekonomika prinuditel'nogo truda,* ed. L. I. Borodkin, P. Gregory, and O. V. Khlevniuk. Moscow: Rosspen, 2005. Also published as "Corruption in the Gulag: Dilemmas of Officials And Prisoners." *Comparative Economic Studies* 47 (2005): 456–475.

Helmke, Gretchen, and Steven Levitsky. "Informal Institutions and Comparative Politics: A Research Agenda." *Perspectives on Politics* 2 (2004): 725–740.

Hendley, Kathryn. "Rule of Law, Russian-Style." *Current History* (October 2009): 339–340.

Herzen, Aleksandr. *A Herzen Reader.* Translated and edited by Kathleen Parthé. Evanston, IL, 2012.

Hessler, Julie. "A Postwar Perestroika? Toward a History of Private Enterprise in the USSR." *Slavic Review* 57 (1998): 516–542.

———. *A Social History of Soviet Trade: Trade Policy, Retail Practices, and Consumption, 1917–1953.* Princeton, NJ, 2004.

Heyman, Josiah, and Alan Smart. "States and Illegal Practices: An Overview." In *States and Illegal Practices,* ed. Josiah Heyman. Oxford, 1999.

Hirsch, Francine. "The Soviets at Nuremberg: International Law, Propaganda, and the Making of the Postwar Order." *American Historical Review* 113 (2008): 701–730.

Hoch, Stephen. *Serfdom and Social Control in Russia: Petrovskoe, A Village in Tambov.* Chicago, 1989.

Hoffman, David L. *Stalinist Values: The Cultural Norms of Soviet Modernity.* Ithaca, 2003.

Holmes, Leslie. *The End of Communist Power: Anti-Corruption Campaigns and Legitimation Crisis.* New York, 1993.

———. *Rotten States? Corruption, Post-Communism, and Neo-Liberalism.* Durham, NC, 2006.

Holquist, Peter. "'Information Is the Alpha and Omega of Our Work': Bolshevik Surveillance in Its Pan-European Perspective." *Journal of Modern History* 69 (1997): 415–450.

Hooper, Cynthia V. "A Darker 'Big Deal': Concealing Party Crimes in the Post–Second World War Era." In *Late Stalinist Russia,* ed. Juliane Fürst. London and New York, 2006.

———. "Terror from Within: Participation and Coercion in Soviet Power, 1924–1964." Unpublished PhD dissertation, Princeton University, 2003.

Humphrey, Caroline. *The Unmaking of Soviet Life: Everyday Economies after Socialism.* Ithaca, 2002.

Huskey, Eugene. *Russian Lawyers and the Soviet State.* Princeton, NJ, 1986.

Iakovlev, A. N., ed. *Reabilitatsiia—Politicheskie protsessy 1930–1950 godov.* Moscow, 1991.

Jancsics, David. "'A Friend Gave Me a Phone Number'—Brokerage in Low-level Corruption," *International Journal of Law, Crime, and Justice* 43 (2015): 68–87.

Jansen, Marc, and Nikita Petrov. "Mass Terror and the Court: The Military Collegium of the USSR." *Europe-Asia Studies* 58 (June 2006): 589–602.

———. *Stalin's Loyal Executioner: People's Commissar Nikolai Ezhov.* Palo Alto, CA, 2002.

Jones, Jeffrey. *Everyday Life and the "Reconstruction" of Soviet Russia during and after the Great Patriotic War, 1943–1948.* Bloomington, IN, 2008.

———. "Every Family Has its Freak: Perceptions of Collaboration in Occupied Soviet Russia, 1943–1948." *Slavic Review* 64 (2005): 747–770.

Jordan, William Chester. "Anti-corruption Campaigns in Thirteenth-Century Europe." *Journal of Medieval History* 35 (2009): 204–219.

Kamenskii, F. "Sledovateli po vazhneishim delam." *Sotsialisticheskaia zakonnost'* no. 11 (November 1949): 34–39.

Kaminskaia, Dina. *Final Judgment: My Life as a Soviet Defense Lawyer.* New York, 1983.

Kaplan, Cynthia S. *The Party and Agricultural Crisis Management in the USSR.* Ithaca, NY, 1987.

Karpushin, M. P., and P. S. Dmitriev. *Vziatochnichestvo—pozornyi perezhitok proshlogo.* Moscow, 1964.

Katsenelinboigen, Aron. "Coloured Markets in the Soviet Union." *Soviet Studies* 29 (January 1977).

Kazantsev, Sergei. "The Judicial Reform of 1864 and the Procuracy in Russia." In *Reforming Justice in Russia, 1864–1996: Power, Culture, and the Limits of Legal Order,* ed. Peter Solomon. New York, 1997.

Kelly, Catriona. "Self-Interested Giving: Bribery and Etiquette in Late Imperial Russia." In *Bribery and Blat in Russia,* ed. Stephen Lovell et al. New York, 2000.

Khlevniuk, Oleg. *In Stalin's Shadow.* Armonk, NY, 1995.

———. *Master of the House: Stalin and His Inner Circle.* New Haven, CT, 2008.

Kirschenbaum, Lisa. *The Legacy of the Siege of Leningrad, 1941–1995.* New York, 2004.

Kivelson, Valerie. *Autocracy in the Provinces: The Muscovite Gentry and Political Culture in the Seventeenth Century.* Palo Alto, CA, 1996.

Kondrat'eva, Tamara. *Kormit' i pravit': o vlasti v Rossii XVI-XX vv.* Moscow, 2006.

Kotkin, Stephen. *Armageddon Averted.* Oxford, 2001.

———. *Magnetic Mountain: Stalinism as Civilization.* Berkeley, CA, 1995.

———. "The State—Is it Us?: Memoirs, Archives, and Kremlinologists." *Russian Review* 61 (January 2002): 35–51.

Kozlov, V. A. "Denunciation and its Functions in Soviet Governance: A Study of Denunciations and their Bureaucratic Handling from Soviet Police Archives, 1944–1953." *Journal of Modern History* 68, vol. 4 (December 1996): 867–898.

Kozlov, V. A., and S. V. Mironenko, eds. *Osobaia papka I. V. Stalina.* Moscow, 1994.

Klitgaard, Robert. "Gifts and Bribes." In *Strategy and Choice,* ed. Richard Zeckhauser. Cambridge, MA, 1991.

Kollmann, Nancy S. *Crime and Punishment in Early Modern Russia.* Cambridge, UK, 2012.

Kornai, Janos. *Economics of Shortage and the Socialist System.* Amsterdam, 1980.

Kramer, John M. "Political Corruption in the USSR." *The Western Political Quarterly* 30 (1977): 213–224.

Krastev, Ivan. *Shifting Obsessions: Three Essays on the Politics of Anticorruption.* Budapest, 2004.

Krementsov, N. L. *The Cure: A Story of Cancer and Politics from the Annals of the Cold War.* Chicago, 2004.

Kucherov, Samuel. *The Organs of Soviet Administration of Justice, Their History and Operation.* Leiden, 1970.

Kudryashov, Sergey, and Vanessa Voisin. "The Early Stages of 'Legal Purges' in Soviet Russia (1941–1945)." *Cahiers du monde russe* 43 (2008): 263–296.

Lampert, Nick. "Law and Order in the USSR: The Case of Economic and Official Crime." *Soviet Studies* 36 (July 1984): 366–385.

LaPierre, Brian. *Hooligans in Khrushchev's Russia.* Madison, WI, 2012.

Lawal, Gbenga. "Corruption and Development in Africa: Challenges for Political and Economic Change." *Humanity and Social Sciences Journal* 2 (2007): 1–7.

Ledeneva, Alena V. *Russia's Economy of Favours: Blat, Networking and Informal Exchange.* Cambridge, UK, 1998.

Leibovich, Oleg. *V gorode "M."* Moscow, 2008.

Lenoe, Matthew. *Closer to the Masses: Stalinist Culture, Social Revolution, and Soviet Newspapers.* Cambridge, MA, 2004.

Levesque, Jean. "Into the Grey Zone: Sham Peasants and the Limits of the Kolkhoz Order in the Post-war Russian Village, 1945–1953." In *Late Stalinist Russia,* ed. Juliane Fürst. London and New York, 2006.

Lewin, Moshe. "Rebuilding the Soviet Nomenklatura 1945–1948." *Cahiers du monde russe* 44 (2003): 219–251.

———. *Russia/USSR/Russia: The Drive and Drift of a Superstate.* New York, 1995.

Linz, Susan, ed. *The Impact of World War II on the Soviet Union.* Totowa, NJ, 1985.

Lovell, Stephen. *The Shadow of War: Russia and the USSR, 1941 to the Present.* Chichester, UK, 2010.

Lovell, Stephen, Alena V. Ledeneva, and Andrei Rogachevskii, eds. *Bribery and Blat in Russia: Negotiating Reciprocity from The Middle Ages to the 1990s.* New York, 2000.

Luryi, Yuri. "The Right to Counsel in Ordinary Criminal Cases in the USSR." In *Soviet Law after Stalin, Part I: The Citizen and the State in Contemporary Soviet Law,* ed. D. Barry, G. Ginsburgs, and P. Maggs, no. 20(1). Alphen aan den Rijn, the Netherlands, 1977: 105–117.

Lustiger, Arno. *Stalin and the Jews.* New York, 2002.

Magnusdottir, Rosa. "Keeping up Appearances: How the Soviet State Failed to Control Popular Attitudes toward the United States of America, 1945–1959." PhD dissertation, University of North Carolina, 2006.

Manley, Rebecca. *To the Tashkent Station: Evacuation and Survival in the Soviet Union at War.* Ithaca, NY, 2009.

———. "'Where Should We Resettle the Comrades Next?' The Adjudication of Housing Claims and the Construction of the Postwar Order." In *Late Stalinist Russia,* ed. Juliane Fürst. London and New York, 2006.

Markevich, Andrei. "How Much Control Is Enough? Monitoring and Enforcement Under Stalin." *Europe-Asia Studies* 63, no. 8 (2011): 1449–1468.

Mars, Gerald, and Yochanan Altman. "How a Soviet Economy Really Works: Cases and Implications." In *Corruption: Causes, Consequences and Control,* ed. Michael Clarke. New York, 1983.

Maslov, V. P., and N. F. Chistiakov. *Vopreki zakonu i spravedlivosti.* Moscow, 1990.

Mauss, Marcel. *The Gift: The Form and Reason for Exchange in Archaic Societies.* Translated by W. D. Halls. New York, 1990.

McDonald, Tracy. *Face to the Village: The Riazan Countryside under Soviet Rule, 1921–1930.* Toronto, 2009.

Merridale, Catherine. *Ivan's War: Life and Death in the Red Army, 1939–1945.* New York, 2006.

Millar, James. "The Little Deal: Brezhnev's Contribution to Acquisitive Socialism." *Slavic Review* 44 (Winter 1985): 694–706.

Montias, J. M., and Susan Rose-Ackerman. "Corruption in a Soviet-Type Economy: Theoretical Considerations." In *Economic Welfare and the Economics of Soviet Socialism,* ed. Steven Rosefielde. Cambridge, 1981.

Moyal, Dina. "Did Law Matter?—Law, State and Individual in the USSR, 1953–1982." Unpublished PhD dissertation, Stanford University, 2011.

Nasmyth, Peter. *Walking in the Caucasus.* New York, 2006.

Nekrich, Aleksander. *Forsake Fear: Memoirs of a Historian.* Boston, 1991.

Neznansky, Fridrikh. *The Prosecution of Economic Crime in the USSR.* Translated by Robert Sharlet. Falls Church, VA, 1985.

Noonan, John. *Bribery.* Berkeley, 1988.

Nove, Alec. "Some Aspects of Soviet Constitutional Theory." *Modern Law Review* 12, no. 1 (January 1949): 12–36.

Osborn, Robert J. "Citizen vs. Administration in the USSR." *Soviet Studies* 17 (1965): 226–237.

Osokina, Elena. *Ierarkhiia potreblieniia. O zhizni liudei v usloviiakh Stalinskogo snabzheniia: 1928–1935 gg.* Moscow, 1993.

———. *Za fasadom "Stalinskogo izobiliia": Raspredelenie i rynok v snabzhenii naseleniia v gody industrializatsii, 1927–1941.* Moscow, 1998.

Pardo, Italo. *Between Morality and the Law: Corruption, Anthropology and Comparative Society.* Aldershot, UK, 2004.

Parrish, Michael. *The Lesser Terror: Soviet State Security, 1939–1953.* Westport, CT, 1996.

Payne, Matthew. *Stalin's Railroad: Turksib and the Building of Socialism.* Pittsburgh, PA, 2001.

Penter, Tanja. "Collaboration on Trial: New Source Material on Soviet Post-war Trials against Collaborators." *Slavic Review* 64 (Winter 2005): 782–790.

Pikhoia, R. G. *Sovetskii soiuz: Istoriia vlasti, 1945–1991.* Moscow, 1998.

Pinkus, Benjamin. *The Soviet Government and the Jews, 1948–1967.* Cambridge, 1984.

Pisar'kova, F. "K istorii vziatok v Rossii (po materialam sekretnoi kantseliarii Kn. Golitsynykh pervoi poloviny XIX v.)" *Otechestvennaia istoriia* 5 (2002): 33–49.

Pollock, Ethan. *Stalin and the Soviet Science Wars.* Princeton, NJ, 2008.

Pomeranz, William, and Max Grutbrod. "The Push for Precedent in Russia's Judicial System." *Review of Central and East European Law* 37, no. 1 (2012): 1–30.

Pomorski, Stanislaw. "Perversions of Soviet Administrative Law." In *Soviet Administrative Law: Theory and Policy,* ed. George Ginsburgs et al. Dordrecht, the Netherlands, 1989.

Pomorski, Stanislaw, and George Ginsburgs. "Enforcement of Law and the Second Economy." Occasional Paper no. 118 (Kennan Institute for Advanced Russian Studies), 1980.

Potter, Cathy J. "Payment, Gift or Bribe? Exploring the Boundaries in Pre-Petrine Russia." In *Bribery and Blat in Russia,* ed. Stephen Lovell et al. New York, 2000.

Pyzhikov, A. "Leningradskaia gruppa: Put' vo vlasti (1946–1949)." *Svobodnaia mysl'* (2001): 89–104.

Qualls, Karl. *From Ruins to Reconstruction: Urban Identity in Soviet Sevastopol after World War II.* Ithaca, 2009.

Randall, Amy. *The Soviet Dream World of Retail Trade and Consumption in the 1930s.* Basingstoke, UK, 2008.

Retish, Aaron. *Russia's Peasants in Revolution and Civil War: Citizenship, Identity, and the Creation of the Soviet State, 1914–1922.* Cambridge, 2008.

Rieber, Alfred J. "Stalin, Man of the Borderlands." *American Historical Review* 106 (December 2001): 1651–1691.

Rigi, Jakob. "Corruption in Post-Soviet Kazakhstan." In *Between Morality and the Law: Corruption, Anthropology and Comparative Society,* ed. Italo Pardo. Aldershot, UK, 2004.

Rittersporn, Gabor. *Simplifications staliniennes et complications sovietiques: Tensions socials et conflits politiques en U.R.S.S.* Paris, 1988.

Roberts, Geoffrey. *Stalin's General: The Life of Georgy Zhukov.* New York, 2012.

Rose-Ackerman, Susan. *Corruption and Government: Causes, Consequences, and Reform.* Cambridge, 1998.

Rubenstein, Joshua, and Vladimir Naumov, eds. *Stalin's Secret Pogrom: The Postwar Inquisition of the Jewish Anti-Fascist Committee.* New Haven, CT, 2001.

Ruthers, Monica. "The Moscow Gorkii Street in Late Stalinism: Space, History, and Lebenswelten." In *Late Stalinist Russia,* ed. Julianne Fürst. New York and London, 2006.

Schwartz, Charles. "Corruption and Political Development in the U.S.S.R." *Comparative Politics* 11 (1979): 425–443.

———. "Economic Crime in the USSR: A Comparison of the Khrushchev and Brezhnev Eras." *International and Comparative Law Quarterly* 30 (1981): 281–296.

Scott, Erik R. "Familiar Strangers: The Georgian Diaspora in the Soviet Union." PhD dissertation, University of California, Berkeley, 2011.

Scott, James C. *Comparative Political Corruption.* Englewood Cliffs, NJ, 1972.

Shapoval, Iurii. "The Mechanisms of the Informational Activity of the GPU-NKVD: The Surveillance File of Mykhailo Hrushevsky." *Cahiers du monde russe* 42 (2001): 207–230.

Sharlet, Robert. "The Communist Party and the Administration of Justice in the USSR." In *Soviet Law after Stalin,* Part III of No. 20, Law in Eastern Europe Series, ed. Donald Barry et al. Alphen aan den Rijn, the Netherlands (1979): 321–392.

Shattenberg, Susanne. "Kul'tura korruptsii, ili K istorii rossiiskikh chinovnikov." *Neprikosnovennyi zapas* 42, no. 4 (2005).

Shearer, David. "Elements Near and Alien: Passportization, Policing, and Identity in the Stalinist State, 1932–1952." *Journal of Modern History* 76 (2004): 835–881.

———. *Policing Stalin's Socialism: Repression and Social Order in the Soviet Union, 1924–1953.* New Haven, CT, 2009.

———. "Social Disorder, Mass Repression, and the NKVD during the 1930s." *Cahiers du monde russe* 42 (2001): 505–534.

———. "Wheeling and Dealing in Soviet Industry: Syndicates, Trade, and Political Economy at the End of the 1920s." *Cahiers du monde russe* 36 (1995): 139–160.

Simis, Konstantin. *USSR: The Corrupt Society.* New York, 1982.

"A Small Handbook for the Bribe Giver: Tokens of Gratitude." *Survey* 29 (Autumn 1986): 195–198.

Smith, Gordon B. "Procuratorial Campaigns against Crime in the USSR." In *Soviet Law Since Stalin,* ed. Donald Barry et al. Leiden, 1979.

Smolentsev, E. A. "Na strazhe sotsialisticheskoi zakonnosti." In *Verkhovnyi sud SSSR,* ed. L. N. Smirnov et al. Moscow, 1974.

Solnick, Stephen. *Stealing the State: Control and Collapse in Soviet Institutions.* Cambridge, MA, 1998.

Solomon, Peter H., Jr. "The Case of the Vanishing Acquittal: Informal Norms and the Practice of Soviet Criminal Justice." *Soviet Studies* 39 (1987): 531–555

———. *Soviet Criminal Justice under Stalin.* Cambridge, 1996.

———. "The USSR Supreme Court: History, Role, and Future Prospects." *American Journal of Contemporary Law* 38 (1990): 127–142.

Soloviev, Vladimir. *Empire of Corruption: The Territory of the Russian National Pastime.* London, 2014.

Staats, Steven J. "Corruption in the Soviet System." *Problems of Communism* 21 (January–February, 1972): 40–47.

Suvenirov, O. F. "Voennaia kollegiia Verkhovnogo Suda SSSR (1937–1939)." *Voprosy Istorii,* no. 4 (1995): 137–146.

Swain, Geoffrey. *Between Stalin and Hitler: Class War and Race War on the Dvina.* London, 2004.

Timasheff, N. S. "The Impact of the Penal Law of Imperial Russia on Soviet Penal Law." *American Slavic and East European Review* 12 (December 1953): 441–462.

Treml, Vladimir G., and Michael Alexeev. "The Growth of the Second Economy in the Soviet Union and its Impact on the System." In *The Postcommunist Economic Transformation: Essays in Honour of Gregory Grossman,* ed. Robert W. Campbell. Boulder, CO, 1994.

Tromly, Benjamin. "The Leningrad Affair and Soviet Patronage Politics." *Europe-Asia Studies* 56 (2004): 707–729.

Tumarkin, Nina. *Lenin Lives! The Lenin Cult in Soviet Russia.* Cambridge, 1983.

Varga-Harris, Christine. "Forging Citizenship on the Home Front: Revising the Socialist Contract and Constructing Socialist Identity during the Thaw." In *The Dilemmas of De-Stalinization.* London, 2006.

Verdery, Katherine. *What Was Socialism, and What Comes Next?* Princeton, NJ, 1996.

Ward, Chris. "What Is History? The Case of Late Stalinism." *Rethinking History* 8 (2004): 439–458.

Weiner, Amir. "Making of a Dominant Myth: The Second World War and the Construction of Political Identities within the Communist Party." *Russian Review* 55, no. 4 (1996): 638–660.

———. *Making Sense of War: The Second World War and the Fate of the Bolshevik Revolution.* Princeton, NJ, 2002.

Weiner, Amir, and Aigi Rahi-Tamm. "Getting to Know You: The Soviet Surveillance System, 1939–57." *Kritika* 13 (2012): 5–45.

Weissman, Neil. "Regular Police in Tsarist Russia, 1900–1914." *Russian Review* 44 (1985): 52–59.

Werth, Alexander. *Russia at War, 1941–1945.* New York, 1964.

Werth, Nicholas. *La terreur et le desarroi: Staline et son système.* Paris, 2007.

Wortman, Richard. *The Development of a Russian Legal Consciousness.* Chicago, 1976.

Zhukov, Iu. N. "Bor'ba za vlast' v rukovodstve SSSR v 1945–1952 godakh." *Voprosy istorii,* no. 1 (1995): 23–39.

Zima, V. F. *Golod v SSSR, 1946–47 godov: Proiskhozhdenie i posledstvie.* Moscow, 1996.

Zubkova, Elena. "Kadrovaia politika i chistki v KPSS (1945–1956)." *Svobodnaia mysl',* nos. 3, 4, and 6 (1999).

———. *Poslevoennoe Sovetskoe obshchestvo.* Moscow, 2000.

———. *Russia after the War: Hopes, Illusions, and Disappointments, 1945–1957.* Armonk, NY, 1998.

Index

Page numbers in *italics* refer to figures.